D1457344

The Baker Who Pretended to Be King of Portugal

The Baker Who Pretended to Be KING OF PORTUGAL

RUTH MACKAY

The University of Chicago Press
Chicago and London

Ruth MacKay works as an editor and writer at Stanford University, where she is also a visiting scholar. Her previous books are *The Limits of Royal Authority: Resistance and Obedience in Seventeenth-Century Castile* and *"Lazy, Improvident People": Myth and Reality in the Writing of Spanish History.*

The University of Chicago Press, Chicago 60637
The University of Chicago Press, Ltd., London
© 2012 by The University of Chicago
All rights reserved. Published 2012.
Printed in the United States of America

21 20 19 18 17 16 15 14 13 12 1 2 3 4 5

ISBN-13: 978-0-226-50108-6 (cloth)
ISBN-10: 0-226-50108-6 (cloth)

The University of Chicago Press gratefully acknowledges the generous support of the Program for Cultural Cooperation between Spain's Ministry of Culture and United States Universities toward the publication of this book.

Library of Congress Cataloging-in-Publication Data

MacKay, Ruth.
The baker who pretended to be king of Portugal / Ruth MacKay.
p. cm.
Includes bibliographical references and index.
ISBN-13: 978-0-226-50108-6 (hardcover : alkaline paper)
ISBN-10: 0-226-50108-6 (hardcover : alkaline paper) 1. Sebastião, King of Portugal, 1554–1578. 2. Portugal—Kings and rulers—16th century. 3. Portugal—History—Sebastião, 1557–1578. 4. Portugal—History—Spanish dynasty, 1580–1640—Biography. 5. António, Prior of Crato, 1531–1595. 6. Philip II, King of Spain, 1527–1598. 7. Espinosa, Gabriel de, d. 1595. 8. Ana, Queen, consort of Philip II, King of Spain, 1549–1580. I. Title.
DP612.M36 2012
946.9'02—dc23

2011036115

♾ This paper meets the requirements of ANSI/NISO Z39.48-1992 (Permanence of Paper).

"*We* can't help the way a king smells; history don't tell no way . . .

"Well, anyways, I doan' hanker for no mo' un um, Huck. Dese is all I kin stan'.

"It's the way I feel, too, Jim. But we've got them on our hands, and we got to remember what they are, and make allowances. Sometimes I wish we could hear of a country that's out of kings."

What was the use to tell Jim these warn't real kings and dukes? It wouldn't a done no good; and besides, it was just as I said; you couldn't tell them from the real kind.

—Mark Twain, *Huckleberry Finn*

CONTENTS

ILLUSTRATIONS

Color Plates (following page xxii)

Maps

Figures

Map 1. Iberia in the Sixteenth Century. Courtesy of Dick Gilbreath, Gyula Pauer Center for Cartography and GIS, University of Kentucky.

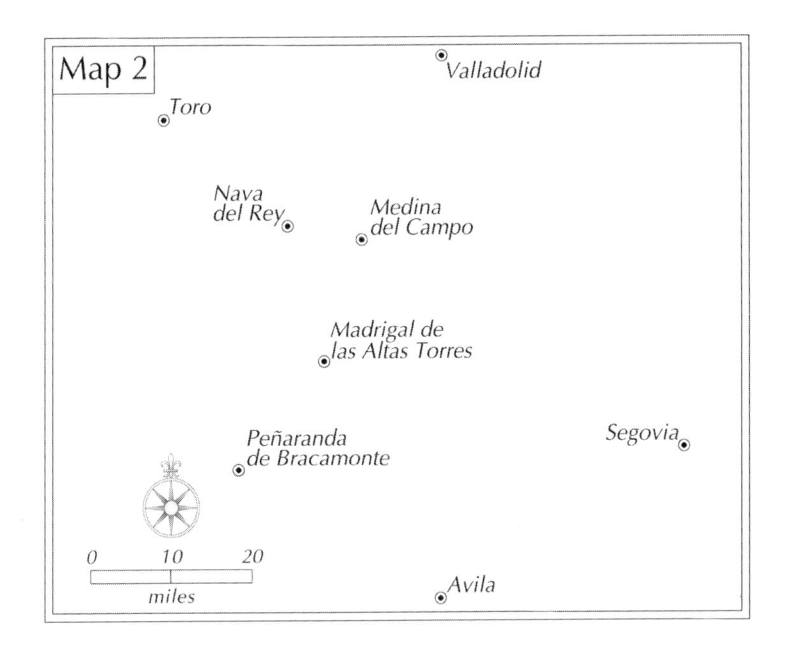

Map 2. Madrigal de las Altas Torres and Neighboring Towns. Courtesy of Dick Gilbreath, Gyula Pauer Center for Cartography and GIS, University of Kentucky.

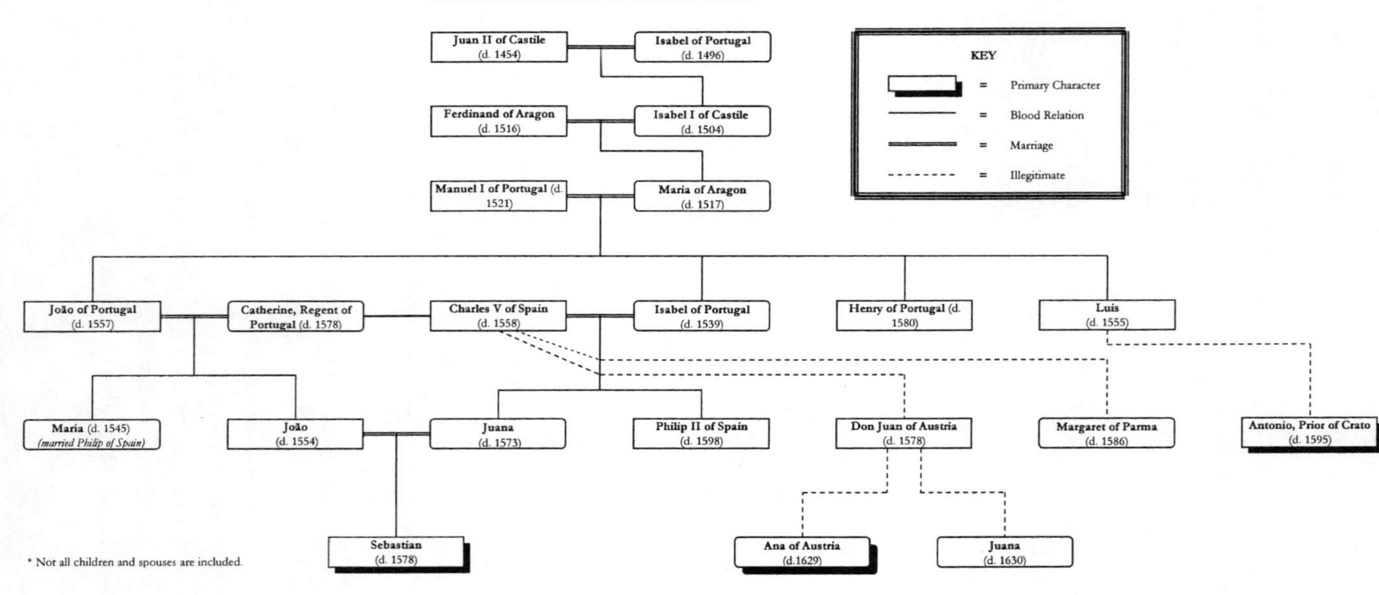

Figure 1. An abbreviated version of the Avis-Hapsburg line.
Courtesy of David Nasca.

CHARACTERS

Note on spelling: In general, royal names have been Anglicized; exceptions are don Juan of Austria; his daughter Ana of Austria; and don António, the prior of Crato. My sources are nearly all Spanish, so some Portuguese names may appear in their Spanish versions.

Abd al-Malik. Ruler of Morocco, widely praised for his knowledge and culture; dies at the battle of Alcazarquivir.

Abu Abdallah Muhammed. Ruler of Morocco usurped by uncles Abd al-Malik and Ahmad al-Mansur; dies at the battle of Alcazarquivir.

Ahmad al-Mansur. Malik's brother and successor.

Alba, duke of, Fernando Alvarez de Toledo y Pimentel. Leads Spanish invasion of Portugal.

Albert, Cardinal Archduke. Nephew of Philip II, viceroy of Portugal and later of the Netherlands.

Aldana, Francisco de. Poet, soldier, aide to Sebastian; dies at the battle of Alcazarquivir.

Ana of Austria. Nun, daughter of don Juan of Austria, niece of Philip II.

Angeles, Fray Agustín de los. Portuguese friar in Madrigal.

Antolinez, Fray Agustín. Augustinian friar, aide to the provincial, Gabriel de Goldaraz; eventually becomes archbishop of Santiago de Compostela.

António, prior of Crato. Illegitimate son of Luís, Infante de Portugal, and nephew of King Henry of Portugal; pretender to the Portuguese throne.

Ataíde, Luís. Portuguese viceroy of India.

Aveiro, duke of, Jorge de Lencastre. Dies at the battle of Alcazarquivir; succeeded by son-in-law Alvaro, third duke of Aveiro.

Azebes, Isabel de. Nun.

Barajas, count of, Francisco Zapata de Cisneros. President of the Council of Castile, later dismissed; married to María de Mendoza y Mendoza.

Bayona, Luisa. Nun.

Belón, María. Nun.

Benavente, Juan de. Augustinian, enemy of the provincial, Gabriel de Goldaraz.

Blomberg, Barbara. Ana's grandmother, Juan of Austria's mother.

Borja, Juan de. Philip II's ambassador to Portugal during Sebastian's youth.

Caetani, Camilo. Papal nuncio in Spain.

Camargo, Juan de. Augustinian, prior of San Agustín de Medina.

Catherine. Sebastian's grandmother, regent of Portugal.

Cerda, Fernando de la. Jesuit, thought to be the author of the 1595 chronicle (*Historia de Gabriel de Espinosa*).

Cid, Inés. Gabriel Espinosa's lover and the mother of two of his children.

Clara Eugenia. Daughter of Inés Cid and Gabriel de Espinosa.

Corso, Andrés Gaspar. Corsican merchant based in Algiers; used by Philip II as mediator in Morocco.

Escobedo, Pedro de. Barbara Blomberg's secretary; son of Juan de Escobedo, don Juan of Austria's secretary, who was murdered.

Espinosa, Ana (or Catalina). Nun.

Espinosa, Gabriel. The baker.

Fonseca, Antonio. A lawyer from Lisbon, held as an alleged accomplice of Fray Miguel de los Santos, later released.

Francisco. Ana's alleged brother, who was kidnapped.

Fuensalida, Juan de. Jesuit, accompanied Gabriel de Espinosa in his last days.

Goldaraz, Gabriel de. Augustinian provincial; tries to block the inquest into the conspiracy, eventually sacked; has enemies within the Augustinian order and links to Navarre.

Gomes, Francisco. Portuguese merchant, arrested on suspicion of being an accomplice of Fray Miguel de los Santos, later released; works for the count of Redondo.

González, Gregorio. Cook who worked with Gabriel de Espinosa in Ocaña.

Manoel Gonzalves. Portuguese courier.

Grado, Luisa de. Nun; close to Ana of Austria, sister of María Nieto and Blas Nieto.

Henry. Cardinal, regent, king of Portugal; Sebastian's great-uncle.

Idiáquez, Juan de. Councilor, ambassador, and close aide to Philip II.

Idiáquez, Martín de. Secretary of Spanish Council of State.

Isabel Clara Eugenia. Infanta, Philip II's daughter, eventually marries Albert.

João of Portugal. Bishop of La Guarda, leading supporter of don António, prior of Crato.

Juan of Austria. Philip II's half-brother, Ana of Austria's father.

Juana. Ana of Austria's younger sister.

Juana of Austria. Sebastian's mother, Philip II's sister.

Llano [or Llanos] de Valdés [or Valdéz], Juan de. Apostolic judge, canon, inquisitor.

Loaysa, Garcia de. Philip II's chaplain.

Mendes, Manoel. Portuguese merchant, supposed ally of Fray Miguel de los Santos and don António, prior of Crato; never located.

Mendes Pacheco, Manoel. Portuguese physician; supposedly treated Sebastian after the battle of Alcazarquivir, later appears in Arévalo; arrested and acquitted.

Mendoza, María de. Ana's mother.

Meneses, Duarte de. Governor of Tangiers.

Moura, Cristóbal de. Close aide to Philip II, later viceroy of Portugal under Philip III.

Moura, Miguel de. Aide to Sebastian and later to Albert.

Nieto, Blas. Ana's servant; arrested and acquitted.

Nieto, María. Nun. Sister of Luisa de Grado and Blas Nieto.

Ortiz, Fray Andrés. Vicar after the fall of Fray Miguel de los Santos.

Pérez, Antonio de. Philip II's one-time secretary; imprisoned, escaped, a fugitive and traitor.

Philip of Africa. Son of Muhammed, the usurped ruler of Morocco; before his conversion to Christianity, he was known in Spain as Muley Xeque.

Philip II. King of Spain

Philip III. King of Spain, Philip II's son.

Posada, Junco de. President of the royal chancery court.

Quiroga, Gaspar de. Archbishop, patron of the Madrigal convent.

Redondo, count of, João Coutinho. High Portuguese nobleman, ally of don António, prior of Crato.

Río, Bernardo del. Spy and courier disguised as a friar, working for Antonio Pérez.

Roda, Francisca de. Nun.

Roderos, Juan de. Ana of Austria's servant.

Rodríguez, Fray Alonso. Nuns' confessor.

Rodríguez, Gabriel. Innkeeper in Valladolid.

Rosete, Fray Alonso. Another confessor at the convent, Portuguese.

Ruiz, Simón. Merchant banker in Medina del Campo.

Santillán, Diego de. Brother of Rodrigo de Santillán; has a post at La Mota castle.

Santillán, Rodrigo de. Judge at the chancery court; appointed by Philip II to oversee the Madrigal inquest.

Santos, Fray Miguel de los. Portuguese Augustinian, royal confessor and preacher, later vicar of the Madrigal convent.

Sebastian. King of Portugal; dies at the battle of Alcazarquivir.

Silva, Juan de. Count of Portalegre. Philip II's ambassador in Lisbon; accompanies Sebastian to Morocco, later becomes governor of Portugal.

Silva, Pedro (aka Luís). Arrested August 1595.

Sosa (Sousa), Fray Antonio de. Augustinian, ally of Gabriel de Goldaraz, probable author of the anonymous letters to the judges.

Sotomayor, Luís de. Dominican, ally of don António, prior of Crato. One of the religious authorities supposed to oversee the last will and testament of don António.

Tapia, Ana de. Nun.

Tavora, Cristóvão de. King Sebastian's closest friend and aide; dies with Sebastian.

Ulloa, Margarita de. Guardian of don Juan of Austria and his daughter, Ana of Austria.

Vázquez de Arce, Rodrigo de. President of the Council of Castile.

Zayas, Gabriel de. Royal secretary.

Zuñiga, Fray Diego de. Churchman in Toledo who preaches against Philip II and says Sebastian is still alive; identity never established.

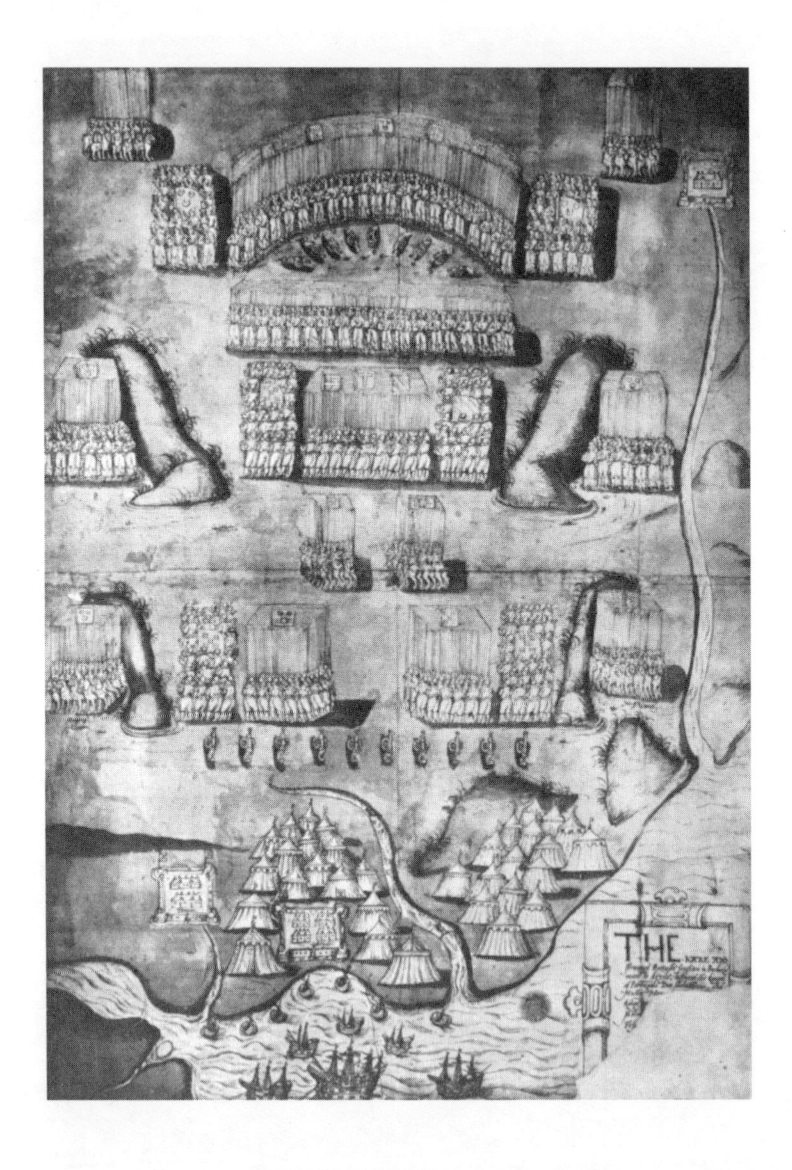

Figure 2. Anon., *The Battle of Alcazarquivir* (sixteenth century?). Original at Hatfield House, Hertfordshire, England.

PROLOGUE

On August 4, 1578, in the blazing Moroccan sun, King Sebastian of Portugal led his troops to slaughter. When the young king died, so too did Portugal's independence, for he left no heir. His uncle Philip II, king of Spain, took the throne after a brief power struggle followed by an armed invasion. From the blood and dust of the battle of Alcazarquivir arose some of Europe's best-known and perpetual royal imposters, the false Sebastians. This book tells the story of one of them, perhaps the least credible, even in an age when prophecies and marvelous occurrences formed the natural structure of people's imaginations.

Sixteen years after the battle, a man appeared in a town in Spain who said he was (or was thought to be) Sebastian. His name was Gabriel de Espinosa. As far as anyone can tell, the mastermind of this imposture was the Portuguese vicar of an Augustinian convent for well-born women, and the immediate objective of the plan was to convince one of the nuns, who happened to be Philip II's niece, that this man, a former soldier and occasional baker (*pastelero*), was her cousin. From there, the plan involved putting a Portuguese pretender on the throne. The principals and a large cast of nuns, monks, and servants were confined and questioned for nearly a year as a crew of judges tried to unravel the story, but the culprits went to their deaths leaving many questions unanswered.

The conspiracy took place at a moment of high political tension. Relations between Spain and Portugal, like those between any neighbors, were both close and fractious, and there were Portuguese who had not resigned themselves to being ruled by a Spaniard, even by one whose mother was Portuguese. The 1590s were unstable years not only in Spain and Portugal but throughout much of Europe, and not just in the political realm but also culturally, even subjectively. Assumptions were proving fragile. The weather was terrible, the king was dying, wars were going badly, and Spain's fortunes were waning. So it was a time for grasping at straws. When the world appears to be collapsing, people cling to whatever they have at hand, to whatever seems likeliest to help. They seek explanations. The phenomenon of the false Sebastians is called *sebastianismo,* a strain of millenarianism sometimes regarded as evidence of frustrated nationalism or proof that Portugal was a tragic, vanquished madhouse. I do not subscribe to this interpretation, but this is not a book about *sebastianismo,* among other reasons because it leans toward Spain rather than Portugal, because that is where the deception was staged.

The conspiracy to remove Philip from the Portuguese throne in favor of a Portuguese ruler may have had no chance of succeeding, but that does not make it a mere anecdote, and though there is little doubt that King Sebastian was an odd character, there is more to be gleaned from his short life than can be found in the often tendentious historiography, which veers from adulation to dismissal with little in between. In the pages that follow, I try to right this wrong by creating a bridge between the story and politics, between the structures of narrative and the demands of diplomacy. This story of a false Sebastian has a great deal to teach us about news and politics and about how people manage to live among forces they might not understand.

The story, in other words, matters. People then, as now, were dying for news. They were eager to hear a good story, an important one, and they were equally eager to turn around and tell it to somebody else. Telling stories, including this one, tied people to a place and time. In an era when news began traveling throughout the Iberian peninsula and hardship and intrigue put people on the road, commoners and elites spoke and read about national independence, intrigue, the cause of Christendom, visible truth, royal authority, and the limits of the possible. In retelling the story of the *pastelero* of Madrigal, this book points to the signs of recognition that helped people interpret their world. In its illogical folds, the story contained familiar sequences of adventure and redemption that made some sense to the victims, observers, and judges who became entangled in or fascinated by the events in the Castilian town of Madrigal de las Altas Torres.

Though I may at times give in to temptation and paint this conspiracy and its actors in comic tones, I want to make clear that I do not consider these people amusing. The story of the *pastelero* has been told for centuries as a curiosity; it has been held up as an example of the exoticism and credulity of the past, something to make tourists and readers see history as entertainment. In my view, the characters in the story display fearless imaginations, they rise to conceptual, political, and physical challenges we cannot conceive of, and they are very, very serious. They should be taken on their own terms, not as simple curiosities or curious simplifications. Their choices, even those choices punished by death, reveal what they thought was right or possible, and their descriptions and memories were a way of stating opinions. Though their lives embodied what we might consider contradictory approaches to the world—devotion and lies, political acuity and blunders, confinement and wandering—such inconsistency should lead us not to dismiss them but to grapple with the ambiguities of the past.

The story teems with characters who are someone other than who they appear to be. Commoners are disguised as kings, kings are disguised as hermits, royals believe they are commoners, several phony friars drift through, and travelers claim to be related to the royal nun, which probably they were not. This was an era, the dawn of the age of Quixote, when the distinction between truth and fiction was of great philosophical concern. It also was a practical religious consideration; one of the Inquisition's primary tasks was to ferret out false Christians, as neither Jews nor Muslims could legally practice their religion but might be doing so secretly. Spain's playwrights during this Golden Age of literature filled their stages with characters dressed up as someone else. Imposters plagued many of Europe's royal families. And politics was understood to be the legitimate exercise of guile and deception.

The conspiracy relied on news. Chronicles circulated throughout Europe recounting the tragedy of Alcazarquivir and, years later, its wondrous second act. We will see that people wrote and received letters constantly; the precursors to our newspapers were called newsletters for a reason. The Madrigal case file includes anonymous letters, forged letters, coded letters, love letters, translated letters, official letters, and letters containing testimony, some of which ended up in personal letters and then in news accounts, copied and reworded and then passed on, orally or in writing, assisted by the startling number of people traveling along the Iberian peninsula's network of roads. Friars, spies, vagabonds, deserters, officials, and couriers all come and go, and they all carry tales. The literature of the time invariably features travelers who, in every sheltered cove, every inn, every chance encounter, seize the opportunity to exchange stories. Some of this world can be seen in the following pages. The boundaries of good history were a matter of concern in the late sixteenth century, and eyewitness testimony frequently was invoked to assure readers and listeners that these fantastic tales were really and truly true; thus newsletters often represented the best of both worlds, truth and falsehood. But though facts and veracity were important, few spinners were not also guided by belief in God's providence, knowledge of the lives of the saints, and a sense of tradition born from belonging to a people or a nation. They owed allegiance to all these things.

The book begins with the story's origins in Morocco, and from there moves to Portugal, to Castile, and to Madrigal de las Altas Torres. We go from King Sebastian, who lost his kingdom to folly, to don António, the Portuguese pretender who never attained one, to Philip II, the most powerful monarch in the world. And we move from Fray Miguel de los Santos, the saintly vicar, to Gabriel de Espinosa, the itinerant baker, to Ana of Austria, a young nun who deserved better.

Plate 1. Cristóbal de Morales, *Don Sebastian de Portugal* (1565). Monasterio de las Descalzas Reales, Patrimonio Nacional, Spain. Photograph: Oronoz.

Plate 2. Alonso Sánchez de Coello, *Juana de Austria* (after 1557). Monasterio de las Descalzas Reales, Patrimonio Nacional, Spain. Photograph: Oronoz.

1

Morocco: King Sebastian

Sebastian was an unlikely figure to excite the romantic imagination, and it was his death, rather than his life, that ensured his narrative survival. He was the last of the Avis dynasty, which came to power in 1385 after the Battle of Aljubarrota, in which Portugal won its independence from Castile. The Avis dynasty's first ruler was João I. A ready supply of able seamen, adventurous merchants, and financial resources enabled overseas exploration and conquest during the next century. On a religious crusade and in search of wealth (the material objectives often draped in the spiritual), the Portuguese in the early fifteenth century began venturing into Africa. First came the conquest, in 1415, of the strategic jewel of Ceuta, just opposite Gibraltar, where the stronghold's owners could control traffic in and out of the Mediterranean and the Atlantic. The capture of Ceuta by one of João's many sons, Prince Henry, "the Navigator," was followed by the seizure of Atlantic islands and incursions down the West African coast and inland in search of gold and slaves. The Portuguese in 1471 captured the Moroccan towns of Asilah and Tangiers, and they rounded the Cape of Good Hope in 1488. In 1497, Vasco da Gama reached India, opening up the sea routes to Asia and its spice trade, which Portugal dominated for the next century. Vasco de Gama's voyages were the basis for the greatest work of early Portuguese literature and its national epic, Luís Vaz de Camões's *The Lusiads* (published in 1572), which, as it happens, was dedicated to Sebastian:

> And you, my boy King, guarantor
> Of Portugal's ancient freedoms,
> And equal surety for the expansion
> Of Christendom's small empire;
> You, who have the Moors trembling,
> The marvel prophesied for our times,
> Given to the world, in God's eternal reign,
> To win for God much of the world again.[1]

Sebastian was born on January 20, 1554, eighteen days after the death of his father, the seventeen-year-old João, also an only child.[2] Sebastian's mother was Juana of Austria, sister of Spain's King Philip II. His parents' marriage was part of a centuries-long strategy by Spain to keep a foothold next door. Chroniclers who knew how the story ended recounted Sebastian's beginnings as having been marked by dreams and visions, "fulfillment prophecies" typical of late medieval monarchs who were destined to be saviors of the faith.[3] Juana's alleged visions as she awaited the birth of her child seemed to point toward Africa. By one account, she saw a group of Moors wearing robes of different colors enter her room. At first she thought they were her guards, but when they left and then entered again, she swooned into the arms of her servants.[4] Portraits of Juana depict a stern but possibly beautiful woman whose intelligence leaps off the canvas. She was educated by the Portuguese servants brought to Castile by her mother, the Portuguese-born empress Isabel, and she married a Portuguese prince, her cousin João, in 1552. (The future Philip II had married João's sister María.) Just five months after João's death and her son Sebastian's birth, Juana was summoned back to Spain while Philip II went to England to marry Mary Tudor (María of Portugal having died in 1545). The nineteen-year old princess never saw her son again. She went on to be one of her brother's most trusted advisers, acting as regent in his absence. She established Madrid's most elite and beautiful convent, the Descalzas Reales, where there are several portraits of Sebastian, which

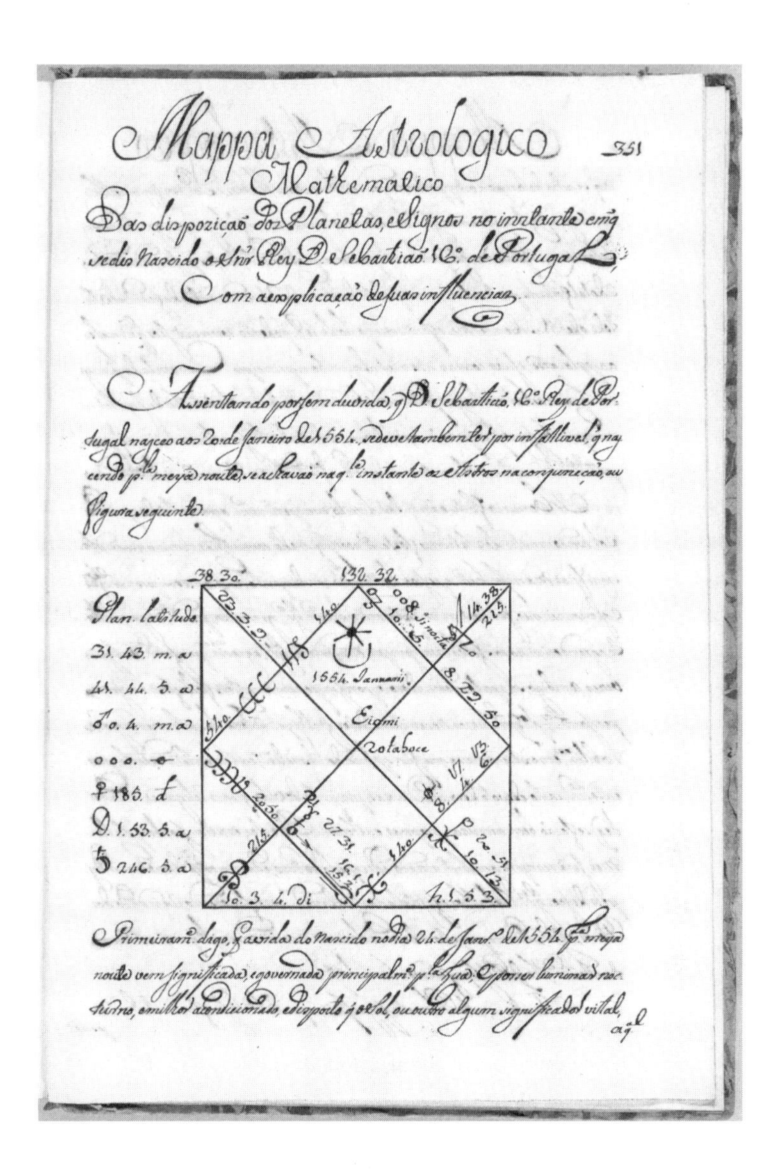
351

Mappa Astrologico Matematico

Das disposiçaõ dos Planetas, e Signos no instante em q se dis Nascido o Snr Rey D. Sebastiaõ 16º de Portugal; Com a explicaçaõ de suas influencias

Assentando por sem duvida, q D. Sebastiaõ 16º Rey de Portugal nasceo aos 20 de Janeiro de 1554, se deve tambem ter por infallivel, q nacendo pto meya noute, se achavaõ naqle instante os Astros na conjunçaõ, ou Figura seguinte

Plan. latitude

1554. Januarii

Eigmi

Primeiramte digo, q a vida do Nascido no dia 20 de Janro de 1554 pta meya noute vem significada, e governada principalmte pla Lua, q por ser luminar nocturno, e milhor acondicionado, e disposto q o Sol, ou outro algum significador vital, aql

Figure 3. "Mappa Astrologico Matematico," drawn on the occasion of Sebastian's birth in 1554, from "Collecção curioza das profecias e controversias sebasticas. . . . ," vol. 2 (MS; Lisbon, 1766). Courtesy of the Fernán Nuñez Collection (Banc MS UCB 143), the Bancroft Library, University of California, Berkeley (vol. 145, fol. 351).

he periodically sent to his mother. Deeply spiritual, she was possibly the first woman allowed into the Jesuits.[5]

As a child, Sebastian was "fair, blond, and beautiful, with a happy disposition. In his time, navigation was very prosperous, with no shipwrecks," stated a history of Iberian royalty, pointing to a contemporary priority.[6] Lisbon, the capital of his kingdom, was the largest and most imposing of Iberia's cities; the historian Fernand Braudel said that had Philip II made Lisbon his capital instead of Madrid, he could have transformed it into another London or Naples.[7] Sebastian was raised by a series of Jesuit tutors and confessors and by two relatives: his grandmother, Catherine, who was both his father's mother and his mother's aunt, and his great-uncle Henry, who had entered the priesthood at fourteen, was an archbishop by twenty-two, and donned the red robes of a cardinal at thirty-three. The two in-laws had deeply opposing attitudes toward child-rearing, education, religion, and national allegiance. Catherine's primary loyalty was to Spain, whose ruler, Philip (her nephew and one-time son-in-law), was her constant correspondent and one of her few remaining relatives; she and her husband, João III, buried all nine of their children, only two of whom had survived long enough to marry. João III died in 1557, and three-year-old Sebastian was sworn in as king. Catherine served as regent until 1562, at which point Henry took over, marking a shift toward more Portuguese interests. He handed the throne to the fourteen-year-old Sebastian in January 1568.

Though the young Sebastian was an avid sportsman and rider, he also was reported to be sickly.[8] The first indication we have is that he suffered severe chills after a day of heavy hunting when he was eleven. The incident was blamed on excessive exercise, but soon it became apparent that there was something urogenital about the ailment, though successive doctors could not decide what it was. Juana sent one of her most trusted aides, Cristóbal de Moura, from Madrid to investigate in 1565, and Philip II sent his own team of doctors. The symptoms appear to have involved involuntary ejaculation, vertigo, fevers, and chills. At least one medical report referred to gonorrhea.[9] The question on everyone's mind, of course, was whether he could have heirs; sadly, the question appears never to have been put to the test. The Spanish ambassador, in the midst of later negotiations to arrange an appropriate marriage for Sebastian, told Philip II in 1576, "It has been shown that the king has not proved himself nor has he ever tried." Furthermore, he said, voicing the opinion of all Spanish emissaries throughout Sebastian's life, "he so hates women that he cannot bear to look at them. If a lady serves him a drink, he tries to take it without touching her. . . . The Jesuits who educated him taught him that contact with women was tantamount to the sin of heresy, and in absorbing this doctrine he lost the capacity to distinguish virtue and gentility from offenses to God." Enemies of the Jesuits as well as those simply concerned about the rocky Portuguese ship of state accused the boy's tutors of essentially holding him captive.[10]

If Sebastian did not like women, he adored activity, both spiritual and physical. Chroniclers and biographers all make note of Sebastian's athleticism and his admirably enthusiastic religiosity. He "was by nature extremely bellicose and since childhood inclined toward weaponry and war games."[11] The Spanish playwright Luis Vélez de Guevara around 1607 depicted a servant asking the young monarch if he wished to dance, paint, or fence, suggesting that dancing would be the correct choice:

> Mi corazón
> tales cosas no apetece.
> Soy colérico y no quiero
> estar dos oras o tres,
> moliendo el cuerpo y los pies
> al compás de un majadero.
> A armas mi estrella me yncita,
> quanto es flema lo aborrezco,
> y si la caça apetezco,
> es porque la guerra ymita.[12]

There probably was no Christian in mid-sixteenth-century Iberia (or anywhere else, for that matter) who was not devout, but there were degrees, and Sebastian's piety was of the militant brand. In particular, he was consumed with a passion for taking back portions of North Africa that his grandfather João III had been forced to relinquish in the 1540s.

That retreat was regarded by many as a shameful episode, one Sebastian felt duty-bound to rectify. This deeply religious young man who, judging by his mother's visions, was born to fight the infidel was called *O Desejado,* "the desired one." Son after son and cousin after cousin had died, and few courtiers would dare criticize or tether the only royal male heir left to Portugal. (His most famous dead cousin was don Carlos, son of Philip II and María of Portugal, who was imprisoned by his father and died in suspicious circumstances in 1568 at the age of twenty-three.) An account of Sebastian's childhood written by his confessor informs us that the boy was "endowed with such extraordinary force that he exceeded all others of his time." He was gifted at sports and "incomparable in the agility of his arms and legs. . . . He was of good stature, with proportionate limbs . . . with absolutely no defects [and with] grace and beauty."[13] The adulation was such, Spanish ambassador Juan de Silva informed a colleague in Madrid, that "they will tell him he's the tallest man in Portugal, or the best musician, or anything similar. His wit is sharp but confused, he imagines things he cannot understand, and thus monsters are born and they tell him he is better than [Cicero]." Later that month Silva told Philip II that Sebastian's education had been so "barbarous" that his virtues would remain forever hidden. Silva cannot have been surprised; he had been warned by his predecessor, Juan de Borja, that he would have to walk on eggshells with his sensitive compatriots (Silva had Portuguese blood) and their king, always reassuring them of Spain's love for them.[14]

In Search of a Land to Reconquer

Persistent inbreeding, ideologically rigid education, religious excess, vanity and adulation, and a proven inability to reason with much intellectual capacity are not the sorts of elements advisable when launching a military expedition. But those, according to chroniclers, ambassadors, and relatives, were the characteristics that defined the teenage monarch, increasingly obsessed with the religious mission of his family and his nation.[15] In the summer of 1569, when a fierce epidemic obliged the royal family to leave Lisbon (some fifty people a day died in Lisbon for weeks; one historian says that half of Lisbon's population perished),[16] he

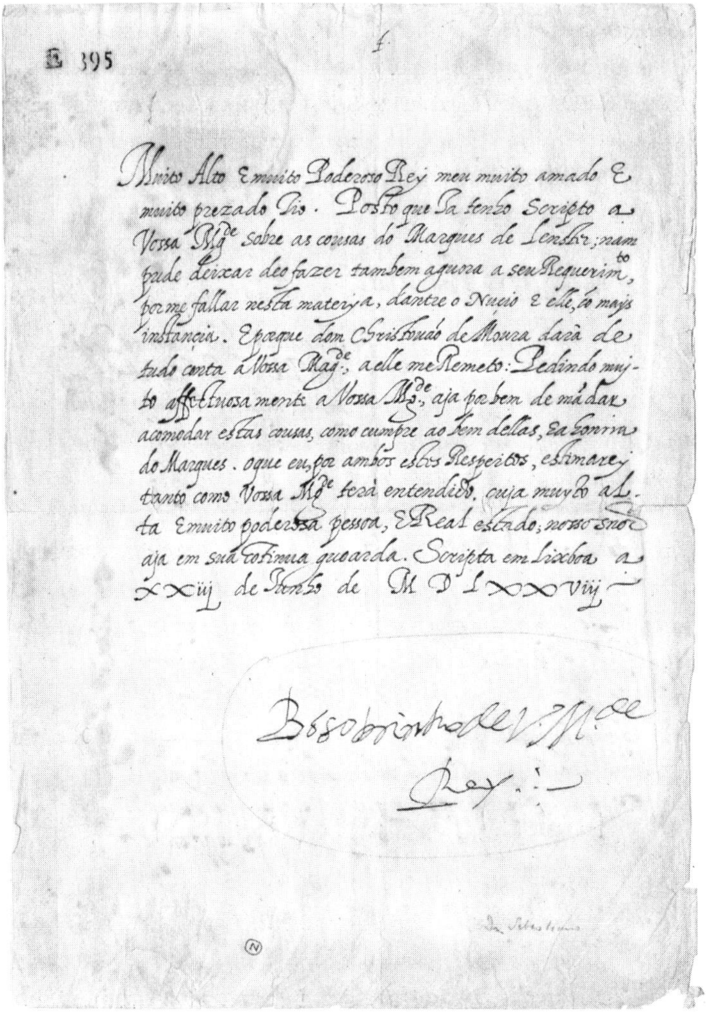

B 395

Muito Alto E muito Poderoso Rey meu muito amado E
muito prezado Tio. Posto que Ja tenho Scripto a
Vossa Mg.de sobre as cousas do Marques de [illegible]; nam
pude deixar de o fazer tambem agoora a seu Requerimento,
por me fallar nesta materya, dantre o Nuçio e elle, co mays
instançia. E porque dom Cristouão de Moura dará de
tudo conta a Vossa Mag.de, a elle me Remeto: Pedindo muj-
to affectuosa mente a Vossa Mg.de aja por bem de mãdar
acomodar estas cousas, como cumpre ao bem dellas, e a honrra
do Marques. o que eu, por ambos estes Respeitos, estimarey
tanto como Vossa Mg.de terá entendido. cuja muyto al-
ta E muito poderosa pessoa, E Real estado, nosso Snor
aja em sua continua guoarda. Scripta em Lixboa a
xxviij de Junho de MDLXXVIIJ

Bõ sobrinho de V. Mde
Rey.

Figure 4. Sebastian's autograph, "Your Majesty's good nephew, King." From a letter dated June 28, 1578, to Philip II (HSA MS B113). Courtesy of the Hispanic Society of America.

traveled throughout Portugal and decided to open up the tombs of several of his ancestors at the beautiful Alcobaça monastery. Over the protests of the Cistercian monks who guarded the royal remains, he swore to the unearthed bodies, including those of Afonso II and Afonso III, that he would restore Portugal's glory. According to later accounts, he was impervious to the voice of reason: "Sire, these Kings and your ancestors did not set for you an example of conquest of other kingdoms but rather they taught you to conserve your own," counseled Father Francisco Machado, of the University of Paris, who happened to be at Alcobaça. "May God grant you a long life and give you a name and a tomb as honorable as these."[17]

Sebastian's religious enthusiasm was further fueled by the famous battle of Lepanto on October 7, 1571, the hero of which was don Juan of Austria, Sebastian's uncle. Don Juan had just suppressed the Moriscos (converted Muslims) in the Alpujarras mountains outside Granada, who revolted in 1568 over increased and repressive restrictions. After his victory there, don Juan took command of a Holy League fleet organized by Pope Pius V and secured a dramatic and audacious victory against the Turks, capturing some two hundred of their galleys and thousands of men, as well as freeing fifteen thousand galley slaves. As many as forty thousand men may have been killed at Lepanto. The league promptly fell apart, and the Turks rearmed, but Lepanto nonetheless became a benchmark for both victors and vanquished, a latter-day battle of Actium where West defeated East and Christendom triumphed over the infidel.[18] The following year, in July 1572, the Portuguese viceroy of India, Luís de Ataíde, returned to Lisbon to huge celebrations and processions. This, too, fired Sebastian's imperial visions, and he commenced efforts to raise troops and ships, though it was unclear who exactly the enemy would be.

There were bad omens, though, which everyone would remark upon later. The 1569 plague was later interpreted as the first of these signs. On September 13, 1572, a vicious storm struck Lisbon, and thirty warships in the harbor were dashed to pieces, while houses and structures up and down the Tagus River were destroyed. And the young king continued to show alarming signs of bad health. Philip II's ambassador during Sebastian's youth, Juan de Borja, regularly informed his master of the chills, fevers, and bleeding.

Yet with the triumphant backdrop of Lepanto and Ataíde's return to Portugal, Sebastian in the summer of 1574 began planning his own crusade. The Spanish royal chronicler Antonio de Herrera wrote that Sebastian initially wanted to go to India but his advisers talked him down to Morocco, never dreaming he would actually go.[19] His plan was to recapture the territory from the Moors, an objective the chroniclers said he had cherished since childhood and for which, it will be remembered, he was destined. Though the bolder of his ministers counseled him to abandon the plan, really not much of a plan at all, the king resisted, ordering recruiters to raise men, all the while trying to keep the project a secret. Borja wrote Philip II on August 14, "The king left Lisbon for [the nearby royal retreat of] Sintra on 3 August, and though people have suspected for days that he sent don António with soldiers to Tangiers [in July] in order to later go there himself, it seemed so crazy I did not even inform Your Majesty, having had the same suspicions last year. . . . But this time there is so much evidence that it is true that I am obliged to write, although the king has not yet informed the queen [Catherine] of his objective." Indeed, Sebastian's grandmother, from whom he was estranged, was kept in the dark until it was too late. "My grandson sailed yesterday and everyone tells me he will go to Africa. He always hid it from me and he also hid his departure, and though today I was given a letter from him saying he will go to Algarve [southern Portugal], I fear what everyone says and I am suffering and in great sorrow," Catherine wrote to Philip II.[20] Cardinal Henry, "tired and distressed because the king would not listen to him," instructed Sebastian to first produce an heir and only then go to war, if he insisted. Sebastian ignored him.[21] There were, it was said, noblemen on board the king's ship who had no idea where they were bound, and news of the arrival in Africa of the paltry expedition, numbering some three thousand men, was received with shock and anger in Lisbon and Madrid. A young monarch with no heir in sight had no business putting his life in danger.

The expedition, based in Tangiers, lasted around three months and was marked by its obvious lack of purpose. At one point Catherine sent a messenger to Sebastian telling him that if he did not come home right away she would go and fetch him. Another person who corresponded with Sebastian was Abu Abdallah Muhammed, "Lord of the Lords of the Monarchy and Empire of Africa and all its inhabitants," and he would not be the last Moroccan ruler to advise Sebastian to stay away. He had been informed that the king of Portugal, moved by his "royal and generous spirit," had decided to visit his lands. "We are very grateful for this noble act" and are willing to help him in all possible ways, he wrote. "But if your intent is other" than noble, Muhammed cautioned him, "you will find our people waiting, ready to show their force against your rash impudence."[22] While in Tangiers, Sebastian deposed don António as governor of that outpost, replacing his cousin and the eventual pretender to the throne with Duarte de Meneses. The adventure finally came to an end in October, when the weather turned cool and Philip II refused to send the young king's forces a shipment of grain to replenish their exhausted food supply. A bit on the defensive after spending three months harassing bewildered North Africans who mostly left him alone, Sebastian wrote several open letters to Portugal's cities upon his return explaining that he had really only meant to visit his forts. He also wrote a chaotic, fifty-three-page account of the adventure.[23]

Morocco in the sixteenth century was governed by the Sa'did sharifs; the Sa'dians were a family from southern Morocco who first rose to prominence precisely in opposition to the Portuguese, and sharifs were those who claimed descent from the Prophet. The dynasty established a state that laid the framework for modern Morocco. Its capitals were Fez and Marrakech, from where they ran important trading centers on the Atlantic coast. The Sa'dians also pushed inland, eventually capturing Timbuktu in 1591, enabling them to control markets of slaves and gold. Morocco's importance to Portugal derived not only from its geographic position at the entrance to the Mediterranean, but from its increasing wealth and its symbolic place as the home of the infidel Moors who once occupied Iberia. It also possessed potentially vast deposits of saltpeter (potassium nitrate), a critical component of gunpowder, which was of keen interest to all the European powers. The sharifs generally managed to play the Turks, the two Iberian nations, and the English against one other, each member of this finely tuned diplomatic quartet in turn distrustful, greedy, and careful.

The opportunity for Sebastian to return to Morocco (and upset the balance) arrived in 1576, when Muhammed was deposed by his uncles, Abd al-Malik and Ahmad al-Mansur, because of Muhammed's tainted bloodline. Malik, who would rule from 1576 to 1578, was a sophisticated and cultured man who spent many years in exile in the bustling cities of Constantinople and Algiers, and he was largely funded by the Turks. Then in his early thirties, he was one of the great examples of the cross-fertilization of Mediterranean Christianity and Islam. After the battle of Lepanto, he briefly was a captive of Spain. Another Lepanto veteran, Miguel de Cervantes, knew Malik in Algiers and wrote of the Westernized Easterner that "he speaks Turkish, Spanish, German, Italian, and French, he sleeps standing, eats at a table, sits like a Christian, and above all is a great soldier, liberal, wise, comprising a thousand graces."[24]

The deposed Muhammed, who earlier had begged Sebastian not to invade, now turned to Spain and Portugal for help against his uncles. (In Lope de Vega's version, the Moroccan flattered the young Portuguese king by comparing him to his imperial grandfather: "You, the famous Sebastian, in whose face I see the image of the Fifth Charles . . .")[25] While Muhammed awaited Iberian assistance, he was a guest in Ceuta. Philip II was reluctant to get involved in the struggle; subsequent writers would speculate as to his ulterior motives (he stood to gain whether Sebastian won or lost), but there were good reasons for shifting his attention away from North Africa. The Turks by then really were in decline and were anyway looking covetously eastward to Persia, and Philip in 1578 ended up signing a truce with them. He also probably figured it was best for Spain to remain friends with as many Moroccans as possible and avoid the establishment of a Muslim alliance in the western Mediterranean. His most immediate tasks now lay north and in the Atlantic: to combat the Dutch Protestants fighting for their independence, keep an eye on England and France, and protect the American fleet, all while managing a budget in continual crisis.

Sebastian, however, insisted, and the two monarchs, uncle and nephew, met in December 1576 in the company of their closest advisers to discuss both the impending African campaign and long-standing attempts to find Sebastian a wife. The site of their ten-day meeting was the huge and wealthy Hieronymite monastery of Guadalupe, in western Spain near the Portuguese border. This was one of the greatest shrines in sixteenth-century Castile and a frequent destination of pilgrims. Columbus went there to give thanks after returning from America; so did pilgrims in works by Cervantes and Lope de Vega. Essentially a royal town unto itself, the complex included hospitals, a school, the monastery and church, workshops, and some seven hundred inhabitants. In light of subsequent events, the meeting would be the subject of chronicles and dramatic productions that traced the tragic denouement back to that majestic encounter in the shadow of priceless relics.

Family Matters on the Eve of Battle

The meeting was prefaced by twin journeys. It took Philip eight days to travel to Guadalupe from his monastery-palace of El Escorial, and he arrived before his nephew to take charge of assigning rooms. With him were many of Spain's leading churchmen and nobles, including the duke of Alba and Philip's loyal aide Cristóbal de Moura, who served as translator.[26] Sebastian took a couple of days longer, leaving Lisbon on December 11. Philip went to receive him and his huge entourage as they arrived in Guadalupe, waiting by the side of the road for nearly half an hour as his nephew approached.[27] When they saw each other in the distance, the two monarchs descended from their respective carriages, removed their hats, walked toward one another, and embraced. Sebastian, according to the account I am using, was unmistakably a Hapsburg and was a couple of inches taller than his uncle. Philip also removed his hat in greeting the high Portuguese noblemen. Sebastian, however, left his hat on his head as the Spanish dukes and counts greeted him, a practice that he continued throughout his stay and that annoyed Spanish critics, always quick to point to Portuguese affectations. "Asked how many people the king [Sebastian] brought," went a contemporary doggerel, "he boldly replied, 'no more than eight hundred; we travel light.'"[28] Like his uncle, Sebastian came accompanied by the most outstanding members of his nobility and church, including the duke of Aveiro, and in every town he had passed through there were triumphant celebrations and elaborate festivities. A composition called "Very Famous Romances" about the king's arrival in the Spanish border city of Badajoz depicts Sebastian as "pale, blond, and very handsome, with a proportional body."[29] Vélez de Guevara chose to make Guadalupe the center of his early seventeenth-century play about Sebastian (the first part transpired in Lisbon, the third in Morocco), inserting that most typical of Golden Age scenes in which the king, disguised as a commoner, encounters a nobody who speaks truth to power. Tell the king, this particular nobody, Baquero, advises Sebastian, "that this campaign he wants in Africa is crazy (*loca*) and that the Moors have neither hurt nor insulted him." Tell him to look at the omens, he adds. Tell him to give us an heir.[30]

Conversations about Sebastian's marriage prospects probably began the minute he was born.[31] During the twenty-four years they lasted, the plans of the various and interrelated royal houses of Europe were continually upset by premature deaths that reshuffled the marriage deck. The strongest candidates for marriage to Sebastian were Margaret of Valois (his initial preference) and Elizabeth of Austria. Both girls were Philip's nieces and Sebastian's cousins. For strategic reasons, the French option was replaced by the Austrian plan, which itself fell apart after don Carlos and Philip II's wife, Elizabeth of Valois, both died, meaning Philip had to remarry. He chose another niece, Anne of Austria (originally betrothed to don Carlos), which meant Elizabeth of Austria went to France to marry Charles IX, sending Margaret to Sebastian. By then, though, the young Portuguese king no longer was willing to marry Margaret, even though the pope was keen on the idea so as to ensure France's cooperation with the Holy League. Sebastian dithered, possibly influenced by his Jesuit advisers, and Charles IX, anxious to get his sister married, paired her off with the future Henry IV of France. Shortly thereafter, Charles IX died, leaving Elizabeth of Austria a widow, but she entered a convent rather than remarry. Candidates were swiftly disappearing. "To speak to him of matrimony is to speak to him of death," remarked one of Philip's envoys to Lisbon.[32] No doubt Sebastian frequently changed his mind, but it is also logical to assume that he was fed up with other people making up his mind for him. To his mother, Juana, he wrote, "I was shocked that you are now trying to persuade me to cede powers regarding my marriage in France, having previously worked so hard to block those plans."[33] Sebastian "has been very hurt since this matter first began," the same envoy wrote, "because of the changes that took place after his first marriage plans were so advanced and he was inclined in that direction. Though his character makes him difficult and the king is young and distrustful, it seems to me he is like children, with their complaints and feelings, who are made content with a toy."[34] Ambassador Borja in 1570 said explicitly to Philip that his nephew was not homosexual (*vicioso*), but he could not come up with a logical explanation for the young man's aversion to marriage, and some of Sebastian's behavior, such as refusing to let anyone see him half-dressed, disturbed the ambassador and prompted jokes in the palace.[35]

By the time of the Guadalupe meetings in December 1576, the only marriage candidate left was Philip's own daughter, Isabel Clara Eugenia, the option favored by Catherine, though it in no way benefited Spain. Three of Philip's sons were dead, and the remaining one, Philip, was weak. If he, too, should die, then Isabel Clara Eugenia would become queen. Philip was not enthused about marrying his daughter to this particular cousin; Sebastian's health and probable impotence were serious concerns, and Juan de Silva, who by now had replaced Borja as Philip's ambassador, informed his master of "secret meetings of many doctors in Lisbon."[36] In fact, Philip probably never seriously considered the option of marrying Sebastian to his daughter, though he said he would, but Sebastian undoubtedly saw the demand as a means of obtaining concessions at Guadalupe regarding the Moroccan adventure.

The content of their meetings was not recorded by anyone. The two monarchs were actually face-to-face—the only time they ever met—five times, for a total of around twelve hours out of the ten days the gathering lasted. The rest of the time there were musical performances, religious services, and meals, "with fowl, goats, pheasants, rabbits, veal, venison, beef, and so much wine one would have thought [the Portuguese] were Flemings or Germans," during which Philip took care to place Sebastian on his right, a sign of respect and a gesture that Spanish critics later said the Portuguese would have been wise to imitate. They were full of slights, arrogant as only those inferior can be, it was said. As a Spaniard and a Portuguese were walking by a cloister, for example, and the Spaniard suddenly saw Philip approach, he warned his companion, "Here comes the king." "What king?' replied the Portuguese.[37]

Sebastian, who was reported to be nervous and inattentive (not surprising, under the circumstances), was housed in a grand hall festooned with silk banners and bejeweled tapestries depicting biblical stories, the seven deadly sins and holy virtues, and battles among mythical gods and creatures. Nearby were nearly twenty smaller rooms occupied by his aides. A diplomatic crisis erupted when a (Spanish) cat managed to get into the rooms and soil the bedding such that it was completely unusable, "and the Portuguese were up in arms over this as if they had been greatly insulted." For their part, the possibly unreliable chronicle went on, the Portuguese left the monks' quarters an absolute pigsty, spent the nights making noise, and even locked the monks in their cells. Coming upon a cistern of rain water in the infirmary, which the monks had deliberately covered with large, heavy stones so the water would stay inside, a few Portuguese gentlemen urinated in it, and they also defiled a stairway in a matter so unsuitable that the chronicler could not bring himself to describe it. "And if they behave like this here, imagine what they do at home." Or so the Spanish writer said. Meanwhile, all Philip would promise Sebastian was fifty ships and five thousand men plus supplies on condition that the Moroccan campaign take place the following August (impossible to fulfill), that Sebastian himself raise fifteen thousand men, and that the expedition land in Larache, on the Moroccan coast, and stay there. One account said Sebastian was so annoyed at his uncle's refusal to sign on to the expedition that he planned to leave at the crack of dawn of the last day without even saying good-bye; Philip II got wind of his plans, and arose extra early.[38]

In Sebastian's absence, an enormous fire burned through Lisbon; among the dead was the wife of the secretary of state, Miguel de Moura. Another omen. Upon returning to Lisbon, Sebastian prevailed upon his nobles to disregard their better instincts, though they—particularly his closest friend, Cristóvão de Tavora—did manage to talk him out of leaving in fall 1577. Another calming influence was Francisco Aldana, a military officer and poet who was not only also talking to Juan de Silva (who described him as "a man of such good character") but was employed by Philip II as a spy in Morocco, principally to show Sebastian the folly of his plans.[39] A third nobleman who resisted Sebastian's militaristic pressure was Viceroy Luís de Ataíde, who chose to return to India rather than participate in the Moroccan adventure. Silva later reported that Sebastian envisioned "a hundred thousand difficulties for his enemies and none for himself . . . and at present there is no human means by which to dissuade him."[40] Over the following months, the Portuguese nobility, clergy, and cities were pressured to "donate" funds; converted Jews also donated in exchange for a ten-year commitment by the crown not to seize their properties if they were later convicted of offenses against the church. (This last arrangement was particularly distasteful to Juan Luis de la Cerda, duke of Medinaceli, whom Philip II sent to Lisbon to restrain Sebastian and who wrote back that Portugal was "one big synagogue.")[41] The hurry to obtain supplies and fit the ships wreaked havoc on local markets, according to one contemporary, as greed was unabated, prices suffered alterations, and Lisbon was crowded with newcomers.[42] The Genoese chronicler Gerolamo Franchi di Conestaggio's starkly anti-Portuguese account reported that Sebastian ignored all the contrary advice of those who "lay before him that he was without heirs, that Christians should rather employ their arms against heretics than infidels, that his forces alone were too feeble for so great an action, strengthening their reasons with many examples. . . . [But] there was neither reason nor example [that] could prevail against the king's opinion, but, fortified in his resolution by men who (either for their own particular [reasons], or for want of judgment) did counsel him to war, it was concluded."[43]

Warnings from Heaven and Earth

It was not just his own men who were warning him. There were also the epidemics, the fire, and the alarming weather. "The most miserable and unhappy year for Portugal was 1577, when the doors were opened to huge and frightening calamities affecting much of Christendom. Observers said that there appeared to be larger and more frequent mutations and strange occurrences than had been seen in many centuries."[44] Worst of all, that most fearful (and predictable) of omens, a comet, appeared around November 7, 1577, and lasted some two months, "the largest and most extraordinary Comet that men had seen in many years."[45] Comets were known to signal imminent alterations in the affairs of nature and societies, generally for the worse. Much depended on how and when the comet appeared. If the great lights should appear in many parts of the sky at once, a contemporary scholar wrote, then "drought and great turmoil in the air and attacks of armies or war" could be expected. "If Comets separated from the Sun by eleven signs should appear in the angle of a King or kingdom, . . . then the King or a grandee of that Kingdom will die. If they appear in the following house, then his treasure and belongings are safe but the Governor or administrator of his kingdom will change; if they appear in a ruinous house, illness and sudden deaths will follow." Ptolemy and other ancient authorities, on whom these theories were based, were not always correct, the scholar admitted. But sometimes they were.[46] In the case of 1577, "Great judgments were issued, most aimed at the King of Portugal because he was seen to be so immersed in war and so ill prepared for such an important matter. . . . But as the ancients also would interpret such wonders in their favor, to urge on their soldiers, . . . the Portuguese said that their blood was boiling and that the Comet was telling the king, attack, attack [*acometa, acometa*] rather than predicting misfortune."[47] The play on words was allegedly used by Sebastian himself: "Using an ingenious paronomasia and a play on words, the never sufficiently mourned King don Sebastian replied to those who wished to divert him from his doomed objective by pointing to the always fatal comet and saying, with remarkable sharpness and wit, 'No, you've misunderstood; the Comet is telling me to attack (*acometa*).'"[48] When chronicler Fernando de Goes Loureiro wrote of the "horrifying and terrible Comet in the Sky," it is striking to note that he placed the comet after, not before, his account of Sebastian's death, as if to make sense of chaos and tragedy. "There were many judgments and opinions," he wrote, "and some said the Comet surely announced the calamity and ruin which later befell the kingdom, yet it could not dissuade the unfortunate King Sebastian from his purpose and campaign, though the Heavens themselves warned of the sentence they had passed."[49] For Pero Roiz Soares, it was "the most terrifying comet ever seen."[50] Another of the clergymen present at the battle of Alcazarquivir, Fray Bernardo da Cruz, said in his 1586 account not only that the terrifying comet literally pointed to Africa, "where it promised to take effect," but also that many people in Penamacor (near the Spanish border) that same year saw armies of men in the sky.[51] Ambassador Juan de Silva described the comet to the king's secretary, Gabriel de Zayas, saying it was a "bright, shining star emitting so many rays and creating such a large ball that it was wondrous, growing every night and traveling toward the east. Some say it is not a comet," he wrote. "I'm not an astrologer, nor do I believe in them."[52] It is worth noting that Philip II ordered a report on the comet to be written by the cosmographer Juan López de Velasco, who turned in a reasonable set of arguments proving, basically, that nobody really knew much about them. But López de Velasco was quite sure that there was no basis whatsoever to the theory that comets announced the death of princes and kings.[53]

At any rate, Sebastian did not let the comet get in the way of his plans. The restraining influence of Catherine disappeared in February 1578, when the weary former queen and regent died. (His mother, Juana, had died five years earlier at the age of thirty-eight; Uncle Henry still hovered in the background.) In March, Sebastian wrote to the Santa Cruz monastery in Coimbra for authorization to carry into battle the sword and shield of Afonso Henriques, Portugal's first king, whose twelfth-century tomb was (and is) there. An eighteenth-century account describes the conditions under which these treasures were delivered to the king, but for unknown reasons they were, mercifully, not taken into battle.[54] Military recruitment was slow and, as everywhere else in early modern Europe, a magnet for corruption. As Portuguese ambassadors were dispatched throughout Catholic Europe to collect commitments of men, munitions, and money, the streets of Lisbon became choked with soldiers and merchants, and the ceaseless drums were heard day and night. Even those who were not going to war pretended they were, so as to please the king, and not for the last time in this tale, clothing became a way of identifying character and motive: "There was nobody who had not changed outfits; even the oldest ministers and most respected men of letters . . . who would wear long, honest, and authorized clothing, decent for their persons and dignity, now all wore short outfits . . . with medals and decorated feathers and many other mad and luxurious elegancies."[55] Philip II sent emissaries to Lisbon to reason with his nephew, who was increasingly resentful that he was not getting what he wanted. "He's on fire," Philips's ambassador Silva wrote, "and it is impossible to dissuade him." Though Philip had instructed that he was not to even think about marching inland once he landed on the Moroccan coast, Silva learned that Sebastian was collecting what he described as portable trenches and tanklike vehicles obviously meant for the desert. In Silva's opinion, the monarch was seeking as many difficulties and as much danger as possible; the appeal of the thing lay in its difficulty. When Sebastian asked Silva if Philip suspected he was planning to march inland, Silva replied (he told Philip) that Philip suspected nothing because a decision like that would be sheer madness. According to a May 13 letter, Sebastian's closest friend, Cristóvão de Tavora, pleaded with Silva to ask Philip for more military aid, as it was clear there was no stopping Sebastian, and he could not go unprotected.[56] Silva's missives got more and more desperate: "the king is on fire," he repeated on at least four occasions in May. On June 8, a week before he was scheduled to embark, this supremely loyal and intelligent man wrote Secretary Zayas, "I am leaving for war, His Majesty's ambassador, with no weapons and no tents. . . . I can only hope to die in the coming six days.[57]

The Moroccan ruler, Abd al-Malik, also begged Sebastian not to embark on the unwarranted venture, not only because it would endanger the fragile balance of power in the region but because the Portuguese would lose. Subsequent descriptions of Malik are universally positive, consistent with the Spanish tradition of admiring worthy enemies. The descriptions stand in contrast to those of Sebastian, for whom *youthful, impetuous, and devout* were the best adjectives writers could find. Fray

Luis Nieto, a Spanish mendicant preacher present at the battle of Alcazarquivir, wrote of Malik at length and, like Cervantes, he admired the Moroccan's linguistic skills:

> He was a man of medium stature and good posture with a broad back; . . . he was as white as milk, with rosy cheeks and a stiff beard, with large green eyes, and in all other ways he was a most attractive and gracious man. In addition, he was very strong and was continually skirmishing and working his horses hard and shooting arrows. He spoke our Spanish very well, and he wrote it. He also knew Italian and he spoke Turkish better than any other language except his own, which was Arabic, in which he was an outstanding poet. He was extremely clever and very measured and discreet in all things, particularly regarding the government of his kingdoms. He played several instruments and danced with grace; he was very fond of weapons and strategy, and with his own hands fabricated some artillery pieces. In all pursuits he was gifted, and though an infidel, was so fond of Christians, and of Spaniards in particular, that I cannot praise him enough.[58]

An anonymous chronicler described him as "a strong man of medium stature with a broad forehead, large light-colored eyes, a round chubby face, a Roman nose, wide mouth, thick lips, narrow teeth, somewhat hunched, with skin the color of brown paper."[59] And a third described him as a man of "ordinary stature, well made and lean, . . . with a pleasant presence . . . and a serious yet happy appearance. He was a brave soldier."[60]

Malik probably wrote three letters to Sebastian: one in late 1577, a second in April 1578, and a third in July, after Sebastian arrived in Morocco.[61] No originals survive. In his first missive he patiently explained the succession rules in his country to demonstrate that he was the legitimate ruler of Morocco. "I offer you this brief account because I know, as the soldier I once was, that before one attains kingdoms through arms, one must use reason," he wrote. He asked Sebastian to send envoys so he could better know the young king's pretensions and could explain his own, and he warned him that Muhammed was unworthy of Sebastian's trust.[62] The second letter arrived with a Captain Zúñiga, who had been captive in Morocco and was released as a messenger. Again Malik pointed to his legal right of succession, and again he requested that Sebastian send a negotiator.[63] The third letter, the most widely circulated, judging by the number of copies remaining, was written just before the battle.[64] "May one god be praised everywhere," it began, signaling that both writer and recipient were followers of monotheistic creeds. Again he counseled Sebastian that his war was unjust, this time adding that if he really wanted to conquer land that was not his, he should do so alone and not in the company of Malik's nephew, who was a dog, a pagan, and a traitor unworthy even of "the slave of my slaves." Malik reminded Sebastian that Muhammed had slain previous emissaries from Portugal and was promising what he could not deliver. Malik, on the other hand, could deliver, and he promised Sebastian land for tillage beyond Portugal's fortresses, a valuable offer that would alleviate the garrisons' isolation. "They tell me that you are bringing [Charles V's] banner with you and that you plan to crown yourself emperor of my kingdom," he wrote, well-informed as always. (Muhammed had promised to make Sebastian emperor in return for his help.) "I don't know who is deceiving you, for I want only your friendship and neighborliness. Let us meet in a place where you are safe, and you can give me your banner, and I promise I will fly it from the highest walls of my cities to confirm you are emperor, as they say you wish to be; anything to avoid your perdition, which otherwise is certain." Think of how many soldiers are needed to expel someone from his own home, Malik wrote, and how much advantage natives always have over invaders. "You do not bring one-tenth the number of men I have, and I am warning you in good time. May God be my witness and judge, for He helps those who have justice on their side." Finally, he wrote, "you come in search of me with no right and you want to wage an unjust war against me, which neither serves nor pleases God. Know that this will cost more lives than grains of mustard can fill a sack. You are young and incxperienced and ill-advised."

Sebastian's fleet—between five hundred and eight hundred ships—left Lisbon on July 8, 1578, after nearly two weeks in the city's wide-open port awaiting favorable winds. (The Tagus was "curdled" with ships, one observer said.[65]) Behind him the king left three men in charge of his government "during my brief absence."[66] According to Nieto, the king took with him fourteen thousand foot soldiers (of whom eight thousand carried picks, "the most useless weapon one could have in Berberia"), two thousand cavalrymen, three thousand former prisoners, one thousand drivers, and an "infinite number" of servants. All told, twenty-six thousand souls. The soldiers included three thousand Germans, three hundred Italians under the command of the Englishman Thomas Stukeley, and two thousand Spaniards (fewer than Philip had promised).[67] There were also two thousand five hundred "adventurers," gentlemen who paid their own way and served under Cristóvão de Tavora. Along with them went wagons, coaches, weaponry, and hundreds of horses and livestock. Juan de Silva calculated that there was enough equipment for an army five times its size; a Portuguese chronicler who survived the battle estimated that there were forty thousand people, most of them "of no use whatsoever for the purposes of warfare."[68] Unlike in other wars, one observer noted, men boarded the ships unsmiling, grim-faced. "As if they could see the coming disaster, they ached at being taken against their will. In the port there was a leaden silence, and in all the time the great number of ships were being readied, not once was a fife or a trumpet heard."[69]

And the signs kept coming, even as the ships pulled out of "Ulysses's famous harbor," a reference to Lisbon's alleged founder.[70] The royal ship, as it turned toward the sea, was caught by a current and its prow smashed up against another ship, causing an artillery piece to fire, killing a sailor. Another lesser mishap, widely commented on, occurred when a churchman attempted to attach the expedition's flag onto a mast and the flag was upside down, with the image of the crucified Christ and the royal coat of arms facing downward. Following that, a lieutenant stumbled twice, and the flag was dropped altogether. Once they were finally on their way, Sebastian asked a musician, Domingos Madeira, to sing, and he obliged: "Yesterday you were king of Hispania, today you have no castle," warbled the apparently clueless man, singing a tune commemorating Rodrigo, the last of the Spanish Visigothic kings, whose defeat by the Moors ushered in eight hundred years of Muslim occupation. As everyone knew, Rodrigo's body was never recovered from the battle of Guadalete, though some said he managed to escape.[71] For Conestaggio, "The King of Portugal's departure from Lisbon was so mournful that it gave apparent signs of evil success."[72] But there was an immediate precedent for bad omens ending with a glorious voyage: in *The Lusiads,* which Sebastian's chroniclers were sure to have read, the Portuguese captain recounts his fleet's solemn departure from Lisbon, where "The people considered us already lost / On so long and uncertain a journey." In one of the most moving and puzzling episodes of the epic, an "honorable" old man in the port delivers a remarkable ten-verse rant on vanity and hubris just as the ships are setting off, undermining the imperialist thrust of the entire poem:

> 'To what new catastrophes do you plan
> To drag this kingdom and these people?
> What perils, what deaths have you in store
> Under what magniloquent title?
> What visions of kingdoms and gold-mines
> Will you guide them to infallibly?
> What fame do you promise them? What stories?
> What conquests and processions? What glories?'[73]

"Here Died the King Who Killed Himself . . ."

After several stops and delays along the way, the fleet arrived at Asilah in mid-July, as disorderly at sea as it had been in port, according to Juan de Silva, who continued writing letters as he sailed. "The Moors played with us and captured a couple of ships at the back with thirty or forty men on board," the ambassador reported from Cádiz, "and what seems most incredible, the king [Sebastian] is moored in an open bay with no protection from the sea." The fleet was sailing in bits and pieces as it moved southward at the mercy of the winds.[74] Sebastian's forces were joined by some two thousand men loyal to (or at least in the employ of) Muhammed, the dethroned sharif. Sebastian's aides, allegedly among them Afonso de Portugal, count of Vimioso, insisted the army should sail down the Atlantic coast twenty miles to the fort of Larache, the recovery of which was, in theory, the point of the expedition (and one of Philip II's conditions), and engage the enemy there.[75] Sebastian, as Silva had suspected he would, instead decided to march inland through the desert from Asilah toward Alcazarquivir (al-Qasr al-Kabir), a town of several thousand inhabitants around twenty-five miles away, and there turn northwest back to the coast and to Larache. Spies reported that Malik was massing tens of thousands of well-armed men; Sebastian decided the information was false.[76] Malik, who, in Conestaggio's words, weighed "how much better an ill peace is [than] a just war," sent his last letter, which, as we saw, was rejected. (An anonymous correspondent said of Malik's offer quite remarkably that "the Moor justified himself like a Christian and the King responded like a Moor.")[77] One of Conestaggio's critics, the Spanish cleric Sebastián de Mesa, in terms similar to Conestaggio's, lamented that the "energetic king [Sebastian] did not see how certain peace is worth more than a doubtful victory."[78] Silva, of course, knew all of this. He wrote to the king from Asilah, "I just learned that the sharif himself has asked [Sebastian] to stay put . . . which had absolutely no effect. Thus we set off, so lacking in every way that soldiers from Andalucia were just sent home because they have no weapons. . . . No other nation would go so cheerfully in search of danger."[79]

On July 29, the overland expedition that Silva so feared began. In the blazing summer heat, the Portuguese forces plodded through the desert. By the fourth day, exhausted under the weight of their body armor, they had consumed most of their food and water. Confronted with the now indisputable fact that Malik's army indeed vastly outnumbered their own and was gathered just ahead, the royal councilors fruitlessly beseeched Sebastian to withdraw. As they awaited action, Sebastian's men were hungry, thirsty, unruly, and terrified they were about to be massacred.[80] Two days later, after the troops had marched a few more miles, the captain and poet Francisco Aldana appeared with five hundred reinforcements and yet another letter, this one from the duke of Alba, whose great military prowess Sebastian must have admired. Aldana also brought a precious gift, the helmet and silk tunic of Charles V, Sebastian's grandfather who, as Malik knew, Sebastian wished to emulate. (Camões had written that Sebastian's two grandfathers, Charles and João III, "both look to see resurrected in you / their times and heroic works."[81]) "May God grant you

Figure 5. Present-day Asilah, on the Moroccan coast. Photograph by Mari MacKay-Sefton.

success in your campaign and a safe return," Alba wrote, though adding, "It appears you went to Africa without informing me." This was the last warning Sebastian would receive. The famed military hero offered some tactical advice and a reminder that "you take the enemy with you, for Africa is a flatland, not good for positions."[82] Indeed, spies by then were informing Malik of his adversary's inadequacies and inferiority and, as one chronicler put it, "the Moors began to lose their fear."[83] On the night of August 3, the hungry soldiers clamored for food, having consumed eight days' rations in four, and Sebastian responded to their entreaties by ordering that an ox be slaughtered and biscuit distributed.[84]

The following morning, August 4, camped near the confluence of two rivers north of Alcazarquivir, the Christian forces confessed their sins and heard exhortations to die for the faith. The royal aides, having spoken their final words of advice, had nothing left to say. Sebastian's last speech was recorded in the chronicles in accordance with the classical norms of antebellum oration:

> I can only say how happy you should be on this occasion, for today we commence that just and holy undertaking so desired by all, entrusted to us and longed for by my ancestors. You well know the hourly affronts to Christianity in this land of the infidel, by an enemy so near to us he is practically a thief in our own house, and well you know the danger posed by the men whom [Malik] brought here upon the Turk's orders. . . . I believe you and everyone else knows that the holy Catholic faith, the protection of the faithful, and the clemency owed to the suffering all oblige me to undertake this mission. I hope God helps me, and I am sure that you all will be with me . . . because Christ's soldiers, when they have sufficient faith, are lords of the battlefield." The speech closed with an Ave Maria led by Father Alexander of the Company of Jesus.[85]

At noon the first cannon shot was fired. According to Nieto, one of the battle's first eyewitness chroniclers, the sound of all the gunfire going off at once, "with such strange fury and such horror and fright, made it truly seem that the earth, with enormous rumbling, and the sky, with fire and thunder and the roar of the artillery, all wanted to sink inwards."[86] The Christian forces fled in terror, prompting an alarmed Aldana to tell Sebastian that his forces were young and inexperienced and needed someone to rein them in and remind them of who they were. "And thus the King rode among his men calling to them, 'My Portuguese, such a small event has provoked such a large show of fear? This is not how wars were won by those Portuguese who came before you, whose honor and bravery is known the world over.'"[87]

But in a "blink of an eye" it was over.[88] The Moors—actually Arabs, Berbers, Turks, and renegades (former Christians)—at first appeared to break ranks and withdraw, but it was merely an astute tactic by Malik. It was his last. He had been gravely ill for at least a month, possibly the effect of poison, and in the chaos of the battle, he collapsed and died, though his death was kept secret until the end of the battle.[89] His forces returned, and the Christians, quickly surrounded, ran out of ammunition and were so crowded that many trampled or stabbed each other. Nieto and other Spanish writers reported that Portuguese noblemen dismounted and hid under their wagons and then broke and fled for the coast to escape death, the dust, and the insufferable heat. In just four hours, anywhere from three thousand to eight thousand Moroccan combatants were slain, along with twelve thousand Portuguese forces, including the cream of the Portuguese nobility. The captive commoners mostly ended up as slaves, to be dispersed throughout the Magreb, many for the rest of their lives. The nobles—among them Juan de Silva (who was badly wounded) and don António, prior of Crato, one-time governor of Tangiers and future claimant to the Portuguese throne—eventually were ransomed, making Ahmad al-Mansur, who succeeded his brother Malik, a wealthy and powerful man. Ahmad secured Moroccan independence and remained a close friend of England until his death in 1603.

Sebastian may have been unstable and a terrible commander, but it appears he was not a coward and was determined to be the last man standing. Suitably, false news and misread signs led to his death, which became a set piece for chroniclers. Surrounded by chaos and death, the young and reckless king galloped round and round, taking on one attacker after the next. His standard bearer, at some point aware that a number of Moors were heading their way, alerted his lord, who replied that there were fewer enemies than it seemed. The bearer was immediately killed, after which the Portuguese forces had no means of following the king, leaving him "as a man lost," in Conestaggio's words. "All the Portuguese were surrounded by an infinite number of Moors, and so they lost sight of the king, deceived by those who said they had seen him elsewhere." Some said the Portuguese army believed Sebastian had been taken prisoner or was in another part of the battlefield, so no one bothered to protect him. The Moors may also have thought he had been taken or killed. (So Sebastian was alive and his enemies thought he was dead; Malik was dead, and his enemies thought he was alive.) Fray Antonio San Román wrote that Christian soldiers were mistakenly following the standard of don Duarte de Meneses. Round and round Sebastian went, covered with dust and dirt. His horse was shot from under him, and one of his men offered him his. The king rode off again, promising that the man would be recompensed, and again his horse was shot. Most chronicles and fictional accounts said three horses were killed from under him. The correspondent in Lisbon of the great Fugger banking dynasty, writing a few weeks later, was one of those who counted three horses, and he added a story that appears nowhere else, that the Turks mistook the son of the duke of Braganza, inexplicably driving a gilt coach in the midst of the battle, for Sebastian, and the man escaped death only by promising them a huge ransom.[90]

Fighting like a lion, Sebastian went on and on, and suddenly the Moors realized who he was, "and for every Christian there were three hundred Moors." Sebastian was down to just four aides surrounding him, among them Tavora. "My Lord, what can we do?" Tavora asked his best friend. "What Heaven wills, if we are deserving," and with that, sword in hand, he threw himself back at the Moors, ignoring Tavora's pleas. Then the king (or Tavora, or another soldier; all versions exist) "put a handkerchief on the point of his sword as a sign of peace, and he rode toward the Moors like an ambassador, but the barbarians captured him and don Cristóbal." Tavora was killed immediately. The count of Vimioso also went down. No surviving member of the Portuguese army witnessed the king's death. Malik's men squabbled for a few minutes over who should kill him, an honor they ended up sharing. According to Nieto, they were not Berbers but Arabs, who did not properly understand the sign of peace.[91]

"Do not trust anyone who says they saw things that day and wants to tell the story, . . . because it was a bolt of wrath from God that blinded us all."[92] The bolt of wrath spelled the end of Portuguese independence: "Oh unhappy patria! O unfortunate king of lamentable memory! For when your Empire and your name were most widely known in the world and your virtue offered the greatest hopes, you launched this insane adventure, scene of such tragic tales in which all the world's evils conspired against your Kingdoms. Here died the King who killed himself, his own hangman, his vassals' own dagger."[93]

Here died the king, but here too were born myths that arose from older myths and memories. If such a thing as Alcazarquivir could be true, then anything could be true. Two days after the battle, the new sharif told Sebastian's servant Sebastián de Resende that he could win his freedom by identifying the royal cadaver, certainly an incentive (it was said) to point out the first plausible candidate among the thousands of decomposing bodies and body parts piled and scattered on the battlefield. The remains he chose had been stripped of clothing.[94] Like Christ's body, this one bore five gashes (though not from arrows, like those suffered by Sebastian's beloved and martyred namesake). There were also two musket wounds in the torso. The corpse was carried to a tent, now the resting place of three dead kings: Malik, Sebastian, and Muhammed, who drowned in a river as he was trying to escape. "This was the most sorrowful spectacle ever seen, enough to make even the most hard-hearted burst into tears, to see three Kings, so powerful, all dead in battle," Nieto wrote.[95] Malik was buried in great triumph. Sebastian again was identified by a group of captive comrades, this time led by Duarte de Meneses, who "carefully viewed" the body, in Conestaggio's words. *Sebastianistas* later would say that a pale, badly decomposed, nude body with no royal insignia or accessory could easily have belonged to a Swiss, Flemish, or German soldier in the Portuguese army. The Portuguese offered Morocco's new ruler, Ahmad, ten thousand ducats for the body, an offer he found insulting. Rather, he suggested, he would like Asilah, Ceuta, Mazagan, and Tangiers to be returned. As that was not possible, Sebastian was buried with honors in Alcazarquivir on August 7. Yet again, two countrymen were called upon to recognize the body, but by then it was so badly decomposed that it was completely unrecognizable.

Philip II later that year called upon the services of Andrea Gasparo Corso to help transport Sebastian's body to Ceuta. One of five Corsican brothers who worked throughout the Christian and Muslim Mediterranean as merchants, agents, and middlemen, Andrea managed the family's Algiers office. Not surprisingly, he also worked for Malik (and knew Cervantes), and immediately after the battle he began helping Philip with the ransom effort. Sebastian's body was disinterred in Alcazarquivir, and was buried on December 4 in the Trinitarian church, in Ceuta. One of the witnesses at the disinterment was Juan de Silva, who lost the use of one arm on account of his wounds. The new Moroccan ruler had ordered Silva's release almost immediately, but he remained in North Africa under medical supervision until late December. "I pray God punishes that young and proud king, as his uncle and those who loved him told him He would," Silva wrote secretary Zayas.[96]

As for the third king, Muhammed, his body was flayed, salted, stuffed, and displayed throughout the kingdom that he had betrayed and lost. He left a son, whom we will meet again. The great Portuguese poet Camões died two years later, on June 10, 1580, just before his country fell to Spain. The heroic age of his epic had ended long before he began writing it.

"Thus was the end of this unfortunate prince in whom were found all things to make his death lamentable: youth, a quest for virtue, lack of succession, a violent death, and his body imprisoned. He had excellent qualities, but they did not help him. . . . But the intentions impelling him toward this reckless end were those of generosity, magnanimity, religious piety, a desire for military glory, gallantry, and a strong heart. It is not unlike what was said of Alexander: he had the virtues of nature and the vices of fortune . . ."[97] This great tragedy, the chasm between what was and what might have been, evokes what Paul Fussell called "irony-assisted recall," referring to the recollections and memories of World War I and the belle époque that preceded it. Even though the latter war was ultimately won by the Allies, participants, as if recounting a defeat, often returned to those points at which things could have been done differently. Such was the case with Alcazarquivir, momentous and unthinkable but also entirely predictable: If only Sebastian had listened; if only we had heeded the omens. The contrast between the glorious optimism and the senseless slaughter, the long build-up and the sudden defeat, the moral certainty of victory and the physical certainty of catastrophe, was all too much to bear.[98]

The news could not be believed. At the same time, stories that could not possibly be true were taken as fact. *Novedades*, one way of saying "news" in Spanish (it also means "novelties"), were never a good thing. No less an authority than Covarrubias, author of the first Spanish dictionary, said *novedades* were new, unaccustomed things, "usually dangerous, for they signify changing old ways."[99] On August 8 a Portuguese agent in Puerto de Santa María, near Cádiz, heard from Ceuta that Sebastian had been defeated but perhaps was taken captive.[100] Rumors of the disaster reached the courts of Lisbon and Madrid on August 10 (six days after the event) and quickly spread through the peninsula. Philip II, who was in his palace in El Escorial, in the mountains outside Madrid, learned the news late on the night of August 12; he immediately prayed in his chapel and then went to bed but could not sleep, and the following day more messages arrived saying Sebastian had been captured alive. Subsequent letters reconfirmed the young king's death, but doubts lingered in Philip's mind until probably August 18.[101]

In Lisbon, meanwhile, what was left of the Portuguese authorities scrambled to manage the story.

> Fearing trouble [*novedad*], the governors said only that there had been a battle, but people guessed the bad news. . . . It was impossible to cover up something of this import, because the news had already arrived, and people saw the governors' sad faces and knew there were meetings every day. Mail was halted, and outsiders were not allowed anywhere, and all the roads and entrances to Lisbon were guarded. . . . The entire city was filled with fear; the men were yellow, sad, confused, some struck dumb, and they did not know what to say or what to imagine, each one providing his own version of these events as it seemed to him, huddling in groups . . . [and speaking of] the bad signs that had been there from the very beginning.[102]

From the very start, then, the circulation and control of news was a crucial component of this story. The sixty-six-year-old Cardinal Henry, now apparently the next king, stayed in Alcobaça, north of Lisbon, and awaited confirmation. According to Diogo Barbosa Machado, Henry was one of many people (St. Teresa supposedly was another) who had visions on August 4; he saw the bishop of Coimbra, don Manoel de Meneses, lying in a pool of blood.[103] Meanwhile, on August 18, a Vatican official in Lisbon, Roberto Fontana, wrote to Rome that he had received word that Sebastian, along with don António and the duke of Aveiro, were all safe. The following day another interlocutor told Rome that Sebastian was probably dead.[104]

On August 24 at last it became official. Church bells in Lisbon tolled all day. "The city has become Troy, burning amid wails, noble tears and illustrious sighs, while the common people are beside themselves with pain and sorrow."[105] The cruel death of a young monarch and the loss of Portugal's national sovereignty was punishment far exceeding the crime of hubris.

> At once, the city exploded in shouts and wails, tears and mourning, not only in Lisbon but throughout the kingdom; . . . some lost their fathers and others their husbands and others their sons and brothers . . . In the streets and in houses one heard nothing but sobbing. . . . For many days, the women did not want to believe that their husbands and King Sebastian were dead, and throughout the kingdom it was believed that he would appear and that the body they said was the king's was actually a German's, but as time went by they realized this was ignorance.[106]

This was not the only writer to point to women and the lower classes as the origin of foolish and desperate beliefs. Even illustrious women were taking "new license" in their sorrow and their prayers, the author of the anonymous "Los ytenes de Portugal" wrote. "There is no devotion they will not practice, no witchcraft they will not believe, no holy women who will not rob them with their superstitions, and the worst part is that they have become so restless and troublesome that if their husbands, wherever they are, knew about this, they would choose to remain captives." In Conestaggio's account,

> It was a pitiful thing to hear the women (whereof the most noble in their houses) from whence you might hear the noise, and the rest in the streets, powering forth their cries and tears unto heaven, the which they redoubled so often as the news was confirmed by any new advertisement. And as it often happens that minds suppressed do oftentimes turn to superstition, so they and likewise many men did not believe what was said, but hoping beyond all hope, and trusting more than they should (although it were verified unto them that their husbands and kinsfolk were dead, yet would they have them still living) and deceived by sorcerers and witches, but most of all by their own desires, remained long without their widows habit, expecting in vain news of him which was passed into another life.[107]

News traveled quickly. In Avila, the future St. Teresa wrote just two weeks after the catastrophe, "I grieve for the death of such a Catholic king and am angry at those who let him place himself in such great danger," showing she knew about the battle but not its political prelude.[108] A Fugger agent informed his masters in Augsburg of the calamity: "The men went about as if dazed. The wailing of the women was so loud that it can be compared with that which arose at the taking of Antwerp. It is a woeful matter to lose in one day the King, their husbands, their sons, and all the goods and chattels they had with them." But, he added, assuming a more practical tone, "what is even more terrible is that this kingdom now must fall under Spanish rule, which they can brook the least of all."[109]

The Portuguese incredulity, at least as it was depicted in chronicles, had historical precedent. When the Athenians first heard their army had been vanquished in Sicily, they too, according to Thucydides, refused to believe the accounts of soldiers who had escaped. Later, "they turned against the public speakers who had been in favor of the expedition, as though they themselves had not voted for it, and also became angry with the prophets and soothsayers" who had promised victory.[110] Plutarch, in *Nicias* and also in "On Talkativeness" in the *Moralia*, recounted a tale ("it is said . . .") in which the Sicilian news first arrived from a stranger who sat down in a barber's chair and began speaking of the defeat, assuming it was not news at all. The horrified barber ran out of his shop and began broadcasting the story, whereupon the unlucky stranger was ordered to explain his sources. "And he, giving no satisfactory account, was taken for a spreader of false intelligence and a disturber of the city, and was, therefore, fastened to the wheel and racked a long time, till other messengers arrived that related the whole disaster particularly."[111] In a similar case, Venice received word of the fall of Negroponte on July 31, 1470, when a shipwrecked sailor arrived in the city with a bundle of rain-soaked letters describing celebratory bonfires along the Turkish coast. At first, people were just puzzled, and uncertainty reigned, but soon more reports arrived, and there were church bells, lamentations, and processions to allay fears, as there would be in Lisbon a century later. "And then murmurs were heard that Negroponte had been lost. The news spread throughout the country. It is impossible to describe how terrible were the groans and sighs," which got only worse once survivors trickled back, each with his own terrible account.[112]

If Sebastian's body was buried multiple times, the slain king also had several funerals. At 6 A.M. on August 27, a Wednesday, Lisbon's city councilors and other officials, dressed in mourning, walked solemnly from the town hall to the steps of the cathedral accompanied by a horseback rider dragging behind him a large black flag. Among the official mourners were three old judges, each holding a shield high above his head. When they reached the church, one of the judges walked up the steps and turned to the crowd as a municipal notary cried out, "Weep sires, weep citizens, weep people for your king don Sebastian. . . . Weep for his youth cut short, for he died in the war against the Moors in the service of God and for the good of his kingdom." Then the judge put the shield on the ground and broke it into bits. All the men, accompanied by crowds, then walked behind the horseman dragging the black flag until they reached the Rua Nova, where again the convocation was uttered and another shield was broken in front of Our Lady of Oliveira. The ceremony was repeated a third time in front of the royal hospital, after which the procession returned to the church and heard a funeral Mass probably delivered by the great Jesuit preacher Luís Alvares.[113] The day after the shields were broken, Henry was crowned.

Sebastian's second funeral was in the grand Hieronymite church of

Belém on September 19 or 20, an occasion of great pomp presided over by the new, elderly king. Historians disagree on who delivered the funeral Mass. The confusion is the result of statements by Fray Miguel de los Santos years later when he was under arrest for masterminding the imposture, and of semifictional works by Camilo Castelo Branco in the nineteenth century. Fray Miguel, who at the time of Alcazarquivir was provincial (chief of a religious order in a province) of the Augustinian order, told the judge in the Madrigal case that it was he who preached in Belém, and most chroniclers follow this version. Before speaking, he said, he had been warned by someone to be careful because Sebastian himself was in the church and would be listening. One account has Fray Miguel scurrying off to ask Henry what to do—was it really a *funeral* Mass he was delivering?—and the king allegedly told him to go ahead and preach.[114] But historians generally believe the funeral Masses were presided over by Luís Alvares, not Fray Miguel.[115] The story might have read better had it been Fray Miguel, but Alvares certainly knew how to orate. It was hubris that had led Portugal down this path ending in three hours of butchery, he admonished his listeners. It was the end of "so many dreams of so many men of so many estates of so many offices of so many sacrifices, . . . the end of so much madness, such lying, such pride and such arrogance, such hope and so much nothing." Damn you, he told the people crowding the enormous church, for it was they who had squandered Portugal's fortune. "You killed the bishop, you killed the cleric. . . . You killed the grandee, you killed the commoner, you killed the people, you killed them all, we all killed them." It was only just that they suffer so enormously for their sins, he said, and the worst was not over, for "God has the custom of announcing a great evil by sending lesser ones." This was the lesser one; the next, he implied, would come from Spain.

The third funeral was in late 1582, also in Belém, and this time, finally, there was a body. Philip II, by then king of Portugal and preparing his return to Spain, ordered that his nephew be disinterred in Ceuta and transported home, among other reasons to make it clear that he was dead, very dead. (In similar fashion, after stories that Richard II of England had not really died in 1400, his successor, Henry IV, organized a procession throughout the country displaying the body, including the king's face.)[116] The procession carrying the body (or, as one writer put it, "the body said to be that of King don Sebastian") stopped on its way north from the Algarve at Evora, where two of Sebastian's ancestors were disinterred in order to join him in Lisbon. Philip ordered that a total of twenty bodies of fathers, sons, and grandsons of King Manuel I be gathered up from around the kingdom, and they (including Cardinal Henry) were all reburied with "sumptuous ceremony and great spectacle" in the royal necropolis of Belém.[117] And still there was one more move. After Portugal regained its independence from Spain in the late seventeenth century, King Pedro II in 1682 ordered that Sebastian's remains be transferred to a monumental tomb in the same church, and there they still reside. Vasco de Gama's and Camões's tombs flank the entrance to the church, and at the far end of the nave the royals surround the high altar. Catherine and Henry are both there, and so, too, is Sebastian, though with a caveat. The inscription on his tomb reads as follows:

> Conditur hoc tumulo si vera est fama Sebastião
> quem tulit in Libicis mors properata plagis
> Nec dicas falli regem qui vivere credit
> Pro lege extincto mors quasi vita fuit.
>
> In this tomb, if rumor be true, lies Sebastian,
> Whom untimely death carried away on the Libyan plains.
> Do not say that those who believe the king lives are deceived,
> For according to law, death is like life for he who has been killed.

The King's Miraculous Survival

Already on August 13, a Spanish notary in Ceuta had informed Philip II that former comrades (in particular the Alencastros, or Lancasters) were saying Sebastian had escaped on horseback and ridden toward Asilah.[118] Immediately the king dispatched Cristóbal de Moura to Lisbon. Like Juan de Silva, whom he essentially replaced as ambassador at this time, Moura was the product of a Spanish-Portuguese noble family; he had been sent to Spain as a teenager with Sebastian's mother, Juana, when she moved to Spain in 1554 and was used as an envoy during the marriage negotiations and as a translator at the Guadalupe talks. Now back in Lisbon in those spooky days after the battle, in which he lost a brother, he wrote to Philip, "There are so many different and diverse opinions, with honest men affirming that the king is alive and in this kingdom, saying they had witnesses. And though it is usual for commoners [*el vulgo*] to believe such things, in this province [Portugal] it is more common than anywhere else in the world."[119] Even Henry was said to have his doubts. As ransomed men began returning from Morocco to Lisbon like latter-day Lazaruses, each carrying his own rumors, miracles seemed possible. "Ignorant people believe he is alive and hidden," according to one account, and that was exactly what Fray Miguel de los Santos had in mind.[120] As long as there was no body, there was hope. Enter Rumor, painted full of tongues.

The trouble apparently began in Asilah, though if it had not started there it would have started elsewhere. The night after the battle, three or four Portuguese men approached the coastal fortress town (today an artsy getaway destination) demanding to be let in. When those inside proved reluctant to open the gates, the visitors said they had escaped from the battle and had Sebastian with them. The gates were immediately opened. One of the men, apparently wounded and partially hidden beneath a large cape, was the object of enormous deference by his comrades, who accompanied him to a dwelling in the walled city. News of the miraculous appearance reached the city's governor, Diogo da Fonseca, who demanded to see the wounded man, who turned out not to be the king at all. It was all an unfortunate misunderstanding, the young man explained to Fonseca, as he and his friends merely meant to say they had arrived from the king's army, not that the king was with them. Fonseca angrily ordered the men on board the next ship home, which turned out to be a mistake, because by the time the *San Martinho* docked in Portugal, the story had a life of its own "among the ignorant and the malicious." Though Fonseca obtained written testimony by the witnesses who identified Sebastian's body, which he then gave to Henry when he arrived home (Henry may have organized the second funeral precisely to make plain that Sebastian was dead), the stories of the latter-day Rodrigo spread, "partly because people wished these false imaginings to be true, because desire, when unregulated by reason, imagines that even impossible causes are probable; and partly because those who supported don António's uprising wanted there to be disquiet and unrest."[121] The circumstances of the identification of Sebastian's body after the battle were sketchy enough to inspire all manner of survival epics, particularly given that public statements were prohibited, leaving gossip and letters as the only source of news.

A man soon appeared in Lisbon saying he had offered something to drink to a wounded man five kilometers from Asilah who escaped the battle on horseback and perhaps was the king. The carrier of this tale managed to get an audience with Henry.[122] Just two weeks after the old cardinal assumed the throne, he was visited by another news bearer, this one a Hieronymite monk named Manuel Antonez, "who confided to don Henrique the startling intelligence that don Sebastian was not killed in the conflict of Alcazar but was then an inmate of their monastery and dangerously ill from the severity of the wounds which he had received in battle. As a guarantee of the truth of this statement, Antonez gave the king a confirmation signed by the prior of the monastery. He further stated that, sick and broken-hearted at the disgrace of his overthrow by the infidel, don Sebastian had no present intention of resuming his scepter until time had allayed the poignancy of his grief." According to this version, here from a nineteenth-century author, Sebastian had lain beneath a pile of bodies until nightfall, after which he arose, dressed himself in a robe and turban, wandered to the coast, and somehow made his way to Lagos, in southern Portugal.[123] A late seventeenth-century fictional account has Sebastian rescued from a pile of bodies by a Moorish princess who takes him to her palace, where her brother, the evil sharif, claps him into chains for a year and then sets him free, after which he shows up in Venice, reunited with his lover and ready to become the Charlatan of Calabria, the most famous of the false Sebastians.[124] An eighteenth-century account has Sebastian surviving the battle in the company of Cristóvão de Tavora (who was dead), the count of Redondo (whom we will meet again), and Jorge Tello, one of Sebastian's pages, who all managed to get to the Portuguese port of Cabo de San Vicente, where they dressed in the clothing of "ordinary men" (one wonders what were they wearing on their escape), deeply affected by what had transpired. "The king, who was honorable and proud, was especially affronted, ashamed of his errors, and therefore no longer wanted to be known or to reign. . . . So, dressed in Hieronymite robes, they wandered through the kingdom and the world."[125] In the reassembled account in the *Historia de Gabriel de Espinosa*, the best-known pamphlet on the conspiracy, Fray Miguel de los Santos says that Sebastian (i.e., Gabriel de Espinosa) told him he had stanched his bleeding battle wounds with sand.[126] Three or four months later, Cristóvão de Tavora's widow asked a certain Dr. Manuel Mendes (sometimes called Mendes Pacheco) to accompany her to Guimarães, in northern Portugal, to tend to a wounded nobleman in a remote hillside hut. Mendes went with her, finding a man with a wounded leg and four Portuguese aides. He spent one or two weeks, depending on the account, attending to the patient, though he never saw his face, which was covered with a brown taffeta mask. He was led to believe he was Sebastian. The doctor later was arrested for propagating the story of the king's survival. We will meet him again.[127]

Much later, when Fray Miguel de los Santos's audience had been reduced from crowded Lisbon churches to just one very skeptical judge, he outlined all the good reasons he had for believing Sebastian was alive.[128] First, at Belém, where he said he preached, there was no Mass said for Sebastian's soul, a technical but crucial omission. Second, the day before the Mass, as we have seen, a gentleman warned him that Sebastian himself would be present at the sermon after leaving his Discalced monastery in Cabo de San Vicente. Third, an Augustinian colleague of Fray Miguel had told him Sebastian was in a Cartusian monastery near Badajoz, which was known because of all the game being carried into the monastery even though the monks did not eat meat. Fourth, Francisca de Alva, Tavora's widow, had sent a bundle of linens to the Discalced monastery in Caparica, near Lisbon, which was for Sebastian. Fifth, don Diogo de Mesa (or Sosa or Sousa), an admiral with the fleet that went to Morocco, returned to Lisbon the very day of the battle without staying to help, which he could only have done because he had the king with him, fully proven by the fact that Henry did not punish him for having left Morocco early.[129] Sixth, he had heard from reliable sources that a man told Henry that he had given something to drink to the wounded king after the battle. Seventh, a man on the other side of the Tagus crossed paths with two men on horseback and a bit later with a third man on foot, who asked him if he had seen two men on horseback, and the first man replied that he had and immediately got down on his knees. Why are you kneeling? asked the rider. Because I recognize you as King Sebastian, the man replied, and the rider put his finger to his lips to tell him to remain quiet, but the man told his story anyway. Eighth, when Fray Miguel was in an Augustinian monastery in Castel Blanco, the monks told him that in a nearby Franciscan monastery (the fifth religious order mentioned, for those keeping track), a monk on his deathbed said he had heard Sebastian's confession at Alcazarquivir and that the king was alive. Ninth, a couple of years ago (meaning in 1592), a soldier and former Alcazarquivir captive had come through Madrigal de las Altas Torres, and he said Sebastian survived the battle and escaped on a boat with two or three other men.

This brings us to the end of Sebastian's story, as we will assume that he did indeed die on that broiling day in August. From here on, his life belonged to others. Fray Miguel's list of nine good reasons for believing the king was alive offers pretty much the complete repertoire of sightings and tropes that appeared again and again over the subsequent decades. Whether or not they were believed does not matter; they were repeated, they were told. We now turn back to Portugal, home of Fray Miguel and his master, the pretender don António, prior of Crato, who naturally had no interest whatsoever in Sebastian being alive. The themes of hubris and folly, faith and omens, and nationhood and reliable history that have such a prominent place in Sebastian's story were reworked over the subsequent years to help people somehow make sense of Portugal's catastrophe and prepare the way for its alleged resolution in a small town in Castile.

2

Portugal: Don António and Fray Miguel

On several occasions we have mentioned António, prior of Crato, whom we left on the battlefield at Alcazarquivir. Unlike Sebastian, he was alive. Don António occupies a curious position in this story. Physically he may or may not have been in Madrigal, though probably not. Unlike Sebastian, he does not seem to have inspired much lasting emotion on the part of his compatriots. But once Philip II was on the throne of Portugal, António was pretty much the only alternative, and it would seem that Fray Miguel's sole objective was to get him crowned, with or without his consent. That was the point of the plot.

António was the son of Luís, duke of Braganza, the brother of King João III. He and Philip II thus were both nephews of the former regent, Catherine, and of Cardinal Henry. (When Catherine died, Philip wrote António a letter of condolence, addressing him as "my dearest cousin.")[1] António's mother, Violante Gomes, allegedly had Jewish blood, and his parents allegedly were not married, though there is uncertainty on both counts. There was precedent in the Portuguese and Spanish royal genealogy for a successful illegitimate claimant or even for one with Jewish blood, starting with the first Avis himself, King João, the victor at the Battle of Aljubarrota and the illegitimate son of King Pedro. Nonetheless, António, possibly with the help of Fray Miguel, would try to prove that his parents had been married.

He was born in 1531. As a young man he studied at Coimbra's famed Monastery of Santa Cruz and later at the Jesuit university in Evora, though he was neither a willing nor a good churchman, much preferring warfare. After his father died in 1555, he received the wealthy priory of Crato, Portuguese headquarters of the Knights of Malta. He refused to take his solemn vows, arguing (like his distant relative Ana of Austria years later, though with more success) that he had been forced into the church against his will when he was too young. Cardinal Henry particularly disliked António and his disorderly lifestyle, throughout which he accumulated debts and fathered around ten children. He eventually was freed of the clerical prohibition against carrying arms, and Sebastian named him governor of Tangiers, but, as we have seen, he was deposed in 1574 in favor of Duarte de Meneses. Family feuding, especially with Henry, led him to find refuge, ironically enough, in Madrid with Philip II, setting off a minor diplomatic and family crisis between the two royal houses in the 1560s, in which the ubiquitous Cristóbal de Moura was one of the intermediaries. Another family scuffle erupted in 1578, just before the departure for Africa, in which António became upset because the king's friend Cristóvão de Tavora poached one of his servants, and Sebastian took Tavora's side. Initially, this caused António to refuse to accompany the king to Morocco, but he was finally persuaded to go.[2]

On the eve of the catastrophe, according to some accounts, don António was among the members of the nobility who urged Sebastian not to cross the Loukous River, figuring it would provide them with a line of defense. Opposed to this idea, Sebastian whipped out his sword with a great flourish, cut the cords that held their tents, and ordered his troops to cross.[3] Somehow, António survived the ensuing battle. The stories of what happened next became the foundational narrative of his subsequent adventures, escapes, and disguises. Soon after Cristóbal de Moura arrived in Lisbon, he wrote back to Philip that every day there was news about who had been taken captive in Morocco. "It is assumed that for sure don António is among them, and that he knew a Jew who paid sixty thousand maravedies in ransom and then hid him, but none of this can be confirmed, as there are so many stories with so little basis."[4] Indeed, the new sharif, Ahmad, immediately ordered that captive noblemen be held in the homes of Fez Jews who spoke Castilian, the better to negotiate with Philip. António, however, eluded this dragnet and was taken to a prison camp somewhere between Asilah and Tangiers. As he removed his ragged, filthy clothing once he arrived, the insignia of the Knights of Malta appeared, and his captors asked what it meant. With the help of another captive gentleman, who was bilingual, he improvised a story saying it showed he owned a small benefice, and he told them he was very worried that if he were not freed before the end of the year, the pope would give the benefice to someone else. A deal was worked out with his captors for three thousand cruzados, to be paid by Abraham Gibre, a Fez Jew who owed António favors from his time as governor of Tangiers.[5] A similar version has António and the other gentleman convincing the Moroccans that if they took him to Asilah, he would pay them three thousand ducats there. António's own version, published abroad, states he spent forty days in slavery until he finally managed to escape, disguised as a priest, "which one must say is a sort of miracle." Whatever the sequence, António reached Asilah, and from there went to Lisbon.[6]

By the time António landed in Portugal on October 12 (some sources say he was the first captive to return), Henry had the throne, and António, who was forty-seven years old, immediately got to work to claim it for himself. The period between autumn 1578 and Henry's death in January 1580 was one of conspiring, lobbying, and judicial inquiry, while the cardinal basically kept the seat warm for his successor. There were three serious claimants: Philip II, through his mother; Catherine of Braganza, through her father (the option that most appealed to Henry, though he did little to help her); and António, who, if his parents had been married, would have had a strong case. In the aftermath of Sebastian's death, Philip was cautious, despite advice from advisers to seize the moment. Typically, he wanted to take his time, and his intentions were not clear: an Italian ambassador commented in January 1580 that it was like "a masquerade of many parts, and one cannot with any confidence predict how it will turn out."[7] As autumn wore on, and with Moura handing out money and promises as well as urging his master to authorize a work of history documenting the legitimacy of his succession, Philip induced Catherine and the rest of what remained of the Portuguese nobility to his side, leaving just António between the Spanish king and the Portuguese throne. Henry, who despised António and was resigned to the inevitable annexation by Spain, though he refused to grant Philip's request for official recognition, asked Pope Gregory XIII to rule that illegitimacy excluded António from the throne. The ailing sixty-seven-year-old cardinal also tried to obtain papal dispensation to marry so he could produce an heir, that being the only conceivable way of stopping Philip. The pope, along with the rest of Europe, was worried at the specter of an even more powerful Philip, but at the same time did not want to anger Philip by pleasing Henry. So the pope dithered (or matched Philip II in prudence), and the unprecedented, not to mention ambitious, dispensation request went nowhere. Henry on his own declared António to be a bastard (in both senses of the word) and dismissed his appeal that his parents had been married. He ordered the arrest of António's witnesses and ordered António never to speak of the matter again.[8]

The country's representative assembly, the Cortes, opened in Almeirim in April, and it was evident that the Portuguese did not want a foreign king and that Philip would face opposition. One correspondent, probably the duke of Osuna, wrote back to Madrid: "These days in Santarém, [five kilometers] from here, friars preached that the people should not obey their king [Henry]. . . . They were not punished, which means it is likely they will do it again with greater enthusiasm, which will harm the ignorant, as the natives of this Kingdom make common cause. . . . Among the lower classes I suspect there is great affection for don António, as they naturally favor changes [*novedades*] to improve their position." A week earlier Osuna had written to the king's secretary, Antonio Pérez, "The preachers' intentions are crystal clear and the king does nothing, though he did react to the complaints of don Cristóbal [de Moura], who ordered that they be punished, though we have seen no sign of that. Nor do we see signs that the Cortes will ever end in a hundred years, because all they talk about is the ransom payments."[9] The Spanish crown interceded on behalf of the leading Portuguese noblemen, but ransoming generally was outsourced to the religious orders of the Mercedarians and Trinitarians or even to the captives' families, who had to come up with money, goods, or, more often, a captive they could swap.[10]

António swore allegiance to Henry and the Cortes on June 13, 1579, but the Cortes adjourned when yet another epidemic arrived. On at least two occasions, Henry banished António from Lisbon to Crato, capital of his military order, and ordered him to observe perpetual silence regarding his claim to the throne. According to a sentence issued by Henry on November 23, 1579, António was "disobedient and stubborn" and continued to campaign among the lower classes and the lower clergy, leaving Henry no choice but to strip him of all titles, rights, and privileges; declare him to be foreigner ("*desnatural de mis Reynos*") and "feared as if he had not been born here"; and order him to leave the kingdom in two weeks.[11] António did no such thing. The Cortes reassembled in January 1580, and that same month one of Philip's envoys reported that António was moving from place to place, sleeping in different monasteries every night, and using friars as couriers because he did not trust the mail. "I promise you the prior don António has the common people of Portugal on his side," he wrote.[12] Three weeks after the Cortes opened, Henry died without having named an heir. Instead of recognizing Philip, he had appointed five governors to run the country until his survivors sorted things out. (According to a contemporary doggerel, he should have been born later or ruled earlier.[13]) The Cortes adjourned, though the third estate, António's base of support, remained in session in Santarém, insisting, with some basis, that Portuguese medieval precedent provided the assembly with the right to elect a successor to the throne.

The following months were marked by more indecision and a vacuum of leadership, the country's most prominent men having been killed or captured in Morocco or bought off by Spain. The Portuguese, according to a Fugger correspondent, "refuse point-blank to become Spanish, though I should like to know what they are going to do about resisting. They have not a single soldier in Portugal who has ever seen any fighting or would know how to lead properly. They have no arms, for they lost them all in the African war. They have no money, and there is fearful scarcity in the country. Moreover, the plague is raging everywhere. Yet, with empty hands, they think themselves strong enough for the Spaniards." Later the same correspondent wrote, "I am credibly informed that don António is plotting in all directions. However, the struggle cannot last long, for all the best people here are in favor of Spain but dare not let it be seen. . . . I have no doubt that Spain will take possession of Portugal, as is fitting."[14] One of Philip's sources of information in these months was Andrea Gasparo Corso, the wily Corsican agent who had arranged many of the ransoms. At least as early as January 1580, he was in Lisbon and apparently in touch with everyone.[15] He had a "friend" who was at Henry's side as the old king was close to expiring (possibly Henry's confessor, whom he knew). He met with Catherine of Braganza. He had informers at the ongoing Cortes meetings. He worked side by side with Moura and thought he might get a face-to-face chat with don António, whose arrival in the capital, he said, inspired little enthusiasm thanks to the work of his "friends." Andrea's brother Philippo, meanwhile, was in Marseilles and sent him news about the queen of France's position on the Portuguese succession, which Andrea duly forwarded to Madrid. (In later, bitter letters from Corso, he complained that while others were rewarded, he was not. People who were no better born than he "are eating hens in their houses, and here I am, away from home and spending my own money; they get favors and I get nothing.")[16]

By this time, Philip was ready to make his move. He ordered troops from Italy and Germany to join the Castilian forces making their way to the border. On March 13, 1580, Philip ordered António to swear allegiance and acknowledge "the right and acknowledged justice I have to the succession of the kingdoms of this crown." If António did so, Philip said, then the Portuguese people would follow. Instead, in Alcobaça, António was carried throughout the city as the people proclaimed him king, crying, "*Real, Real, por el Rey don António, Rey de Portugal*."[17] Philip was not the only one to recommend that the pretender stop his trouble-making. The bishop of Salamanca, who appears to have had some sympathy for the rebel just over the border, wrote him in April to explain delicately that it would be best if don Diego de Cárcamo, a Castilian working as head of António's household, returned home "until this is settled." (Cárcamo did indeed opt to return to Castile, and in the following months, with the duke of Alba, acted as an intermediary, to no avail.)[18] More important, Alba himself on April 6 wrote a flowery but unmistakable warning. He had been so very happy to hear of António's release from Morocco, he said, and regretted that he had been too busy to travel to Portugal to kiss António's hands. After much affectionate prologue, he told António that he could not help but dare to suggest that "in these high seas [he] trim his sails a bit." Philip was absolutely determined to vanquish him, Alba warned him, and Philip's forces were "Christian yet at the same time terrifying." The eventual conqueror of Portugal added, "With all the forces of [Philip's] great power and his kingdoms, he is so powerfully inclined in this direction. I take no pleasure in seeing Your Excellency on the other side, nor is it any consolation to say that great men are destined for great things."[19] He also wrote to distant relatives on the other side of the border, advising them to pick the winning side. One such recipient was Manoel de Portugal, one of the four sons of the count of Vimioso and one of Lisbon's representatives in the Cortes. Look at the beautiful city of Lisbon, Alba cautioned his cousin. Now imagine it burning, its noblemen howling, its women raped, its churches in ashes.[20]

Not far from the bishop of Salamanca, in the seigneurial town of Alburquerque, close to the border, a local woman experienced in royal and saintly visions was visited on Palm Sunday by St. John the Baptist, dressed as a pilgrim. He told her to tell Philip II that the king must complete Sebastian's mission. If the king did not first defeat the African infidels with an army of men from Spain and Portugal, he would die in the attack on Portugal, the pilgrim told her. (He had visited her once before, when he led her to the gates of paradise, which she opened with him and saw St. Michael, "just as he is painted here in the world.") She confided to a local friar that St. John the Baptist and his companion also told her things about Portugal that they prohibited her from repeating except to certain people in Portugal, and "even if she were tortured a thousand times," she would remain silent. The pilgrims visited her again a few nights later, this time telling her to go to the bishop and reveal all so he could organize a meeting of the appropriate people in Portugal. The friar was of the opinion that the woman had "imagination rather than revelation," but just in case, he passed the word along to his superiors.[21]

Two months later, as the Castilian troops were massing at Badajoz, the Jesuit preacher Luís Alvares—he of the fiery and mournful funeral Mass for Sebastian—preached another of his inflammatory sermons, this one in Evora on the Day of Ascension, around May 12.[22] The "great evil" he had promised in his funeral Mass had come to pass. "Oh glorious, oh timid, oh renowned Kingdom of Portugal, what sad news is this I hear? They tell me you want to toss the crown off your head, fling the scepter away and, as if that were not enough, . . . they tell me they want to place you in captivity and servitude. Are we not going mad?" When the great Jewish warrior Judas Maccabeus and his men were outnumbered, they fought all the more heroically, he reminded the faithful. The time had not yet arrived when the Portuguese had to eat cats, or rats, or lacked water, so how was it that they were not resisting? One reason might be, of course, that the country had lost a generation of men just two years earlier. But, Alvares said, "Do not be cowed by the strange events of Africa." That was a dandy's war conducted with kid gloves and camp followers; this would be a pure, honest war. Finally, he cited an unlikely source, Abd al-Malik, the cultivated leader of the Moors who died at Alcazarquivir and whose letters to Sebastian had circulated so widely. Remember what he told Sebastian, may he rest in Holy Glory, he said: "If it requires at least four men to drag a dead man from his home, how many will be necessary to remove a live Portuguese, separating him from his wife, his children, his belongings?"

On June 19 or 20 (depending on the account), two days after the first Portuguese town surrendered before the invading army, Santarém, where don António had established his headquarters, acclaimed him as king in an explosion of wild enthusiasm led by the bishop of La Guarda. ("In the view of many," according to a 1582 assessment of the bishop, "it was wondrous that such a respected person, blinded by the passion of friendship, should allow himself to be dragged down these crooked paths.")[23] In a scene that takes us back to the final moments of the battle of Alcazarquivir, the contemporary Spanish historian and political theorist Juan de Mariana wrote that among the crowd of enthusiastic spectators, "a shoemaker, holding aloft a pike with a handkerchief on its tip, waved it like a flag and proclaimed António king of Portugal."[24] Conestaggio tells the same story: "The ceremony was no sooner begun but that Anthony Barachio, an impudent fellow (holding a handkerchief upon the point of his sword) proclaimed Anthony King, being followed with great noise and acclamations. . . . At that time Anthony, feigning a certain modesty, or thrust forward by his own irresolution, cried no, no, and stepped forward as if to stay the people. . . . He was amazed and trembled, giving notable signs to his followers, [and] at the first step he stumbled and almost fell, in sign of presaging ill."[25]

From there, António went to Almeirin, where he lodged in a Dominican convent and took all Henry's properties, and on to Lisbon, trailed by hundreds of supporters who cheered, shouting "*real, real*" as he went from church to palace to fortress.[26] At his proclamation ceremony in Lisbon, one of his supporters, Emanuel Fonseca Nobreza, embellished on António's providential escape in Morocco, preparing the narrative ground for the escapes to come. "I will lay aside the disgraces he suffered with King Sebastian at his departure for Africa," he said, a reference to the squabble with Tavora,

> which others would have taken for an excuse to stay, yet acquainted with the frowns of fortune, although he did judicially foresee that he went to his ruin, he chose rather (with so great danger of his person, following the rashness of another) to remain a slave unto the Moors than to blemish his honor with any reproach, how small so ever. He remained prisoner as he had foreseen in that unhappy day. . . . But the King of kings, although he seems sometimes slack, yet does he equally weigh and execute all things, providing so, that while king Henry enjoyed the realm, in those few days of his life which remained, he miraculously delivered from the hands of the Moors him whom he intended should be our true king. . . . He returned into the realm where fortune not yet weary of him crossed him with a thousand afflictions, all of which he has overcome and surmounted by his virtues.[27]

By June, Philip II was in Badajoz, five miles from the border, with his army led by the duke of Alba. Philip had hesitated before appointing Alba, who had fallen into disgrace and was living on his estate ill, old (he was seventy-three), and retired. But the duke's cruel governorship in the Netherlands, a prime component of the Black Legend of Spain, was sure to strike fear into the defiant Portuguese, and so he was recalled.

The king, for the first time calling himself Portugal's "natural king and lord," issued an edict prohibiting anyone from giving António shelter or aid; violators would be considered guilty of treason and be condemned to death, infamy, loss of honor, and confiscation of property. The king ordered authorities to post the edict in the "usual squares and places, and on the gates of cities, towns, and villages, and in churches and monasteries and in all other public places."[28] The governors appointed by Henry had urged the Portuguese to accept Philip as their king; António's proclamation of himself as king and his entry into Lisbon finally pushed the rest of the Braganzas into doing just that, leaving Philip's way that much easier.

The Pretender On the Run

The Spanish-led army, some twenty thousand troops, entered Portugal in late June just as António was proclaiming himself king, and it marched west as the Spanish fleet sailed around from Cádiz and up the Portuguese coast. On July 18, Setubal, one of don António's strongholds, fell and was sacked. On August 1 it was Cascaes, whose military defenders were executed. On August 25, the Spanish forces, wishing to avoid the spectacle of an attack on Lisbon itself, instead assaulted Alcántara, just outside the city. (Lisbon's authorities had pleaded with don António to fight outside the capital, and he accordingly withdrew his men from Belém.) His makeshift army had several thousand men, including Moroccans from the losing side in Alcazarquivir and at least 109 noblemen or other elites, among them the bishop of La Guarda (João de Portugal, another of the Vimiosos; the family did not heed Alba's warning) and members of the Meneses, Coutinho, Alencastro, Melo, Mendonça, and Mascarenhas clans. But chroniclers all emphasized that António's strength lay with the rabble. Conestaggio described, even worse, how women followed his cause, wielding frying pans as weapons and "seeming to remember the ancient battle of Aljubarrota betwixt the Castilians and the Portugals, where, these being conquerors, they vaunted that a baker's wife had slain seven Castilians with a frying pan." Between five hundred and three thousand Portuguese were killed as Lisbon fell.[29]

Fifteen years later, the impostor Gabriel de Espinosa, the *pastelero,* who by then had been prisoner for five months and tortured more than once, told judge Rodrigo de Santillán that he had met Fray Miguel de los Santos during the siege of Lisbon. He was a soldier before he was a baker and, as we will see, he fought on many fronts for the Spanish monarchy. In August 1580 he was among Alba's troops. According to his account, he and some fifty other soldiers took it upon themselves to defend the Monastery of Grace, Lisbon's Augustinian headquarters, which he said was in danger of being sacked by German troops under Spanish command. (Philip and Alba had expressly forbidden pillaging, to little effect.) This account meshes nicely with that of the contemporary chronicler Pero Roiz Soares, who described how the duke of Alba, hearing rumors that don António was hiding in a convent, unleashed anti-Antonian residents of the capital onto the city's religious houses, including Our Lady of Grace. "Sensing their good fortune, they went straight to the Monastery of Our Lady of Grace, running through the buildings and cells, waving swords and shouting, 'let's get that Jew, don António, who is hidden here . . . ' and other infamies."[30] The site of the presumed encounter of the protagonists of the Madrigal conspiracy is atop a hill on the edge of Lisbon's famed Alfama district. Today the monastery is used for government offices, but the church, first established in 1271, is still open, though obviously rebuilt. What draws visitors is not the building, and certainly not the history, but the sweeping view. Philip II visited in November 1582, when he resided in the Portuguese capital, remarking that the church and monastery "are very good."[31]

"At the time [of the assault], Fray Miguel was the provincial," Judge Santillán later wrote, "and he was very grateful, and so when Espinosa came to Madrigal, Fray Miguel recognized him and received him kindly."[32] So the Lisbon monastery, in the absence of any other explanation, was where everything began. Santillán's apostolic colleague, judge Juan Llano de Valdés, never got Fray Miguel to admit he had met Espinosa in Lisbon. "The two of them [Espinosa and Santos] agree on everything except on if they met in Lisbon," Llano told the king. "Fray Miguel still insists they did not. I think this is a matter of small importance, with far weightier matters to consider in this matter, so I have not pushed further." And, he added, referring to the Augustinian, "the diabolical resolution of this man is truly remarkable."[33] Santillán, whose usual job was as a judge at the royal chancery courts but who had a special appointment by the king to take care of the Madrigal matter, was more astute than Llano; he said of Fray Miguel's version, "Fray Miguel vaguely denies he met Espinosa in Lisbon, and in my opinion he is denying this in order to cover up the fact that it all began then."[34]

Don António, meanwhile, in his own account described being hidden in a priest's house in the days before the assault on Lisbon, then hiding in the Belém monastery as the Castilian troops approached. He fought heroically, receiving "two great wounds in his head," which did not prevent him from saving someone's life. After the battle, by one account, he made his way to a dense olive grove on a nearby hillside and began walking away from the city. He washed his wounds and bandaged himself. Then he put on a cape and walked the fifteen kilometers to Sant Juan de la Talla, where he entered the church. The dean of Evora arrived shortly with forty horsemen. They were later joined by the new count of Vimioso (son of the count slain at Alcazarquivir) and his brother, the always reliable bishop of La Guarda, who brought more men. In another version, the duke of Alba said António went from Lisbon to nearby Vila Franca de Xira, where eighty to a hundred horsemen, including Vimioso and Diogo Botelho, an aide of António's, had arrived.[35] In any case, António and his men moved north to Santarém, which was about to surrender, so they continued northward, living off the land and people's generosity, until they reached the great university town of Coimbra. There, according to one chronicle, "the students, preferring not to study, joined up with him like riffraff." Don António slept in fields or was sheltered in the homes of widows and peasants, aided by faithful servants. More than once he escaped the Castilian soldiers by an hour or less, leaving his poor hosts to answer the invaders' violent and insolent questions, often paying with their lives for having protected their king.[36]

Here begins the second series of providential escapes of the man who, in his edicts and fundraising letters, now referred to himself as "I the King." Despite Philip II's instructions to Alba to move quickly, the pretender slipped away. From Coimbra, he went north, establishing his headquarters in Oporto, where he appointed Diogo Botelho as governor.

(Botelho later became his roving ambassador in Europe; his final duty was to witness don António's last will and testament.) The Oporto government lasted just three weeks. On October 23, the troops of the new Spanish commander, Sancho Dávila, entered the city, which had hoisted white flags, but the pretender, who at that point had some ten thousand men, again got away.[37] For seven months, despite a price of eighty thousand ducats on his head, monks, nuns, and common people opened their homes to don António and told tales.

> The Portuguese wept at their ill fortune, at not having defended themselves well or surrendered well. . . . Some believed [António] had been killed by the Castilians, who kept the death a secret because they had stolen his jewels. Other said he was awaiting ships from France and England. . . . Others wanted him to stay hidden until [Philip], who, it was said, had little time left to live, died, because then he could take the kingdom. And though some thought he had left, most said no, that he was still trying to leave, afraid of being taken prisoner.[38]

According to the duke of Alba, António's forces captured Portuguese ships on their way back from Brazil loaded with sugar and other merchandise.[39] He also received weapons and supplies on English and French ships.

"In this land, they promise much and deliver nothing," Sancho Dávila wrote in October, complaining to Alba about how little support he was getting as he tried to hunt down don António.[40] Throughout the autumn, he reported on frequent arrests of António's supporters, including servants, gentlemen, and clerics ("they emerge into the sunlight like snails"),[41] but they yielded little valuable information. After the pretender's forces in Oporto had been toppled, and the pretender was once again on the run, Dávila told the duke that one of his men had run into a suspicious friar carrying letters for "Ana de Miranda" and later a messenger with a letter for don António's daughter Luisa and a long list of other recipients in Coimbra, including one from "the fat brother" acknowledging receipt of the Ana de Miranda missive. But all the questioning in the world could not get the friars to reveal what was behind all this coming and going, he said. So the second messenger was given "the rope treatment," allowing

Dávila to learn that António was still in Portugal, going back and forth among convents and monasteries, and that a network of Franciscans and Dominicans all seemed to know where he was. Dávila organized sting operations by which the letters would be delivered to their intended recipients, who would immediately be arrested. The messenger was told that if anyone was tipped off, he would lose everything: belongings, children, life. Dávila told the duke that he wanted to obtain permission from the papal nuncio to take criminal action against this insolent army of friars. "If they are squeezed, I am sure we will find [António], but otherwise this will never end; these things always get worse the longer they go on." To the royal secretary Gabriel de Zayas he wrote, "Don António's voice is everywhere, and the people do not want to give up hope, and this shamefulness grows every day, especially among friars and nuns, who are planning uprisings."[42] The trick with the false messenger had worked, he reported, and Luisa was under control, though he wished she could be sent elsewhere. But by the end of the month, his prey was still at large. Of his supporting role in this Portuguese version of *The Scarlet Pimpernel*, Dávila wrote to Zayas, "Every day we get a thousand bits of news, but we can't catch him. The nuns and friars must have buried him alive, because no amount of promises or threats have brought him to light."[43]

The outside world, too, was watching the Castilians chase the man whom Philip II now referred to as a tyrant.[44] A Fugger correspondent in Cologne complained that the Italian letters were unreliable but that he had good sources in Portugal. "They are informed that [António] and his adherents, after being routed by the Spaniards near Oporto, embarked on an English ship at [Viana do Costelo], in order to sail to France or England," he wrote in January 1581. "But they could not do this owing to contrary winds, so they left the ship perforce and went to Galicia by land. They were overtaken and robbed by Spanish soldiers. The Spaniards made no mention of their death, fearing to be deprived of the loot. This news has lately reached the Portuguese from Antwerp and meets with universal credence. So there is little need to fear the reappearance of don António and the other rebels."[45] His account of the failed escape and the premature announcement of António's death were in part echoed by a 1596 chronicle: "[António] embarked with his followers in a boat given to him by the bishop of La Guarda. Because of a storm and strong winds, they were forced to return to land. And walking among Sancho Dávila's soldiers, who had occupied the marina, he was not recognized, as he was dressed as a poor sailor. He escaped and then spent months hidden in the kingdom before going to France, where he was well received by the queen mother and her son, Henry III." A Fugger cousin wrote from Portugal at around the same time, also prematurely, that with the help of Franciscan monks, António, "who has been living in want and in the clothing of a boor," had set sail from Galicia on a Venetian ship bound for France.[46]

He was never betrayed. For nearly eight months, don António managed to elude the vigilance the Castilians kept on all ports and border posts. He finally left by sea for France in May 1581, embarking from Setubal, near Lisbon, thanks to a wealthy widow, Beatriz Gonçalves, who paid the captain of a Dutch ship to take him and a group of his loyal followers aboard. (António later wrote that Philip II ordered that the widow's picture be hanged, the widow herself having fled.)[47] With him, he took some ten servants and a good lot of the crown jewels, with which he financed his later efforts to capture the throne. He made his way to Paris and the welcoming court of Henry III and the king's mother, Catherine of Medici. In June 1581, Philip II swore before the Portuguese Cortes (in Tomar rather than in Lisbon, because of the continuing plague) to uphold the laws, customs, and privileges of Portugal, and the monarch entered the capital later that month. As his procession reached the Rua Nova in Lisbon, it was said, a street vendor approached him: she and her compatriots received him as their king, she said, "until King Sebastian arrived, and once he arrived, Philip would have to return with God to Castile and leave their kingdom." Philip smiled. He stayed for nearly two years, finally having succeeded in unifying the peninsula under one crown.[48]

Patriots and Neighbors

Despite António's departure and Philip II's presence in Portugal, the common people of Portugal awaited the return of don António, that very intolerable and most atrocious tyrant.[49] In June 1581, Esteban de Ibarra, an aide to the duke of Alba, offered royal secretary Matheo Vazquez an eloquent and disturbing picture of the country the pretender had left behind. England and France were circling, waiting to pounce, and Philip should never, ever let his guard down, he wrote.

> I swear to you, these are such barbarous and senseless people they are capable of any sort of great evil, out of vanity and commitment, without considering either the danger or the method. They so hate His Majesty and so desire don António they cannot stop themselves from declaring that without Our King they would be free of the Castilian yoke. I am sure you will think this is nonsense, but God knows I do not think so . . . I see the people loose, with no fear of justice, unrestrained, with hatred and complaints for the King, with sorrow for not having fought for the patria and now finding themselves subject to Castile. For all this, they blame their lack of unity and leadership, and they regard themselves as dishonored for being so diminished, and they want to recover themselves. There are an infinite number of poor and indebted people with no way of making a living; all that, and the love for don António, for whom they weep, and they pray for his return.[50]

After Philip left, appointing his nephew Archduke Cardinal Albert as governor (the duke of Alba died in December 1582), things did not improve. Many people still thought Sebastian would return, Albert told Philip, or that he had in fact already returned and was hiding in Lisbon.[51] In general, the high clergy supported Philip, though they were not all enthusiastic. (The bishop of La Guarda was the exception.[52]) It was the middle and lower clergy, particular those from the religious orders, who continued their agitation, and they had a potentially dangerous hold on a people reeling from defeat, epidemic, and the loss of independence. As Cristóbal de Moura disbursed gratuities among church officials after Henry's death (Philip was especially suspicious that the Jesuits supported the Braganza option), he regularly reported back to the king about priests and friars whose sermons were inciting parishioners. Around that time, a memo discussed the appropriate punishment for the regular clergy who were making trouble. They should all be sent to the most remote and most reformed monasteries possible, the writer suggested, each separated from the other, with no say in the governance of their new homes. Dominicans, Franciscans, Carmelites, Hieronymites, Trinitarians, and Augustinians were all guilty, and among the latter was "Fr. Miguel dos Anjos [Angels], provincial, who engaged in skirmishes on horseback and went armed and was a great councilor to don António." This is our Fray Miguel, "angels" erroneously replacing "saints."[53] So the Spanish authorities had taken note of the future vicar. The papal nuncio in Portugal, Cardinal Riário, issued an edict on February 11, 1581, when don António was still wandering, condemning the pretender's religious enablers: "With no fear of God, causing grave damage and danger to their souls and scandal throughout this Kingdom of Portugal and the Algarve, they leave their monasteries and churches to take up arms, and many of them shed their regular habit to participate in wars and disturbances in favor of don António, prior of Crato."[54] Three months later, the bishop of Tuyd wrote to Philip's secretary, Gabriel de Zayas, in Madrid, reporting further disturbances: "I think the solution is to remove them from Portugal, scattering them throughout Castile in prudent religious institutions," he wrote, which in fact is what happened.[55] Fray Luis de Granada, one of the greatest figures of sixteenth-century Iberian Catholicism, wrote to Zayas in November 1580 to report on the bad behavior among his brethren in Portugal, some in his own Dominican order, whom he had to discipline. "A very learned master of theology . . . preached in the Belém church before don António's army . . . that it was a mortal sin not to take up arms for him, saying that if sons were obliged to go back for their fathers [most likely a reference to the *Aeneid*], much more so were they obliged to go back for their *patria*, and he gave more reasons, and in this same tone all the other preachers are preaching, deceived by lies, saying that fighting Castilians is like fighting Lutherans." As for the papal order that the clergy remain neutral, Fray Luis wrote, a professor at Coimbra had announced that such an order violated natural law and that all men were obliged to defend their country. He also told Zayas that an Augustinian, obviously not Fray Miguel, had preached to his followers that Castilians were men just like they were, setting off a near riot in the Monastery of Grace, and the Augustinian was imprisoned upon orders by the "bad bishop of La Guarda."[56]

The motivation of the clergy in opposing the union of the crowns is worth thinking about. The historian João Francisco Marques explains Fray Miguel's determined scheming (and, by extension, the troublemaking of the rest of the clergy) as evidence of nationalism: "He acted out of patriotism, with sincere ends and unscrupulous means. Blinded by his nationalist aversion to Castile, he was impelled to fight for the restoration of the independence of the Portuguese crown, spurred on by collective memory."[57] Not for the first time in early modern European history, the lower clergy took upon itself the burden of national defense ("in these Portuguese matters I have seen that friars and clergy are at the root of it, and in this business it looks the same," Judge Santillán remarked grimly as the Madrigal case began),[58] but patriotism surely is not the most useful term for examining their motives. The Madrigal story, unlike the two earlier appearances of false Sebastians, is not one of messianic nationalism and thus is really not an example of *sebastianismo* at all. It is simply one of replacing one ruler with another, of replacing a "foreigner" with a "Portuguese." In the great revolt of the *comuneros* in 1520, when Castilian cities rose up against the absent Charles V, surrendering only eighteen months later, it was the clergy who gave the uprising the religious language that bound and inspired the cities in their multifaceted (political, fiscal, social) struggle. When Catalonia rebelled in 1640, again the clergy did the same, and that same year Portugal finally would begin fighting off the Spanish crown, also with the support of the clergy. In our case, in 1580, the Portuguese religious orders had many reasons for resisting Philip; they were the shepherds of grievously wounded flocks; they were guardians of ancient traditions and values; they spoke for the common good; and, on a more practical level, they surely were worried about the inevitable church reforms under his rule.

Patriotism is never a simple matter, but in the case of Portugal and Castile it is particularly difficult to pin down. Portugal as such came into existence after winning its freedom from Castile just two hundred years before the events we are describing, when "The noble standard of sublime Castile / Was trampled under the Portuguese heel."[59] But even at Aljubarrota, the great Portuguese hero Nuno Alvares had two brothers who fought with the other side, and there were other members of the Portuguese nobility who did the same. We have seen the extent to which the upper Iberian aristocracy was intermarried; indeed, had they not been so, none of this would have happened. It is unclear if the royal cousins even considered it intermarriage. They were simply all members of one family. (Don António, as we have seen, turned to Philip II in his youth to get away from his oppressive family.) Many of Philip II's leading courtiers and advisers came to Spain from Portugal, either with his mother, Isabel, or with his sister, Juana. When Philip argued that he was the "*rey natural de Portugal*," we should remember both that *natural* means native and that the annexation was an act of royal will, not national sentiment; Philip was simply taking what by right and bloodline belonged to him. Spanish writers at times seemed to think "Portuguese" was a subcategory of "Spanish;" thus one could be a Spaniard from Andalucia or one from Portugal. The Vélez de Guevara play referred to earlier, for example, has a soldier being asked, "You, Christian, where are you from?" The answer: "I'm Spanish and Portuguese." In the same play, Sebastian himself describes himself as Portuguese and Spanish.[60] If there were feelings of loyalty among the Portuguese upper classes, they were not easily identifiable with national boundaries. That said, Spain's impact in Portugal was far greater than the reverse, and this was not an affair between equals. Poor neighbors generally resent rich neighbors. (In the Iberian peninsula, they do to this day.) But neither was there a consensus in Portugal among any class, including the clergy, regarding the supposed enemy. When don António ended his published manifesto with a fusillade of invective, using the word *hatred* (ancient hatred, natural hatred, general hatred) four times in two pages to describe the Iberian relationship, one thinks he does protest too much.[61]

The border was permeable, as most early modern borders were. There was lots of smuggling, and rural workers, artisans, and soldiers routinely made their way back and forth. The mingling of Spanish and Portuguese can be seen clearly in the town of Madrigal de las Altas Torres, the site of the conspiracy. Fray Miguel himself, it seems, was the grandchild of Andalusians; his paternal grandfather left Spain after killing a man.[62] Judge Santillán believed the people who worked in Espinosa's bakery were Portuguese. Portuguese travelers visited Madrigal, as we will see from the testimony. One of Ana of Austria's messengers from the convent, Miguel Pérez, was Portuguese. But though there was intermingling, there also was distinction. Testimony from Portuguese witnesses always included references to their background: Fray Alonso Rosete "said . . . his father [was] from the town of Pereña, near Ledesma, and his mother was born in the town of Magadorio, in the kingdom of Portugal, where this witness was born." In the margin someone noted, "born in Portugal."[63] Judge Llano later noted of the same witness that his father was Castilian but that Rosete "was all Portuguese."[64] On the Spanish side of the border, Portuguese were always identified as such. The label might seem to question loyalty, and under the circumstances of this story, that would seem logical. But saying "Miguel Pérez, *portugués*," is not much different than saying "Miguel Pérez, *de Segovia*." Nonetheless, Spanish accounts of the Guadalupe meetings and the battle of Alcazarquivir do not show much respect for the Portuguese, regardless of social class. Golden Age literature often portrays them as excessively vain, laughably proud. Chroniclers several years after the unhappy events in Morocco probably felt they had good reasons for disparaging their presumptuous neighbors, whose behavior was in line with the words of Juan de Borja, Spain's ambassador to Lisbon in the 1570s: the Portuguese court was prickly, he told Philip, quick to discern imagined slights without considering all the reasons for a particular act of negligence and wrongly convinced that Spain needed it more than the reverse.[65]

Aware of the chip on their shoulder, Philip took pains after 1580 to not antagonize the Portuguese more than necessary, though there was no doubt in his mind that Portugal belonged to him and that its acquisition was part of a "vital step on Spain's road to global mastery."[66] This was a question of dynastic inheritance and imperial mission. It was also a question of God's will. But Portugal and its people were not the enemy, and there was no point in regarding their Iberian neighbors as subjects. The Portuguese royal house remained more or less intact, a good way of integrating the elites of that country. Portuguese laws would not be changed, new taxes would not be levied, Castilians would not replace Portuguese in civil or religious posts, garrisons would not be established, and the Portuguese empire would remain Portuguese, though these conditions all began withering by the end of the century.

To rope together the protests of the 1580s and 1590s that nonetheless occurred as acts of desperate nostalgia for don António or Sebastian deprives such events of their fertile mix of economic, religious, and even imaginary motivations. The rhetoric of patriotism may mean many things. Positing nationalist impulses for the series of disturbances that began in the 1580s and continued intermittently during the sixty years during which Portugal was governed by Spain amounts to answering the question before it is asked.[67] Similarly, positing Castilian chauvinism as the driving force behind the actions of the Spanish crown cannot explain the complicated ways in which the monarchs governed their complicated monarchy. The fact that Portugal eventually would rebel in December 1640 should not be read backward to explain agitation whose motivations and origins owe little if anything to what we call nationalism.[68] There are references now and again in the documents to hatred on the part of Portuguese, but I am not sure we can take them literally. A tiny indication of sensational lies about Castilian cruelty—an António supporter in London wrote that Philip had ordered the president of the Council of Castile to strangle and burn two dukes, two counts, the bishop of Jeréz, and the archbishop of Córdoba—suggests that they were short of good material and had to work hard to incite hatred against the victors.[69]

Fray Miguel's Long Journey to Madrigal

There would seem to be an obvious and intrinsic conflict between those interested in putting António on the throne and those propagating the stories of Sebastian's survival. Yet the two currents appear to have merged, or it appeared logical to some people that they might have merged. Archduke Albert suggested they were the same people and, as we will see, Fray Miguel would proclaim the return of the one only to engineer the return of the other. Sebastian was hidden, disguised, waiting for the right moment to return; and so too was António, wandering in his own sort of desert, the European royal courts. Both awaited recognition. Both were on their own, helped only by the kindness of the clergy.

So now let us go to Madrigal de las Altas Torres, where the chief figure in the conspiracy was a Portuguese friar who had worked for both Sebastian and don António. There was no doubt among the judges after the first few weeks that the plot had been hatched by Fray Miguel de los Santos. The judges did not have to understand his motive or make sense of the plot, which was fortunate for them because, given the evidence we have, it made little sense. They did not have to figure out what Fray Miguel was thinking, who his audience was, or why he thought don António was fit for the throne. All they had to do was establish that he was plotting to remove Philip. Our task is harder and more frustrating. Fray Miguel would not have gotten where he was had he not been highly intelligent, which makes one think there was more to it than we know. There must have been. But we do not know what he thought about Spain, or Portugal, or patriotism, or how he justified what he did or made it conform to his faith and his vows. We know, simply, that Judge Llano and others thought him "so intelligent and cunning."[70]

Miguel de los Santos probably was born in Santarém in 1537 or 1538. Judge Rodrigo de Santillán was of the opinion he was descended from Jews (a frequent accusation against the Portuguese, though Fray Miguel's Portuguese ancestry was very short), but there does not seem to be any evidence, and Santillán also was of the opinion that the friar was the devil incarnate. "I don't think there has been a man of such evil conscience since Judas," Santillán pronounced. "He schemed away while saying Mass every day, and on the outside he performed acts of such saintliness that he fooled everyone. People in [Madrigal] took him for one of the apostles, although it is true they never saw him fast or eat fish in all the time he was here."[71] In May 1591, Philip II solicited letters of recommendation regarding the newly or almost appointed vicar of Madrigal, and we have the valuable testimony of Fray Agustín de Jesús, a colleague of Fray Miguel's for many years during their religious training and student years in Coimbra. "No one can give better testimony than I about his life, customs, knowledge, and abilities," declared Agustín, the archbishop of Braga. Fray Agustín had it on good authority that Fray Miguel had no trace of Jewish blood; his grandparents were from Jeréz de los Caballeros and Seville, in southern Spain, and they claimed to be related to the great soldier Gonzalo Fernández de Córdoba. After his grandfather killed his own cousin, the family fled to Portugal, where they settled in the Algarve and had two sons, one of whom was Fray Miguel's father. He married a good woman, and the future vicar grew up in a good family; a list of Augustinian professions gives his parents' names as Diogo Fernandes Arjono and Inés Alvares de Campos.[72] Fray Miguel professed at the Monastery of Grace in Lisbon in 1554 (Fray Agustín professed the following year) and did extremely well, though his teacher was later burned by the Inquisition for Lutheran heresies.[73] He was "an example of virtue and religion," modest and serious, according to his school friend. He was a gifted Latinist, the best in the class in many subjects. He also was a renowned preacher, which led to his being summoned to the royal court, where he worked for Catherine, Sebastian, Henry, and don António in various religious capacities. Although he had never been in charge of a monastery, he was elected provincial of the order in May 1574 at an unusually young age. In May 1578 he became prior of the Monastery of Grace, where, according to some historians he spoke out against the imminent African campaign.[74] Not a single sermon of his survives. According to some historians, he was the author of the letters to Pope Gregory XIII pleading the case of don António's legitimate birth. Just before the fall of Lisbon, he was elected provincial a second time, in April 1580. He was present when António was acclaimed king in Lisbon, and, as we have seen, he took up arms at Alcántara on his behalf.

After the fall of Lisbon, he was imprisoned in Coimbra. Philip issued preemptive general pardons, starting in mid-July 1580, and ended up excluding just fifty-two people from his final amnesty of April 18, 1581.[75] Fray Miguel was one of them, considered among those too guilty to pardon. In August 1581, the king wrote that he had first thought to send Fray Miguel to Burgos but then decided to send him to a convent in the Kingdom of Toledo, and he asked the Castilian provincial of the Augustinians to make a suggestion. The monastery "must be secure so that he not be able to leave or communicate in any form with anyone outside the convent, and as for food and daily needs, he must be treated like the other religious and remain there until His Holiness or your general (aware of his crimes) order what to do with him."[76] We do not know what Philip's doubts were or what the provincial replied, but Fray Miguel was sent to Salamanca, which is not in the kingdom of Toledo but was the principal center of learning for the Augustinian order. One of the witnesses in the Madrigal case reported he had run into Fray Miguel at the Augustinian monastery in Salamanca in late 1581.[77] Two years later, on Christmas, Fray Miguel wrote an unctuous congratulatory letter from Valladolid (*sic*) to the Augustinian prior general in Rome concerning the order's internal affairs, in which he explained he had suffered the accusations of "iniquitous men of a wicked time."[78] After two years in exile, one of them in "seclusion" (it is unclear what he means), "I have [now] been restored to my former liberty by royal favor" on condition that he not return to Portugal. "Having been expelled from my country, although in this province of Castile, I have been treated very honorably and reasonably by the Fathers of the same province, and I do not doubt I will remain here among them," he said. But he also wished to go to Rome, as well as home to Portugal, and he requested most humbly, mentioning in passing that he had twice been provincial and had taught at Coimbra, that the prior general help him in these desires. However, he was still in Salamanca in August 1586, when Philip II wrote to the prior of his monastery instructing him to release Fray Miguel. For some reason, the process was moving slowly. "Having learned from Father Agustín de Jesús, vicar general of your order in Portugal, that Fray Miguel de los Santos, a native of that Kingdom, who resides in your convent, has behaved such that he deserves clemency and kindness," the king wrote, "and having received a request from the vicar general, I have decided to grant [Fray Miguel] permission to go to Portugal, and I am writing to inform you of this so that you allow him to leave when he wishes.[79] So Fray Miguel's old friend Agustín had been helping him for a while; possibly the prior general in Rome had not. According to Fray Miguel himself, he then spent ten months in the Portuguese town of Castelo Branco, equidistant between Salamanca and Lisbon.[80] Fray Miguel also said he was in Madrid in around 1588 and, indeed, another witness, who worked as a servant to the count of Redondo, don António's most fervent noble supporter, reported he had seen Fray Miguel in Madrid in around 1589 at the Augustinian headquarters of San Felipe, just off the great crossroads of the Puerta del Sol, one of the best places in Spain to hear news.

In the fine words of Peter Burke, "The crucial point of contact and tension between public and private was the news."[81] Every town and city has spots where news is invented, channeled, or transmitted, and the sort of spot generally corresponds to the sort of news. Rivers where washerwomen gather; water pumps or wells; the square in front of the palace or courthouse; and taverns, mills, pharmacies, and marketplaces each attracted a crowd with specific interests, social networks, and routes, and each could mark an intersection of palace, convent, court, road, market, and battleground. The Puerta del Sol was the greatest of all Spanish crossroads. It was the exact geographic center of the country, and the steps outside San Felipe, soon to be known as the gossip shop (*mentidero*) of San Felipe, were notorious as the birthplace of news and rumor. Cervantes, Vélez de Guevara, and Quevedo, among other writers, mentioned the steps, providentially situated near both a large monastery and Spain's first post office, which was used by individuals as well as by officialdom. The Calle de Postas began (it is still there) right next to San Felipe (which is not). A few decades later, shops printing *avisos*, or newsletters, would be set up in these blocks; in the 1590s, however, print news culture of the sort growing in London and Venice still took a back seat in Spain to private letters and gossip. *Ruidos* (noise) and *murmullos* (murmurings) of reborn kings, Castilian atrocities, unhappy nuns, miraculous apparitions, and catastrophic battles were born or echoed here.[82] Unlike in other European capitals, Madrid's courtiers, ministers, and servants often did not live at the royal palace, so they carried their *novedades* with them as they traversed the city on their way home. Soldiers in particular were prone to loiter, and the origin of the word *mentidero* (*mentir* means "to lie") could well be the tales of exaggerated bravery they told one another as they waited for new assignments, gambled away their pay, or lay concealed from recruiters. The pollen gathered in the Madrid gossip mill would be disseminated wherever the soldiers went, which was everywhere.

A second news-mongering site in Madrid, on nearby Calle León near the Plaza de Antón Martín, was a gathering place for artists and actors. The tale of the *pastelero* of Madrigal is littered with disguises, surprise appearances, and a preoccupation with distinguishing truth from fiction, theatrical devices familiar to audiences at the time. It is impossible to know if our players wandered down that way, but it is tempting to find inspiration for the conspiracy there and also to imagine resonance there after the fact. Madrid was the center of theatrical activity in Spain, and the 1590s was the start of the great era of the *comedia*, the name given to Spanish dramatic works, of which Espinosa was fond. Finally, these hubs of circulation, obviously, were meeting places. An extraordinary number of witnesses in this case told the judges they had run into some other witness elsewhere in the peninsula, and there were no people more itinerant or talkative than soldiers and clergymen. Gabriel de Espinosa was a soldier, and Fray Miguel was an Augustinian; both were sighted in Madrid in the late 1580s, and both later appeared in Madrigal. If news could be conveyed, plans could also be hatched.

Fray Miguel of course was not the only Portuguese national to be transported to Castile during these years. One of the best known of his fellow *exceptuados*, the name given to those excluded from Philip's amnesty, managed to escape, at least at first: this was the bishop of La Guarda, João of Portugal. According to the head of the University of Coimbra, the bishop had crossed the border into Castile disguised as a sawyer with a large saw strapped to his back. "If so little attention is paid and people are not asked who they are, don António might choose the same route," he sensibly warned.[83] Escaping into, rather than out of, enemy territory may not appear to be a prudent move, but lists of prisoners show that most of the bishop's family (he had as many as four brothers and seven sisters) was being transported in the same direction, so perhaps he wanted to remain close to them. His brother Francisco—third count of Vimioso, present at both Guadalupe and Alcazarquivir—died fighting for don António in the Azores in 1582, but brother Luís was imprisoned in the duke of Francavilla's castle in Castile.[84] The women of the bishop's family, like nearly all the women in this tale, were sent to convents. There were tentative instructions to take the bishop's mother and sisters to the Augustinian convent in Madrigal, which would have been quite a coincidence, but that did not happen, and I do not know where they ended up.[85] Female relatives of don António's leading advisers (the wives or widows of Diogo Botelho, Manuel Fonseca Nobreza, and Diogo de Meneses among them), as well as António's own daughters, were distributed in convents throughout Spain. So, too, were troublesome clerics, male and female, whose arrival was heralded by letters from Philip II to priors and royal authorities in the provinces along the way warning them that prisoners under armed guard were en route, by land or by sea.[86] As for the bishop of La Guarda himself, he bought a few years by disguising himself as a sawyer, but in April 1585 he was captured near Evora, this time dressed as a hermit. He was stripped of his rank, benefices, and nationality, and sentenced to life in prison in Setubal, where he died.[87]

Fray Miguel, unlike the bishop, served his time. Somehow he then went to Madrigal de las Altas Torres, probably just after staying in Madrid. Madrigal, in the far north of the province of Avila, is a town whose location and appearance belie its erstwhile importance. The reliable 1591 census reports 670 households (approximately 3,350 people), compared to 2,826 households in Avila and 870 in nearby Arévalo. By 1751, according to the important mid-eighteenth-century census known as the Catastro de Ensenada, it had 357 habitable dwellings.[88] Situated on the harsh and beautiful Castilian plain, it was one of many royal outposts established at a time when courts were always on the move. The town sided with Charles V during the *comuneros* revolt.[89] Isabel of Castile's father had a small palace there; that building eventually became the convent where Fray Miguel now set up shop. The convent sits at the bottom of the town, hugging the once magnificent town walls, which boasted dozens of towers built by the town's former Muslim inhabitants. Just on the other side of the walls was another monastery, previously inhabited by Augustinian nuns, but after the nuns moved into the palace in 1525, it was taken over by Augustinian friars. Despite housing royalty, it was not a luxurious or beautiful town, and today it is impossible to imagine the rich and famous gathering there. In the words of Judge Juan de Llano, it is a "sterile, poor place."[90] Close to Arévalo, the town lies twenty-five kilometers from the once-great fair town of Medina del Campo and an additional forty kilometers from Valladolid along the same road. Going west, it is around seventy kilometers to Salamanca, and from there another hundred to the Portuguese border. It thus sat in the center of a densely traveled network, though traffic and business had declined sharply in recent decades. Medina del Campo, for example, in 1561 had nine couriers; by 1597, there were only two, plus a postmaster and postman.[91] Still, Madrigal had access to news. It was not isolated.

Quite obviously, Philip II made a stupendous error in allowing Fray Miguel to be appointed to a convent housing a royal, though there is confusion regarding the mechanics of the actual appointment. The vicar told Juan de Llano he had known Ana of Austria four years before being appointed. "He spoke to her twice, and this must have led to her desire that he be vicar, and she achieved this, and he does not know the reason, except that she was not content with the past vicars," the judge wrote. A summary of Ana's testimony reported that "at her urging, His Majesty ordered that Fray Miguel be vicar."[92] One version of the widely circulated chronicle usually called *Historia de Gabriel de Espinosa* recounts that the Augustinian "had been ordered taken prisoner and brought to Castile in a coach guarded by musketeers, and after much time, he showed repentance, and His Majesty wanted to demonstrate his trust in him, and [Fray Miguel] asked that he be appointed vicar of the said monastery and confessor of doña Ana."[93] Chronicler Luis Cabrera de Córdoba wrote that Fray Miguel had been appointed vicar in Madrigal "at the urging of important gentlemen."[94] The provincial difinitor, Juan de Benavente, on several occasions insisted that Fray Miguel's appointment was improper and anyway had exceeded the stipulated term of three years. Llano also suspected hanky-panky; probably in March 1595 he asked María de San Vicente, the subprioress, about a papal brief Fray Miguel either had or had tried to obtain for a perpetual post. He also asked Fray Miguel how long he had been in Madrigal, how he got the appointment, and why, "being that he is Portuguese and this province has so many excellent friars of his order who could do the job, . . . and why he proposed coming here as vicar, being an outsider, and why he retained the job for so long when it is the custom of his order to not stay more than three years."[95]

Fray Miguel was by all accounts a brilliant theologian, a capable leader, a charismatic personality, and someone whose quick promotion to the Lisbon palace was richly deserved. He does not seem like the sort of man to whom things happen. He made them happen. And somehow, he landed in Madrigal. There may have been royal intervention on his behalf; there may have been a deliberate attempt by one of Philip's enemies to place a fox in the hen house; there may have been a plan hatched during conversations in Madrid. Or maybe he had no idea who was in the convent and arrived there by chance; he stumbled upon Ana, and said, "Hmmm, what can I do with this?" Once there, maybe he arranged for Gabriel de Espinosa to arrive in the summer of 1594 and appear to be King Sebastian. Or maybe not. Maybe, he just waited, like Mr. Micawber in *David Copperfield*, for "something to turn up." Patience was a virtue, after all. And he was inexplicably rewarded.

Conspiracy in the Convent

Fray Miguel's tenure as the vicar of Nuestra Señora de Gracia la Real came to an end on October 15, 1594, when he was placed under house arrest. He was first held in the home of a local official, then in the home of the priest of the Church of San Nicolás, on the town's main square, and then in the fortress of La Mota in Medina del Campo. He was ferried back and forth to Madrigal to testify. His final weeks were spent in Madrid, nearly a year later. At the friar's first testimony (*confesión*), which began at five in the morning on October 17, Judge Rodrigo de Santillán told the prisoner after writing down "three pages of lies and contradictions" that he would be tortured if he didn't tell the truth, whereupon the friar said his fellow prisoner was, as a matter of fact, King Sebastian. The Portuguese monarch was fulfilling a vow he made after the battle of Alcazarquivir "for having brought so much ruin upon his kingdom and lost so many men by doing what he wanted instead of listening to others." Santillán listened to this until two in the afternoon, when he was rudely interrupted by the Augustinian provincial, who barged in claiming jurisdiction, and then he went to lunch.[96]

Thus began the last twelve months of Fray Miguel's life, during which he spun lies and dropped alluring hints about the architecture and purpose of his project, sending the king's ministers chasing through the Iberian peninsula in search of confirmation. Starting in January, when indeed he was tortured, and many times, his stories changed nearly every time he met with Juan Llano, the apostolic judge who took jurisdiction of the ecclesiastical witnesses. Each new version prolonged his life. Among the many enigmas in this case is what a man renowned for his great knowledge and piety thought he was doing lying through his teeth to a nun. For the success of his plan (for lack of a better word) depended on the unwitting collaboration of Ana of Austria. Lying, said Juan de Aranda in his 1595 encyclopedia of wisdom, “is one of the most abominable vices that exists.”[97] Like everyone else writing about lying at that time, Aranda turned to St. Augustine, of whose order, it should be remembered, Fray Miguel had twice been a provincial. Augustine wrote two books about lying, on which he took a hard line: under no circumstances was lying ever to be tolerated, wrote the saint. Never, not even (especially not even) if it is close to the truth, not even if the aim is to praise God.

The vicar's first appearance in the case came with two letters he sent to the *pastelero,* Gabriel de Espinosa, who, unbeknownst to Fray Miguel, had been arrested in Valladolid on October 8, 1594. The letters, along with two letters from Ana, which we will look at later, were picked off by Rodrigo de Santillán before they reached the imprisoned baker.[98] They were intriguing, to say the least. Addressing the prisoner as “Your Majesty,” Fray Miguel brought him up to date on the state of health of his lady (*mi señora*) and the little girl and the nanny, all of whom were well and desirous of Espinosa's return. The little girl was the recipient of lovely clothes and presents. He said his lady wished for the nanny and the nanny's servant to leave town. He referred to the expected arrival of a group of men in disguise who were bound to cause gossip in town, which was of grave concern. The men would be led by a servant of someone named Barbara Blomberg, and they would stay in a tavern in a nearby village. One was named don Francisco, another don Carlos, another Benamar, and His Majesty too would be among them. There is talk of an imminent journey, and a sense that something complicated is afoot and should not be discovered. “My king, my lord,” one of the letters says at one point, and one wonders: Why was this written? The audience of the letters ended up being the judges, the king, and his ministers, but in principle they were going only to Espinosa, who presumably knew who he was. Unless, of course, he was supposed to show them to someone else.

During the first week of November, Santillán held preliminary conversations with both Espinosa and Fray Miguel in which the latter insisted the former was Sebastian. The vicar had prayed so fiercely for Sebastian to return, and Espinosa knew things only Sebastian could know, he said, making him almost certain it was true, though he did admit the Portuguese monarch had shown up four years before the end of the twenty-year vow of penitence he took when he went to Jerusalem.[99] His explanations, certainties, and theories were muddled during the early weeks. But by the time Llano and the vicar sat down on January 18, 1595, for a long chat full of interesting revelations and more lies, much more was known, offering the judges a basis for grounding their questions. The three-year-old girl referred to in his letter was the daughter of the "nanny," Inés Cid, who in fact was Espinosa's companion. The girl's name was Clara Eugenia. The identity of the men who were to have ridden into town disguised remained a mystery, though don Francisco turned out to be the man Ana thought was her brother. Throughout autumn, Rodrigo de Santillán heard from civilian witnesses, and Llano (and Augustinian authorities, who elbowed their way in early on) spoke with the nuns. Between them they put together quite a drama: daily, it appeared, Espinosa had met with Ana in the convent, speaking through the *grada*, the grille separating nuns from visitors, entertaining her and her friends with tales and promises. They nuns adored the little girl, whom Ana called *hija*. Fray Miguel, like a master of ceremonies, seemed to guide the players, and it was said that he had overseen a sort of marriage ceremony between Ana and the man she believed was her cousin, the fallen king of Portugal. In the words of the early twentieth-century British historian Martin Hume, "the mean little town was full of gossip" about the visits between Ana and Espinosa.[100]

Fray Miguel had never met Espinosa before the latter arrived in summer, he assured the judge in January, denying Espinosa's story about the fall of Lisbon.[101] He was pretty sure Sebastian was dead, he said now, and in his opinion, Espinosa was a liar, though at the same time, he confessed he had sort of believed him at first and had told Ana that the baker appeared to be Sebastian but probably was not. Actually, he clarified, Ana obviously wanted to believe he was Sebastian, so he told his Portuguese colleague Fray Agustín de los Angeles (later arrested) to tell her that in Portugal lots of people thought Sebastian was alive. Ana, he added, had told a local judge (unconnected with this case) that she was not really a nun and was going to leave the convent to reign and govern. It was she who had come up with the idea for Fray Miguel to marry her and Espinosa, which the vicar did, standing by the church grille. He admitted now he should never have consented to that, or to asking the pope for a dispensation, being that the bride and groom were first cousins, and he begged forgiveness. (The *Historia de Gabriel de Espinosa* adds the detail that Espinosa promised Ana he would get a dispensation, "which is easily obtained by royalty, and it would not be the first time.")[102] The vicar and Ana had arranged for Espinosa to leave town for a few days, the idea being that he would travel to the French border via Valladolid and meet up with the gentlemen, including Ana's brother and someone "who had taken possession of England."[103] Asked by Llano why he did not alert Philip II about the impostor, he said he figured Espinosa would soon disappear anyway. Ana's servant, Juan Roderos, also had asked Fray Miguel why Sebastian did not announce his presence to one and all; Fray Miguel told Llano that he had told Roderos that Espinosa had told him that all would be revealed once Philip died.

Ana, who in Fray Miguel's early version organized most of the conspiracy, had heard the story of Dr. Manuel Mendes, whom we last saw treating the wounded Sebastian in a remote mountain hut in Portugal. As part of her effort to confirm that her cousin Sebastian was alive, she asked that the Portuguese doctor come to Arévalo, which needed a doctor, and, presto, he came. Mendes later told Santillán he had come "at Fray Miguel's orders" and had known the vicar "since the time they went to school at Coimbra."[104] In his January interrogation, when Fray Miguel was still pretending the royal presence was all Ana's idea, he told Llano he had asked Mendes if Espinosa appeared to him to be the Portuguese king, and Mendes replied that he did not. Mendes was arrested almost immediately in October and spent all of autumn sick in bed. According to his final sentence, the doctor always insisted on Fray Miguel's evil pretensions and always insisted Sebastian was dead; indeed, he said, Ana did not want to believe him: "You Portuguese are so vain that just because he's dressed like that, you won't recognize him," Ana told him, disgusted with his lack of faith. Mendes told Santillán he now thought the entire mountain-hut escapade was "a joke." He was one of the few to be acquitted.

On March 7, 1595, assisted by torture, the judges learned more from Fray Miguel, and this time a more coherent picture began to emerge.[105]

The *Historia de Gabriel de Espinosa* resembles docudrama both here and elsewhere, but its account of Fray Miguel's first encounter with the instruments of torture reads true, though it appears nowhere in the case file. The Augustinian was taken from Medina to Madrigal, where the torturers (executioners, or *verdugos*, often did both jobs) had their installation ready. They placed Fray Miguel in front of the rack (*potro*) and other devices, and he was warned (the pamphlet uses indefinite plural subjects, though the warning must have come from Llano and Llano alone) to tell the truth, or he would be stripped of his clothing.

> He stuck to his guns, saying he had nothing more to say. That man was King Sebastian, that's who he thought he was, as he said before, and neither torture nor death would make him say anything more, and if he did say something, it would not be the truth. And with that, he was ordered to the test and given a brutal torture [*recio tormento*] from which he suffered as if he were a robust young man, saying nothing more, after which the cords were again tightened and the torture increased, and he could no longer resist, and he said, loosen the cords, I will talk, and that is what happened.[106]

Fray Miguel had been the deceiver, not the deceived, Llano confirmed to the king, and the vicar ratified his confession twenty-four hours after the torture, as required by law. The *Historia de Gabriel de Espinosa* says the Augustinian had spent the previous twelve years looking for a double and planting rumors that Sebastian was alive. According to Llano's report, when Espinosa arrived in Madrigal (the vicar continued denying they ever met in Lisbon), Fray Miguel saw a certain resemblance between him and Sebastian. It was not perfect, but it was his best shot, and time was running out. So he proposed the imposture, saying he would work to convince Ana. Espinosa agreed. Fray Miguel told Espinosa things about Sebastian that only Sebastian would know, which Espinosa then told Ana. Slowly over the summer of 1594, he made her believe she had a cousin and, even more important to her, a way out of the convent.

> The said Fray Miguel took Espinosa to meet and know the said doña Ana by the monastery grille, telling her he was disguised because of a vow he

> had made in Jerusalem to not return to his kingdom for twenty years on account of the battle he had lost in Africa, and though the said doña Ana did not believe him for some time, Fray Miguel put so much effort into persuading her and used such cunning until finally she was convinced and persuaded, and once that was established, the said Fray Miguel talked with her about marrying the said Gabriel de Espinosa, pledging themselves in a promise of matrimony, as was done, and the said Gabriel de Espinosa wrote a document signed with his name as King don Sebastian and gave it to the said doña Ana in the presence of the said Fray Miguel and doña Luisa de Grado, saying he took her as his wife, and he gave the said document to doña Ana, all upon the orders of Fray Miguel.[107]

This part of the story did not much change after this point. Given that the hidden King Sebastian did not intend to declare himself until after Philip II died, the plan had been nipped in the bud. Though it was scandalous and traitorous, it was no longer dangerous. On the other hand, during this same session with Llano, Fray Miguel also talked about his alleged accomplices and his long-range objectives, which were of far more importance. Previously, he had said he had never corresponded with anyone in Portugal except for a few prelates and archbishops who were old friends. Now it turned out he had. These stories kept the judges interested, and hence kept him alive, but because he kept changing them, torture became a regular feature of his miserable existence. In March, April, May, June, and July he was questioned repeatedly, each time saying something new, each time saying he had made the previous statements only because of the torture.[108] Santillán said several times that these repeated sessions only made things worse; in the words of a secretary, Santillán believed that "asking Fray Miguel the same things over and over only gives him an opportunity to change his story."[109]

The Pretender's Involvement

From the very start, Rodrigo de Santillán suspected an Antonian connection, which only makes sense, since he knew António was alive and was pretty sure Sebastian was not. Already on October 12, 1594, he reported that the detained *pastelero,* who by then had received the letters in jail from Ana and Fray Miguel addressing him as Your Majesty, was probably António himself, whom, of course, he had never seen, not even in a likeness.

"I think it must be don António," Santillán told Philip, referring to Espinosa, "because no other person who lets himself be called Majesty could be hidden in Spain so long without being missed in his own country and because this man has the distinguishing marks [*señas*] they say don António has; he is a smaller rather than larger man, with a lean face, blue eyes, one of which has a cloud [probably a cataract], and he is around sixty-four years old." The same day he wrote to Cristóbal de Moura, "I remember seeing the description [*señas*] of don António in the wanted posters distributed during the war."[110] Five days later, Fray Miguel also was detained: "[Fray Miguel] was imprisoned and exiled because he corresponded with don António during the war of Portugal. . . . He was preacher to the kings of Portugal, and I tell you [writing to Moura] that he is far from stupid, and therefore it is impossible that the man I am holding prisoner [Espinosa] could have deceived him by saying he was don António or King Sebastian."[111] Moura, who had spent a great deal of time in the Portuguese court, evidently wrote back telling him Sebastian could not possibly be sixty-four (he would have been almost forty-one) and that don António did not have one clouded eye. But the pretender was in his early sixties, so that made some sense. While Santillán insisted Espinosa was don António, he also told Moura that Fray Miguel, a serious and holy man, had said Espinosa was King Sebastian. (In one of the more bizarre points of the case, Fray Miguel much later told Llano that Espinosa had written him after the latter's arrest begging Fray Miguel to tell the authorities who he really was [meaning anything], being that "some said he was don António and others that he was don Sebastian, and others that he was Drake.")[112]

We will return to the impressions the judges and others had of Espinosa, but once it was established that he was not don António, the problem still remained of determining the pretender's true involvement. He had not been idle since he left Portugal by boat. He spent the rest of his life going back and forth between France and England seeking financial and military assistance, and both those crowns used him as a bargaining chip in their three-way standoff with Spain. The Azores Islands fought Spanish annexation until 1583; the resistance there largely was organized by the clergy and partially financed by France, whose enthusiasm (António had dangled Brazil as an incentive) waned after a naval defeat at the hands of the marquis of Santa Cruz in June 1582. The following year the Portuguese islands, which occupied a strategic location for the Americas trade, accepted the inevitable. In 1585 António left France for England. Queen Elizabeth was not inclined to anger Philip by aiding the man who wished to topple him from the Portuguese throne, but she also wanted to keep António in her arsenal of Spanish vexations, so she paid off his debts and humored him. After 1588, when England famously defeated the Spanish Armada, Elizabeth could afford to be more generous. Heeding don António's assurances that the people of Portugal would rise up angry if an anti-Philippine attack were to be launched, she agreed to help fund an assault led by Sir Francis Drake, a hugely expensive disaster. In April 1589 Drake wasted time sacking La Coruña on his way to Portugal, further enraging Philip, who was well informed of Drake's plans because he had informers in don António's circles. When the British reached Lisbon, they found deserted streets rather than the crowds of supporters they expected, though Cabrera de Córdoba reported that more than three hundred clerics and friars joined the attackers there, probably not the sort of support the invaders were hoping for. The British ships were unable to maneuver their way up the Tagus, so, discouraged and angry, they withdrew, sacking Vigo on their way back.[113]

Philip was keenly interested in physically eliminating the potentially dangerous pretender. Already before don António escaped from Portugal, the former ambassador, Juan de Silva, had considered drastic measures: "A determination should be made if he is to die or not, and if he is to die, the type and fashion [of death] must be resolved," he wrote. António was, after all, Philip's cousin and a cleric. Options were considered: decapitating him wherever he was caught, or perhaps taking him to Oporto and doing the deed there in his very own house so no one could say there was any doubt about it. (One Portuguese royal back from the dead was enough.)[114] António's published manifesto, his apologia, accused Philip of sending many Castilians and Portuguese to France to try to kill him, which was probably true.[115] Philip's ambassador in London, Bernardino de Mendoza, kept the king well informed of António's activities there. In France, the Treaty of Joinville in 1584, promising Spanish aid to the Catholic League, included a clause requiring the duke of Guise to return the Portuguese pretender to Spain if he were found, and António's chief agent in France, Antonio de Escobar, code name Sampson, was actually on Philip's payroll.[116] Messengers and spies regularly made their way from Portugal to England and France and back again, and all were under control. In 1587, Juan de Idiáquez, one of Philip's top aides, again suggested to ambassador Mendoza that António be killed; Mendoza wrote back that it would be easy to kill his servants by dropping poison into their beer but that the pretender kept his libations separate. "Two Englishmen are busy in the matter now, and they say that as don António frequently visits a countess who lives near the village where he is, they will find some opportunity of giving him a mouthful," he wrote in March 1587.[117]

Eight years later, evidence emerged during the investigation that the man himself, by now back in France, had been in Madrigal de las Altas Torres. In a two-day interrogation on October 19–20, conducted by Augustinians rather than by the judges, the nuns were all asked if they thought or had been told that the baker courting Ana was don António in disguise, or his servant, or his spy, and if they knew if don António had ever visited Madrigal.[118] Several of the women confirmed that they had thought or had heard that the baker was indeed, in the words of María Belón, "don António or some other prince." Ana de Espinosa (no relation to Gabriel) had heard in the convent that the baker was don António's spy, but she thought that was a huge lie, and she could not remember who had told her. She also had heard in the convent that people in town were saying don António had visited the baker, but she did not believe that either. Augustina de Ulloa, and Inés de Cangas, and María Belón also heard that the baker had hosted António in his house. Augustina de Ochoa had heard from another nun, Isabel Manjon, who had learned it in a letter posted six leagues away, that Ana of Austria was corresponding with don António; Isabel Manjon, asked to confirm this information, clarified that the letter came from just two leagues away, from her brother, an Augustinian friar named Alonso Gutiérrez, who lived in the town of Cabezas (probably Cabezas de Alambre) and for some reason had told his sister that there it was said that Ana and António were in touch.

On March 21, 1595, a summation of Fray Miguel's confession one day earlier stated the objective of the conspiracy quite clearly and confirmed that the nuns knew what they were talking about: "The intention and motive of this matter was to create rumors that Espinosa was King don Sebastian and then, after persuading the Kingdom [of Portugal] and inciting it, to summon don António and make him King of Portugal, and Espinosa would work for him, or don António would see what to do with him as long as he did not kill him."[119]

But for any of this to work, don António would have to approve the plan firsthand. (According to the *Historia de Gabriel de Espinosa*, the pretender was on the other side of the border awaiting word from Fray Miguel that he had found a good double; the double would then travel to France to meet with the original, which may have been what Espinosa was doing in Valladolid when he was arrested.)[120] So, the vicar told Llano, António stopped off in Madrigal on his way from England to Portugal via Galicia. Fray Miguel set up the visit by writing to Fray Alvaro de Jesús, procurator of the Order of St. Augustine, who passed the letter on to Manuel Tavares, a Lisbon merchant, who ensured that it reached don António. (Fray Alvaro was used as a mail conduit on more than one occasion; he also allegedly received and forwarded letters that Fray Miguel and Ana sent to Fray Antonio de Santa María, a leading Augustinian, member of the Alencastre clan, uncle of the duke of Aveiro, and future bishop.) The pretender arrived in Madrigal on August 20 or 21, 1594, disguised (*desfrazado*) in a multicolored outfit covered with a Manchegan cape; another interrogation refers to the visitor being "disguised, his face covered with a colored or purple cape."[121] He and one of his companions, a Franciscan friar named Diego Carlos, who was not wearing his usual habit, stayed at a tavern in town. Fray Miguel was strolling near the convent when don António came up to him and removed his cape, and the two old friends embraced and then took a long walk in the fields outside town. The pretender told Fray Miguel this was the third time he had been in the Iberian peninsula since he went into exile. As they walked, the vicar explained the plan, by which Espinosa would marry Ana and claim the throne, after which António would expose him as a fraud and dispose of him. António said the plan was a good one, and, despite the difficulties, he wanted in. He agreed to let it be known among his followers that he had seen Sebastian alive in Madrigal. A couple of days later, he and his travel companions met with the vicar in the friar's cell for an hour, and they all agreed to move forward. (One of the nuns who testified in October, María del Portillo, said she knew about this meeting because Rodrigo de Santillán talked about it as soon as he entered the convent to start the investigation; it is not clear how Santillán had acquired this knowledge so early on.) Later that evening, they met again in the cell and then left for the surrounding countryside, where they walked until two or three in the morning and apparently crossed paths with the baker. "Don António said [to Fray Miguel], very happy and laughing, that he had seen Espinosa without the baker's knowledge, and though his *señas* were not similar to those of don Sebastian, other factors would ensure that the plan would be successful." (In a later version, on June 23, Fray Miguel said one of don António's party had actually visited Espinosa in his house.)[122] The entourage left town the next day without having been identified: "In Madrigal, [don António] was so careful that those who accompanied him pretended they were linen vendors and they carried their wares under their arms," Fray Miguel said later.[123] In subsequent weeks a series of letters between António, his followers, and Fray Miguel allegedly established the network that would guide the conspiracy.

Rodrigo de Santillán was finally content. "This cake appears to have more layers than we thought," he wrote Cristóbal de Moura, "and now all we have to do is give a good torture to those two Lisbon merchants and find out where don António is."[124] But there are many reasons why the scenario is implausible, though if a Fugger correspondent could write in October 1587 that the pretender, in disguise, was on his way from England to Constantinople via Danzig and Moldavia, from whence he would travel to Cairo, Persia, and India, then the prospect of his making his way to Madrigal is less problematic.[125] But if don António were interested in taking the throne, it is hard to believe he would choose such a risky and indirect route as that described by the vicar. The sixty-three-year-old pretender is unlikely to have been traveling to Portugal at all, much less via Madrigal. According to the always sensible Juan de Silva—by now the count of Portalegre, captain general, and one of five governors of Portugal—who in May was in Lisbon investigating a long list of Fray Miguel's alleged accomplices and the continual clerical noise in favor of don António, you cannot prove a negative, no matter how unbelievable. That said, Silva did his best, suggesting that the king take a close look at António's calendar, which was surely within the ability of the king and his spies to do. Was it really possible for him to have made this voyage from June to September? Silva asked. "If Your Majesty knows from any source that don António was in France or England during those four months, then the friar is obviously lying. I think he should be questioned again on this point."[126] Which he was, repeatedly. Fray Miguel quickly retracted the story, blaming it on his fear of torture, though he reinstated it when Llano announced a new round of interrogation and threatened to starve him.[127] In July and August he would again retract it. Llano, it should be pointed out, believed that don António had been to Madrigal and deeply resented Silva's second-guessing from afar. In Silva's opinion, the follow-up regarding the tale of don António's visit and his alleged network of supporters had been negligible, and if a Portuguese judge (rather than Llano, one assumes) had been in charge, the truth quickly would have emerged. Llano begged to differ: "It makes perfect sense that things happened thus, because given the minimal sense, possibility, and consideration with which don António has conducted all his affairs, it seems we should judge these and other actions in a similar fashion, especially being that he probably is not being well received elsewhere. . . . The count's incredulity regarding Fray Miguel's confessions is the result of his not knowing the basic facts about this matter."[128]

The Specter of a Network

Philip II and his aides wanted to determine the extent to which don António was involved in Fray Miguel's scheme, but they also, given the increasing probability that the pretender himself was not involved, needed to figure out what sort of support network the vicar did have. Starting in January 1595, Fray Miguel's confessions included tantalizing lists of visitors, correspondents, and messengers.[129] One of don António's companions when he came to Madrigal was, the vicar said, Francisco Gomes, who worked for the count of Redondo. Manuel Tavares, the merchant who supposedly acted as a conduit in Lisbon, turned out to actually be a lawyer named Antonio de Fonseca, in whose home don António stayed and who was an acquaintance of Fray Miguel from his days in Salamanca. On March 9, Fray Miguel named Francisco Mascarenhas, Juan Coutinho, and Martín de Alarcón, all members of noble Portuguese families. He also mentioned the duke of Aveiro (Alvaro de Alencastre, a descendant of the English Lancasters; the previous duke, who was at the Guadalupe meeting, was killed at Alcazarquivir), Rodrigo de Noronha, Jorge Barbosa, and Alvaro de Medeyros. Alvaro de Jesus, the Augustinian who allegedly notified Tavares (now Fonseca), also had sent on a letter with the news to Jorge de Alburquerque, in Goa. Regrettably, Fray Miguel had burned all their replies, and he never showed them to Espinosa, he told the judges, so there was no material evidence of the correspondence.

On May 22 he retracted some of the names: "Upset as a result of the torture, he had said he wrote to Rodrigo de Noronha, Jorge Barbosa, and Alvaro de Medeyros, but in fact he had not written to them nor had they responded, and he says this to ease his conscience, but he wrote to the rest and they responded as he has declared." But he also added new names: the count of Monsanto (of the Castro family), Juan Gonzáles de Ataíde, Luís de Portugal (brother of the bishop of La Guarda), the archbishop of Lisbon, Antonio de Melo, and a man in Lisbon named Manuel Mendes who was not the same Dr. Manuel Mendes who allegedly cured Sebastian. Don António had assured Fray Miguel that the duke of Aveiro, count of Redondo, and don Luís were on board. Don António was planning to go to Paris a few months after his visit to Madrigal to meet with "*el de Béarne*," otherwise known as Henry of Navarre, Henry IV, King of France, in whom the pretender placed great hopes. Correspondence among all these men was constant and fluid, the vicar indicated, and don António's letters were signed Fray Juan Peregrino (John the Pilgrim), "his usual signature among his friends since he disappeared."[130] On June 23, Fray Miguel dropped Melo from the list: "Thinking back, and to ease his conscience, he stated that Antonio de Melo, a resident of Lisbon, one of those to whom he wrote, replied only that no one would ever hear him [Melo] say that King don Sebastian was alive because he saw him in the battle of Africa in such a state and in such danger that unless a cloud came down from heaven and lifted him up it was impossible to escape."[131]

These men, who were supposedly alerted that Sebastian had been discovered alive in Madrigal, or who were aware of the imposture itself, were all plausible accomplices. Some, like Luís de Portugal, had been *exceptuados.* The count of Redondo, João Coutinho, fled Alcazarquivir with the ill-fated Muhammed, though he got further than the usurped Moroccan king.[132] Redondo also fought against the Castilian forces in 1580 and was captured after the fall of Lisbon but released. He then was involved in the failed uprising of 1589 (when Drake arrived), as was Juan Gonzáles de Ataíde, and the count was again imprisoned. Redondo's aide, Francisco Gomes, who supposedly accompanied don António to Madrigal, was a merchant born, interestingly, in Asilah, the Portuguese-Moroccan town that served as the base for Sebastian's doomed military campaign. Gomes, it turned out, had two brothers who were Augustinians and had lived in Fray Miguel's old monastery in Lisbon, though now they were in the Indies. He spoke with Fray Miguel in Madrid at San Felipe six years earlier, when he was there to oversee the count's lawsuits, but, he insisted in his testimony after he was arrested, he had no correspondence with Fray Miguel or don António.[133] Rodrigo de Santillán interviewed the innkeepers where Fray Miguel's visitors had allegedly stayed, and they confirmed that indeed the "disguised Portuguese" had arrived in July 1594 asking for directions to the convent (which is hard to miss). The innkeepers did not know who the men were, but they saw them walking from the town square, where the inn was, to meet Fray Miguel.[134]

On the last day of August 1595, by which time he was imprisoned in Madrid, and the two Portuguese suspects, Gomes and Fonseca, had testified they had nothing to do with him, the former vicar decided to jettison the whole story. All seven of his past confessions were false. Actually, he said, don António had never been in Madrigal, and he (Fray Miguel) had no accomplices. None.[135] Once again, he attributed his past tales to his fear of torture.

The logic of the rules of torture were being tested here, as Llano well recognized. "The law provides that those who retract their confessions can be sent back for more torture [*tormento*] to make them tell the truth," he wrote the king, "but if we send Fray Miguel back for more, he will ratify his earlier confessions and retract what he says now, as has always been the case, and therefore I think it best that we finish this matter off once and for all because it seems he changes his story solely to extend the matter."[136] Confessions gained under torture were inadmissible as evidence, a principle included in Castile's medieval code of law, the *Partidas*. Hence the need for the defendant to ratify the information the following day. Like scientists who must replicate results, judges had to replicate confessions, and changes in testimony necessarily led to a new round of questioning and torment. Strictly speaking, torture was not a matter of punishment but of utility. It was a means, the only means, for confirming something for which there was incomplete proof. Some people were usually exempt from torture; these included the nobility, doctors of law, pregnant women, the very young, the very old, and the clergy. But certain crimes exempted the exempt, and lèse majesté was among them. If a clergyman was tortured, he might have the privilege of clerical executioners, but not necessarily. A seventeenth-century manual states that though it might be thought indecent for a layperson to lay hands on the cleric, "it would be far more indecent for a cleric to exercise such a vile office." In our case, Llano, whose titles included chaplain to His Majesty, member of the Oviedo cathedral chapter, and commissioner of the Supreme Council of the Holy Inquisition, oversaw the torture of Fray Miguel; those who actually tortured the principal defendants were executioners or town criers. A notary also would have been present. There are references to turning or tightening cords, which suggest the rack (*potro*), the most common device after the sixteenth century, although the Cortes complained in the 1590s about "new sorts of exquisite torments, both cruel and extraordinary and never imagined by the law."[137]

Fray Miguel's guilt was long established; he was questioned and tortured repeatedly—always only at the orders of the king—solely in order to obtain the names of his accomplices. They, along with Espinosa's little girl, were what made this case matter to Philip II, for in them lay the potential threat to his rule. In January, once the basic facts of the conspiracy were known, Moura and Juan de Idiáquez wrote a memo saying there was no more need to torture anybody as the identity of the principals was established: "The truth is well known by now, and the world will be persuaded more by judicial confessions gained without force than by those conducted with torture, which the malicious will doubt," they wrote.[138] But the king was not satisfied, and in March he wrote a series of instructions and notes regarding how the questioning should proceed. By this time, he knew Espinosa generally told the truth, and Fray Miguel generally lied. But Fray Miguel also had lied to Espinosa, possibly infecting the latter's testimony. Ask Espinosa when Fray Miguel told him about the letters to the Portuguese accomplices, he instructed the judges. Ask Fray Miguel the same. Ask Fray Miguel if he ever showed the letters to Espinosa (we have seen that he did not). Ask him why he was in such a rush to contact all these people and how he dared write them about the marriage of Ana and Espinosa when it was not even a necessary part of the plan and only endangered him. Tell Fray Miguel "to tell the truth and not trouble his conscience any more with any more crimes and confess if what he says about the accomplices is an invention just like the revelations, and if he told Espinosa all this just to encourage him, and if he is now giving false evidence with these names, thinking it will help him escape or postpone the case."

> Ask him, finally, as a man capable of reason, especially a learned man like himself, what he thought to accomplish with such a tangled affair and what he thought he was doing raising such a low subject to such a high station with such difficulties, and if by chance his intention was to use these stories to deceive and attract the simplest and most gullible people and then, once they were stirred up, get rid of this man, who was being used as bait, and join a revolt on behalf of don Antonio.[139]

At some point, though, the questions had to cease. The president of the Council of Castile, the kingdom's highest body of royal justice, which stepped in at the end as a formality, wrote on September 7, 1595, "In no way is it believable that this friar created this extraordinary invention without including those who could help him. He could not have succeeded [without help], and it is possible he intended to communicate with them later on." But it really did not matter anymore, he agreed: "May justice be done."[140]

The Bandit Who Became a Spy and Dressed Like a Friar

One of the strangest facets in this case is the possibility that Antonio Pérez also was entangled. Very briefly, Pérez was Philip II's secretary of state and one of the leading figures, with Ana de Mendoza, princess of Eboli, of one of two factions that dominated Philip's court in the 1570s; the other was led by the duke of Alba. In one of the greatest scandals of Philip's reign, Pérez organized the murder of Juan Escobedo, the secretary of don Juan of Austria, Philip's half-brother. Philip assented to the murder, but later, after the death of his half-brother, he realized Escobedo had been unjustly killed. In 1579 (amid the political jockeying before the Portuguese annexation) Pérez and the princess of Eboli were arrested. But Pérez had proof that the king was complicit in Escobedo's death, putting Philip in an awkward position. In 1590, Pérez escaped his captivity and fled (disguised) to Aragon, where the king's law could not reach him; the "escape to Aragon" was a trope in Castilian literature whose parallel in the Madrigal story is refuge in Béarn, the other side of the French border. Pérez was then accused of heresy, enabling the intervention of the Inquisition, whose jurisdiction extended into Aragon. In May 1591, when he was being transferred from one prison to another, he again escaped, and Aragon rose in revolt against Castile, the most serious uprising in sixteenth-century Spain other than the 1520 revolt of the *comuneros*. The antiroyalist disturbances, put down only after Philip sent some seventeen thousand Castilian troops to Aragon (almost as many as were required to annex Portugal), were triggered by the Pérez affair but had deep roots in resentment over taxation and constitutional matters as well as in class conflict within Aragon. Like the prior of Crato, Antonio Pérez spent the rest of his life going back and forth between the courts of England and France raising funds, organizing failed invasions of his homeland, writing his memoirs (published in 1592), and lurking in the back of Philip's mind. The princess Ana of Eboli, daughter of the duke of Francavilla and widow of a Portuguese nobleman, Ruy Gomez da Silva, was a prominent member of the Mendoza clan and the object of undying hatred by the king and many of his ministers. She spent the last thirteen years of her life under house arrest.

Antonio Pérez's linkages to the Madrigal conspiracy are murky, probably nonexistent. He and the prior of Crato, both exiles, certainly were interested in each other's existence and to some extent, as enemies of Philip II, were natural allies, but they also were competing for the same support. The doctor who reported from London that Philip had ordered the strangulation and burning of noblemen and bishops may not have been the most reliable of sources, but he also said Antonio Pérez had met secretly (*sic*) with the king of France, which was "good news for the king our lord," that is, don António.[141] When Antonio Pérez was in Pau (France), he allegedly wrote to don António in England to propose that together they encourage Queen Elizabeth to attack Spain.[142] The two Antonios cohabited for awhile in Eton College in the company of Dr. Lopes, a Portuguese Jew who later was executed for treason.[143] Don António favored couriers dressed in monk's habits (the Venetian ambassador reported the arrest of one such friar in February 1591), so it should come as no surprise that Pérez used similar methods or that they should, in fact, share messengers.[144]

One of those men, Bernardo del Río, among the most fascinating of the witnesses in the Madrigal case, placed the two Antonios together in Toulouse.[145] In early February 1595, officials in Olmedo (thirty-five kilometers from Medina del Campo as the crow flies) picked up a couple of suspicious friars who appeared to be traveling together, though one was walking a few days behind the other. The arrests set off a clattering scandal, exactly what the judges did not want, when word got out they were spies in the pay of France. There also was a lot of noise when the Augustinians claimed jurisdiction after del Río demanded they intervene; given the two friars' possible connection with France, and given the Augustinian provincial's well-known links to Navarre and France (on which more later), Santillán immediately informed the king of the matter and did a first round of questioning with the imprisoned friars in Medina. In that conversation, del Río said he was walking from Segovia to Avila (apparently taking the long way around), where he needed to clear up his status with his order. Ordered to read from a book in Latin, he explained his linguistic deficit by saying that in France they did not require those of his profession to have competency in Latin. Santillán then moved on to other things (March was spent interrogating Espinosa and Fray Miguel), and not until April did he get back to the monks, who remained locked up.

The first one, Francisco Montenegro, turned out to be a vagabond (though actually a friar) who lived off alms and had nothing of interest to offer. But the second one, del Río, was another matter. He was dressed as a Trinitarian lay friar but had demanded that the Augustinians help him. He first said he was Catalan, but Santillán thought he was a Galician disguised as a Portuguese. In fact he was French. This was his story, which he told under torture and later ratified. On his travels through Spain, when he was in Torrelaguna, north of Madrid, he ran into another Trinitarian, who immediately detected fraud. The true Trinitarian took the false one by the arm in the direction of Alcalá de Henares, where matters would be sorted out at Trinitarian headquarters, and when they crossed a bridge, del Río tossed away a bundle of letters. The Trinitarians ordered him to cease wearing their habit, but at some point after that, del Río must have joined up with Montenegro and once again was dressed as a friar. Around that time he was spotted in Segovia, speaking good French. The truth was, he told the judge, he was not a friar at all. He was a former bandit. The thirty-four-year-old prisoner told Santillán that his gang in Zaragoza, led by one El Pintado, participated in the tumultuous and successful effort to free Antonio Pérez from his Inquisitorial jailers in 1591. Del Río caught Pérez's eye during the melee (according to Santillán's version, "Antonio Pérez took a liking to this Bernardo when he saw him behave like a true man"), and the bandit joined the entourage that accompanied the disgraced royal secretary to France. There, in Béarn, they joined the court of Henry IV's sister, Catherine, referred to as Madama. This was the period at the tail end of the French Wars of Religion when Philip II was sending troops to fight Henry IV, and it was then that the two Antonios met in Toulouse, del Río said. Soon, del Río began carrying messages between France and Portugal. The letters he threw off the bridge were from Antonio Pérez to a Manuel Mendes in Lisbon, the same Mendes, it would seem, whom Fray Miguel named in his confessions. Mendes, in turn, had given del Río letters for Pérez as well as for don António, prior of Crato.

After del Río was arrested in Olmedo, he told Santillán, he received a visitor on Palm Sunday in his jail cell named Fray Antonio, a tertiary Franciscan monk. This man, whose existence Santillán confirmed, told Bernardo that he, too, was a messenger between Manuel Mendes and Antonio Pérez and was on his way to Lisbon and stopped in Madrigal "because he was very friendly with Fray Miguel de los Santos." His advice to del Río: "Just say you're a vagabond friar, and they'll release you." Fray Antonio went on to tell del Río that his people in Lisbon (among them don António himself) had told him that next summer the French and the English were going to attack Spain.

So was Fray Miguel lying about Mendes? Juan de Silva never found him and insisted that he and others of Fray Miguel's supposed contacts in Portugal were inventions, but the name is a very common one.[146] Was Bernardo del Río lying? Was the Franciscan monk really an Augustinian? Was the man "who had taken possession of England" and who appears in several witnesses' testimony actually Antonio Pérez? Del Rio's is among the most intriguing of the many collateral tales in the Madrigal conspiracy, but I am convinced that trying to track down all the names and clues is not productive, given the information we lack and the probability that witnesses lied or repeated other witnesses' lies. The point here, as elsewhere, is that Madrigal formed part of a physical and discursive world of disguises and adventure, politics and diplomacy, and that correspondence and messengers traced the lines connecting the parts. The erstwhile bandit Bernardo del Río was one of those connectors. In July 1595 when Santillán was working on the sentences, he admitted that all he had on del Río was a confession, "which by law is not enough to convict him." But in the case of lèse majesté, he went on, less proof is required. So del Río was sentenced on August 2 to two hundred lashes and ten years on Spain's galley ships. His *pregón*, the statement of his guilt read aloud in public, said he was convicted "for being a criminal and for having come with letters from Antonio Pérez for someone in these Kingdoms to the detriment of His Majesty."

"The Whole Kingdom Is Watching"

Bernardo del Río's letters from Antonio Pérez got tossed off a bridge, but four surviving missives shed new light while casting more confusion on the conspiracy. They remind us that the investigation was very much in the public sphere, no matter what the king and the judges did to muffle the noise, the interminable *ruidos*. The letters were anonymous and first appeared in early January 1595.[147] The first arrived at the Medina del Campo home of the famed merchant banker Simón Ruiz, where Santillán lodged. The one-page letter, in tiny, neat script, suggested that the judge consult religious experts as he unraveled the strands, exactly the sort of advice Santillán did not want ("They think one can't do anything without the opinion of a theologian," Santillán grumbled to the king). If he was interested in more, the writer told Santillán, he should attend Mass in a certain church the next day as a sign. Santillán did so, and on the following day was rewarded with a second letter. A few weeks later Santillán and Llano received a third and fourth. The author was well informed and had access to a great deal of background information. It was quite clear to the judges as well as to Philip and his advisers that the writer was a man of the church. "Do not pay much attention to the anonymous letters," Moura wrote to Llano on February 16, "because it is clear they are from friars and people who want to place obstacles in justice's way."[148] Friars were possibly Santillán's least favorite sector of the population, and the behavior of the Augustinians over the Madrigal scandal probably destroyed any remaining sympathy he may have had for men of the cloth. "The intention of the writer was good, but the advice was not," Santillán said. "It is obvious he is a friar. Their opinion in matters of republican government is usually not on target because their constitution strives for perfection and purity, as is only right among those who profess that life, and their government is a matter for a small group of people, and even there, as we can see [a pointed reference to inter-Augustinian squabbles] it is difficult to preserve a perfect and pure spirit. So there is no comparison between their mode of government and that of the republic." Llano, a member of the clergy himself, was in theory more kindly disposed, but the anonymous letter hectoring him to "consult with some serious theologians" on matters of law and God's justice must have annoyed him.

"The whole kingdom is watching," began the first letter, a disheartening thought. This was the shortest of the four letters, which basically served only to insist on the necessary role of theologians and to find out if Santillán wanted to hear more. In addition, it made two interesting points: everyone knew that Santillán and Llano wrote to the king constantly, several times a day. And the letter-writer was "not Portuguese nor is he related to anyone from that nation."

The second letter, five and a half pages of tiny script, got into the particulars of the imposture, showing off the writer's skills of rhetoric and reasoning. The evil baker (*este negro Pastelero*) was a low commoner. Everybody knew that Fray Miguel had been very close to King Sebastian. Everybody also knew that the vicar had performed a marriage ceremony uniting Ana of Austria and the baker. It was impossible for Fray Miguel to think that this vulgar commoner was the king, but at the same time he must not be a vulgar commoner if the vicar performed the marriage ceremony. Therefore he was someone else, but of high social standing: "He cannot be a low man but rather a grand, very grand person." Another indication that the prisoner (Espinosa) was not a vulgar commoner was that he had refused Ana's offer of jewels. No commoner would do that. Furthermore, the prisoner had not been tortured (though he would be soon, which the letter-writer did not know), showing he was exempt. Though the writer was sure that Fray Miguel could not be deceived into thinking the prisoner was Sebastian, let us assume for a moment, he posited, that the prisoner really was Sebastian: then why remain in hiding? If the Portuguese people should find out (and they would find out) that their king was sitting in a prison cell in Castile, they would revolt. So the prisoner definitely was not Sebastian. "It is laughable to say that don Sebastian has been hidden for all these years and that now he can find no better protection than Fray Miguel nor a better position than that of a baker nor a better place than Madrigal," he wrote. The king would be safer and more suitably attended in a thousand homes in Portugal, he pointed out. And the business about Sebastian having taken a vow not to rule or enter Portugal for twenty years was even more laughable; no priest in his right mind would accept such a vow or, if it had been accepted, he would easily commute it. Then who was the prisoner? The writer was coy, referring to "many secret papers" that would reveal all. But in his opinion, the man was don António. Nobody else fit the bill. "We know this friar and don António had a very close friendship, so there would be no reason for amazement if António, wandering around as he does, sought him out to speak with him and that the friar introduced him to doña Ana, and little by little they spun this tapestry, or perhaps they had already spun it through letters, which is what brought him here to get a sense of how things were going in the Kingdom." There is an uncharacteristic, though inevitable, flaw in the writer's reasoning here, for sheltering don António for whatever reason would be a direct attack on Philip II, and thus the theory does little to protect Fray Miguel, which was clearly the writer's objective. Or perhaps, as Moura said, the objective was merely to slow things down.

In late January the second set of letters was delivered, one for Santillán and one for Llano. The writer started off by reminding Santillán that everyone was watching and that he could use some help: "Many eyes, as Your Grace knows, see a lot, and it would be both presumptuous and arrogant to trust only what one's own eyes see and to think that others might not see more." He praised the judge's restraint (though that was due to Santillán's duties rather than to the judge's taking the writer's advice) and urged more of the same; rushing heedlessly forward would lead nowhere, he said, "like an exhausted swimmer drowning at the river's edge." By then the writer had learned of Philip's order to torture the two principal suspects. "Ropes will not yield results in this sort of matter or reveal the truth. I greatly fear the blood they draw will hide the truth, like covering it over with dirt." He knew the prisoners would have to be tortured at some point, he said, just not yet, not until all other methods had been tried. His logic again deserted him for a moment in this third letter to Santillán when he referred to the impending torture of Fray Miguel: "I once again plead with Your Grace a thousand and one times in all possible earnestness that you stop and realize that in matters like these it is far wiser to display calm and maturity than the spirit of the law."

Finally, to Llano he appealed as a fellow churchman to whom he knew

God had granted great abilities (but not so great that he couldn't do with a bit of outside theological opinion). To him he praised the good vicar. "I can say no more than to tell you who Fray Miguel de los Santos is. I assure you I have known few if any people with more gifts and better qualities. He is a man of great understanding, rare prudence, wide learning, and has always been known as a great man of religion and a servant of God, and nothing has been found against him for many years." And now, the writer said, this beacon of religious discretion is about to face his maker accused of having been deceived by a lowly baker, "dishonored and taken as a madman and killed as such, or punished not as a madman but as someone who has committed one of the hugest and most harmful lunacies one could imagine, which cannot be the case either, for nobody could believe such a thing of Fray Miguel. And thus there being no basis in truth, the door is open for everyone to think and say what they want."

At several points throughout the letters, the writer suggested, almost threatened, that unrest in Portugal was on the verge of turning ugly and that "infinite harm" was on the horizon. Certainly everyone saying and thinking what they want was a dangerous prospect. If word should get out—and it would—that Sebastian or António were hiding in Spain or that Fray Miguel had been tortured, Portugal would revolt. In the third letter to Santillán, even the specter of Antonio Pérez was summoned. The impending disturbances "would be much greater than those of Aragon, being that Antonio Pérez had neither the reputation nor the authority in Aragon that Fray Miguel has in Portugal, and the Aragonese nation is less credulous than the Portuguese and felt less violated by the [Castilian] government, nor did they miss their natural king like the Portuguese do." These repeated implicit and explicit references to the coming violence are not logically argued (nor are the António theory or the Fray Miguel exculpation), and one gets the sense that, as Moura said, the writer was throwing everything he had in the judges' way, hoping that talk of bloodshed just might scare them into slowing down.

At the start, Santillán was worried that searching for the author of these letters might set off more bells in an already talkative town. "I did not want to investigate so as not to make noise [*hacer ruido*] and give rise to suspicions that the letters contained things they did not," he told

Philip. But after the second pair was delivered, Santillán began making inquiries. Immediately he discovered that, in a remarkable coincidence, a guest in one of the town's inns was a student who had been don António's servant in Portugal until the fall of Oporto in 1581, fourteen years earlier. Either he was a very young servant or a very old student, but in either case he had an alibi for the night the anonymous letters were left at Santillán's door, his handwriting did not match, and anyway he said he was studying to be a Benedictine. So that led nowhere.

Given the author's evident desire that the investigation be detained, there was no doubt in Santillán's and Llano's minds that he was Augustinian, most probably Fray Antonio de Sosa (or Sousa or Sossa), who lived in Valladolid and was a close friend of the provincial, Gabriel Goldaraz. The principal source for this theory was Fray Juan de Benavente, the Augustinian difinitor for Castile, who believed the reason Sosa so feared the torture of Fray Miguel was that the vicar might start singing about his Augustinian accomplices in the conspiracy. In autumn, Benavente began writing letters to the judges about Goldaraz, whom he hated, and the provincial's friends, who he said were involved in unsavory and possibly traitorous activities. Llano had known Benavente for years and trusted him, and on February 18 the two men met in Medina del Campo to talk about the anonymous letters. The handwriting, style, and clarity all told Benavente the author was Sosa, whose literary skills were widely known, and the fact that some of the letters had been left at Simón Ruiz's house only increased his certainty, given the friendship between Ruiz and Sosa and between the servants of the two men. Benavente "does not know anyone in the entire province who is more reckless and daring in such things than the said Fray Antonio de Sossa, who publicly preached in Valladolid against His Majesty's order against the two prisoners," according to a summary of Llano's findings, referring to the arrests of Fray Miguel and Espinosa.[149] If one looked through the papers on his desk, surely one could find a draft, which Benavente said he was certain would have Goldaraz's fingerprints all over it. Furthermore, Benavente said, in a coup de grâce, Sosa came from a Portuguese family. Llano and Santillán wanted to go to Valladolid immediately to arrest Sosa and confiscate his papers, but permission was denied.[150] Moura and Juan de Idiáquez, as well as the king, were of the opinion that a more undercover approach was called for. Philip II, though quite ill at this point, continued to be informed: "As for Fray Antonio de Sosa, I think I know him," he wrote in the margin of a memo. "He's very old, even older than I am, so I don't know how his handwriting is so good." Sosa faded away as the judges turned their attention to other matters and disregarded his advice to avail themselves of the wisdom of the living clergy rather than relying on "dead papers" (*papeles muertos*).

The Jesuit Who Knew Everything

Another piece of correspondence floating around during these months was written not by a worried Augustinian but by a Jesuit.[151] Like the anonymous writer, the Jesuit was in Medina del Campo, and he assumed Espinosa was Sebastian because otherwise Fray Miguel would have to be a liar, which was impossible. At the very least, Espinosa was a gentleman. The Jesuit's account is significant because much of the wording is identical to that which appeared in the only known pamphlet about the case, published in 1683 but thought by some to have circulated in a previous version as early as 1595. We will return to the pamphlet, but for the time being we can assume that the extraordinarily well informed author of this account was either the author of the pamphlet or the source. The document, called "An account of what is known of the pastelero de Madrigal who is being held prisoner in Medina del Campo on His Majesty's orders," was written between December 1594 and February 1595. There is no indication if it was part of a letter or to whom it was addressed. It begins by describing a visit to Madrigal "a few years ago" by a group of disguised men who met with Ana of Austria. They spoke with her at length until they realized their presence had been detected and even that Philip II had been notified, at which point they became frightened and left. One of those men, the writer says, later opened a bakery in the nearby town of Nava; he was a "very bad baker" though not at all greedy, undercharging for his goods, and from Nava he moved to Madrigal. So, although the judges always insisted Espinosa had never been to Madrigal before, the Jesuit had been informed otherwise. In Madrigal, the Jesuit wrote,

Espinosa spent most of his time, day and night, in the convent parlor with Ana or in Fray Miguel's cell. When Espinosa was arrested in Valladolid, he was on his way to Burgos; the Jesuit knew Espinosa had reserved horses for that purpose. At this early point in the supposedly secret investigation, the author knew not only about Santillán's work habits (private notaries, interrogations lasting as long as eleven hours), he also had dissected the arrest down to its finest details, knew the content of much of the testimony, and was familiar with just about every point that would appear in everyone's subsequent account and speculation: linen shirts, jewels, captured letters, Ana's brother, Espinosa's cell, the vow after Alcazarquivir, the doctor, Sebastian's funeral Mass. There was nothing he did not know. These were the narrative signposts, the syntax of both the conspiracy and its unraveling. The Jesuit therefore probably was ground zero. But though he may have established the syntax, his writing also reflected a general sensibility of which signs would be useful interpreters of confusing events. This case, which relied so much on both the written word and oral accounts, illustrates beautifully how literary structure and political/legal chronology cohabited in the telling. The Jesuit's account is one of the first and best examples of this, and we will return to it later.

In addition to denouncing Sosa and Goldaraz, Fray Benavente mentioned a third Augustinian who was taking the king's name in vain: Fray Diego de Zúñiga, a preacher in Toledo who Benavente said was going around saying there was no reason to think King Sebastian was dead. Two weeks later, Santillán relayed this information to the king, remarking on the obvious danger of encouraging the Portuguese to continue waiting (or hoping; *esperar* means both in Spanish) for Sebastian.[152] In Toledo, "they are speaking about the Madrigal matter in ways other than they should," Moura and Juan de Idiáquez said to the king, and they suggested that the local governor investigate Zúñiga. But Philip II was ahead of them; in his handwritten notes on their memo, he added, "Here we all know who Fray Diego de Zúñiga is. He says he's the son of don Diego de Zúñiga, who was ambassador to France, and thus it would be best . . . to carry out this investigation with great dissimulation and secrecy."[153]

Exactly who Diego de Zúñiga was is not clear. The dukes of Béjar, among Spain's oldest and grandest noblemen, were Zúñigas, and indeed the current duke had been Philip's ambassador to France, but around half the male members of the family appear to have been named Diego, many of them were religious, and many used alternate surnames. There was one who was appointed difinitor of the Augustinian Order in May 1595 (replacing Benavente), but it is unlikely our rabble-rouser would have been chosen.[154] Another Augustinian was regarded as a saint and died in 1599 caring for plague victims in Valladolid, the wrong city, and yet another appeared as a hostile witness (some said perjurer) at the 1572 Inquisition trial in Valladolid of Fray Luis de León. That Zúñiga has been placed in Madrigal in 1568, but he also has been confused with the Diego de Zúñiga who was a famous astronomer and philosopher in Toledo during these years; it is unlikely that Philip and the other authorities would not know the astronomer, so he probably is not our man either. On March 4, the Toledo governor, Alonso de Cárcamo, was told to find out very discreetly what Zúñiga was up to. On July 11 (the task was delayed for some reason) Cárcamo wrote to secretary Martín de Idiáquez that the friar was "very persuaded that the man being held prisoner in Medina del Campo is King Sebastian and that His Majesty [Philip II] will order him killed as he has ordered many others, and he calls His Majesty cruel, vindictive, and a bad governor. In a place so attuned to news as Toledo, such a free and rash person is a very bad thing." In Cárcamo's opinion, this called for an inquisitor, to which Philip assented.[155]

Sosa and Zúñiga together, Benavente insisted, were enough to raise a disturbance and make the community rise up (*levantar una comunidad*), fearful words for a ruler whose father's kingdom had been set afire by the *comuneros* and who now at the end of his life faced a shaky succession, widespread hardship, challenges throughout Europe, and direct criticism of his rule at home. During the very weeks that Philip and his ministers were corresponding about the French spy Bernardo del Río and the possibly seditious friars, Venetian agents reported that Lisbon had been evacuated out of fear that the English were on their way to sack it.[156] Philip was a busy, distressed man.

3

Castile: King Philip II and the Baker, Gabriel de Espinosa

Spain was at war virtually every day of Philip II's reign. As the king got older, sicker, and more uncomfortable, he could derive no satisfaction from seeing any resolution ahead. The 1590s commenced with Antonio Pérez's escape; that was followed by a series of domestic protests, resistance in the Cortes, and continual bad news from France, the Netherlands, and the Atlantic, all punctuated by frequent bouts of alarming and painful illness in the royal body. The military, fiscal, and constitutional crises were related, of course, and they seemed to be compounded by natural disasters and the inevitability of God's punishments. "There are malcontents of all sorts in all Spain's kingdoms," remarked the outgoing Venetian ambassador in 1595.[1]

Reports on the king's comings and goings during the last decade of his life read like medical bulletins. As he lay or sat in pain, he also worried, for the king knew better than anyone the dangers of an extinguished dynasty. The safe succession of the monarchy depended on the good health and good sense of Prince Philip, who in 1595, during the Madrigal case, began attending government meetings and participating in official ceremonies on his own (another king-in-waiting, this one legitimate). It was common knowledge among court observers that the prince was not especially gifted, unlike his sister Isabel Clara Eugenia, and the king's advisers worried about the bad influence of the duke of Lerma, Francisco Rojas de Sandoval, who eventually would become the new king's powerful favorite. Already in the 1580s, after the Portuguese annexation, Philip II's bad health became the subject of widespread speculation, whether out of wishful thinking or loyal concern. He caught the same influenza that killed his young wife in October 1580, and don António's forces in northern Portugal weighed rumors that the king had succumbed as well.[2] In the wishful-thinking category, a pamphlet printed in London in 1590, allegedly written by a French Catholic, remarked that the Portuguese and Flemings "never enquire for any other news" than the imminent demise of the king, "whose aged yeares breede continual danger."[3] By October 1594, the papal nuncio in Spain, Camilo Caetani, could write to his secretary of state in Rome, "The king is old, and continually ill."[4] Though Philip still inserted himself into the management of the monarchy, he doubled his cabinet of advisers from three to six members, and contemporaries generally commented that Cristóbal de Moura and Juan de Idiáquez were now directing the government. The king acknowledged that he ailed from what he called melancholy, "a very bad thing, though fitting for these times and for what is happening in the world, which cannot but affect me, for the state of Christianity pains me greatly."[5]

Castile, the belly of the beast from where Fray Miguel de los Santos chose to launch his conspiracy, was a cold and unpleasant place in the 1590s. There was more rain than usual, inadequate harvests, and hunger and poverty. Population plummeted, especially in the heart of Castile. The tax burden continued to grow, though it could not grow enough to satisfy the crown's wartime needs. The deficit thus steadily increased, and Philip in November 1596 would declare his fourth suspension of payments. But before doing that, he turned to the Cortes, which sat in session in Madrid from 1592 to 1598. The principal tax levied during these years was the *millones*, lump-sum assessments generally financed by taxes on local foodstuffs. Many city councils, to whom the Cortes representatives at this stage were accountable, refused to sign off on these taxes, among other reasons because the first and second estates were not exempt from *millones* as they had been from previous taxes.[6] But even a rich man like don Pedro Tello de Guzmán, Seville's representative to the Cortes, understood that the crown simply could not squeeze any more wealth out of desperately poor constituents. In a speech in May 1595, as the Madrigal case was dragging to a close, he said, "The poor exist on sardines and cod, which they eat all year. With that and fried bread they survive, with no stew pot with meat. They know nothing of turkey, hens, rabbits, partridges, fancy cakes, blancmange, and other exquisite and expensive foods, which are only for the rich and grand. With such inequality between one and the other, one so much more valuable than the other, we take much from those who have little, and nothing from those who have everything."[7]

In rejecting what the Venetian ambassador reportedly called the king's "insidious request," Cortes representatives naturally had motivations other than defending the interests of the poor, though there is no reason to think Guzmán was not sincere.[8] I. A. A. Thompson has written persuasively that their motivations transcended finance.[9] Constitutional considerations regarding the respective rights of a monarch and his vassals hovered in the background. In denying Philip II the taxes he requested (though eventually he got them), they were making clear their unhappiness with his government. The late sixteenth century in Spain marked a moment of important political devolution, as finances and military recruitment drifted into the hands of municipalities, lords, and contractors, in part an organizational response to the growing crisis but also a recognition of the unwieldy nature of the monarchy and its peculiar genesis. The *millones* mark the defining point of this devolution. But fiscal stinginess throughout the reign not only of Philip II but of his father also reflected Castilian discomfort with the Hapsburg imperial agenda. The annexation of Portugal constituted a piece of that agenda, and though the Cortes supported it in 1580, it is not far-fetched to think that a decade later there might have been people of influence in Castile who would not have objected to the return of Portugal to the Portuguese. There certainly was sympathy for disengagement elsewhere. On May 19, 1593, one of Madrid's representatives to the Cortes, Francisco Monzón, responding to the crown's long-running request for revenue, said, "His Majesty should bring back the armies he has in France and Flanders, and that way the rebels who don't wish to abide by the holy faith will be thoroughly and rigorously punished. If they want to be abandoned, let them go." Fray Antonio de Sosa, the man suspected of writing the anonymous letters to

Rodrigo de Santillán and Juan de Llano, was said to have announced in his Medina del Campo monastery, "It is heresy to say that the king in good conscience can defend the states of Flanders at the cost of the kingdoms of Spain, and I said so to his face."[10] What Geoffrey Parker has called Philip's "messianic vision" essentially equated his mission with that of God, which of course made lèse majesté, the crime in Madrigal, all the worse.[11] But there were those who were not so sure God was on Philip's side.

Dissent in the Cities

The present-day provincial capital of Avila, one of Europe's greatest walled cities, is some fifty kilometers from Madrigal and was the seat of royal and religious authority in the region. It also was the site of some of the most worrisome unrest in the decade, aside from the Aragonese uprising; this was particularly disquieting, given the participation of members of the nobility. Palace factions and small rebellions by noble families, followed by banishment to their estates, were not unknown during Philip's reign (in fact the duke of Alba came out of house arrest to lead the army that annexed Portugal), but the prospect of alliances among commoners, urban elites, and aristocrats surely summoned up thoughts of the 1520 revolt of the *comuneros*. Already in 1589 the Avila town council refused even to meet to approve taxes or free their Cortes representatives from having to consult with them before voting (a key struggle between the crown and the cities, which the former eventually won). Now nobles and members of the clergy were angry about not being exempt from the *millones* and about the creation of new city posts, the purchase of which helped the royal coffers but diluted the powers of existing councilors.

On October 20, 1591, the royal governor announced at the city council that pamphlets or broadsheets had appeared overnight regarding the standoff with the king. They read as follows:

> If any nation in the world had good reasons for being favored, esteemed, and given freedom by their king and lord, it is ours. But the greed and tyranny of our days make that impossible. Oh Spain! Spain! How your services are being acknowledged, drenched with noble and plebeian blood!

Yet in payment, the king intends to tax nobles as if they were commoners! Recover yourself, and defend your liberty, for justice is on your side. And you [*tú*], Philip, be satisfied with what is yours and do not covet what others have or make those to whom you owe your honor defend theirs, so long preserved and defended by the laws of these kingdoms."[12]

In just a few days, Philip II sent law enforcement officials to Avila to take charge of the situation, and there were immediate arrests of aristocrats, city council members, a priest, and leading professionals. The punishments were brutal: Diego de Bracamonte, a member of one of the city's most prominent families, was beheaded in the city square. Even the king's chronicler, Luis Cabrera de Córdoba, allowed that "some said the king went too far in the investigation and sentencing, especially with don Diego." Cabrera held a variety of court appointments over the years and was intimately knowledgeable about palace life. The king sent him to Avila to investigate, and when he reported back that the city was by and large loyal and always had been, and that similar pamphlets had appeared in other cities, the king (according to Cabrera) replied, "Really? Wasn't it there that they deposed King Henry? And didn't they side with the tyrant [and *comunero* leader] Juan de Padilla?"[13]

Earlier that same year, noblemen and artisans also found common ground in Madrid. One day in March after the midday meal, as many as one thousand angry shoemakers, carpenters, hatmakers, and the like marched to the palace of the Condestable de Castilla, Spain's highest-ranking grandee, and demanded that he speak on their behalf with the count of Barajas, president of the Council of Castile. The tradesmen were angry about the city's stiff new rules governing where they could sell and manufacture their wares, and they argued on constitutional grounds that the king had no right to treat the poor in that manner. One can assume they had good reason to believe that the constable, Juan Fernández de Velasco, whom they acclaimed as their defender, would be on their side. They were right, for he told the crowd he would speak to the king in the palace, and off he went, followed by a crowd shouting slogans about justice and mercy. The papal nuncio reported to Rome shortly thereafter that exceptions had been made to the new rules because of the poverty and need suffered by Madrid's artisans. Among the ringleaders, several artisans were banished, whipped, or sent to the galley ships. After the episode, the constable went on to an important diplomatic career, and the count of Barajas, Francisco Zapata de Cisneros, was removed from public life; he reportedly spent the entire next year without budging from his estate in Barajas, where he lived with his wife, María de Mendoza y Mendoza.[14]

The Portuguese, meanwhile, resisted the temptation to revolt in 1589 when Drake visited their shores, but that did not signify they were content or had forgotten their subjugation. In 1584, the first of the false Sebastians appeared. He was a young former monk who had been expelled from his monastery and then became a hermit, finally settling in Penamacor. He said he had been at the battle of Alcazarquivir, giving rise to the belief that he was the king, and he did nothing to squelch the story. In fact, he acquired two aides, whom he named Cristóvão de Tavora and the bishop of La Guarda, and he established royal councils. He eventually was arrested, but because he had not intended to propagate the lie (though the appointment of his aides would suggest otherwise), he was sent to the galleys rather than executed; his aides were not so lucky. The following year—seven years since Alcazarquivir, the time of penance some said Sebastian had assumed—there was a second appearance, far more dangerous. This imposter, Mateus Alvares, also had abandoned his monastery to become a hermit, and he actually looked like Sebastian. But rather than harmlessly entertain the neighbors as his predecessor had done, Alvares raised an army of some one thousand men and was proclaimed king, taking as his queen the daughter of his chief supporter and organizer, a wealthy farmer who had made a name for himself as an opponent of Spain. The new king next ordered the Archduke Cardinal Albert to leave the country. This clearly could not continue, and government troops under the command of Diogo da Fonseca (who seven years earlier had commanded the fortress of Asilah, where the earliest of Sebastian's survival stories was born) marched on Ericeira, the rebels' base. There were many executions, many more sentences to the galleys, and Alvares was hanged, drawn, and quartered in Lisbon on June 14, 1585, and his head was mounted on a post in public view for a month.[15]

Despite or because of the repression, anti-Spanish tempers remained high. In June 1586, "the King gave audience to a Portuguese woman, and was subsequently informed that she and some companions were spies of don António and had plotted to stab the King with a sharp dagger which she concealed in her pilgrim's staff." She was arrested but confessed nothing.[16] In January 1592 Juan de Silva warned the king from Lisbon that the Portuguese continued being most disobedient vassals. "It is impossible, having grown up with their own king, hating our Nation and Your Majesty's grandeur, that they should now feel consoled," he wrote. And, he added, the common people were crazy (they suffered *locura*), still awaiting don António's return (and Sebastian's, one assumes).[17] Sure enough, two years after the Aragonese, Madrid, and Avila episodes, there was trouble in southern Portugal, in the town of Beja.[18] Albert, viceroy of Portugal, departed Lisbon for Madrid in August 1593, leaving in his place five governors (one of them Silva). Two weeks later, some "abominable papers" appeared. Don António's supporters had seized the moment. The pamphlets "say [Philip II] treats his vassals in an insufferable fashion and that the people should rise up and seek another king," Silva wrote to Cristóbal de Moura.[19] They needed no false Sebastian to inspire them. Unlike the protesters in Avila, the would-be insurgents in Portugal were commoners, though they probably were in close touch with noblemen abroad and, through them, with don António. They insisted, as the Portuguese had during the Cortes meetings before the annexation, that Portugal's ancient laws gave them the right to elect their own king. Silva—also the country's military chief—immediately ordered troops to Beja, inspiring new protests, and some were arrested, including a man said to be one of don António's sons. But the pamphlets and the noise continued to circulate.[20]

Prophecies of Doom

In Castile, in retrospect, this was the start of the long disenchantment, the realization that Spain was retreating, or had to retreat, and it was the start of an era when learned and not-so-learned tracts (called *arbitrios*) proposing solutions to the monarchy's ills were circulated, discussed, and then often ignored. As the century's last decade began, there were signs that Spain might be at a breaking point. People dared to voice fears and doubts, and many blamed Philip II for the relentless calamities. As if a spell were being cast off and sight suddenly returned, certainties were exposed as frauds, and the glitter was recognized for what it was. Spaniards' conviction that things were seriously amiss was confirmed by a new round of comets, though we have seen that comets, eclipses, and other omens could be read as good news or bad, the harbingers of wonders or the promise of punishments. A comet in March 1590 lingered for eight days and was blamed for months of bad weather and storms that kept ships in their harbor; another appeared in July 1593, staying in the sky every night for two hours.[21] As was the case with chroniclers sorting through the dead bodies at Alcazarquivir to read signs of the foretold disaster, however, maybe comets were not to be trusted.

If some men turned disenchanted, others became enchanted, for this was also one of the great eras of visionaries and seers. Among them was Miguel de Piedrola, a former tinker and soldier who wandered widely through the Spanish empire in Europe and managed to escape from prison more than once, thanks to the voices that guided him.[22] Like other seers, he found the allegorical meaning of his visions and voices in Scripture, and the interpretation generally was linked to injustice and royal error. Philip II was aware of Piedrola's prophecies, though not entirely convinced. He wrote on a memo that Piedrola was not quite sane, yet invited him to an audience, but the two never met. Piedrola had prominent supporters, some of whom had been supporters of Antonio Pérez. His popularity peaked in 1587, when the Cortes actually recommended that Philip create the office of Royal Prophet and appoint Piedrola to the post, which does not seem to have happened, though it indicates the degree to which prophecy was considered potentially beneficial and certainly not criminal. After his arrest that year, Piedrola grew progressively less cocky, finally admitting to the inquisitors that he was not a prophet at all, only "an illiterate idiot who has studied the Bible only a little bit."[23] Pleading ignorance and delusion was a common tactic by those facing the Holy Office. The prosecution—which probably heard the case in 1588, the year of the Armada—disagreed, saying he was a "heretic, apostate, disturber of the peace in the republic, usurper of divine and celestial authority, arrogant, seditious, scandalous, a trickster, and a con man who had a pact with the Devil and who declared and signed himself to be a true prophet of God, neither false nor meritorious, . . . and who claimed to be subject neither to His Holiness nor to His Majesty in Earthly things."[24] Yet, as was common in these cases, the authorities found imagination, not revelation. False prophets generally were ignored, not punished. Piedrola's sentence was lenient: he served two years in a fortress and was banished from Madrid forever. He also was forbidden from ever again reading the Bible, owning paper, writing letters, or speaking on religious matters.

We have seen that a humble woman in Alburquerqe communicated with St. John the Baptist about the imminent annexation of Portugal. Two years earlier, the always skeptical Juan de Silva told Philip II he had heard talk of a Franciscan in Fez who prophesized a Christian victory there in 1578; Silva was keeping the news away from Sebastian, he said, so as not to "whet his appetite."[25] A more prominent example of Portugal as a topic of conversation with the saints was María de la Visitación, sometimes called "the nun of Lisbon," who declared Philip would be punished for taking what was not his. (Her eventual trial took place at the same time as Piedrola's, and one of her visitors was the man later held responsible for the seditious pamphlets in Beja.[26]) A resident of Madrid named Juan de Dios, who identified himself as St. John the Baptist, also predicted Spain's imminent ruin and proclaimed himself the king who would save it. Many of these figures knew each other or knew of each other, and their proclamations and visions were recorded and circulated in pamphlets and, of course, orally, either as gossip or as material criticized (and thus further circulated) in sermons.

Among the best-known of the visionaries during these years was Lucrecia de León, a young, middle-class woman in Madrid.[27] Lucrecia was literate, she knew her history and theology, and, having worked in the royal palace, she had access to lots of news. (She knew about María de la Visitación, for example). She also had relatives in America. So her world was quite broad. From November 1587 to May 1590 she dictated hundreds of apocalyptic dreams populated by a regular cast of characters to a small group of prominent supporters and stenographers, among them a churchman named Alonso de Mendoza, an extremely well-connected member of one of Spain's most powerful noble clans. Richard Kagan has suggested that Mendoza, acting as Lucrecia's godfather and stage manager, used her dreams to pressure the king to release the princess of Eboli and Antonio Pérez, whom many of the Mendozas had championed during the scandal. Lucrecia's dreams featured locusts, Moorish invasions, and burning palaces. There were appearances by Philip II, royal ministers (including Juan de Idiáquez and Cristóbal de Moura), Sir Francis Drake, Queen Elizabeth, and Miguel de Piedrola (whom she knew). There were predictions of destruction and revolt, and dramas of royal neglect and righteous vengeance. The overriding theme was Spain's utter and deserved destruction. Eight months before the defeat of the Armada, Lucrecia witnessed the fleet being vanquished. The characters who guided Lucrecia through these dreams had nothing but contempt for the king, whose injustice, blindness, decrepitude, and corruption they deemed responsible for the collapse. He was depicted as a bad father, a bad husband, and possibly a murderer, a latter-day Rodrigo (the last Visigothic king) provoking the demise of Christian Spain. All this and more was written down and circulated by Lucrecia's circle of advisers, and Philip might have been willing to let it go on had Antonio Pérez not escaped from his Madrid prison in April 1590. Enough was enough, and Lucrecia was arrested. Her Inquisition trial dragged on in fits and starts from summer 1590 until August 1595, the same month Gabriel de Espinosa was executed. After receiving her sentence, she disappears from the historical record.

So there was fertile ground for notions such as that Sebastian might have returned or that the Spanish monarchy was off-course and nearing the end of its grandeur. Though the king was certainly attuned to the dangers of too much imagination, he himself was not immune. People were prepared to believe unusual things. Prophetic scripts might even provide comfort, though they announced worse calamities ahead; at least they pointed in a direction, at least they provided explanations. It surely is no accident that right at this time the king's top aides suggested to him that now might be a good moment to commission an official history of his reign.[28]

Wonders on the Road

Judging from the testimony collected by the Madrigal judges, the Iberian peninsula's roads were crowded in the 1590s. This was a common lament of the time, and treatises bewailed an alleged plague of vagabonds. The denunciations may have exaggerated, but roaming artisans, fieldworkers on their way to a meager harvest, soldiers awaiting assignment or absent without leave, and inhabitants of villages that no longer could support their population were all on the road, on their way to someplace else. After the war of annexation, many Portuguese were forcibly uprooted to Castile, as we have seen. And though a 1595 handbook defined banishment as "one of the worst calamities that exists," it was one of the most frequent punishments by civil and Inquisitorial judges.[29]

Starting in 1561, defendants in Inquisitorial cases had to describe to the judges what their lives had been like up until their alleged wrongdoing, and these autobiographies (*discursos de la vida*) are like travel guides. (They are also, not incidentally, similar to Golden Age novels in which characters suddenly launch into tales of adventure and mishap frequently corroborated by witnesses. The legal and romantic narrative structures were not all that different; both assumed speeches and stages.) Satoko Nakajima has compiled a series of data on demographic movement taken from a representative sample of Inquisitorial cases.[30] Taken together, the narratives reveal constant motion, at least among members of the lower classes, the likeliest to be defendants in these mostly petty cases. Nearly all left their hometowns at some point, and they had covered great distances, sometimes hundreds of kilometers. Most people who left their towns never returned, either because they were banned (runaway apprentices, for example, or deserters), had no relatives (most defendants did not know who their grandparents were), or could not find work. Their loyalty was to the place they lived in, not to the place where they were born. All this transit made it possible—necessary, even—for wanderers to invent new identities, new spouses, new pasts. Or maybe the wandering was the result of the new identities, not the cause. At any rate, as they wandered, they carried and created news; laws against vagrancy therefore also may have been attempts to keep the noise level down.

But the wandering and displacement was not solely a sign of crisis. Though Inquisition defendants may not be typical, these swearing, fornicating laborers were not all that exceptional, and their movements indicate a more general interconnectedness of people and places in sixteenth-century Iberia. Nobody seemed surprised that Fray Miguel could move to Madrigal, or that Gabriel de Espinosa (like Piedrola, a former artisan and soldier) could just show up, or that Bernardo del Rio, the false Trinitarian who was don António's messenger, should run into both a real Trinitarian and another messenger for the pretender. The coincidences and chance encounters that emerged through the judges' questioning seemed remarkable to no one. (Though it may be that the judges found the coincidences so alarming they chose not to investigate further.) Fernand Braudel remarked on the "complicated internal and external structures and weighty institutions" that maintain a culture of transhumance; he was referring to financial and legal structures, but I think the same can be said of culture or knowledge.[31] Underlying the demographic movement, allowing and propelling it, was a culture of news and linkages. In inns, for example, itinerants shared their stories and created ephemeral communities that vanished the next morning as the travelers set off anew on their journeys; "wonders always seemed to happen" there to the heroes of one of Cervantes's novels.[32] When don António and his friends allegedly visited Madrigal, they stayed in an inn, and so did don António's former servant, the aspiring Benedictine, and so did Espinosa in Valladolid. Innkeepers' testimony was frequently of use to Rodrigo de Santillán and Juan de Llano as they figured out who had visited whom over the past months and how it was that everybody seemed to know everybody or knew someone who did. Inns were held in low regard and were the targets of innumerable complaints to government authorities. But the proprietors were an invaluable source of information. As Adam Fox put it, ale houses were "revolving doors" of news; indeed, throughout Europe, innkeepers often were postmasters.[33]

One of the most intriguing tales of itinerancy in the Madrigal case is that of a Portuguese priest picked up in July 1595 at an inn in Medina del Campo who called himself Luís de Silva, though it turned out his name was Pedro.[34] Santillán told Moura that the suspect had no sooner arrived in Medina than he began asking about what was going on in Madrigal. He was around fifty-eight years old. With him was a young woman whom he first identified as his daughter Catalina, though others called her Luisa, and actually, he admitted, she was not his daughter at all. He gave his testimony in a private home in Madrigal owned by Beatriz Espinosa (no relation to Gabriel). He was born and raised in Lisbon, where he still resided. He studied theology at Salamanca and had held various posts in Portuguese churches. Asked to explain what he was doing in Medina, he said he left Lisbon in November 1594 and traveled to Seville and from there to a small town outside Córdoba to attend to some religious legal business. There he heard that there were two ships docked in Málaga ready to leave for Italy, and he went there to see if he could get a ride to Rome, where he wanted to discuss a matter of conscience with His Holiness. But the ships were gone by the time he got to Málaga, so he decided to visit his cousin Luís in Sanlúcar de Barrameda. This possibly was the same Luís de Silva who was Sebastian's ambassador to Spain; he was wounded at Alcazarquivir, ransomed, and then retired. (He also was the brother-in-law of Cristóvão de Tavora, Sebastian's closest friend.) Luís told him there was a boat docked in Cádiz on its way to Venice. For some reason that did not work out either, so Silva traveled to Salamanca (via Cáceres), where he fell ill, and from there to Madrid, where he wanted to continue trying to find a way to get to Rome. But on his way to Madrid he stopped off at the monastery of Our Lady of Virtues, near Peñaranda (probably Peñaranda de Bracamonte), where the monks told him it was far better to go to Madrid via Medina (decidedly not the case.) He followed their suggestion but fell ill in Medina, spending nine days there before his arrest.

In the judges' mind, Silva's credibility was low, as he twice tried to escape from jail using files and made no effort to offer convincing answers. Asked why, if his name was Pedro, he signed papers as Luís, he said he just felt like it. During his testimony, Silva showed he knew some very influential people, including the duke of Lerma and the duke's brother, the archbishop of Seville. His own relatives included not only Luís but members of the Mascarenhas family and the duke of Aveiro, names all too familiar to the judges. He also had a visitor, a Portuguese friar who arrived in Medina on a mule and left town the minute he heard his friend was in jail.[35] Silva did not know Fray Miguel de los Santos, he said, but it turned out he did know about the Madrigal case. When he was in Salamanca, he recalled, he had been in a bar owned by one Rincón, on the main square, and the innkeeper was saying that in a nearby town (Madrigal) a man who they said was prince don Carlos had been arrested along with some nuns, and the authorities had summoned the count of Fuentes (Juan de Silva's predecessor as captain general of Portugal) to identify him. Pedro de Silva said he told the barkeeper to stop talking nonsense, because he had been at don Carlos's funeral.[36] But later, he told Rodrigo de Santillán, when he was in Our Lady of Virtues, he could not keep from telling the friars there about this conversation, and he asked if by chance they knew anything about the case. Indeed they did; one friar said that in Madrigal there were nuns and a friar and another man held prisoner, and it seemed to Silva that the friar told him they had been tortured for heresy or something along those lines and that the man who was imprisoned (Espinosa) had a relative who was an Inquisition familiar, which was why an inquisitor was handling the case. Pedro de Silva's role in the conspiracy, if he had a role at all, is a mystery. He might have shown up intending to assist the prisoners but arrived too late. By the time Silva spoke to the judges, Espinosa was dead, and Fray Miguel was in Madrid. Not knowing what else to do with Silva, the judges found him guilty of concubinage.

Enter the Baker

Let us now turn to the imposter himself, Gabriel de Espinosa, the *pastelero de Madrigal*, whose widely circulated chronicle announced his arrival with these words: "Near the end of September 1594 a man named Gabriel de Espinosa, dressed in the clothes of a common man, arrived in Valladolid." His companion, Inés Cid, will recount their travels together in the following chapter, but before he met Inés, he already was on the move. He probably was born in Toledo; he said he was forty-three, though Santillán thought he was in his sixties. (As the months passed, grey and white roots began showing, so he had dyed his hair.[37]) When he was a young man, like so many others, he joined the army. He told Ana of Austria and her friend Luisa del Grado he had fought with don Juan of Austria's forces and had been as far as the Holy Land. We know he was in Portugal in 1580, still fighting; after that, he told Ana and Luisa, he had been captured by don António's forces and taken to France. By Drake's 1589 attack on Galicia, he was back on Iberian soil. Along the way, he acquired some (scanty, according to witnesses) skills as a baker and cook. Inés Cid's testimony suggests that Espinosa was still a military man a year or two before the Madrigal case, though he could have been cooking for the troops rather than fighting.

We should not be surprised that witnesses who, in theory, were completely unrelated to Espinosa offered the judge information regarding his whereabouts. The Augustinian Fray Marcos de Amador, for example, told his superior on October 18, 1594, as the case began, that when he arrived in Madrigal just a couple of months earlier, he immediately recognized Espinosa as the man whom he had hired to cook dinner after a Mass he delivered in Pamplona.[38] He had been shopping for food in Pamplona's main marketplace when a man came up to him and asked what he was buying and why, and he offered his services; this was Espinosa. During the interrogation, the Augustinian provincial, Gabriel de Goldaraz, asked Amador what Espinosa generally wore in Madrigal (sometimes a brown baker's garb, other times velvet). Amador said he knew nothing else of Espinosa's background or even his first name. Fray Luis Ortiz, at the same monastery, confirmed Amador's testimony by adding that he had run into Espinosa cooking in Madrid seven or eight years earlier. Ortiz was eating with his friend Fray Gerónimo de Guevara, and there he saw Espinosa "dressed as a cook putting on a stew and preparing hens with his sleeves rolled up," though he could not remember exactly where the restaurant was. The nun María del Portillo, in the same round of testimony, said she had heard from people inside the convent but also elsewhere that Espinosa had been a baker and cook for the duke of Alburquerque.

Gregorio González, currently working as a cook for the count of Niebla, said he had worked with Espinosa in Ocaña, near Toledo.[39] Around six years ago, he said, he was working for the marquis of Almazán, preparing a meal for members of the Council of Orders, and because he did not feel very well, he was given an assistant, Espinosa, who arrived badly dressed with a son of around sixteen years old. (This was the first confirmation that Espinosa had other children.) After preparing the meal, Espinosa ate with González and González's wife, María de Torres. Now, just recently in September, González had been walking down Calle de la Comedia in Valladolid on his way to the theater, when who should he run into but that very same cook. Valladolid was a prosperous and bustling university city (it would soon, albeit briefly, become Spain's capital), headquarters for the royal appeals courts, and home to many noble families; it had around forty thousand inhabitants. González recognized Espinosa from afar, he said, a man of medium stature, with grey hair and two clouds (probably cataracts) in one eye, dressed in old brown velvet trousers and a jerkin with gold trim. González called out to Espinosa, who was talking to a group of people. Espinosa broke off his conversation and took González aside. Times have changed, brother, Espinosa said, and if there was anything he could do for his old friend, he would be happy to oblige. González took him home to eat with María and some neighbors. María also recognized him right away and reminded him of the good old days. Oh that, Espinosa said. I was disguised then. No, González said, you told me you were a baker in Ocaña, and you showed me your credentials. True, Espinosa replied, but '"kings and princes wander disguised,' and if [González] wanted to be with him he would do him and his wife many favors, and the cook laughed because he and his wife thought [Espinosa] was crazy because he also said he had transported His Majesty's weapons into Navarre. Espinosa left but he came back another day . . . and he showed [González] things of value," including a watch, some cameos, a silver box, and a portrait of a beautiful lady, perhaps of the sort called *naipes* because they were the size of playing cards. "When [González] praised her beauty, [Espinosa] said that although she was a nun she could marry and that the prince our lord had no one to marry except her, and when the neighbors asked how a nun could marry, he said, 'There are no laws for kings,' and that she was a nun against her wishes and had said so to a bishop when she entered the convent."[40] He visited a few times more, always telling stories and showing off jewels. González decided to stop inviting Espinosa over, and some days later, when he heard he had been arrested, he gave his statement.

Espinosa was a man of his times: a soldier of the monarchy, a wanderer with a few marketable skills—cooking, baking, weaving—someone liminal, a charmer and a risk-taker, the future protagonist of romantic poetry and drama. As Cabrera de Córdoba nicely put it, "He had many skills, having learned none of them."[41] He could be anyone, and that was the problem. In the Medina del Campo public jail on February 17, 1595, he told Juan de Llano his name was Gabriel de Espinosa and then immediately changed his mind.[42] He could not give his true name, he explained, because he had vowed not to reveal it until he died. A furious Llano replied with threats and thunder, invoking apostolic law and punishments for perjury to no effect as the defendant confirmed he would neither give his name nor those of his parents, who he said were dead. He never knew his father, though he remembered his mother, as indeed was the case with King Sebastian. (Later, however, Espinosa would say he did not remember his mother either.) Yes, it was true he had told Rodrigo de Santillán his name was Gabriel de Espinosa, he told Llano, but that was because at that time (just after the arrest) he was working as a baker and that was the name on the document issued by the guild attesting to the carrier's skills. This is all we will ever know of his identity from the prisoner himself: his name was not Gabriel de Espinosa.

He told Llano he arrived in Madrigal in June 1594. Previously he had a shop in the nearby town of Nava, and he was hoping to do better.[43] He began making pastries for the convent, and he met doña Ana and the other nuns when he went to get paid. He admitted he sometimes spoke with them near the *grada*, the latticed iron grille dividing the nuns' quarters from the visitors' parlor; a similar grille divided the public and private sections of the church. They asked him how he was doing in town, and he offered to bring his little girl to play with them. He also met with Fray Miguel in the vicar's cell from time to time. But according to Ana's servant Juan de Roderos, just two days after Espinosa's arrival in Madrigal, Fray Miguel summoned him to his cell, and the two men later met with Ana. "He thinks [Espinosa's] arrival in Madrigal was at the orders of Fray Miguel, and I believe that too," Santillán told the king.[44] According to the *Historia de Gabriel de Espinosa*, the first thing Santillán did when he arrived in Madrigal was go to Espinosa's house, "in which he found no sign of a bakery, just an oven and wooden implements. All the rest had disappeared." (Something else that disappeared was Espinosa's portable desk, which had been full of papers; Santillán determined that someone had picked it up and taken it to the convent, but he never found it.)[45] Santillán's investigations led him back to Nava, where people said Espinosa had been a bad baker who undercharged his customers, and, really, he was not a baker at all; someone else was doing the work, though from time to time he tried his hand at it. How could he bake, people in Madrigal asked, if he was at the convent all day?[46]

In Espinosa's February interview with Llano, he denied he had ever said he was Sebastian but admitted that Ana and Fray Miguel treated him as if he were:

> He saw they wanted to regard him as such, and the witness [Espinosa] told them that was badly done and wrong because it was treason against the king our lord because in no kingdom can someone else be called king and not be called a traitor. And because of that, and also because of a letter from the Augustinian provincial to doña Ana telling her she was entertaining a baker [one of Ana's chief crimes was to have been intimate with a low commoner], he decided to leave town, as in fact he did, not wanting to offend the king our lord.[47]

He was not Sebastian, he told Llano. Then why would they think he was? the judge asked.

> Because of the signs [*señas*] remarked upon by Fray Miguel and recognized by him as belonging to Sebastian, and doña Ana said the same thing to the witness [Espinosa], recognizing his signs. And the witness told them they were fooling themselves because he was not the king, and doña Ana replied that he should watch what he was saying because she had spent six years awaiting the said King Sebastian and had prayed and made vows and had been told he would arrive in the year 1594, and if he had not arrived by St. Michael's Day, he would never come. And he had arrived just then, and the *señas* confirmed it.

Espinosa's explanation of why he left town refers to his visit to Valladolid, which led to his arrest. He stayed in Valladolid at least a week and probably two, judging from Gregorio González's testimony. According to Espinosa, the plan was to leave Madrigal and never return, though the judges discovered immediately that a plan was afoot involving the disguised visitors whom Espinosa was supposed to pick up somewhere and take back to Madrigal. In fact, Ana and Fray Miguel appear to have thought he was in Burgos, not Valladolid. The arrest, which led to the unraveling of the conspiracy, took place on the night of October 8, 1594, when Rodrigo de Santillán got word that a man, "badly dressed (*en mal hábito*), appearing to be an outsider (*extranjero*), carrying many jewels" and talking loudly about his royal connections, was causing a bit of an uproar in the local bars. Santillán had to track him down, being that Espinosa had moved from inn to inn, but after a few hours, the judge found his man: "a man of medium stature, somewhere between redhead and grey, with a blow or cloud in one eye," who immediately attempted to escape. Santillán's men grabbed him, demanding what the rush was. "I'm in enemy territory and anything could happen to me!" he exclaimed.[48] He gave his name and said he was a cook and baker for Ana of Austria and was in Valladolid at her behest. He was struggling to get dressed as Santillán came in, perhaps to ensure that the luxurious clothes Ana had sent him—Santillán discovered his shirts were of fine Holland linen—did not get left behind. In his rooms he had objects of value, including a portrait of Ana (probably the one he showed González), leading the judge to assume he was a thief, and he took him off to jail. In the later conversation between Espinosa and Llano, the judge asked about information he had received that Espinosa had stayed at an inn in Valladolid near the city's theaters that was owned by Gabriel Rodríguez. It was Rodríguez who carried letters from Espinosa in Valladolid to Ana and Fray Miguel in Madrigal. Before Rodríguez left on his epistolary mission, Espinosa asked him to tell the recipients that actually he (Espinosa) was writing from Burgos. Furthermore, Rodríguez should say that years earlier he had known Espinosa in Burgos "wearing a different outfit, accompanied by certain gentlemen who served him at the table, respectfully and with no head covering."[49] (Espinosa more or less acknowledged all this to Llano but said there was no harm meant.) After the arrest, Santillán picked up Rodríguez as he returned from Madrigal with the replies, addressed to Your Majesty, and promptly informed the real king.

Immediately, the president of the royal appeal courts, located in Valladolid, got involved.[50] The president, Junco de Posada, was terrified that news of the presence of disguised Portuguese royalty (whether Sebastian or don António) would get out, and he implored and ordered Santillán to ensure that Espinosa be strictly guarded. But in Santillán's opinion, more guards would just call attention to the prisoner, the last thing he wanted. He was working very hard on the case, he assured Cristóbal de Moura, and did not need interference from Posada or anyone else: "I beg your grace to not allow injury to me by those who spend their time sleeping and whoring while I work all day and conduct rounds all night." He's a good man, he said of Posada, but he can't keep a secret.[51] But, as it turned out, it appears there was traffic in the Valladolid city jail, which Santillán himself admitted later on, though he blamed the jail staff.[52] Whoever was at fault, it is likely Espinosa communicated with the outside world during his first week of confinement.

Signs of Recognition

There were many reasons for thinking Espinosa was, as the anonymous letters had put it, "grand, very grand," and the authorities took a while to decide how much to suspend disbelief. Those who spent the most time with Espinosa were the slowest to relinquish thoughts of his grandeur. Those who made his acquaintance only briefly resisted seduction: Junco de Posada, for example, was sure from the start he was nobody, though a potentially dangerous nobody. Another chancery judge, Martín Hernández Portocarrero, also was not fooled; in October he told Philip, "I believe this man is no more than a very low baker or a cook who was encouraged by the ignorance or malice of the friars, and his deeds deserve very rigorous and most severe punishment."[53]

Around ten days after the arrest, the prisoner was moved to the public jail in Medina del Campo. Accompanying him on the journey was Rodrigo de Santillán's brother Diego. At two in the afternoon he bundled the shackled prisoner into the coach and set off with armed guards riding alongside. Espinosa was melancholy and asked Diego why a poor baker was being transported with such finery. Diego felt sorry for him, he later told his brother, and asked one of the guards, Cervatos, to join them in the interior of the coach. When Cervatos told the prisoner that he had been in France,

> the good man began to speak with him in French so well that Cervatos said he had never heard a man speak better. And then he began to speak German and Tudesco [another word for German] very well, according to Cervatos. And he said he knew all languages a little and I, being malicious, asked him if he spoke a little Portuguese, and he fell quiet and said, 'Not a word, though I have been in Portugal.' And I promise you that that silence was mysterious, because he had been joking around and suddenly got quiet and melancholy again, and for the next two hours we couldn't get him to say a word.[54]

Finally he was persuaded to emerge from his cocoon, and he said he'd like to meet with Rodrigo for three or four hours. His brother the judge was very busy, Diego said, but perhaps Espinosa could write him a letter. The baker agreed but then said he did not know how to write and could not trust anyone else with the information. He also said he wanted to speak with Philip II. They spent the night in Valdestillas, and arrived in Medina at ten in the morning. Upon entering his cell, Espinosa asked that the curtains be drawn and the doormen be dismissed, as he did not want anyone to see him. "And in all this time," Diego told Rodrigo, "I assure you that in my entire life I have never met anyone who appeared so grand though he makes all efforts to appear to be a baker." The talkative Cervatos lost his job over this episode.[55]

According to Rodrigo de Santillán, his apostolic colleague Llano in December was still not sure to whom he was speaking. Bluntly, he told the king on December 4, "Doctor Juan de Llano has affirmed that my prisoner in Medina is King Sebastian."[56] Repeatedly the king had warned the two judges to play nicely together, and Santillán was trying hard, he assured the monarch, but Llano's obstinacy on this point was making it difficult. Llano was so convinced of the prisoner's identity that he had stopped investigating properly. A few days later, a palace memo read, "Don Cristóbal [de Moura] and don Juan [de Idiáquez] believe [Your Majesty] should reply to Doctor Juan de Llano disabusing him of this error toward which he is inclined and refresh his memory regarding the confession of Fray Agustín de los Angeles," who had told the judges that Fray Miguel told him to lie to Ana that Sebastian was alive.[57] As for Santillán himself, on December 20 he told the king, "I still think he is not a baker, though the Augustinian friars say he is, and they saw him baking cakes here and in Pamplona. But," he pointed out, using his notable common sense, "if he wanted to pretend, he had to do something to make the pretense credible."[58]

That week, Llano had just finished talking with Ana and Fray Miguel, who both "confessed affirmatively that the prisoner was who they say he is," a way of avoiding the word "Sebastian" in correspondence that could fall into anyone's hands. So Llano decided he wanted to see for himself if there was anything to what they said. This was when he finally figured out the truth. He had seen some portraits of Sebastian, he told the king, though quite a bit younger, and it seemed to him he would not be tricked. "I was with the prisoner alone for three or four hours, and I think in no case can we say he is who they say he is. On the contrary, his aspect and appearance is quite different, because this prisoner is a very small man with a thin face and very different color skin, hair, and beard, besides which he has a large and visible cloud in his right eye, and his age does not fit. He speaks the Castilian language very well with no accent of any sort, which rarely happens with people from other kingdoms."[59]

Not a single person in Madrigal other than Fray Miguel had ever seen the real Sebastian. In an era of few mirrors and virtually no access to portraits, what did people remember about faces? What markers did witnesses, judges, neighbors, and nuns use to decide who somebody was? Was there something inescapably visible about a king or a gentleman? This story is full of people in disguise: António in Morocco, Portugal, and later throughout Europe; the Portuguese who visited Madrigal; Ana's brother (still coming); friars (either not friars at all or from another order); Sebastian (a hermit or a baker) and Espinosa (a king or a baker); and of course nuns and friars are not entirely visible. For centuries, literature has depicted kings mingling or conversing among their subjects disguised as commoners, as human princes. These scenes often take place in forests, territories apart from normal civilization; we saw one such case with Sebastian before the Guadalupe meeting. Those humble interlocutors are usually fooled by their monarchs' disguise, otherwise they would not be so truthful and wise with them. Ana accused Dr. Mendes of being deceived in this manner; distracted by Espinosa's shabby clothes, she said, he could not see the king beneath them. Yet others were not fooled (though, of course, the reverse is true); they believed they detected royal blood beneath the rags. The stories that circulated in the weeks after the battle of Alcazarquivir about Sebastian's survival and don António's escape from captivity were based on people seeing through disguises, ignoring ripped clothing, distinguishing nobility through the dirt and grime, like Joan of Arc picking out the disguised Charles VII of France. Indeed, Valentin Groebner has written, "Identifying the unrecognized was a prevalent theme in medieval and Renaissance literature. Literary charades were played by challenging visitors at court to identify the real sovereign among three identically dressed characters and treat him appropriately."[60] If a rose by any other name would smell as sweet, then nobility too, even without its ephemeral trappings, should be easy to detect.

According to the widely circulated *Historia de Gabriel de Espinosa* and most of its variations, Espinosa was dressed in the "habit and clothing of a common man" or the "habit and clothing of an ordinary man." (Sebastian and Tavora escaping from the Moors also were dressed as "ordinary men.") The *Historia* quotes Fray Miguel saying that Espinosa arrived in Madrigal wearing his baker's garb. The Jesuit correspondent writing during the investigation (probably the author of the pamphlet) said Espinosa "arrived in the habit of a common man."[61] Junco de Posada, commenting to the king on Espinosa's arrest, said that though he had been captured in "a humble habit," Santillán suspected he was of high rank (probably because he had seen Espinosa's luxurious linen clothes at the inn).[62] Of course, anyone with money could buy good linen. But good linen did not *belong* on a baker. Clothes might or might not conceal true identity—in fact, clothing in this tale both identified and camouflaged people—but, beyond that, the reason witnesses were asked to describe clothing was that people should be wearing certain outfits and should not be wearing others. That was the theory. In practice, sumptuary laws show that if people constantly had to be reminded not to wear certain things, it is likely they were wearing them. A commonplace of criticism and satire in Spain and elsewhere in Europe during this era was that no one was as he appeared to be. Yet Sebastian (like any king) played a range of roles—soldier, hero, tragic youth, penitent hermit—each with its own costume, so at the same time an unstable relationship between clothing and rank was accepted, something that also emerges with the witnesses' inevitable descriptions of Espinosa's dress. Any moderately literate inhabitant of sixteenth-century Spain was familiar with Byzantine adventures of pilgrims, rogues, and kings whose disguises confused or blinded people they encountered along the way. The drama of Madrigal cannot have seemed much different.

Literacy and languages are another social marker. We have seen that Espinosa could (or would) not speak Portuguese. Normally this would clinch the matter, but this was neither the first nor the last case of royal imposture in which trauma and time were considered powerful enough influences to wipe the linguistic slate clean. The most credible of the various men claiming to be the son of Marie Antoinette and Louis XVI, who either died in prison as a child in 1795 or was smuggled out by royalists, spoke French with a heavy German accent he attributed to the passage of time. The famous impostor of 1550s France, Martin Guerre, "spoke only a few stolen words" of the Basque language he learned as a child, though the judge decided Guerre had moved to Francophone lands too early for this to account for much.[63] The *Historia de Gabriel de Espinosa* embellishes Espinosa's relationship to language: "his manner of speaking to others, the sharpness of his understanding, the nobility of his speech, the way he linked one thought with the next, and one was never able to find fault with what he said, and he spoke many languages," which was not quite true.[64] Espinosa said in the carriage with Diego de Santillán that he could not write. This is not plausible, given his travels and training as a craftsman of one sort or another. But we have seen his signature, and he did not write well. Ana at one point in their relationship obtained a written statement from Espinosa pledging himself to her. It read, "I, don Sebastian, by the grace of God, king of Portugal, receive as my wife the most serene doña Ana of Austria, daughter of the most serene don Juan of Austria," and he signed it "I the king." When Ana saw his signature, she crumpled up the paper and threw it on the floor, angry at how messy it was: "You should be called don Scribbles, not don Sebastian!" she exclaimed.[65] The king also noticed the odd writing.[66] On March 2 he wrote on a transcript of Espinosa's February 17 confession to Llano (which contained Espinosa's confusing explanation of his non-name), "There is something very strange about the signature." Espinosa first had written in very shaky, awkward letters, "I, the prisoner" (*Yo el preso*). Below that he wrote (though it is hard to make out) "who is not Es[p]inosa" (*q. no es es[p]ynosa*). The content is obviously meant to perplex the authorities; the shaky hand may be due to illiteracy or to the torture he had undergone. By late July, the day before his execution, he could no longer sign at all (see figure 6).[67]

Finally, another indication that Espinosa might be someone other than a baker came with a skill fitting for a nobleman. The last time anyone saw the real Sebastian, he was on horseback, riding expertly around and around as waves of enemy soldiers tried to knock him down, hopping back onto new horses as his were shot out from under him. The scene, one of the great set pieces of the Alcazarquivir chronicles, had been told and retold, and one of the first things Santillán told the king about his mysterious prisoner was that he was an excellent horseman.[68] The judge had been informed that the previous Tuesday (probably five days earlier) in Valladolid's Campo Grande, today a city park, Espinosa had watched some men trying to break an angry horse. He called out to them and offered his help, and then mounted the horse with amazing ease. News of the event circulated. The author of the *Historia de Gabriel de Espinosa*, with access to the same documents we have but probably others as well, said Espinosa "mounted [the horse] with such skill and gallantry that those who were present, as well as the groom, said they had never in their lives seen a better horseman in all of Castile nor in Italy nor anywhere else. And as the groom praised him, he asked the horseman who he was,

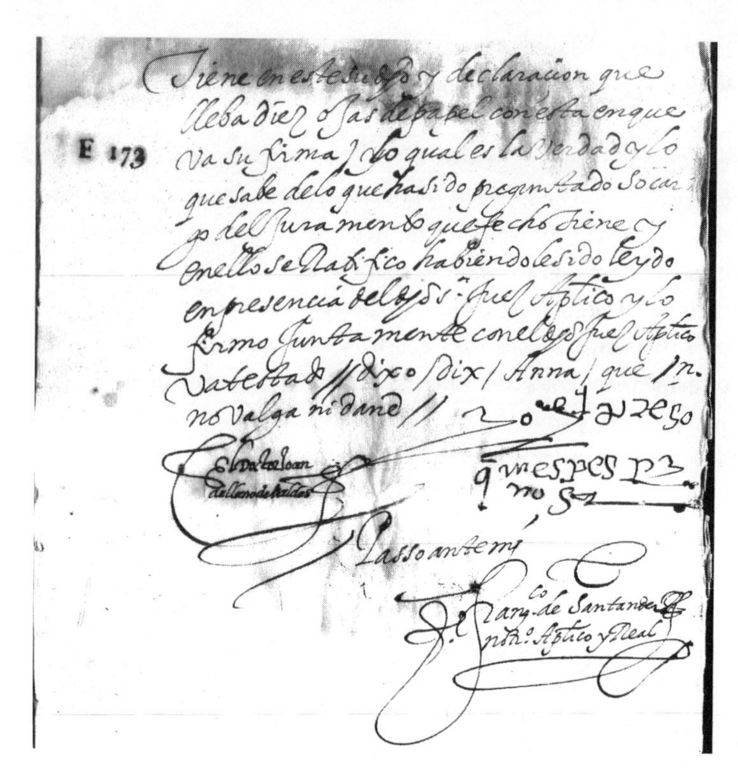

Figure 6. Gabriel de Espinosa's autograph (1595), "I the prisoner, who is not Espinosa. . . ." (AGS E, leg. 173, doc. 239). Courtesy of Archivo General de Simancas, Ministerio Español de la Cultura.

and when he replied he was a baker in Madrigal, the groom laughed and said, 'You a baker? Right, and I'm one too!'"[69]

What the Nuns Knew

Less than a week after Espinosa was arrested, the Augustinian provincial, Gabriel de Goldaraz, held a two-day interrogation of all the nuns and monks under his jurisdiction in Madrigal.[70] His objective was to take charge of a situation that even then showed signs of spinning out of control. He was well aware of what had been going on in the convent (his enemies, it will be remembered, said he was a co-conspirator) and he did not want outsiders—especially not an arrogant, anticlerical judge like Rodrigo de Santillán—taking over.

The first of the twelve questions addressed to the religious community asked if they knew or had heard anything about the identity of the town baker. Two legal considerations are relevant here: Spain's medieval and subsequent legal codes specified that women's testimony was acceptable only in those cases in which they were personally involved and only if they were of good reputation. The nuns qualified on both counts.[71] Second, by necessity at a time when documentary proof was tricky, the judges (or, in this case, the provincial) relied on hearsay, a close relative of rumor and noise. The chronology of the law—still a work in progress—and the chronology of memory did not necessarily coincide. One learned of events after they occurred, later remembered learning them, and told the story only after that, and in their testimony people may have been recollecting how events had been recounted rather than how they occurred. They dated events by how long ago they took place.[72] Witnesses referred to the time of year or to points on the religious calendar, but they never gave days or dates. Things happened several weeks ago, eight or nine years ago more or less, during the time of the war, before St. Michael's Day.

This was the same round of questioning that produced Fray Marcos de Amador's recollection of seeing Espinosa in Pamplona and Luis Ortiz's story about seeing him in Madrid. The nun María Belón provided similar information. One day, she said, a visitor named Pedro Dorado came to the convent and told her he had met Espinosa during the war with Portugal when he, the visitor, was a garrison soldier. Espinosa was working as a baker and maybe also, although the visitor was not sure, in a wine cellar. The visitor furthermore assured her that the little girl with Espinosa was the baker's. And he said that when he saw Espinosa in town and told him he recognized him from Portugal, Espinosa became frightened and replied, "you have quite a memory." When Espinosa asked Dorado if he had fought with don Juan in the war against the Moriscos, Dorado not only said that he had but he began asking Espinosa many questions he could not answer, leading Dorado to believe Espinosa was a liar.[73]

All the nuns and friars had opinions about the identity of the man who had arrived just four months earlier. Fray Juan de Avendaño said he had heard that "the said baker is a disguised gentleman and that [Espinosa] had said words to that effect." Andrés de Santa Cruz said he was a "disguised gentleman and a member of a military order, but he can't remember if it was Santiago, which is what many people in town and religious in this house are saying. . . . [Amador] told him he was a cook and that when [Amador] said Mass in Pamplona, he cooked the meal and [Amador] gave him six ducats and the cook asked for four more." Ana de Espinosa (no relation) said she did not know who the baker was but figured "he was a charlatan [from *charlar*, to chat], a fraud, one of those lost people wandering around." María de San Vicente said she had heard he was "a wizard and a con man who had a familiar [in the Inquisition; that is also what Pedro de Silva said], which she had heard inside the convent and from people who visited, . . . and she heard that he had cast a spell on the pastries he made for doña Ana of Austria to make her talk to him." Augustina de Ulloa had never seen Espinosa, but she was worried because she "very unwillingly" had eaten one of the pastries. Leonor de Cartagena had heard he was a "*pícaro*, con man, wizard, the devil's man, and she does not know him." Ana de Tapia had heard he was a "liar, wizard, and con man, and that the son of a thief said [Espinosa] was a colleague of his father's." María de Portillo, who said Espinosa had worked as a cook for the duke of Alburquerque, also said she had heard both in the convent and outside that he was a knight commander whose official costumes were hidden. Luisa del Grado, Ana's closest friend and enabler, who must have known at this point she was in deep trouble, said she had heard he was a baker, though others said he was a wizard and a con man. Her sister, María Nieto, said "she does not know who this baker is other than a baker and a liar, according to what she has heard, though from others she heard he was more honorable than he appeared and had honorable clothing in his house." Gerónima de Arpide said he was a "con man and a wizard, which is what she always thought, and she had heard so elsewhere, referring to Espinosa's time in Nava, and a student told her that another baker told him, 'protect yourselves from that devil you have there,' because Espinosa had cast spells on even the crumbs."[74]

He may have been a wizard, but he probably was not a thief. Fray Antonio de Sosa, the likely author of the anonymous letters, noted that the prisoner's lack of cupidity showed he could not possibly be a commoner, and Llano too was puzzled that Espinosa refused valuable offerings of jewelry from Ana.[75] (It might be, however, that when Espinosa went to Valladolid, he meant to keep going, taking the jewels with him; the fact that he had not moved on to Burgos speaks in favor of that theory.) According to the *Historia de Gabriel de Espinosa*, Espinosa's disdain for material wealth was a deliberate ploy to make people think he was high-born.[76] The jewels and the fact that they were gifts from Ana were a key part of the story as it was retold in the weeks following the arrest. The Portuguese chronicler Pero Roiz Soares chose jewels as the way to introduce Ana; she was "a niece of the king, daughter of don Juan of Austria, a nun in the said monastery and very rich with many very valuable jewels that her father left her."[77] The jewels appear in the very first sentence of Santillán's first letter to Philip II reporting on a man "carrying many jewels, among them a jewelry box with a unicorn on it." Espinosa's drinking buddies "asked him whose was the image on a ring he was wearing [the image was of Philip II] and he said, it is your lord, and they said, isn't he also your lord? and he said no, not my lord, I will be his and yours as well."[78] Just one week later, nearly all the nuns and friars in Madrigal said they knew that when he was arrested, Espinosa was carrying Ana's valuables. The prioress said she believed he was arrested because he did not give a woman a ring he had promised her, leading her to denounce him to Santillán. She also said Espinosa was carrying a golden parrot and other gold objects, including the ring with a portrait of the king, "and she had heard the jewels were doña Ana's because [Santillán] wrote to doña Ana to ask if they were hers and she replied that they were. [The prioress was correct, so her story of the spurned woman in Valladolid may also be true.] Asked why Espinosa took the said jewels to Valladolid, she said only that she had heard he entered Valladolid accompanied by more than twenty men and had twenty thousand ducats of jewels and money, though others said it was only five thousand." Avendaño recounted the story of how Espinosa had shown a woman his ring with the portrait of Philip II. "This is your lord," Espinosa said, to which the woman asked, "he's your lord too, no?" In Avendaño's version of the tale, only a week old and already altered, Espinosa replied, "not my lord, but a cousin or a relative." Luis Ortiz also mentioned the jewels; he heard Espinosa was arrested because "he was a disguised gentleman and he had the jewels because he was going to sell them or pawn them and among them was a ring with His Majesty's portrait."[79] And a few weeks after the arrest, the papal nuncio wrote to Rome saying Ana had given the baker "certain jewels" to sell in Valladolid. The rumor in that city, the nuncio continued, was that with the money, Ana was planning to escape from the convent with Fray Miguel and Espinosa, who was a disguised gentleman. The investigation was causing all sorts of gossip and noise (*gran rumore*), he said.[80]

Ana apparently had jewels to spare. Works of literature from this era often featured jewels as identifying marks for women whose present situation was less than that to which they were accustomed. Women might be captive, disguised, or abandoned, but they invariably had gems sewn into the seams of their garments that showed who they really were. (Their virginity was said to be their most precious jewel.) The stones and pearls were reminders, tokens, and a guarantee of future salvation.[81] Jewelry exchange marked Ana and Espinosa's relationship from the very start. Ana's first knowledge of the baker's existence, she said later, came when he left a cross with relics for her with the convent doorkeeper, Luisa de Vayona, saying he was a servant of don Juan of Austria and asking that the cross be delivered to don Juan's daughter.[82] Espinosa told a similar story in his February confession: when he went to the convent to get paid for his pastries, he said, he gave the wooden cross with relics to Luisa del Grado (Ana may have mixed up the Luisas in order to protect her friend.) The jewels also were used by the vicar, who, according to the nuns and his own testimony, gave Ana gold, silver, jewels, and cash. How he obtained this wealth is a mystery.[83]

Ana's ring with the image of Philip II was a powerful object to give away. In the latter half of the sixteenth century, miniature portraits of rulers began being worn and presented; the fact that they were called *naipes* (playing cards) probably indicates they were meant to be passed around. In 1564 the king gave Francisco Barreto, the former Portuguese governor of India, a portrait of himself on a chain "in order that I be bound to you every day of your life, for whatever you wish."[84] Portraits appeared in pendants, on rings, and on little boxes. Several full-size portraits of the women of Philip II's family show them holding miniatures of the monarch, possibly denoting their regal powers in his absence.[85] Miniatures, often encased in jewels, were collectibles (Queen Elizabeth had many),[86] a way of joining the public spectacle of kingship to the privileged, private realm of those deemed worthy of possessing such an object. They also may have been something of a talisman, like relics or images of saints. Suitors in Cervantes's *The Labors of Persiles and Sigismunda* literally fight to the death over possession of a portrait of the beautiful Auristela as if they were winning the lady herself. So the fact that Ana had a ring with her uncle's image is perfectly consistent with royal practice, as is her making a present of it to a man she believed was her cousin. What surely is less common is that a man such as Espinosa used portraits as a way of, essentially, making friends; he showed royal images to Gregorio González as well as to the people in the Valladolid tavern.

Gift-giving was a serious matter, creating obligations and denoting status, and the judges and ministers paid obsessive attention to the various gifting relationships among the players in this story. Ana and Espinosa exchanged presents; so did she and Goldaraz, and both relationships later were deemed improper and dangerous. Ana's servant Juan de Roderos reported that Goldaraz "was in the habit of sending presents to doña Ana, especially from Navarre."[87] That allegation was confirmed in Llano's investigation of Goldaraz's insubordination and sketchy political contacts. One Fray Juan de Tolosa in Medina del Campo said the provincial had a "close relationship with doña Ana and often gave her presents, especially from Navarre, and this witness saw him sending her a very good jacket and some preserves and ham," which he sent to her in care of the prior of the Augustinian monastery in Medina, Fray Juan de Camargo. Fray Juan de Benavente, Goldaraz's sworn enemy, told Llano much the same.[88] Goldaraz's assistant, Fray Agustín Antolínez, was equally intimate with Ana, and Santillán was of the opinion that there was some mutually beneficial financial relationship between the two Augustinians and the nun.[89]

In a self-serving letter from Goldaraz to a colleague in October 1594, the provincial described the pastries that Espinosa brought to the convent as presents, which allowed the baker access to Ana, Luisa, and the innocent vicar.[90] Espinosa also, as we saw, brought the cross as a present. Ana, then, would reciprocate. As Fray Miguel said in an equally self-serving confession before the torture began, Ana gave the vicar many presents from Portugal "because she thought she should."[91] In October, in Goldaraz's mass questioning of the nuns, Ana confessed she had sent a bedspread and a mattress from her cell to Espinosa's house so his little girl would have a nicer place to sleep.[92] (In the letter she sent to him in Valladolid, she also mentioned having ordered clothes and linens for the child.) In addition, she told Goldaraz, she had sent a servant to Madrid to bring back six fine shirts, three pairs of colored silk breeches, and taffeta garters, all for her brother whom she believed would soon arrive. When he questioned the nuns again, Goldaraz specifically returned to the linen, asking them once again if they knew Ana had sent these gifts to his house, and they all replied that they did. Ana not only gave Espinosa linens, Inés de Cangas said a few months later, but when he left for Valladolid, she gave him gold and silver, and her portrait, and locks of her hair. Indeed, Ana's indictment on March 7, 1595, stated that after she and Espinosa exchanged marriage vows, she gave him gold and silver jewelry, linens, cash, and a portrait of herself, and a lock of her hair. In one of several indications that Ana was not all that popular, Inés de Cangas added that the nuns were disturbed by Ana's friendships but could not say anything because he was the vicar, and she was "*tan exempta*," so privileged, and did not even have to request permission to meet visitors at the *grada*.[93]

Who Was Gabriel de Espinosa?

After the arrest, Santillán left Espinosa alone, busy with other matters in Madrigal, and he finally spoke with him during the first week of November.[94] He arrived in Medina del Campo on Sunday night and heard from Espinosa until four in the morning. On Monday night he interrogated him until three in the morning and finished up late Tuesday. Santillán always preferred interrogating at night; fewer people noticed what was going on, and defendants were tired and less resistant, he told the king. This was when Espinosa admitted that Fray Miguel and Ana seemed to think he was Sebastian; they gave him lots of presents, he said, so he let the charade continue. Espinosa would reveal nothing about his past. In Santillán's opinion, though he had the bearing and carriage of a gentleman, there also were signs indicating a deal with the devil. Espinosa denied any disrespect for Philip II and said he was in Valladolid on his way to collect Ana's brother. It was at that point that Santillán suggested to the king that Espinosa's companion, Inés Cid, be tortured.

Espinosa appears to have been moved around in Medina del Campo, as there are references to his being in the city jail, La Mota fortress, and in the home of the merchant banker Simón Ruiz, as well as in Madrigal, where the torture took place. Judge Portocarrero, who detested Rodrigo de Santillán, complained that the prisoner was being transported from his prison cell to Ruiz's home to dine off silver dishes with Santillán, which appears unlikely, but that is what he said the guards told him. (A week later a friend of Santillán's warned him that in Valladolid word had gotten out; the correspondent did not believe what they were saying, but he thought Rodrigo should know.[95]) Given the experience of Santillán's own brother Diego, it was reasonable for Rodrigo to want to limit Espinosa's regular access to guards who might be seduced by his imperious manner. On the one hand, keeping him in one place might allow a trusting relationship with guards to develop; but on the other, the more guards he encountered, the greater his chances of finding allies. At any rate, Espinosa's increasingly frantic behavior in late fall indicates that he had received news of the outside world, probably through his guards, and was apprised of the lockdown at the convent. A guard at La Mota, Juan Jiménez de Gatica, wrote to Santillán on November 28 in very unschooled handwriting, saying he was beside himself with compassion for Espinosa. The prisoner was feverish and had spent the entire night awake, half-crazy, calling for Santillán. "I beg you to come here if it is possible," Jiménez wrote.[96] Santillán told him not to count on it: "You can tell him I will not give him an opportunity to tell me more nonsense." He would interrogate him as a judge, not chat with him, he told Jiménez, and he reminded the guard of Cervatos's fate.[97] Simón Ruiz himself also wrote to Santillán, advising him that the prisoner was ill and melancholy. Ruiz had called for a doctor, who must have done something, for a week later Espinosa met with Llano.[98]

In mid-December the king authorized torture for Espinosa.[99] The imposter was transported by mule from Medina to Madrigal in the dead of night, confined with two sets of irons, lamenting his fate as he drew closer to the convent town where he once lived. At times on the twenty-five-kilometer drive, he appeared to think he was going to be executed ("I don't deserve this, King Philip") but then suddenly seemed to believe he was on his way to a cross-examination with Fray Miguel and Ana, which excited him and seemed to give him great hope. His feverish monologue amused the guards. When they finally arrived, he was taken to a home and undressed, and the *verdugos* began their work. He succumbed to the pain more easily than had Fray Miguel, quickly confessing to Santillán that he had pretended to be King Sebastian and had married Ana at the behest of Fray Miguel. In essence, he repeated the friar's confession, omitting only that his ultimate destiny was to be killed once don António took the throne, which, naturally, he did not know.[100] In January 1595 the prisoner again became quite ill. Santillán wrote the king that he had not been able to transport Espinosa to Madrigal for more questioning because he had fevers and exhaustion, so much so that the governor of Medina asked that a doctor be summoned. "I am inclined to say no because I want no one to see him," Santillán wrote. Despite having confessed his crimes, the tirelessly inventive Espinosa still was speaking in mysterious fashion to the guards, Santillán complained, and matters would only get worse if he died after having spread his tales. "If he's going to die, the doctor can't do much for him anyway," he remarked.[101]

In February, Llano took the long confession from Espinosa to which we referred earlier. Santillán was furious that Llano was poaching on his territory; it also annoyed Moura and Juan de Idiáquez, but, they said, "what's done is done." The king was less charitable with Llano's interferences, telling him that repeated questioning was just producing new lies.[102] Again in the first week of March, Espinosa was interrogated and tortured. The main topic of conversation appears to have been his daughter.[103] He provided the date and place of her birth and the names of her godparents, and confirmed that Inés Cid—not some mysterious noblewoman in Oporto, as was believed in the convent—was her mother. He again admitted that Fray Miguel had put him up to the imposture and that he had accepted. It would be easy to convince the Portuguese he was Sebastian, he told the judges, because he had some of Sebastian's *señas*. Later that month Santillán had yet another session with Espinosa, which was when the crucial story of his first meeting with Fray Miguel in Lisbon finally emerged.

After that point, the judges knew enough. There had been lies and imposture, an implied threat to the crown, and criminal access to doña Ana. Plenty of details were missing, but Espinosa probably could not supply them. From here on, the king was interested in just two things: Epinosa's little girl, who was referred to in the correspondence as *la niña*; and Fray Miguel's accomplices.

Two of the principal mysteries of the case, the ones that have engaged romantic writers for four hundred years, are who Espinosa was and what he knew. Though the king in November ordered officials to find out where he was from (Toledo was all he would say), who his parents were, and where he had been, no reliable information was obtained.[104] The *Historia de Gabriel de Espinosa* says he left Spain because he killed a man, which sounds familiar, because that is what happened to Fray Miguel's grandfather.[105] It also says he was not a good baker (a *muy mal pastelero*, in fact), which could prove he was not the lowly commoner he was dressed up to be. Or maybe not. His slippery background was not a new development, which is why he was such a perfect find for Fray Miguel; years earlier he had insinuated to Inés Cid that he came from money. He was all things and nobody, and to his very last breath he refused to be more specific. Over and over again he told the guards that the king must be contacted so he could identify him.[106] In one of several instances where we see Santillán's peculiar sense of humor concerning torture, the judge entered his cell sometime in late February to find the prisoner in bed. Espinosa leaped up and began dressing. "As you were, brother," said the jolly judge, "you'll have to be naked for what we're going to do." Espinosa replied, "This cannot be true. . . . I know I must die, but His Majesty must respect the fact that I am an honorable man and he will want me to die honorably and not on a rack."[107] In Espinosa's last conversation, recorded by Juan de Fuensalida, the Jesuit priest, he said, "I was not born to be a prince or a king but an emperor, and despite my troubles I have always been an honorable man. And I [Fuensalida] asked again how, if he was abandoned at the church door, . . . and he laughed, not saying who he was, suggesting he was someone else. . . . And so, not saying who he was, anyone who saw him and spoke with him would say he was someone else."[108]

The prospect of Portuguese gentlemen weeping in ecstasy to see their reborn king may have gone to his head, and that may have been the astute Fray Miguel's intention. One of the most learned theologians of Portugal was insisting he was Sebastian. Who was he to disagree? The king's niece told him he was the answer to her prayers. So maybe he was a king after all. Maybe he was even Sebastian. Six months of interrogation, torture, and fear may have cemented some version of that possibility in his head. Or, if he was not a king, at least he was somebody important. And perhaps he really was. But he would not say, he told his interrogators, except face-to-face to Philip II. What did he know? The Portuguese chronicler Pero Roiz Soares was among those who depicted Espinosa as the one who deceived Fray Miguel, not the other way around, but given what we know about the two men, this is impossible to believe. Roiz himself appears to have had difficulty believing it, concluding that only a pact with the devil could explain how someone as eminent, learned, and virtuous as Fray Miguel could have been taken in.[109] Goldaraz in October also portrayed Espinosa as the Svengali, but he had every reason to push suspicions away from the friar (as Roiz had to push blame onto a Spaniard). The smooth-talking baker, according to the provincial, made the vicar believe he had fought with Ana's father, prompting "the good Fray Miguel" to allow Ana to meet with him.[110] But Goldaraz's version has many holes. It is more likely, as the *Historia de Gabriel de Espinosa* put it, that Fray Miguel was "the lead dancer."[111]

In the nineteenth century, the Portuguese Romantic novelist Camilo Castelo Branco wrote the scene this way:

> "Gabriel de Espinosa, would you like to help me give Portugal a new king?"
> "Me?" asked the baker, clapping his hands to his chest. "Me? Oh Fray Miguel, are you joking?"
> "No! I'm listening to divine orders," confirmed don Sebastian's confessor, with a gesture of inspiration. "Portugal will have a Portuguese king if

> you want it to. . . . It is necessary that don Sebastian, king of Portugal, not have died; and you will be don Sebastian!"[112]

Maybe Espinosa and Fray Miguel met in Madrid and hatched a plan (they were both sighted there in the late 1580s), or possibly Espinosa really did arrive in Madrigal by chance one day only to be recognized by the vicar a few days later, assuming Fray Miguel could recognize someone whom he had met just once, amid chaos, fourteen years earlier in Lisbon. And maybe Fray Miguel himself was there by chance. Or maybe not. As for where the plan was going, possibly Espinosa knew nothing and simply inched himself into trouble bit by bit until it was impossible to extricate himself. Fray Miguel probably hoped the wanderer would do just that, slowly easing into his identity once he learned about his new past. That was chronicler Cabrera de Córdoba's interpretation: "Little by little [Fray Miguel] let [Espinosa] know he believed he was King Sebastian, though he was not, but he had just enough *señas* that, together with the information he gave him, everyone would be persuaded."[113] The most convincing of liars, after all, is he who believes his own lie. The vicar was certainly clever enough, after fifteen years of scheming, to figure that out. Though, of course, there is such a thing as too good a memory; one of the most famous itinerants of the era, Martin Guerre, "remembered" a past not even the real Martin Guerre remembered.[114] Why Espinosa would have accepted whatever offer Fray Miguel made and what he thought he might possibly gain from such an adventure remains an enigma.

The criminal sentences were mostly handed down in July 1595. Espinosa was found guilty of consenting to the vicar's plan to pose as Sebastian and pretend he was disguised and wandering in accordance with a vow he made after Alcazarquivir "with the aim of making himself king of Portugal and persuading the natives of that kingdom he was the king, under the orders of Fray Miguel and on the basis of some corporal signs Espinosa is said to have that are similar to those of the king."[115] Fray Miguel, the indictment went on, wrote to his noble Portuguese accomplices, who sent messengers to Madrigal for whom Espinosa played the part he was told to play, and the visits would have continued had Espinosa not been arrested. The official proclamation of guilt (*pregón*), which was both posted and read aloud, exists in two versions. Madrigal was a small town, and probably the town crier (*pregonero*) had a fixed spot in the main square, though it appears that on execution day he wandered. In a large city, however, there were several intersections and landmarks where the *pregonero* would go at fixed times to cry out, in a clear and loud voice, judicial sentences, price ceilings, police measures, and the like. Lisbon in 1596 had around five such spots; Madrid had a few more. It was through this dissemination that laws and edicts became real; thus justice was written, oral, and visible. In the summary document listing all Espinosa's indictments, the *pregón* says, "This is the justice ordered by his Majesty and don Rodrigo de Santillán in his name for this man for being a traitor to the king our lord and for having pretended to be King don Sebastian." In the subsequent document in the case file, however, the *pregón* says: "This is the justice ordered by the king our lord and don Rodrigo de Santillán in his name for this man for being a traitor to His Majesty and impersonating a royal person when he is a low and lying man."[116] It seems the latter was the version called out by the crier as the ghastly cortege made its way through the town streets. There was no point in even naming the missing Portuguese monarch, and evidently the palace wished to emphasize that Espinosa was, after all, nobody.

News Gets Out

What did the outside world know of all this? Fame's two trumpets, one for falsehoods, the other for truth, could blast at any time, sending *ruidos* shimmering up and down the Iberian peninsula. Prisoners and witnesses were transported and interrogated at night, Santillán used his own private messengers, and Sebastian's name was rarely if ever mentioned in official correspondence. Still the news got out, which can be no surprise, given the dense network of roads in the region, the scandalous nature of the events, and the fact that prisoners were being housed and tortured in private homes. As the anonymous letter-writer said, the whole kingdom was watching, and after watching for awhile, the kingdom put pen to paper or just relayed the news verbally. The news industry in Spain was less developed at this time than elsewhere in Europe, but we can safely assume that items in, say, the reports sent to the Fuggers' banking headquarters or ambassadorial dispatches sent from Spain made their way into private correspondence and from there back into the public stream, perhaps still appearing to be letters, which lent credence and proximity. Diplomats filed reports, but, as surrogate narrators, they also recreated events, turning news into a kind of stylized fiction or tableau. *Se dice*, it is said, one hears, people are saying, one believes . . .

Venetian ambassadors in particular were famous for being on top of all important gossip. In the Middle Ages, diplomats fulfilled particular missions and returned home, but by the sixteenth century, resident ambassadors were information-gatherers, and their masters gathered up all their potentially useful fruits and nuggets to buttress their own power and prestige. In the case of the *pastelero*, however, the Venetian ambassador failed miserably, though, to be fair, he had only just arrived in Madrid. His name was Agostino Nani. His report, dated August 10, 1595, as it appears in the State Papers (indexed under "Portugal, frivolous anti-Spanish plot in"), follows:

> An event has recently happened in Portugal which at first had its origin in feminine frivolity and the superstition of the populace, but ended in matters of moment. In a certain convent was a nun called sister Anne, sister of Don John of Austria; she opened relations, by means of an Augustinian friar, with a pastry-cook, son of a canon in Lisbon of very humble birth. The friar gave out that this pastry-cook, on the strength of his likeness to Don Sebastian, was in fact the King who was erroneously supposed to have fallen in Africa. Matters went so far that a marriage contract was drawn up, and the pastry-cook calling himself King Don Sebastian, and signing himself "I the King," exchanged rings.
>
> The affair came to light, and his Majesty, seeing that there was a nun in the case, requested the Nuncio to appoint a judge. The Nuncio chose one of his Majesty's chaplains, and in drawing up the case, it was discovered that the friar was in correspondence with Don Antonio of Portugal and many leading Portuguese. Their scheme was to seduce the populace under the leadership of this pretended King; an idea which has been tried before in Portugal. The result is that many arrests have been made and some

prisoners, including the friar and the pretended King, have been sent here [Madrid] for examination. The nun has been condemned to five years of rigorous confinement in her cell.[117]

The errors are numerous, of course. The event did not happen in Portugal, Ana was not don Juan's sister; the pastry-cook was not the son of a canon, nor was he Portuguese; the nuncio did not appoint the judge; the judge was not a chaplain; and Espinosa was not sent to Madrid. Furthermore, the report was filed in August 1595, by which time the case was ten months old and Espinosa was dead. Given the other examples of private correspondence we have, it seems Nani was not paying close attention or had lazy sources. The following year, confirming one's suspicion that he was not the most distinguished or serious of envoys, Nani appears to have triggered a near riot in Madrid by harboring a fugitive and then ordering his nephew to beat up a royal judicial officer who came in search of the man. When the matter went to trial (Nani's immunity possibly was revoked), the ambassador's men threw stones at the officers as they approached the courthouse, and then Nani himself whipped out his sword and lunged at them. Nani went on to a brilliant career as Venetian ambassador in Constantinople and Rome, and in 1618 was a candidate to be doge.[118]

The English do not seem to have been better informed, though it would not take long for more accurate information to cross the channel. In early 1596, this item appeared: "*A Portuguese pretender*. The Spanish King's ministers in Portugal executed a man who was very like the former King Sebastian of Portugal in face and form. He had begun to pretend he was in fact Don Sebastian. The affair was fomented by a Father Provincial of St. Augustine and the people had begun to rise. But with the pretender's death, all was quieted."[119] Again, the errors: the event did not take place in Portugal, there was no likeness between Espinosa and Sebastian, there was no popular support, and Fray Miguel's execution was omitted. Possibly the English source relied on Nani.

Our third example is a letter from Bartolomé Gasca de la Vega in Valladolid to Diego Sarmiento Acuña in Madrid. The recipient, later the count of Gondomar, was one of the most distinguished royal servants of his generation, and his letters are an extraordinary document of his times. His friend Gasca de la Vega, part of a well-positioned family, clearly had friends in judicial and church circles, as did Gondomar. On February 12, 1595, he wrote this remarkably accurate and detailed letter:

> The news here is that don Rodrigo de Santillán has arrested a man who is in prison with guards, among them don Diego, his brother. . . . Through some letters that landed in don Rodrigo's hands, he is said to be called Majesty. There are many theories: that he is don António, a spy for [Henry IV], a foreign prince, Prince don Carlos, and even King Sebastian. You can believe whatever you want. Some say he's a royal ambassador. He's in a jail cell in Medina del Campo in a common bed with guards. He says he's a pastry cook, and his name is Gabriel de Espinosa, and he does not know who his parents were. It is said he is forty-four years old, more or less, though he has grey hair, but he is spirited and strong and sometimes very serious. He was a baker in Madrigal and in La Nava, but another baker made him leave because he baked large pastries and his own weren't selling. They took him from here [Valladolid] to Medina in a coach with no irons. Don Diego and five or six constables and eighteen or twenty musketeers accompanied him. . . . He has a cloud in one eye, broad shoulders but is not a large man, and he has a pretty little girl of two and a half whose mother, it is said, was his lover who worked in his shop, and she is also a prisoner. Doña Ana of Austria also is being held, with nuns as her guards. It is said she spoke and wrote to him and was good to the little girl when he was gone, according to a man here whom Espinosa sent to Madrigal with letters when he was a lodger [this is Gabriel Rodríguez], and the replies were seized by don Rodrigo. The nuns' vicar also is a prisoner. He is a very honorable person and he was in La Mota and now he is back in Madrigal. Doctor Llano de Valdés is the ecclesiastical judge, and they say he has removed four nuns from the convent and even tortured one of them with bricks [*de ladrillo*], and he tortured a servant of the friar who fled [this is Juan de Roderos], and it is believed also an *hidalgo* from Salamanca who is a prisoner and also a friar. [It is unclear who this might be.] Your Grace can believe what he wants of all this; none of it is gospel. But they say for sure that don Rodrigo married off his sister to the governor of Medina, and don Diego has married a rich

> widow from Toledo. . . . This man who was here [Espinosa] had two pages, and one of them robbed him of one hundred forty ducats and his shirts, of fine Holland linen. When he was captured, he had jewels and presents that they say doña Ana gave him. He is in prison, and they haven't tortured him, they've just taken his confession, which they say was in public before eight witnesses; he said he was a baker and a low person, etc. [*sic*] But he did not say where he was from or who his parents are. It is worrisome how slowly this matter is moving ahead, even though it goes against the king, and they're not doing anything to him, just taking more depositions.[120]

Gasca de la Vega obviously did not know who Fray Miguel was, and he was wrong about Espinosa not having been tortured. But in general, he knew what was going on. The business of the eight witnesses is somewhat explained in the *Historia de Gabriel de Espinosa*, which says Santillán wanted the confession to be heard by nine (*sic*) witnesses, "but even that was not enough to calm things down and quiet the false opinion created around this man that he was more than he was saying."[121] Gasca de la Vega was familiar not only with the judicial mechanics of the case but, like the Jesuit whose account we saw in the last chapter, with the jewels, the presents, and the linen. He also knew the case was moving at a snail's pace. His sources probably were varied. He either knew the innkeeper Rodríguez or knew someone who knew him. Some information is likely to have come his way via servants, who often were familiar with more than one household. (Simón Ruiz's servants knew Antonio Sosa's servants, for example.) Many of the nuns had relatives in town or nearby, and the convent walls were hardly an obstacle for news; on the contrary, they seem to have been a stimulant. The Santillán family was prominent, which helped; Rodrigo was tight-lipped, but he had at least two well-married siblings who perhaps communicated their brother's doings to their neighbors. The prison guards obviously had talked. Gasca de la Vega may not have had good religious sources, however, for they would have known Fray Miguel's background. In any case, if he knew the narrative this well and was able to put the events into a logical order, then others could, too. In particular, one wonders what the upper-class women of Valladolid were saying; probably a great deal.

The Rising of the Hidden King

Nearly a century before the events in Madrigal, the Iberian peninsula witnessed an upsurge in millenarian beliefs as Christian and Jewish traditions (with Islam in the background as constant menace and interlocutor) converged at a time of particular political tension. Many people in the early sixteenth century thought it possible that a hidden king, a sleeping hero, would rise up to lead them out of their troubles. In Spain and Portugal this king—an example elsewhere is King Arthur—was called *el encubierto* or *o encoberto*, the concealed one, whose return had been prophesized centuries earlier. The revolts of the *comuneros* in Castile and the Germanías in Valencia in the early 1520s seemed to confirm such a moment. In Valencia, in fact, a figure emerged calling himself *l'encobert*, claiming to be the (dead) son of Ferdinand and Isabella, and he raised a band of warriors who fought against Muslims and royal troops.[122] In Portugal sometime between the 1520s and the 1540s, a shoemaker named Gonçalo Anes, who was called Bandarra, predicted the destruction of what he considered a corrupt and unjust regime to be followed by the regeneration of Portugal. Like his Spanish counterparts a few decades later, this shoemaker—Ana of Austria knew of his writings—described the coming of a great king who would restore peace and reestablish the golden age. Also like them, Bandarra landed in front of the Inquisition, accused of crypto-Judaism and "being a friend of *novedades*." In 1545 he was ordered to stop writing and prophesying, which he did, but his prophetic poems, called the *trovas*, in large part dream narrations full of politically and religiously charged dialogues, lived on, circulating in new versions even as they were prohibited. After the battle of Alcazarquivir, logically enough, they acquired new meaning, and the hidden one became identified with *o desejado*, the desired one, the name given to the boy Sebastian who would save Portugal from ruin, the country's last chance for survival. These various strains of thought—the awaited messiah of the Jews, the revelations of Christians, the hidden king, and nationalist sentiment—all streamed together.[123]

Recognition of a king by actual physical markings was only relatively important alongside prophecies and desire. (The Madrigal case is unusual in not relying on birthmarks or scars.) There was no shortage of examples of returned kings in Iberian and European history, usually after a royal body went missing in the chaos of battle. Not all apparitions were messianic ones; there were plenty of cases, like that of Madrigal, in which political machinations rather than prophecies were at work, but the former certainly took advantage of the latter. The example that set the tradition was that of King Rodrigo, Spain's last Visigothic ruler. After he was defeated by the Moors in 711, ushering in eight centuries of Islam in the peninsula, his body was not found on the battlefield, and it was said he escaped to Portugal, to the city of Guarda (where a certain bishop would later cause problems.) It was said too that King Harold of England did not die in the Battle of Hastings in 1066; instead, the wounded man was discovered by a peasant who took him home and cared for him, and the king eventually became a hermit. In the twelfth century, a revived Alfonso I of Aragon reappeared forty years after losing the Battle of Fraga. Like Sebastian, he was overcome with shame and indignation at his defeat by the Moors and had traveled to Jerusalem. He returned to Aragon to reclaim his throne, and the pretender was executed some four years later.[124] Perkin Warbeck, the false duke of York (the real one having died in the Tower of London), launched two unsuccessful landings from France in order to claim the throne; he was executed in 1499. The body of Polish king Wladyslaw III disappeared after the Battle of Varna in 1444, and he also journeyed to the Holy Land, finally settling on the Portuguese island of Madeira. There are multiple cases in Russia: in 1591, the tsar's son Dimitri supposedly escaped an assassination attempt, and at least three false Dimitris appeared. Alexander I allegedly faked his own death in 1825 and lived for thirty-nine more years as a pious Siberian hermit named Feodor Kuzmich.[125]

The king as hermit was a veritable topos during the medieval and early modern periods, when rules of dynastic legitimacy might be undermined by prophecy. In an era when distinguishing truth from falsehood became an obsession, when writers debated the difference between history and fable, when messages were often false, news could not be trusted, and stages were inhabited by characters wearing the wrong clothes, kings pretended they were commoners, and commoners claimed to be kings.

Frequently, the king's penance took place after a catastrophic battle. His body could not be identified, or it was falsely identified, and a peasant (or a Moorish princess, in the case of the Sebastian literature) discovered the wounded king and took him home. In these cases, the king chose to disguise himself, to melt into the land of forgetfulness. His disappearance, the complete absence of a body, could be as much of a disguise as a willful impersonation was. But sometimes he was unwillingly disguised, victim of some terrible accident. Babies were switched at birth, for example. Or a queen fled an evil king, taking with her the true heir. Deathbed confessions frequently were the way these stories emerged, prompting the erstwhile hidden monarch to step forward with new memories and reclaim what was his, always in the name of restoring justice, restoring order. Amadís de Gaula, the greatest of Spanish romantic chivalric heroes, was himself abandoned at birth and spent the rest of his life battling his way through Europe to conquer his lady love and establish his noble identity.[126]

There was no one, rich or poor, who did not know these stories. To believe in them, to believe in magic, was not necessarily a sign of lunacy or ignorance. The stories bound together the realms of faith and the state, with rulers undergoing a metamorphosis that surely sounded familiar to nuns and friars. They often gave women protagonism, disparaged by some, but protagonism nonetheless. They kept alive memories and visions of a just world, and in some cases provided a way of talking about nationhood and tyrannicide. Their ubiquity was evidence of the interconnectedness of kingdoms, the fluidity of correspondence. They made a certain amount of sense, and they helped make sense of events that otherwise seemed unbearable. Neither reductive explanations of miracles, coincidences, or divine providence (figuring out what "really" happened), nor the tendency to treat medieval and early modern witnesses as simply overly susceptible to the bizarre gets at the actual, complex experience and meaning of these events. Observers, literate and not, found a way to simultaneously inhabit the world of incongruity and what we would call the world of logic.

Occurrences like the false Sebastian of Madrigal show how this was possible: the world Castilians inhabited bore a startling similarity to the one they might read about in novels or see on stage. I cannot say what the protagonists knew about literature; I know only that Fray Miguel owned four books, and that Gabriel de Espinosa liked the theater. But the nuns came from prominent families, the friars spent a great deal of time moving from place to place, and the judges had heard everything there was to hear. They all knew history, they all had access to news, and in some way they all must have recognized the events unfolding around them. Aristocratic women, which many of the nuns were, were considered the target audience for the Byzantine novel (which in literary chronology followed the chivalric novel and preceded the picaresque), whose characteristics closely fit the events of Madrigal. Espinosa's journey through life was quintessentially picaresque, but the imposture overlaid his reality onto an older yet equally familiar tale, that of the religious pilgrimage (*peregrinaje*)—in this case Sebastian's. The secular and sacred journeys thus coincided. Don António also referred to his *peregrinaçaõ*, his wanderings in exile, and signed his letters "John the Pilgrim."[127] These journeys required costume changes, subterfuge, confusion, and the overcoming of many obstacles, at the end of which things were supposed to turn out well. Audiences, readers, and the devout were well trained in untangling complicated plots. They could figure out the coherence amid the contingency. And strange events could be made intelligible because such things had happened before. The boundaries between literature and history were thin; indeed, the picaresque genre, which this true story so resembles, often pretended to be history, not fiction at all. The manuscript fortuitously uncovered, the deposition, the letter read aloud before people gathered in an inn, all move the novel away from its identity as make-believe, transforming the author into mere transmitter of truth. As Roberto González Echevarría put it so aptly for our purposes, "The novel dons a disguise."[128]

The only characters in this book who ever saw both Sebastian and don António were Philip II, Cristóbal de Moura, Juan de Silva, and Fray Miguel. Philip saw his nephew just once, in Guadalupe, where Sebastian "looked more as if he were born in Germany or Flanders than in Lisbon," and he had last seen don António in the 1560s.[129] The vicar's interrogators asked him to describe Sebastian: was he "a tall man, or of what height, was he pale and ruddy, what color [were] his hair and his beard, was he fat or thin, how was he proportioned, did he speak Portuguese [*la lengua portuguesa cerrada*] or did he speak Castilian?"[130] But physical recognition was unlikely. Verisimilitude probably was not sought by imposters in general, and certainly not by this one in particular. The case of Martin Guerre proved, wrote the English ambassador to Portugal decades later as he mused over the false Sebastians, that "there is often such a resemblance between persons that, especially when they are not confronted, they may easily be mistaken for one another."[131] In fact, nobody (except the Portuguese visitors whom we know about only thanks to Fray Miguel's probably false account) ever did recognize Espinosa as Sebastian, so that was one old tale that did not come to pass. Nobody experienced that moment when pretense falls away as the truth is literally revealed, a moment familiar from contemporary literary conventions but also a device recognized and criticized at the time as an artifice. It would have been too good to be true.[132]

Hagiographic chronicles about Sebastian often made a point of saying he was proportional, an odd claim explained by the fact that by most other accounts, he was not. Philip's ministers all referred to his physical defects, which the young king may have overcome with strenuous exercise. The man who appeared in Madrigal in the summer of 1594 bore none of these qualities. He was neither imbalanced nor blond, he was charming and seductive, he was able to have children, he was quite old, he did not speak Portuguese. But what did that matter alongside a tradition of revelation? The ways of God were many and mysterious. And who better to appreciate that than a princess in a convent?

4

Madrigal: Ana of Austria

Ana arrived at the convent of Nuestra Señora de Gracia la Real when she was six. She was accompanied by Magdalena de Ulloa, the rich and philanthropic widow who raised Ana's father, don Juan of Austria, the half-brother of Philip II and hero of Lepanto.[1] Doña Magdalena said she was the child's aunt, which was not true, and also said the child had no parents and no surname, also not true. So the child was registered, like all orphans, as Ana "of Jesus." Her dowry was six hundred ducats. No one, herself included, knew she was of royal blood except doña Magdalena, who said nothing and apparently never saw the child again.

Ana's mother was named María de Mendoza.[2] She was related to a branch of the enormous, aristocratic Mendoza clan, the counts of Coruña, with whom don Juan was close, and that was the origin of their brief affair. Ana was born toward the end of 1568 in the present-day province of Soria. Unusually, María raised her illegitimate child herself. She moved to Madrid with her mother, Catalina de Mendoza, and they lived in a house they bought in 1570 near the present-day Plaza de Tirso de Molina, in the Lavapies neighborhood. Catalina died in November 1571, and in her will made a point of saying how much she loved her baby granddaughter, whom she mentioned by name, and she specified her inheritance. Two months later, María herself died. She made two wills. In the first, dated December 18, 1571, she declared that her daughter, "doña Ana de Mendoza," was her only heir and furthermore was the "daughter of the illustrious don Juan of Austria." One of the executors of this will was Alonso de Mendoza, a priest or Dominican friar at Nuestra Señora de Atocha, a Madrid church and shrine. It is possible that this was the same Alonso de Mendoza who nearly twenty years later, by which time he had a highly distinguished clerical résumé, acted as Lucrecia de León's guide as she dictated her hundreds of seditious dreams. If it is the same person, and there is evidence pointing both ways, it is not unlikely that in the early part of his career he would have reached out to a relative in need, or that she would have seen in him a good protector, given his powerful family connections. But several weeks later, still alive, María had a change of heart about her will. In a second version, dated January 15, 1572, the reference to don Juan is gone, though the daughter is still named: "Doña Ana de Mendoza, my natural daughter." Mercedes Formica surmises that Alonso advised María to remove the reference to don Juan in exchange for the family's support. The count of Coruña at that time, Lorenzo, was one of around twenty siblings, including possibly Alonso himself, as well as Bernardino, Philip II's ambassador to London and Paris, and Francisco, chief of Juan of Austria's household. (Also raised in the crowded household was an orphaned cousin, also named María de Mendoza, who later married the count of Barajas.) By the time Ana's mother's second will was signed, Alonso was no longer an executor; instead, the count, obviously a more powerful ally, was named as Ana's guardian. María died three days later, on January 18. The baby was given to doña Magdalena, whose family also was intertwined with the counts of Coruña. Three years later, when Ana arrived in Madrigal de las Altas Torres, she had no name.

Don Juan of Austria died in October 1578. His was a hideous death, and some people assumed he was poisoned, though typhus is more likely. An autopsy revealed that many of his internal organs were black. After his great victory against the Moriscos in the Alpujarras war, don Juan had wanted to be given the title of *infante* and the right to be called His Highness, and he was perpetually discontent that his brother the king deprived him of the honors he thought he deserved. Only after his death, when Philip II ordered that his half-brother's body be interred at El Escorial with that of their father, Charles V, would don Juan receive the recognition he had craved. At some point after don Juan's death, Philip II learned that his brother had offspring. At some point after that, Ana's life changed. The first record that Formica found referring to the young nun as "Ana of Austria" was in April 1583, five years after her father's death, but the notification of her royal blood—which meant the slain king Sebastian was her first cousin—probably came earlier.[3] From then on she was referred to as "Your Excellency" and enjoyed a royal allowance.

When Ana was around fourteen, in the spring of 1583, by which time her identity was known, she took her first vows as a nun, becoming one of a long line of illegitimate and legitimate noble girls to spend their lives in convents. She later insisted she had been too young and therefore was not really a nun. According to the rules of the Council of Trent, she had a point. The high-water mark of the Counter-Reformation, the Council of Trent spent its last session, in 1563, discussing monastic reform, including measures to ensure that vows were freely taken and to allow appeals by those who later claimed they had been forced into a life of seclusion. Girls were to be no younger than sixteen when taking their vows. The church was keen on quashing the trope of the well-born girl stashed away; thus the increased formalities. In St. Teresa's constitutions for the Descalced Carmelites, for example, she wrote, "The novices, like the professed nuns, may receive visitors; for in case they should be discontented, it must be made clear that we do not want them except of their own free will, and so they must be given the chance of letting it be known if they do not wish to remain." In some convents, novices were subject to a series of public questions outside the cloister walls to prove they were going in willingly.[4] Ana's formal vow of profession came on November 12, 1589, and the king asked the bishop of Avila to witness the ceremony to verify that his niece really wanted to take this step: "I, doña María Ana of Austria, daughter of the Serenísimo Prince don Juan of Austria, brother of our King, having completed my probationary time, do profess . . ."[5]

Ana's new home had once been a royal palace. The future Queen Isabel of Castile was born there in 1451, and in 1476 she and her husband, Ferdinand, returned to preside over the Cortes, which met in a large hall crowned by a beautiful Mudejar ceiling. Ana's grandfather Charles V later gave the palace to the Augustinian nuns, and two of his aunts, both named María de Aragon (illegitimate daughters of King Ferdinand by different women), were prioresses there. One of Ana's aunts, an illegitimate daughter of Charles V named Juana, and thus a half-sister of Philip II, may have died there as a child, and her remains, along with those of other royals, are supposedly in the alabaster sepulcher in the nuns' church.[6] Also buried there is Cardinal Gaspar de Quiroga, a town native and the convent's powerful patron, who during his long career was president of the Council of Castile, archbishop of Toledo, and inquisitor general. Despite Quiroga's lofty position, he had his differences with the king. During the Antonio Pérez episode, for example, he was a firm defender of the princess of Eboli, and he also had been sympathetic to Lucrecia León.[7] Quiroga died on November 22, 1594, at the age of nearly eighty-three, and his funeral, in Madrigal, came at a busy moment in the conspiracy investigation. Philip II, worried about the *ruidos*, was sure the crowds of dignitaries who streamed into town after an elaborate procession from Madrid would want to enter the convent, whose inhabitants at that point were under lock and key. Hundreds of friars from different orders all in one place was a recipe for serious gossip, and indeed Judge Juan de Llano had to order certain friars to stop repeating conversations they overheard while there.[8]

According to the 1591 census, there were fifty-five nuns in the convent; by the 1751 census, there were twenty-six, and in 2009 there were thirteen, ten of whom were elderly. The proliferation of religious houses in sixteenth-century Spain was the source of frequent complaint, among other reasons because the clergy was exempt from taxes. In Granada, for example, even the archbishop in 1603 opposed the establishment of a house for mendicant Augustinians, saying "there are fourteen convents for men in this city, more than enough for a city bigger than Granada." In that same year, in all of present-day Spain and Portugal there were a total of 116 Augustinian monasteries and convents.[9] Valladolid alone in 1591 had 350 secular clergy and no fewer than 1,440 friars and nuns, adding up to nearly 4 percent of the city's population.[10] To some degree, the problem arose from inheritance practices; placing a son or daughter in a monastery was a way of ensuring that the family money was not dispersed among too many offspring, though wealthy young women

Figure 7. Present-day Convent of Nuestra Señora de Gracia la Real, Madrigal de las Altas Torres. Photograph by Javier Alvarez Dorronsoro.

entered convents with a dowry. The number of nuns referred to with the honorific *doña,* the presence of Ana and her ancestors, and Quiroga's patronage all point to the pedigree of the Madrigal convent. At the beginning of the case, Judge Rodrigo de Santillán noted that the nuns and the friars had "a lot of influence with people in the town because they have so much wealth here," probably referring to land holdings.[11] Other institutions were far poorer, as can be seen in the minutes of the Cortes being celebrated while the Madrigal case was ongoing. On January 18, 1595, for example, the Descalzas of Badajoz informed the Castilian representative assembly that their roof was falling in, for which they received fifty escudos in alms. Seizing an opportunity to help their own districts, other cities' representatives immediately put forth a series of similar petitions: Santa Isabel in Segovia, Santa Isabel in Córdoba, Santa Ana in Murcia, Santa Catalina in Avila, Santa Ursula in Jaén, the Misericordia Hospital of Guadalajara, and the Santa Lucía hospital of Cuenca all reported extreme necessity.[12]

The Madrigal convent is not large, and it must have been crowded during Ana's time. The nuns' testimony, full of eavesdropping, attests to the close living quarters: "There is so much talk, it is easy to forget what one heard and from whom," remarked María de San Vicente in her testimony.[13] There is one central courtyard, or cloister, measuring forty by forty meters, with a fountain in the center. Surrounding the civil Gothic patio is a vaulted arcade of semicircular arches. On one side, on the ground level, are the meeting rooms and refectory. On an adjacent side is the church, divided into two sections, one for the public, where the priest delivered the Mass, and the other, previously the royal chapel, now reserved for the nuns. Later when she described her conversations with Espinosa, Ana said the *grada,* the dividing point between the two sections, "has two iron grilles, thick and far apart from one another." This is what separated Ana and Espinosa as they spoke throughout the summer of 1594; they also met by the grille in the visiting parlor (*locutorio*). Grilles were of intense interest to church authorities. Hernando de Talavera, the late-fifteenth-century archbishop of Granada, advised Cistercian nuns in Avila that they be separated from visitors by two partitions of wood or iron hung with a cloth so they could be heard but not seen; the Benedictine order specified that no hand or arm should fit through the grillework.[14] Philip received a report in 1581, when he was still in Lisbon, alleging that at a particularly lax Franciscan convent in Zamora, the grille was more ceremonial than effective, allowing for "great offenses to God," including snowball fights between nuns and local gentleman, and apparently there was even worse.[15] After the 1960s reforms of Vatican II, one of the two grilles in Madrigal was removed, and today the wooden lattices are displayed on the wall of a meeting hall as a reminder. Surrounding the main courtyard on the upper level are the nuns' quarters; the stone stairway leading upstairs is crowned by a spectacular Mudejar ceiling. The upstairs corridor is whitewashed, with little wooden doors leading into the private quarters. The nuns probably did not all have the same amount of space; Ana clearly had at least one extra room for servants, probably two, and her rooms may have been in a different section of the convent, today closed off to visitors.

Before entering the convent itself, one passes through a large outer courtyard. In one corner is the entrance into the convent; across sits the *casa de los frailes.* Some of the friars lived in the Augustinian monastery just outside the city walls, but those who attended to the nuns' needs, including the vicar and confessors, lived right next door. In 1590, Philip II expressed concern over excessive fraternization between nuns and monks in general, and he issued decrees limiting or even prohibiting contact. Spain's bishops were very much opposed to these restrictions, judging that they impeded the "common good of the Christian republic." Just as the Christian community cannot be judged by Judas, one bad apple should not condemn the church, they wrote. "Nuns, because they are women, are fragile, and they easily become disconsolate and upset, and to their suffering from pain or worries is added the unhappiness at being confined and cloistered, and thus they are in need of exhortation, consolation, and spiritual guidance," they told the king.[16] Their advice rang true to the Tridentine emphasis on confession and frequent communion. Regardless of what finally transpired with the decree, in Nuestra Señora de Gracia in Madrigal, friars and nuns nearly shared lodging.

Ana knew "that in all of Portugal there was no one more learned in religion, letters, prudence, and saintliness" than Fray Miguel de los Santos.[17] Historians of female religiosity are familiar with cases in which nuns, prohibited from administering the sacraments themselves, were subject to the authority of men less able than themselves or unscrupulous men who subjugated and intimidated them. Fray Miguel certainly was not less able than the women under his charge, but he most decidedly took advantage of his vast learning and experience, as well as his proximity, to mold the imagination and expectations of the young Ana of Austria. He was her guide, her confessor, almost a father.

Vows and Revelations

One day in March 1593, before the plot came to light, Philip II's longtime aide Juan de Silva was traveling from Madrid to Lisbon. On his way, having witnessed "the most beautiful sunshine on the snow that I've seen since the day I was born," he visited Filipa, a nun in Segovia who was a daughter of don António, the prior of Crato. From Segovia, Silva descended the mountains to the plain and went on to Madrigal, describing (in the same letter) his destination as a seminary for princesses in the desert. When he arrived, he met with Fray Miguel de los Santos, "an Antonioan Portuguese friar," who told him he had been ordered there by Philip II to be Ana's confessor and insisted that Silva meet with Ana. Silva obliged, none too willingly, and listened to Her Excellency sing to him for half an hour, which turned into three-quarters of an hour, after which she told him she would commend him to Our Lord. The sharp-tongued count of Portalegre replied that it was news to him that royal prayers were the best sort, and he went off to his inn to get some sleep.[18]

This was the site of the unholy conspiracy, which was already under way when Silva visited. According to Fray Miguel's testimony, obtained under torture, in around August 1593 he began telling Ana—who had asked that he intercede with God to ease her continued dissatisfaction at being a nun—about his revelations and visions.[19] One day while saying Mass, he told her, he heard a voice say three times "Let her be, I want her like that." When he asked God what he meant, God replied that he had grand plans for Her Excellency. On another occasion, standing before the altar depicting the Hill of Calvary, he noticed that the crucified Jesus was flanked by King Sebastian and Ana, dressed in white and holding banners. Again he asked God for an explanation, and this time God told him that Sebastian and Ana must marry and together recapture Jerusalem and destroy the sect of Mohammed, and that this was also the wish of the Virgin Mary along with saints Peter, Paul, John the Baptist, and many more. Another time, he said, he was praying in his cell and God appeared, "as usual," this time with Sebastian and Ana holding hands. When the friar asked God how he could know if he were being deceived, God told him to ask Sebastian himself, which he did, and Sebastian's reply, though marred by ripped paper, appears to confirm that he and Ana were on a mission. Later he saw Sebastian and Ana standing together over Christ's tomb with an angel hovering close by. He also saw a large navy, and one of the ships had a crucifix painted on its sail, and he and Sebastian and Ana were boarding the ships along with other churchmen. For the past year, nearly every day, he told the judge, he had been explaining to Ana that she and Sebastian were meant to marry and save Christianity. Once Gabriel de Espinosa providentially arrived in town, Fray Miguel saw the Virgin Mary pointing her finger at Espinosa, indicating he was Sebastian. Therefore, the judge concluded in his report, "Her Excellency believed him, because of the credit and esteem in which she held Fray Miguel, as if an angel were talking to her." Epic literature typically includes a scene in which the hero is prophetically instructed as to his destiny. This was Ana's scene.

As if it were not enough for this young woman, whose memory of the outside world must have been dim, to believe that God and the saints were lined up in agreement that she must marry her miraculously revived cousin, Fray Miguel sought human assistance as well. Several years ago, Ana told the judges, travelers alleging to be former soldiers and prisoners in Morocco were invited to the convent by Fray Miguel to assure her the king was alive.[20] Fray Agustín de los Angeles, the nuns' confessor, who was Portuguese and had only recently been summoned to the convent by Fray Miguel, told the judges that Fray Miguel instructed him "that if doña Ana should ask him if there was belief in Portugal that the king was alive, he should say yes, but the next day when she continued asking him, he replied that he believed it was madness to think he was alive." The king, reviewing this testimony, remarked that the efforts Fray Miguel had made "to further this invention" by enlisting the aid of other clerics "clearly show his malice."[21]

So Ana nourished a conviction that Sebastian was alive, though we do not know when she first acquired that idea. Miracles often were preceded by long periods of contemplation and prayer, she knew. Her fixed belief might somehow be mirrored by her cousin's long journey through the desert, both ultimately being rewarded. The prospect of being allowed to protect this patient, penitent, wounded relative must have been seen by her as a gift. In November 1594, by then under house arrest, she wrote two letters to her uncle explaining her state of mind in the previous months. "Having learned and been given evidence that King Sebastian my cousin was not dead, and believing that he was traveling about on a pilgrimage, I was moved by pity to pray to God that He show me if this were true or false, and at that time the man named Gabriel de Espinosa came to this town and he revealed himself to Fray Miguel and to me as King Sebastian himself, and he gave good reasons and many different proofs [*señales*], and he persuaded me to believe him," she wrote.[22] In her other letter, she recounted how she had asked Espinosa for an explanation for his long absence. He, no doubt having been brought up to date on Fray Miguel's visions, said he had made a vow as he stood before the holy sepulcher. He could not reveal himself earlier, he explained, which made perfect sense to someone schooled in the practice of holy vows. "He spoke to me with so much enthusiasm for serving Your Majesty," she wrote, "and so lacking in desire to take even one inch of land from your crown, and that was the hook with which he caught me, along with my seeing that he was your beloved nephew and knowing that the day he spoke the truth, he would bring Your Majesty much happiness." She also saw his mother in his face, she said, remembering how good Juana of Austria had been to Ana's father, don Juan of Austria (unlike the king himself). She had doubts, she admitted to her uncle; many times after their visits she would go over their conversations in her head, weighing what he had said. But most of all, she hoped he would keep his promise to bring her her long-lost brother. That was the real hook, guaranteed to snare someone who never had a family. A long-lost cousin was good; a long-lost brother was even better.[23]

Even if the Virgin Mary did not point her finger at Espinosa, his arrival was a godsend for Fray Miguel, assuming it was not arranged. One of the points on which Espinosa and the vicar differed was how they met; Espinosa said it was in Portugal during the Spanish assault on Lisbon, which Fray Miguel denied. The king thought the contradiction important; Juan de Llano did not.[24] Espinosa, always more credible than his accomplice, told the judges in February that he arrived in Madrigal from Nava in June 1594 only because he wanted to set up a pastry shop. The convent ordered pastries, and he went there to collect the money, which is how Fray Miguel saw him, and he called him up to his rooms for a chat.[25] Soon after, he introduced himself to Ana as a former soldier under her father's command and gave her the cross encrusted with relics. Whether they talked about the pastry business, as Espinosa told Santillán, or about the reconquest of Jerusalem, the friendship between Ana and Espinosa grew over the summer. Judging by subsequent testimony, there was no one in town or in the convent unaware of their relationship and its collateral activities. Later on, the nun Inés de Cangas testified that "the main door of the convent was always open, day and night, upon Fray Miguel's orders, and doctors and friars visited in doña Ana's rooms among the nuns with great scandal and indecency, and the nuns were sorrowful but dared not say anything because the said Fray Miguel was their prelate."[26]

The Augustinian provincial, Gabriel de Goldaraz, who quickly would become the judges' chief enemy, was well aware of the chatter. Already on September 17, before the arrests, he wrote to Fray Miguel, first expressing annoyance at the presence of the new Portuguese confessor, Agustín de los Angeles, and then, more importantly, warning him that he had heard "that a baker in this town comes and goes in [the convent] and receives many favors from Her Excellency and yourself, and in the town and in both monasteries [for men and for women] they do not speak well of this." He asked Fray Miguel to ask Ana on his behalf "to moderate her favors to this man and do so in such a way that there is no gossip (*hablillas*)."[27] Goldaraz's wish would not come true. The following month,

Espinosa got sidetracked in the company of non-royals in Valladolid and was arrested. He told Santillán that if he were accused of theft, he would obtain a letter from Ana certifying that the jewels in his possession were hers, and with that, Santillán told the king, "I took him to jail, because I was certain there was something mysterious about this man."[28] While Espinosa was in jail, his courier, the innkeeper Gabriel Rodríguez, was nabbed carrying the letters from Ana and Fray Miguel. Reading Ana's two long letters, whose syntax and handwriting is largely impenetrable, Santillán realized, quite disturbed, that she believed Espinosa was somebody very important.[29] Fray Miguel directly addressed Espinosa as "Your Majesty." The *hablillas* had only just begun.

Ana ached without Espinosa, she wrote in what Santillán referred to as the first letter, and she reminded him of their sacred promise to each other. "I am yours, *señor,* and the vow that I gave you I will honor as I do that of baptism, through life and death." She reported that she had been playing with *la niña,* whom she later refers to as *mi hija*, who had a nanny (*ama*), and she had ordered some clothes for her in Valladolid. She also wrote that the permission (*la facultad*) had not yet arrived because it had to be approved by a bishop or an inquisitor, and she referred fondly to a certain Francisco, whom Espinosa was about to see. The second letter, which indicated she had received news from him, is addressed to "my king, my lord." In it, she spoke of the eternal length of her days spent without him. She referred to "your people," to "my brother," and again reported on the lovely little girl who now called her "mother." "You are my life, *mi señor*, see how I obey you in writing tenderly, as you ordered." She appeared to have made plans for a journey to an inn in a nearby town and was coordinating with servants and sending multiple messages in various directions. Most damning was that she told him, "I want to be a woman" (*quiero hacer oficio de mujer*). Santillán believed the handwriting was deliberately awkward to make it less comprehensible (perhaps the syntax was, too), and she suggested as much in her second letter, saying she was a handwriting "apprentice" and worrying that Espinosa might not be able to read it.

Santillán immediately informed the king that his niece possibly had given birth to a child and was promised in marriage to someone who apparently was royalty. Based on the content of the intercepted letters, Santillán began rounding up people for questioning and sending agents out to all the many places throughout the peninsula mentioned in the letters. The letters and subsequent testimony, much of it false or based on delusions, suggested that Espinosa was going to Burgos or France or both to meet with important people and then bring Francisco to Ana. For some reason, perhaps because he had friends there, he lingered in Valladolid. Maybe he intended to continue the journey as planned, maybe not.

Obstruction of Justice

A few days later, on October 14, quickly armed with a personal judicial commission from the king, Santillán went to Madrigal and got to work. He was convinced that friars and nuns were at the root of the problem, as they generally were: "Never in the history of the world was there a great evil or serious crime in which a religious was not involved," he would say a few months down the road.[30] He arrived in the late afternoon, he told the king, and went directly to the convent. "Fearful that if [Ana] had advance warning she might hide papers, I went in saying I had to speak with her on Your Majesty's orders, and that I particularly wanted to see some windows in her room that open onto the street. I looked for the papers, and though I found many letters, I found none with this year's date, nor last year's. Instead, I found empty drawers, and I ordered her detained in her rooms with four nuns standing guard." She was not to write or receive any letters or messages.[31] Fray Miguel, too, had cleaned out his desk. Somehow the inhabitants of the convent had received word of Espinosa's arrest, as we already saw from their detailed knowledge of the jewels he was carrying. Santillán ordered the arrest of around eight individuals named in the letters and held them in various houses in the town, and he also ordered the transfer of Espinosa from Valladolid to Medina del Campo.

Santillán's forced entry into the religious houses immediately sent Goldaraz into action. On October 17, assisted by Fray Agustín Antolinez, Goldaraz staged his preemptive strike with the marathon interrogation of all the friars and nuns to establish what they knew about Espinosa, his relationship with Ana and Fray Miguel, and the little girl.[32] Content aside, the fact that the hearing took place at all is indicative of the divide between religious and secular authorities and within the Augustinian order. Sixteenth-century Spain was a deeply litigious place with many overlapping jurisdictions (territorial, seigneurial, ecclesiastical, municipal, inquisitorial, and royal), so it is not surprising that there were attempts from the start to halt such a scandalous case or grab jurisdiction away from other parties. Every judge and jurist who intervened in the case—aside from Santillán and Llano, there were two others from the royal chancery court, along with Goldaraz, who acted as such—had nasty things to say about the rest. As a royal aide put it, "These judges in Madrigal are raising quite a ruckus."[33] After Santillán rifled through Ana's papers, or what was left of them, Goldaraz immediately instructed the nuns and the prioress to bar the judge from entering the convent again.[34] Two days later, the king himself ordered Goldarez to quit obstructing justice and allow Fray Miguel (quickly imprisoned in the Mota fortress in Medina) and all the other religious inhabitants to answer Santillán's questions. The king also summoned Goldaraz and Antolinez to Madrid to meet with him, an encounter we know nothing about.[35] Two weeks later, there was word from one of the chancery judges that Goldaraz, despite the royal scolding, had managed to remove the guards from Ana's rooms.[36] It was then, fed up with this game of cat and mouse, that the king sent Juan Llano de Valdés, a canon and general commissioner of the Inquisition, who arrived on November 15 with full powers not only to examine the religious witnesses but to look into the behavior of Goldaraz himself.

Before Llano's arrival, Santillán had the benefit of the opinion of one of the most prominent religious figures of the era, Father José de Acosta, who just happened to be passing through Madrigal in late October.[37] Acosta, a Jesuit, was a native of Medina del Campo and author of the great *Natural and Moral History of the Indies* (1590). Remarkably, he spoke with Espinosa in prison, after which he advised Santillán to go hard on him, "using more rigorous methods than pen and ink." But for access to the convent and its inhabitants, he would need the nuncio's permission, Acosta told him. The papal envoy had been informed of the Madrigal scandal almost immediately; as we saw earlier, he wrote to Rome about the arrest, the jewels, and the gossip.[38] By mid-November, both the apostolic and civil judges had the requisite papal permission to question whomever they wanted wherever they wanted and to remove whatever they wanted from the convent. The nuncio also warned Goldaraz to cooperate.

On December 1, "having understood that [Goldaraz] . . . wanted and attempted through various means and for his own ends to hide the truth regarding this matter," Llano conducted a hearing to get at the bottom of his attitude.[39] Though they were both men of the cloth, there was no love lost between them, probably not untypical of the relationship between authorities of the church and the orders, the former often unable to impose their will over the closed world of the latter. Testimony at the hearing and information from Goldaraz's enemies revealed that he had told just about everyone in the Augustinian monastery in Medina del Campo that he was going to do everything he could to stop Llano. Witnesses also complained he was far too close to Ana and had sent her presents from Navarre. Earlier we looked at this misbehavior as it related to gift-giving; even more intriguing was the fact that Goldaraz was a native of and had worked in Navarre, a datum with a possible whiff of sedition. At the time of the investigation, France was immersed in the so-called Wars of Religion, in which Philip II backed the Catholic League, led by the House of Guise, with an eye to eventually putting his daughter Isabel Clara Eugenia on the French throne. His Bourbon enemy was the erstwhile Protestant, Henry IV, who in January 1595 declared war on Spain. (The eventual peace in 1598 would put an end to Portugal's hope for French aid.) For years, Navarre, especially Henry's homeland of Béarn, a Protestant stronghold, was a contested area between the two European powers. An impressive number of characters in the Madrigal conspiracy had ties to either side of the border region: Espinosa had been in Pamplona and in theory was on his way there when he was arrested; Ana's brother was supposedly there; Bernardo del Río had come from France; Miguel de Piedrola, as it happens, was born in Navarre; both Antonio Pérez and don António, prior of Crato, were known to have met there, the obvious place for any political exile to land; the prior of the Augustinian monastery in Medina, Fray Juan de Camargo, was from Navarre (and was arrested in early December); and so, too, was Camargo's good friend Goldaraz.

Chief among Goldaraz's accusers was Fray Juan de Benavente, who arrived in town for Quiroga's funeral and for some reason stayed, and whose hatred was such that one suspects, as Santillán did, a long backstory.[40] Nonetheless, the story he told in an eight-page document, referred to as his *escrúpulos*, written in tiny script and massively underlined by its readers, makes for provocative reading. Years earlier, Goldaraz had been posted in Pamplona but was expelled by the viceroy, the marquis de Almazán, Francisco Hurtado de Mendoza y Fajardo (for whom Gregorio González and Gabriel de Espinosa later cooked dinner in Ocaña). Goldaraz refused to leave; he was imprisoned, and there was a big uproar. This much is true. But Benavente said he heard from reliable sources that while there, Goldaraz once left Pamplona and traveled to the Pyrenees to meet with Vandoma, the name by which Henry IV was known to Spaniards who would recognize him only as duke of Vendôme. "This is serious," reads a marginal note that appears to be Santillán's, and he was right, as it would amount to an act of treason. Benavente said he would be very surprised if Vandoma did not have a hand in the Madrigal affair. Add this to the known fact that it was Goldaraz who had pushed for Fray Miguel's appointment at the convent, and you have a problem. Goldaraz's main allies, as we have seen, were Antonio de Sosa, probably the author of the anonymous letters, and Diego de Zúñiga, who was preaching in Toledo that Sebastian was not dead, so the provincial was not in a strong position. Benavente said the general of the order had told him he would not support Goldaraz for a second term as provincial (he had been elected in 1592), citing the many complaints he had received, and, indeed he was not reelected. Llano dismissed him during the second week of December.

Ana's Story

Before he lost his job, however, Goldaraz had his day with the nuns and friars.[41] First, he wanted to determine how Santillán got into the convent to begin with. Nuestra Señora de Gracia used to have a gatehouse at the entrance to the outer courtyard staffed by women who oversaw the wheel device (*torno*) embedded in the outer wall through which objects could be passed back and forth to the outside world with no visibility. (Some convents still use them; Nuestra Señora de Gracia does not.) Convents had strict rules about who could open doors, sometimes requiring two or three keys to be operated simultaneously. Nonetheless, Santillán obviously broke those barriers. The prioress, the first of the women to testify, said she had been sick in bed the whole time and could not say who opened the doors on Saturday and Sunday, a nice job of stopping that particular line of questioning. Most of the two days was devoted to the nuns' and friars' opinions of Espinosa's identity, which we saw earlier, and speculation regarding Ana's brother and the *niña,* which we will come to. There was near unanimity that Fray Miguel and Espinosa were very close and saw each other daily and that Ana treated the baker with great respect, leading the witnesses to believe he was of noble birth. Several noted that Fray Miguel would defer to Espinosa when entering doorways, and some said Ana had offered him her chair, which would mean one of them was on the wrong side of the grille.

Goldaraz included Ana in this line-up, the first glimpse we have of her and her perspective. Her conversations with Espinosa, she said, came about because he said he could cure her hurt hand and her pockmarks, though how he knew she had these ailments is unclear. The prescription for the cure was among her papers, if Santillán had not made off with it, she said crisply. Espinosa also instructed Luisa del Grado on how to cure a niece of hers by applying a potion based on ground barley, though they had not yet tried it out. Four months is a long time, Ana noted, so she could not remember everything that had transpired since Espinosa arrived. But she did remember that one day she eavesdropped as Espinosa spoke with Luisa of his travels and adventures. He described an age of crusades to which she was linked by blood. He had been to the Holy Land, he had fought under the command of her father in Granada, where he himself had led companies of troops, he had been as far as Angola, and he had battled don António in Portugal. At this point, surely already aware that she was in delicate territory, Ana made clear to Goldaraz that when speaking of the pretender, Espinosa was disapproving, saying that by chance he knew António's relatives in Oporto, one of whom had a lame hand, and Espinosa "thought badly of them because they did not wish to surrender to His Majesty." She believed the baker was "an honorable hidalgo, based on the years he said he had spent in the war, and a more estimable person than indicated by his dress, which she knew by the way he spoke, and he said he was disguised in this occupation [as a baker] because of a misfortune that had befallen him." Did he ever speak to her about Sebastian? the provincial asked. Yes, it seemed to Ana that he once said he had fought with him in the battle of Africa, she replied. On the second day of testimony, the provincial asked her about the linens she had sent to Espinosa's house, which she insisted were for the little girl and not for an alleged guest (don António?) who, Goldaraz had heard, spoke with her at the grille. This was slander, Ana said. Goldaraz also asked about an errand on which she had sent her servant Blas Nieto (brother of Luisa del Grado and María Nieto) to Madrid, where he was supposed to obtain funds drawn on an account of hers as well as funds taken from her paternal grandmother's allowance. He also was supposed to buy shirts, trousers, stockings, and garters, which she planned to give to her brother for All Saints Day or Christmas. Santillán had seized the cash and the clothing, she said.[42]

The point of this early testimony most likely was to establish Ana's innocence. Goldaraz wanted to make clear that Ana dealt with a lowly creature like Espinosa only because of the little girl who for some reason was in his care. In case there was any doubt of Ana's virtue, the last question was a piece of performance art: Goldaraz asked her if Espinosa had ever said anything disrespectful to her about Philip II. Ana replied

> that if the provincial father were not a prelate and her Father, she would be very offended at a question like this, because she is not a woman who would consent to such insolence by anyone in her presence, because everyone knows how devoted she is to His Majesty and how she commends his life and prosperity to God, and if her father gave his life for His Majesty's service, she can do the same, and His Majesty knows that to the extent she can, she has left her pleasure and her will in his hands and renounced herself to them, and though this matter has been so unpleasant for Her Excellency because of the exorbitance with which Judge Santillán has treated her, no one has heard her utter a single word of complaint or anger about his ministers, who have proceeded with little justice or right.[43]

Santillán himself obtained access to Ana soon after this, overcoming Goldaraz's impediments and spending two full days with her. The first session lasted ten hours, during which she refused food. In the course of the interrogation, she said she wanted to see the two letters she wrote to Espinosa to make sure they were hers, and she reached through the grate that separated them (which would not have met Hernando de Talavera's standards) to take the letters back from him and then began ripping them. Santillán managed to snatch them back and immediately summoned a notary to record the incident. Ana said there was no need for that; she would willingly confess to the destruction of evidence, still visible today. "I was doubting whether to send you the original confession," Santillán wrote the king afterward, "given the dangers of the road," but he decided to give the long document to a notary he knew well, Juan Lopes de Vitoria, to take to Madrid. Notaries recorded everything, making testimony real, but Santillán trusted no one. As for the obstinacy of the Augustinians, which had delayed his access to Ana, he told the king, "Truly, sire, I am filled with sadness to see the world in such a state, where instead of religion and Christian sincerity there is only deep corruption, and we find nothing but schemes and conspiracies that conceal truth and obstruct justice."[44]

Nearly all the inquiries into Ana's and the other nuns' knowledge and actions took place during six weeks, from mid-October to early December, by which time the judges, though still with many loose ends, knew enough. After Llano arrived, he and Santillán went on a hunt for more evidence in the convent and found indications that papers had been burned in the fireplace where the friars' food was cooked.[45] (Luisa del Grado later confessed that Ana had "burned lots of papers in her fireplace and in the convent patio.") That same day, the two judges met again with Ana, which Santillán found instructive. "With people like this, who cannot be obliged by more rigorous methods to tell the truth, one must find a way of tormenting their understanding, using such strong reasoning that they are obliged and must tell the truth," he said, using the word *tormento* as an equivalent of what today we would call torture. "She almost confessed everything, because she confessed the letters were hers," he noted. But her statements were not written down "because Doctor Llano thought it was too late or he had some other reasons," Santillán told the king, annoyed, as usual, with the competition. "And the next day I found that doña Ana was completely changed, and this is because she has someone advising her," he wrote, referring to Goldaraz, who Santillán believed was not only obstructing justice but skimming Ana's royal allowance.[46]

In their conversations as he recounted them to the king, Santillán—who at this point leaned toward thinking Espinosa was don António—asked Ana why Sebastian would want to remain incognito.[47] For the shame he suffered on account of the disastrous battle, she replied. Well, he said, "the matter is a bit past shame at this point, given that he's a prisoner and the state he's in, so this might be a good moment to declare who he is,' to which she replied [he continued writing], [that] he was afraid someone would kill him, and then she said to me, 'Find out what you can and then you can cease all your investigations.'" She also surprised him by saying "that being that the prisoner is her cousin, and she is not a nun, no one should be shocked at their relationship and close friendship. I said, 'What do you mean you're not a nun?' And she replied [that] she had been forced to profess, she had been threatened and frightened, and she had said as much to many of the nuns, and she would provide all the necessary details." Here Santillán scored a point; how did her statement now jibe with her insistence that he, as a secular judge, had no authority over her, a nun? Now you're not a nun? "To this she replied that she had been advised to say that for the time being as a defense tactic, and similar points show she remembers well the provincial's lessons."[48]

On November 18, when Ana met with Santillán to inform him in writing that she did not accept his authority, she also said some very interesting things about the town of Madrigal and the passage of information through the permeable convent walls. She knew, she told him, that he had interviewed many witnesses in the town whom she described as suspicious characters, and she asked that their names be recorded as "declared enemies" of hers and of Fray Miguel. Asked to elaborate, she said her enemies spoke badly of her and her affairs and had requested an inquiry into the activities of certain town councilmen, whereupon she and "the whole town" wrote to the president of the Council of Castile telling him not to send an investigator, and indeed only a minor official was sent, for which reason these men were her enemies. To my regret, I know nothing more of the cloistered nun's surprising involvement in local politics.[49]

In another of her written protests over procedure, Ana again said she refused to answer Santillán's questions because he had no authority over her "and because God gave us the freedom to not incriminate ourselves when there is insufficient evidence." If she had hidden information from the king, "whom I hold in place of a father, with none other alive," it was out of fear that she should have spoken to him earlier. One omission had led to the next. But now, she said (surely because she knew that Llano, who had arrived on November 16, did have jurisdiction over her), "I state and confess and declare that the said prisoner is King Sebastian, for which I have much evidence, which I will describe to His Majesty in a sealed letter."[50] She also told Llano she wanted to address the king directly, and she read to him from the draft she had begun. "It appeared to me that there was little or nothing of substance" in the letter, Llano told the king, "and I told her that if she wanted to tell the truth she should just do it, as the greatness of Your Majesty does not allow you to suffer such a muddled letter."[51] But the two judges, who, despite their harsh behavior, were not unsympathetic to her plight, agreed to let her finish writing the letters she had begun both to the king and to Espinosa, with the king's permission, to see what she would say. Of course, the letter to Espinosa would not be delivered; that would, the king remarked, be an "indecency."[52]

To Espinosa, Ana wrote quite beautifully: "The leaves on the trees cannot move without the will of God, and we must believe, sire, that He who so cares for all creatures must take particular care with those most important, and thus I believe that all that has occurred in this matter is a special providence, though the path be bitter." Philip II, she told Espinosa, was eager to know if the prisoner really was his nephew, and to that end he had sent Doctor Llano, to whom Ana had told the truth, thus putting Espinosa's life and her honor at risk.

> Therefore I beg you in God's name to tell His Majesty and these gentlemen, his ministers, that you are the said King Sebastian, as you told me and Fray Miguel, because you have no other choice. . . . Sire, I find myself with

these tribulations and disgrace for having spoken with you and for having wished to serve you as my cousin, whom I so esteem. The world, ignorant of who you are, slanders me, and what I beg of you is only just. . . . You can tell the truth to [Llano], who wishes this to end well and to tell His Majesty who you are, and in allowing me to [write this letter], it is clear that neither His Majesty nor his ministers will be unhappy if they find you are his nephew.[53]

She gave this letter to Llano, and a similar one to Santillán, in which she again told the prisoner how happy Philip II would be when he discovered that his beloved nephew was still alive. "You owe this to my honor," she told him, begging him to tell the judges who he was. But, of course, there was no reply.

More than a month after the arrests, with no Fray Miguel and no Espinosa, Ana appeared to suspect the dreadful truth. This was not the ending she had imagined. On November 19, she begged the king for mercy. "I erred out of ignorance," she wrote.

> Out of ignorance I did not tell Your Majesty, first because I was not certain he was king, and second because I was waiting to hear about my brother, and I did not want to confess everything and risk Your Majesty's condemnation for not having told you earlier. It was ignorance, not malice, to not know my obligation, for I entered this place when I was six and I know nothing of the world except the bitterness it holds for me. This man deceived me, the devil led him here to disturb my honor and destroy me, removing me from Your Majesty's grace. I humbly beg, for the sake of the crucified Jesus Christ, that you have compassion for me and see that this honor, which Your Majesty's ministers have shred to pieces, is that of a niece, daughter of that ill-fated father. My error was that I was simple, for which this punishment is excessive. Do what you will with this man, be he good or bad, but do not allow this unfortunate woman, this house, and so many innocent prisoners to pay the price.[54]

Four days later she wrote again to the king, this time giving the letter to Santillán. Again she described how Espinosa had convinced her he was

King Sebastian and promised to reunite her with her brother. "Sire, you know well that since I was born I have not recognized any other father than Your Majesty, and as such I have respected and loved you, resigning my wishes to those of Your Majesty," she wrote, adding that someone of her status should not have to deal with these judges, courteous though they may be. Santillán did not use a notary, she said (not quite true), but Llano did (and was more careless), "and so many things have spilled out that if God did not grant me patience, these matters would have put an end to my life." Vile things were being said about her. Her honor and that of the convent were in grave danger, she insisted, and she begged him to put a stop to the interrogations.[55]

What Barbara Blomberg Knew

Of the "innocent prisoners" Ana referred to, few were as pathetic as her servant Juan de Roderos. He was twenty-two and had been working for Ana and Fray Miguel since he was sixteen, he told Santillán when he was interviewed in Medina del Campo in December.[56] He had assumed Espinosa must be someone important, he said, but he didn't know who. He knew a great many other things, though, some through direct observation and some through Luisa del Grado and her sister María Nieto. Roderos placed Espinosa with Ana in the *grada* from eight until ten in the evening on at least two occasions, when he believed they were talking about Ana's brother, Francisco. Espinosa told him he (Espinosa) was going to Burgos and then to Navarre and France to meet with some colleagues and would return by All Saints Day with Francisco and another man who also was very important. And Roderos heard Fray Miguel say that Espinosa appeared to be King Sebastian. Santillán was not very happy with Roderos's first statement: "He said nothing of substance, and it would be a good idea to give him a very good round of torture (*un muy buen tormento*) so that he tells the truth," he commented. Indeed he did just that, and Roderos testified again in January, this time more talkative. He confirmed Ana's and Espinosa's close friendship, though he did not know if the baker had ever been in her rooms. Nor was he sure if Fray Miguel had copies of the convent keys, but he did know that a local locksmith, Juan de Estudillo, visited Fray Miguel several times and made keys for him. (Llano later asked Fray Miguel about these "false keys.")[57] He knew that a local courier, Miguel Pérez, who was Portuguese, carried many messages from Ana and Fray Miguel to Madrid addressed to a certain Fray Antonio de Santa Maria, yet another Portuguese Augustinian once imprisoned for his support of don António. As soon as Fray Miguel learned of Espinosa's arrest in Valladolid, Roderos told Santillán, he immediately ordered Roderos to bring him the portable wooden desk where Espinosa kept his papers, and he "ripped and burned many papers, and he gave many of them to a boy who works in the said monastery named Sebastianillo, who took them to the friars' fireplace to burn."[58]

Fray Miguel had told Roderos, the servant went on, that King Sebastian could not reveal himself until Philip II died, and furthermore that Espinosa would return from his journey to France with colleagues, including "a man who had taken possession of the Kingdom of England," wording that also appeared in Fray Miguel's statements. This group, including Ana's brother, would arrive at night so as not to be seen, and they would leave their horses in the nearby village of Blasco Nuño. In the company of Fray Miguel and Luisa del Grado, Roderos witnessed Ana's and Espinosa's tearful farewell when the latter left for Valladolid to commence this journey. As they went together to Valladolid (for some reason, Roderos accompanied him), Espinosa told Roderos that he owed so much to Fray Miguel that he might even appoint him pope. "He did not go into more detail on this point or give the reason for his debt other than the good works he had done for him in [Madrigal]," Santillán wrote.[59] It was also on this trip from Madrigal to Valladolid that the baker supposedly began singing a *romance* about the battle of Alcazarquivir; the royal chronicler Luis Cabrera de Córdoba says Roderos said that when Espinosa "got to the part about the army's defeat and that no one knew King Sebastian's fate, he gave deep sighs, over and over." The Escorial version of the *Historia* also includes this episode, though the case file does not.[60]

Roderos came to the attention of the judges after Ana, somehow having learned of Espinosa's arrest, immediately sent her servant away to the home of Barbara Blomberg, her grandmother, who lived in Colindres, near the north coast of Spain in the present-day province of Santander.

For Ana had a grandmother. When Blomberg was around twenty, she had a brief affair with Charles V when the emperor was in Regensburg (Bavaria), and in 1547 she gave birth to the future don Juan of Austria. The baby, named Jerónimo, was given to one of the emperor's aides, Luis Quijada, and his wife, Magdalena de Ulloa (who later took Ana). They, in turn, at the emperor's request, handed the child to another couple, a retired court musician named Francisco Massy and his wife, who lived in Leganés, outside Madrid. For the first seven years of his life, don Juan of Austria lived like a village boy. In 1554, when Sebastian's mother, Juana, was summoned back to Spain to be regent, Juan was sent back to Quijada and Ulloa's home in Valladolid, near Juana's court, for a more suitable education. He was in the presence of his father just once. Charles V died in 1558 and did not mention this son in his will, though he did, on his dying day, order an aide to send six hundred ducats to Blomberg.[61] He left a sealed letter for Philip II telling him he had a half-brother named Jerónimo. The brothers met in 1559, and the new king made public the identity of his adolescent brother, whom he renamed and gave the title of Excellency—just as Ana received a new identity and title when don Juan died.[62] Blomberg, by then widowed and living in present-day Belgium, also received a new, enhanced status that included servants, a pension, and the title of Madama Madre de don Juan de Austria. But the subsequent disapproving correspondence to Philip II from the duke of Alba, then the governor of the Spanish Netherlands, who was assigned to keep an eye on her, indicates she did not behave in a manner appropriate to a royal mother.[63] By 1570, the king was keen to place the merry widow in a convent, a plan he said don Juan agreed to, but Alba told him that was harder than it seemed. Philip wrote in November 1571 that the move would have to be effected with subterfuge. In 1573 Blomberg was still throwing her money around, and the duke, busy putting down the Dutch rebellion, reported that no honest woman would cross her threshold. For some reason, four more years transpired until the scheming half-brothers and the duke finally lured her south by telling her that Margaret of Parma wished to see her. In Genoa, she changed ships, thinking she was going to Abruzzo, and she ended up on the northern Spanish coast.

Like her granddaughter, she was placed in a convent. Hers was San

Cebrián de Mazote, near Valladolid—and near Magdalena de Ulloa, who, according to Blomberg, kept her on very short purse strings. Unhappy there, soon she moved north to Colindres, where Philip II gave her the use of the home of don Juan's former secretary, Juan de Escobedo (murdered in March 1578) and the secretarial services of Escobedo's son.[64] During the following decade, Blomberg ceaselessly complained of her dire poverty, saying she was condemned to spend all her meager money on medicine and on paying off the debts of her less famous son (by her deceased husband), Conrad Piramo, also known as Pyramus. Don Juan paid for his half-brother to study for the church, not wanting him anywhere near the court or the army, but Conrad spent years lobbying for a better position. (Even on his deathbed, don Juan referred to this problem, which entailed locking Conrad up in a castle.) In 1591, unhappy and sick in Colindres, Blomberg begged the king to be allowed to leave the damp mountain air and return south to Madrigal, where it was dry and hot, and she could live near her granddaughter, a request which Ana also relayed to the palace. On November 15, a memorandum recorded that a conversation about the matter had taken place in El Escorial "and it appeared that it was not appropriate for doña Ana's peace of mind nor her profession that her grandmother visit her."[65] Nor did the king seem to want to allow Blomberg to move. The visit between Ana and her paternal grandmother never took place, though Ana had some sort of financial relationship with her. Blomberg died in December 1597. Unlike Ana's more modest grandmother Catalina, who wrote in her will, "I have great love and goodwill for doña Ana de Mendoza, my granddaughter, daughter of doña María de Mendoza, my daughter" and who left the little girl a preferential share of her estate (which Ana may never have seen), Blomberg did not mention Ana in her will.[66]

That oversight was undoubtedly the result of the events of 1594. As the first arrests were made in October, Ana sent Roderos off to Colindres with a note asking her grandmother to shelter the servant until further notice.[67] Ana's and Fray Miguel's intercepted letters to Espinosa both mentioned Blomberg: the vicar instructed the man he addressed as Your Majesty to return with the group of men disguised as "Madama's servants, and say they were carrying a message from her to [Ana], and I will contact Mazateve,

Madama's steward."[68] (In fact, Juan de Mazateve probably left Blomberg's service in 1579, showing that Fray Miguel may have been fifteen years out of date.) In her letter, Ana asked Espinosa not to visit Blomberg when he was in the north; she was cross with her and would not do her the favor of writing, she said.[69] Blomberg may not have known about these schemes, or perhaps she did, but obviously she was disturbed at Roderos's unannounced arrival. As he was unable to offer a plausible explanation for being nearly three hundred kilometers from home (there was conflicting evidence whether he had ridden or walked), inquiries were made. In Santander, the nearest city, a churchman who was Blomberg's friend already knew of the events in Madrigal, which had taken place only ten days earlier. According to him, officials in Valladolid had arrested someone who said he was working for don António and who was in Madrigal to speak with Ana. This story traveled from Santander back to Blomberg, who put two and two together, and she immediately wrote to Junco de Posada, president of the royal chancery court in Valladolid.[70]

Roderos, as a result, was arrested and taken back to Medina del Campo, where he sat in prison until August, nearly a year later, when he was sentenced to serve four years on the galley ships. In between he was tortured at least twice, enduring twenty *vueltas*, or turns of the ropes or rack on which he had been placed.[71] He was innocent of the real conspiracy, Santillán admitted, but he knew about Ana's presents to Espinosa, he knew Espinosa's plans to "seat Fray Miguel on the throne of Saint Peter," and he had started off by denying he knew anything, never a wise move. "We tried to get information out of him and they pressured [*apretaron*, which also means to squeeze] him, and he is now maimed [*manco*] in both arms and thus useless for the galleys, and it would cost money to transport him and feed him, and thus I recommend that his sentence be reduced to banishment," Santillán wrote.[72] Nothing more is known of Juan de Roderos.

In early December, Llano spent two days listening to Ana once again. Asked to justify her early denials, she said she had sworn to the man she thought was her cousin that she would not reveal his secret, and she was bound to uphold that promise. The judge was convinced she had been a pawn in a wicked game, the exact point of which he was still trying to figure out. Espinosa might have been trying to "take advantage of doña Ana," he wrote the king, "but he would never dare try such a thing because of the quality and respect of the said doña Ana, nor would she allow it, given her authority and worth, and because she had the intention of changing her status"; that is, she planned to marry him.[73] He also might have been planning to steal her jewels, but the judge also rejected this option, given that Espinosa had had the opportunity to take more and turned them down. If Ana was innocent, which Llano thought she was, then the two men bore all the guilt. But Ana at this point still harbored the belief, or said she did (because really there was no alternative), that Espinosa was Sebastian. During the second day of her December testimony with Llano, according to the judge's summation, she said that "she had not promised to marry anyone; but Espinosa, whom she considers to be don Sebastian, her cousin, told her that once his pilgrimage was finished he would be happy [to marry her] with papal dispensation." She confirmed she had received letters from the prisoner but that they, along with her own writings about "her freedom and the way in which she professed, and some predictions of curious happenings" all went up in flames when she heard Santillán was on his way.[74]

There was one more long round of questioning in January, but by then the judges expected little from Ana, whose only goal was to reestablish her besmirched honor by reiterating why she had believed the two men's tales. "It never occurred to her to speak to the said Espinosa except in *la grada,* and she never did so," the summation states. "She believed he was King Sebastian her cousin because Fray Miguel, whom she believed because he was such a learned person, said he was. . . . Espinosa said he would marry her once his kingdom was returned to him, and she is insulted to think anyone could think otherwise, and God is witness to her conscience and time will bear her out."[75]

The Little Girl

Throughout the autumn, Philip II kept close track of all these conversations and testimony. He read the transcripts, filling the margins with observations and questions, trying to pick apart what his niece said. Llano "has given doña Ana more credit than is advisable," he observed at one point in December, pointing to apparent contradictions.[76] Few days went by without a letter or memorandum with suggestions, which meant the witnesses were questioned again and again and again. But once it became clear that Ana had been a victim of deceit, he lost interest in her. Not once did he write to her. One version of the *Historia de Gabriel de Espinosa* reproduces a letter from him to Santillán referring to "Ana of Jesus, who is said to be the daughter of our brother." Perhaps he was even willing to deny she was his niece.[77]

The king's real obsession, which would keep this case alive far past its logical expiration date, was *la niña.* When the case began, Philip II was sixty-seven years old. Since the 1580s, he frequently had been ill and incapacitated, mostly from gout, which at times was so bad he was unable to hold a pen. On March 7, 1594, his final testament was signed and witnessed, but he recovered; in May 1595 he again spent a full month at death's door, and he passed most of the rest of his life in the sixteenth-century equivalent of a wheelchair, though he continued signing documents right down to his last two weeks.[78] Though his thoughts may have turned to the afterlife and away from everyday matters—by the time of the Madrigal case, he relied more on aides—he also had to think about the future of the dynasty, which could not have been comforting. The king sired fifteen children, only three of whom were alive at this point. He had two beloved daughters: Isabel Clara Eugenia, who in 1599, when she was thirty-two, married archduke Albert; and Catalina Micaela, who in 1585 married Charles Emmanuel of Savoy. The Spanish heir was Prince Philip, who did not live up to his father's expectations of a ruler, physically or otherwise. The king had far more confidence in Albert, whom he raised, but Albert could not be king. In the lottery of life expectancy, Philip II could not count on much. The case of Sebastian showed what could happen when healthy, direct heirs were not in place.

The rules of dynastic succession and the odds against survival were what made phony relatives such a scourge for royal families. An Englishwoman, Anne Burnell, for example, claimed in 1587 that a witch in Norwell told her she (Anne) was Philip II's daughter and had the arms of England imprinted on her body. The Privy Council eventually studied the matter, and poor Anne Burnell was whipped in 1592.[79] The previous year, another alleged daughter showed up closer to home, in the very town of El Escorial. She talked two priests into getting her into the palace, promising she would pay them back generously after she was recognized. Once Philip II was alerted, he ordered a medical examination to find out if the woman was crazy; if she was, she should be sent to the insane asylum in Toledo, and if not, she should be whipped. It was the latter, and the king's real offspring had a good laugh.[80] But the prospect of relatives with claims to the throne generally was not a source of amusement. There were precedents in Spain and Portugal for bastards usurping the throne of brothers; both the Spanish Trastámara and the Portuguese Avis dynasties began with illegitimate rulers. It was too late for don Juan of Austria to usurp anyone, but Ana was his daughter, and now maybe she had a daughter. The rebellion of don António himself, after all, was based on a good claim of dynastic legitimacy. As Rafael Valladares has noted, António "may have been a bastard, but a small but precious amount of Avis blood was running through his veins."[81] In fact, António's extensive brood of children would continue bothering Philip during the last twenty years of the king's life. They deserve a brief detour.

We have met a couple of them already. When Sancho de Avila's troops were hounding António's forces in northern Portugal, they stumbled upon Luisa, and Juan de Silva visited another daughter, Filipa, in Segovia on his way to Madrigal. The best known sons were Cristóvão (who referred to himself as prince and later king of Portugal) and Manoel (future son-in-law of William, Prince of Orange, and the only one with heirs). The two sons spent the 1580s and 1590s fund-raising for their father; in 1588, don António sent Cristóvão to Morocco for three years as a guarantee for a loan from Ahmad.[82] In addition to these four children, there probably were six more, probably all in convents or monasteries. One historian says there was a son, Alfonso, who went into the navy, and another boy, Juan, who died in childhood. He also found two daughters at the monastery of Las Huelgas, in Burgos.[83]

In 1580, as Philip II began moving intransigent Portuguese and their relatives into Castile, Luisa and Filipa were transported from Santarém, where they must have been taken after being removed from their convents. (That same month, don António authorized allowances to both, so he was thinking of them even as he fled.[84]) Luisa was deposited in the convent of Santa Clara la Real, in Tordesillas. She made it clear as soon as she arrived that she did not want to be a nun. A year later, she was still there and still unhappy, and Philip was still insistent ("this is what is best for her").[85] After leaving Luisa in Tordesillas, the guards took Filipa (already a Cistercian nun) to nearby Valladolid, to Santa María la Real de las Huelgas. The king was very specific in his fussings over the sisters' finances and the manner in which they were to be addressed. They were to have no contact at all with anyone from Portugal. Filipa was still in Valladolid fourteen years later; indeed, Rodrigo de Santillán at first thought the nun involved with the baker was Filipa, not Ana, which in a way would have made more sense. "I understand that don António has a daughter in that monastery, and the people who work in the pastry shop are Portuguese, and my servants tell me that some Portuguese have come to my house asking after the prisoner," he told the king.[86] Filipa was not stable, the king said—not surprising under the circumstances. He recommended that the abbess in Valladolid be extra strict with her: she "should not consent to what Filipa wants but only to what is fitting, and [Filipa] must not have dealings with anyone from outside but rather should calm down and accept her vocation calmly."[87] Her life was a miserable one, whether by nature or by imposition. In 1590 she wrote Philip II from Valladolid, "Since the day Your Majesty ordered that I be placed in this monastery, my sorrow and affliction have been intolerable."[88] To her confessor, she signed her letter, "this unfortunate exile," and the abbess of Santa María la Real wrote that Filipa had very few belongings, was "in bad health and extremely delicate," and missed her sister.[89] In 1605, looking back on her tribulations, she said she had been transferred from Valladolid after the "La Coruña business," probably Drake's 1589 attack on Galicia, when another nun insulted don António and Filipa apparently punched her.[90] After that, she led a peripatetic religious existence, going from Valladolid to Segovia, to Avila, to Toledo, and back to Avila. Either she or Luisa may have sent a pair of gloves to Antonio Pérez in 1592, which he acknowledged to an intermediary by saluting the royal hand that made them.[91] As Filipa's life neared its end, she was still enclosed, a self-described martyr and exiled prisoner, still unhappy, deprived of the royal allowance she deserved, in bad health, always writing letters, always complaining about the damp and the loneliness, and perpetually mourning her father. It appears her last home was in Avila, from where she signed a letter "the disconsolate orphan, doña Filipa."[92]

Stray royals were potentially dangerous, no matter how remote the chances of their legitimacy or their claims. In the case of don António's children, there were a lot to keep track of. Before the annexation, he seems to have requested permission to marry. The request was denied, but, Juan de Silva said, "his children, and he has so many, could be given something, but as little as would be fair."[93] Like false kings, false children tended to appear. "It is odd how don António's progeny extend themselves to all the corners of the kingdom," Silva remarked in a letter whose title (written by a secretary) was "the count of Portalegre's opinion on the children of don António, real or false, who are being uncovered." In Silva's opinion, the king should immediately and secretly determine once and for all how many children the pretender really had. The real ones should be transported to Castile, and the fakes should be prohibited from ever claiming parentage.[94] The discovery that prompted this particular correspondence was a boy in Barcelos, in northern Portugal (an especially "bizarre" case in Silva's opinion), who was said to be António's son. Philip ordered that the boy be taken to Coria, in the present-day Spanish province of Cáceres, next to Portugal. In his instructions to the bishop of Coria, the king wrote, "Under no circumstances should this boy be referred to as don António's son, nor should anyone call him that. This matter must be disposed of in such a manner that no one mentions it, and no Portuguese must see or speak to him."[95] As late as 1598, Silva was still dealing with don António's alleged offspring, reminding Archduke Albert that a boy locked up in Saõ Gião (Sangian) castle, who might be another son, should be moved to Castile.[96]

Among the battery of questions Goldaraz asked the nuns and friars of Madrigal during his two-day interrogation was, "Do they know if doña Ana has written to the daughters of don António who are nuns in Segovia and Tordesillas or if she has had letters from them?" Yes, of course the nuns knew all about that. He probably asked the question because it gave him an opportunity to prove how much Ana of Austria loved her uncle. Ana de Espinosa (no relation to Gabriel) knew that Luisa and Filipa wished to communicate with Ana, but Ana was not interested. Augustina de Ulloa knew that Filipa, "said to be the daughter of don António," wrote to Ana, and Ana was angry with the messenger, saying she wanted no contact with someone who opposed His Majesty. Luisa del Grado and her sister María Nieto said Filipa used Ana de Tapia's brother as a messenger, and (again) Ana was angry and refused to receive him. Ana de Tapia clarified that a native of Madrigal currently living in Segovia named Melchor González gave her a letter from Filipa for Ana of Austria, which Ana refused, and Ana de Tapia then opened the letter and read it. Filipa had written six lines, very graciously, saying how much she wanted to know Ana. Then one day Ana of Austria asked Ana de Tapia's brother to tell Filipa to never write again because her father was an enemy of His Majesty.[97]

Even as the king's faculties waned, he remained acutely interested in anything that touched upon his royal authority, particularly in the wake of the Aragonese troubles. Thus the little girl in Ana's convent, the *niña* who arrived with the baker and for whom Ana bought presents, might prove as inconvenient as the little boy in Barcelos. Goldaraz's interviews with the nuns and friars revealed that many of them believed or had been told that the girl was a relative of Ana's and that through her, the convent would inherit a large sum of money.[98] The child's alleged paternity ranged widely through the Hapsburgs; the father was said to be Ana's brother, or archduke Albert, or Albert's brother Ernesto of Austria, or Pyramus, Ana's uncle. Most of Goldaraz's respondents thought the child was Ana's niece, a term which might have been used loosely, as *cousin* was. María Belón said Margarita de Toledo heard Ana tell Mencía Bravo in the confessional that Ana believed the girl was her niece. In his testimony, Fray Andrés de Santa Cruz probably nudged Philip II a bit closer to the grave with his observation that Fray Miguel had told him the child looked like Philip II "from the nose up." The *Historia de Gabriel de Espinosa* states that the little girl was so discerning she would eat only off a napkin, and that Ana thought the girl had an indefinable quality (a "*no sé qué*") of royal bearing.[99] The general assumption that the well-mannered little girl was of a good family helped the nuns believe that Espinosa must also be noble. Furthermore, the child's name was given as Clara Eugenia, an unlikely name for the offspring of a baker but well-chosen to torment the king, whose daughter had nearly the same name. "This name is one of the biggest reasons to make me think she is Ana's daughter. The prisoner [Espinosa] would not have come up with this name, not even to write it, and he should be asked about this," jotted the king on a memo in December.[100]

Espinosa brought the child with him, Llano reassured the king, and there was "not a shred of evidence" the baker had set foot in town before that.[101] (The Jesuit who wrote the pamphlet, of course, thought differently.) Why were the nuns so affectionate toward the child? the king asked again and again. Why did Ana love her so much? He was particularly adamant that Santillán measure one of the windows separating the nuns from their visitors, "for it would not be the first time I've heard of such a thing," referring to lovers squeezing through. (Franciscan ecclesiastics fifty years later specified the dimensions of the *torno* to make sure bodies could not pass through.)[102] It was clear to everyone but Philip II that the child was Espinosa's with Inés Cid, the "nanny" who accompanied him when he arrived in Madrigal. But from October until nine months later, the very day before Espinosa's execution, the king incessantly instructed his judges to make sure. Every single witness was asked, and then asked again, about the child's origins. "Try to find out who the girl's mother is, I'm still not satisfied," he added to a letter to Santillán as late as July 8, 1595.[103]

So Llano went back for one last round the third week in July and interrogated Ana's confidantes Luisa del Grado and María Nieto, along with Inés Cid, about the child. Luisa and María both told Llano that Ana loved the girl, playing with her and buying her clothes, because she thought she was the daughter of her cousin Sebastian. It was true the child called Ana "mother," Luisa admitted, but she called the other nuns the same, and probably Ana encouraged the practice to please her cousin. Both Luisa and María knew the little girl was born in Oporto, possibly to a noblewoman. Both denied, in nearly identical and very specific terms, that Ana was the child's mother. For ten years, Luisa said, "day and night, she has served doña Ana, and in that time she has cured many of her sicknesses, and she has seen her body, and if she had had any impediment of the sort referred to, she would have seen it and known it, and that is true for all the nuns who are with doña Ana, and therefore what the question suggests is impossible because they could not help but see it and know it in the monastery, where the nuns are always with her, and they saw her nude and dressed at all hours." María added that Clara Eugenia could not be Ana's daughter "because the said baker Espinosa had never been here before last summer."[104] Espinosa, meanwhile, even after he received the last rites, had to endure Santillán's questions about his daughter's birth, her godparents, and her midwife.[105] But Espinosa could tell Santillán nothing the judge did not already know, for the child's mother had told him everything.

The Torment of Inés Cid

The story of Inés Cid is one of the most difficult and brutal passages of this tale. She had no friends, having just arrived in town. Espinosa whiled away his hours with the nuns, taking the little girl to the convent as bait, so she must have spent most of her time alone. Thanks to Ana, Inés Cid had decent linens in the house, though they were meant for Clara Eugenia. She probably tended the bakery. When Fray Miguel wrote to Espinosa—the strange letter addressed to Your Majesty, though since the recipient knew who he was, we imagine the vicar meant for someone else to see the letter—he told Espinosa, "The nanny is well, and I met with her, and consoled her and encouraged her, and told her to let me know if she needed money, and if so I could sell four books I have. She said she had enough money for the time being but complained no one would sell her lard in town; an order was given, and now she's provided for. . . . My lady [Ana] wants with all her heart that the shop be closed and removed from the eyes of the town."[106] Ana wanted Inés Cid gone.

As soon as Espinosa was arrested, Inés Cid also was confined, and the little girl was given to the governor of La Mota fortress in Medina del Campo. Already on November 6, Santillán had suggested to the king that Inés Cid was the key. A memo from Cristóbal de Moura summarizing the judge's recent letters for the king stated that "if His Majesty so ordered, the prisoner [Espinosa] could be tortured, though he [Santillán] believes it would be better to start with the *ama*."[107] Two days later, the king wrote back, agreeing with Santillán that Inés Cid be questioned in Medina. "Inquire very carefully about the matter of the girl, for she must know everything," he said, "and if it were necessary to use torture you should do so *in caput alienum*, the same as with the principal delinquent and the other prisoners, except Fray Miguel, to whom you should do nothing without consulting me first."[108] Santillán questioned Inés Cid in December, but the session yielded "nothing of substance," according to the king.[109] Santillán was going to move on to the next level when he made a startling discovery: "I was about to torture the *ama*, but once her clothes were removed it was clear she was pregnant. . . . She is five months' pregnant and she says Espinosa is the father, and though I questioned and requestioned her, she said nothing conclusive."[110]

Inés Cid's pregnancy won her a respite of sorts. The following month, in late January, Santillán asked doctors to examine her because she had a fever, and they said that unless she were removed from her cold cell in the Medina public jail, she would never get well.[111] She probably gave birth in May; the *Historia de Gabriel de Espinosa* says the baby was a boy who looked just like the little girl, which should have put an end to speculation regarding Ana's involvement. But the king's obsession was such that the second child could not save Inés Cid. Around six weeks after she gave birth, the prisoner was "fine" and could be tortured, Santillán told the king.[112] On July 21 she again appeared before a judge, this time Llano, and described to him how she had wound up in Madrigal with a three-year-old. In her earlier testimony in autumn, she said she received the child when it was six months old, which nobody believed. She lied, she explained now, because Espinosa told her to, because they were both frightened they would be punished for living in sin. (Possibly Espinosa was already married; he certainly had children.[113]) Llano now told her three times, as specified by law, that she was being formally warned that if she did not tell the truth she would be tortured.

So she told her story, thanks to which we have a magnificent biography of a young, rootless woman.[114] She was the girl's mother, and Espinosa was the father, she confirmed. She was twenty-six years old and was born in Orense (Galicia), and she had met Espinosa in the town of

Allariz, near Orense, in October 1591. She got pregnant in the town of Monte Rey, in Galicia, while traveling with him. From there they went to Oporto, where she gave birth one morning around three years ago, on a Sunday or a holiday, in a house loaned to them by a soldier in the guards corps in that city, and she seemed to remember the soldier was named Domingo, but she could not remember his last name. Asked to recite the names of the people present at the birth, she said they were Dominga Pérez, who was married to Juan de Barros, a soldier in the company of Captain Pedro Bermúdez (governor of Bayona in the late 1580s; he fought against Drake); and María Rodríguez, who was married to Juan or Pedro Rodríguez, another soldier; and also Inés Rodríguez, the wife of a retired soldier who was missing an eye, whose name Inés Cid could not remember, but she did remember that he was from Bayona. The midwife was there, but Inés Cid could not remember her name either, but she was Portuguese, from Oporto, and she lived nearby; and the godparents were there, and they were Juan de Casares, a soldier, and the aforementioned Dominga Pérez. The baby was baptized in a church used by the guards corps, a bit down the hill, and it was called Our Lady of something, but Inés Cid could not remember what, nor could she remember the priest's name. (Espinosa's recollections of the birth were similar; the child's name was Clara Eugenia, he confirmed, and she was born three years ago this October in Oporto in a house near the guards post near his pastry shop. He could not remember the midwife's name or the names of the two soldiers who acted as godparents.)[115] After around eight days in Oporto, Inés and Espinosa moved on to Viana, still in Portugal, where Pedro Bermúdez took the company of guards, and they stayed there for around two months. Then they went to Salvatierra (Galicia), where Inés Cid stayed while Espinosa traveled in Castile to the cities of Zamora and Toro, after which he sent a message telling her to join him in Zamora. She did so, traveling on a cart driven by a man named Juan Alvarez while nursing the baby. She met up with Espinosa in Zamora, and after eight days they moved on to Toro, where they stayed for eight months in the home of Nicolás Lopez, a baker who lived on the square next to the main church. During that time, Espinosa went with Don Juan de Ulloa to the city of León.[116] Later, the couple moved to Nava, near Medina del Campo, where

Espinosa had a pastry shop, and from there they came to Madrigal. Later in the day, a second round of questioning took place, this time with Santillán. Same questions, same answers, with only slight variations.

But after reading this testimony and learning nothing of interest, Philip II was still not satisfied. On July 24 he wrote to Santillán: "Now that Inés Cid has given birth, the reason for not torturing her no longer exists, so if you think it would help determine whose child the girl is, you may do so."[117] So on July 30, Inés Cid was tortured.

The session took place in the home of Beatriz de Espinosa, who also hosted the interrogation of Pedro de Silva. Those present, other than Inés Cid and Santillán, included the notary, Juan López de Victoria, and two *pregoneros*, or town criers, Pedro de Segovia and Juan Sánchez, whom Santillán summoned from Valladolid to conduct the enhanced questioning.[118] First the judicial decree (*auto*) was read aloud. Inés Cid had been condemned some time ago to torture by water and ropes, but because she was pregnant, the sentence was suspended. Now, "in the service of His Majesty and the administration of justice," it was deemed appropriate to continue. The session itself began with an injunction, also read aloud and then signed by the notary. "The said Inés Cid was told once, twice, and three times, as required by law, to tell the truth of what she knows and is warned that if in the said *tormento* an eye should come out or a leg or arm break or if she should die, it is her fault and responsibility and not that of the said judge."

> Then they undressed her and put a diaper on her and tied her to two bars, passing a girth beneath her arms, and they began turning the *mancuerda* [a racklike device with ropes] once and up to fifteen times, pulling her arms, and she said, "Jesus, they are killing me, Lady of Canto, Lady of Guadalupe, you know the truth, I know no more than I already said, Mother of God take pity on me, Mother of God of Consolation they're killing me, oh my God, judge, have mercy on me, I don't know what else to say, oh God be with me, oh poor me, full of sins, know that I have committed other sins, but in this I have not offended you, and I don't know anything more than what I've already said. God help me, they're killing me, I'm going to die, oh you traitor, I knew nothing of your lies."[119]

(The *Historia de Gabriel de Espinosa* offers details about these lies, though they may be fabrications. According to the pamphlet, Inés Cid told the judge that during her five years with Espinosa he always said to her, "If you only knew who I really am, and if I could only take you to my house in Castile, you'd be really lucky." From time to time, she said, he received money, which she believed came from wealthy relatives. He had never actually made pastries until they arrived in Nava.)[120]

The transcript went on:

> And the judge, seeing that she said nothing she had not already declared, ordered her removed from the said *mancuerda* and placed on the rack [*potro*], and the ropes and garrotes were tightened as usual, and after a few twists she said, "Mother of God of Rosario, I know no more than I've said, judge, for the love of God read me my past confessions, and the last one I gave to Doctor Llanos, and I will say if I know more, the girl is my daughter, and I gave birth where I said I did, and I know nothing more of Espinosa's stories and lies and plots than what I've already said." And the judge ordered me, the said notary, to read the said confessions and their dates, and I read them, and she heard them and said she has nothing to add and that everything she said is true. . . . And she said she is the age previously stated, and she did not sign because she does not know how.[121]

It was not quite over. Though it had not been proven that Inés Cid was guilty of the imposture, her pretense that she was the child's nanny, not her mother, had aided Espinosa's "lies and inventions." Her cooperation earned her the extraordinarily harsh sentence of two hundred lashes and ten years' banishment from the kingdoms of Castile and Portugal.[122] Lucrecia de León, in comparison, who spent several years recounting seditious dreams at the behest of friends of the king's sworn enemies (men who were treated more leniently than she), received one hundred lashes, two years' imprisonment, and banishment from Madrid and Toledo.[123] A late seventeenth-century manuscript account reports that after the flogging and imprisonment, Inés Cid tried to leave one of her children in Medina (the author remarked on the "beauty of both creatures, especially the markings [*señales*] on the boy, which caused great shock and wonder)," but, given the delicate nature of the case and "fearing the king's indignation," no one would help her.[124] Exit Inés. We know no more about the mother of the adorable child with whom Ana and the other nuns played, if she left with her two children in tow, or what her physical state was.

This ill-used woman was one of several figures in the Madrigal saga whose family was broken. Ana was the unmarried, illegitimate child of another illegitimate child, and both she and her father were brought up by nonrelatives. Sebastian never knew his parents and died childless. Espinosa said he never knew his parents. The nuns and friars had no offspring they could admit to, though sometimes there were children raised in monasteries. Don António was illegitimate, and his children had no parents to care for them. Family, or the lack thereof, hovers in the background of both the initial disaster of Alcazarquivir and this sequel. For it was the prospect of family that lured Ana into believing Espinosa and Fray Miguel. They had promised her a brother.

Kidnapped by the Moors

All the nuns and servants knew something about this brother. Among Goldaraz's questions during his mass interrogation were these: Do they know the child with the baker, and do they know whose she is? Do they know if she is the daughter of a man said to be doña Ana's brother? Do they know who this brother is, what his name is, where he is, and if he has ever come to this monastery? Do they know if the baker knows this brother, where he is, and how he got there? Do they know if the baker promised doña Ana to bring her brother to this town?[125]

The brother, whose name was Francisco, held a fantastic place in the collective memory of the convent. His story would fulfill any checklist of the epic or Byzantine genres, which frequently featured accidentally and dramatically separated siblings whose lives then became a mission to find one another and restore order. Fray Luis Ortiz, who saw Espinosa cooking in Madrid, said he had heard Ana's brother was named don Leopoldo, or something like that, and he lived abroad, but he couldn't remember in which country. Mencia Bravo said Ana suggested that Espinosa was her brother's servant. Augustina de Ulloa had overheard Ana and the baker saying he would bring her brother to her before Christmas. Gerónima de Arpide, who believed Espinosa was a sorcerer, had the sensible opinion that it was through the little girl and the brother that they had all been deceived. Ana de Vega said she knew nothing about a brother, but she did know that Ana had a sister living with the Princess of Parma, which was exactly right.

Goldaraz asked the nuns about Francisco, but he knew the story himself. For some reason, he had recounted it in its entirety in a letter to Fray Juan Bautista, a colleague in Valladolid, even before the Madrigal scandal broke.[126] Around nine years ago, he said, a pilgrim (*peregrina*) appeared at the monastery gate. She told the gatekeepers she was on her way from Seville to the holy shrine of Santiago de Compostela to pray for the health of don Juan of Austria, whom she had known in Seville, and she stopped off in Madrigal to see Ana. When the nuns told the visitor she could not see Ana, she complained of their cruelty in not allowing her to see her sister, prompting one of the women to go inside to tell Ana what was going on. Ana, who had not yet formally professed and did not wear a habit, asked the prioress at the time, María Gaytan, to order dinner for the pilgrim in the receiving area and find out what she could. The prioress, accompanied by the already ubiquitous Luisa del Grado, went to speak to the visitor, who wore a shawl that covered her face from the nose down. The nuns later said she had a long, sharp nose, beautiful eyes, and a small and pretty forehead, and from what they could tell she was good-looking. Luisa testified that the visitor wore an extraordinary headdress and little mittens. Based on the way the visitor spoke, María Gaytan believed she was "more than an ordinary pilgrim" and was sixteen or seventeen years old. The pilgrim would not say who she was but continued complaining and weeping because she could not see her sister. María Gaytan explained to her that Ana could not receive strangers who covered themselves. But Ana, the visitor said, did not know she had a brother, the son of don Juan of Austria and María de Mendoza, who had been kidnapped by the Moors when he was growing up in Jeréz. The brother had been rescued and could be recognized by a birthmark on his chest, near his neck, in the shape of a heart, she said. As the pilgrim told her story, Ana entered the *grada* to listen from a hiding place, and her silk clothes rustled just as the visitor said she was traveling with an old man named Iñigo (or Juan, depending on the version) de Mendoza. The visitor heard the silk and immediately knelt, whimpering, again asking to be able to see her sister, and again she was denied. The nuns offered her alms, which she said she did not need, though she said that if Her Excellency herself gave her a crust of bread she would regard it as a relic. Finally, after much crying, she left, and as she did so, the nuns (and Ana) glimpsed her shoes and stockings and "as she walked and took steps it seemed she was a man, not a woman." In the following days, the nuns heard there was a stranger in town complaining she had not been allowed to visit her sister in the convent.

Ever since, Goldaraz told Bautista and the nuns told Goldaraz, Ana believed the visitor had been her brother "and she has lived with this persuasion and with an incredible desire to know if it was him, where he is, and in what habit and clothing he goes about."[127] Margarita de Toledo answered this last question by saying the king had sent the brother off to Malta, where he was to receive a habit of the order of St. John. Knowledge of the brother was "public and notorious throughout the convent," she explained. In her testimony to Goldaraz and in later confessions, Ana repeated much of this story, explaining that she "understood he must have been her brother, for he knew so much about these [family] matters."[128] After Espinosa arrived in town, somehow it emerged that he knew her brother, a remarkable coincidence that struck no one as remarkable. Francisco, it turned out, was concealed in Navarre awaiting the right moment to reveal himself. Goldaraz provides the fascinating detail that Ana was convinced he was wandering around disguised "so His Majesty would not catch him and kill him like he did with her father."[129] So not only did she not have a family, but she believed her uncle had killed her father. Ana therefore gave Luisa's brother, Blas Nieto, money with which to buy fine clothing for Francisco (though other versions suggest the clothes were for Espinosa). Espinosa was to collect him and the other men in Navarre and return, staying in Blasco Nuño, where they could get new horses. They would be disguised as servants of Barbara Blomberg. Espinosa went off to find Francisco and was arrested a few days later.

The story of Francisco's visit to the convent pre-dated Fray Miguel's arrival by around five years. The vicar could not invent a story remembered by the provincial and nearly all the nuns, but he certainly could not have invented a better one. He seems to have incorporated it into his schemes, for in the *Historia de Gabriel de Espinosa*, Fray Miguel told Llano that Espinosa told him that he (Espinosa) had traveled with a dozen men, none of whom sat in his presence while he ate, "and one of them was the son of don Juan of Austria, a gallant lad of around twenty-two, whom they called Francisquito, and another son of his in Italy, called Carlos, who was seventeen."[130] But there is no denying that a stranger did knock on the convent gate around nine years ago, passing herself or himself off as Ana's sister (though never identifying herself as any particular sister) and saying Ana had a brother. Disguised siblings are frequent in literature, though it is rare for men to pass as women, which appears to be what happened here. The nun Gerónima Arpide was right that there was no better way to lure Ana than to promise her a brother, but exactly what Fray Miguel planned to do after that and whether he really could produce a brother, of whom there is no documentary evidence—was Espinosa supposed to return, and if so with whom?—is unknown.

So Ana's defense for having become entwined with a common baker and keeping the matter a secret from the king rested on her belief that her cousin had returned from the dead and her brother had risen from a realm even more obscure. She and her father both were raised with pseudonyms, disguised as commoners, and then announced to the world with new names, so why couldn't the same thing be true for her brother? Tens of thousands of Christians were captured by North Africans during the early modern period, either in warfare or by pirates. Many became Muslims or pretended to convert; others were ransomed by the crown or religious intermediaries; others escaped and returned home years later, often unrecognizable. Maybe Sebastian escaped; after all, don António, the prior of Crato, had. So too had the plaza prophet Miguel de Piedrola. Why not Francisco? Why could siblings not be reunited, as they were in the *romance* in which a gentleman encounters a beautiful woman washing clothes at a fountain and proposes marriage, only to discover she is his long-lost sister who had been captured by the Moors? He joyfully takes her home, calling out to his mother:

Abrid puertas y ventanas,
balcones y galerías,
que por traer una esposa
os traigo a una hermana mía![131]

The perceived likelihood of such events made the false captive (*falso cautivo*) another familiar literary character and one of the first recourses for Mediterranean imposters.[132] But regardless of fraud, in Counter-Reformation Spain it was true that danger and adventure awaited across the Mediterranean, and the same was true for the other side: captives, travelers, adventurers, and refugees went in both directions in practice and in literature. The opposite shores provided both horrors and possibilities, and sometimes the two coincided: St. Teresa recalled that when she and her brother were young, they planned "to go off to the land of the Moors and beg them, out of love of God, to cut off our heads."[133] There were stranger things than a disguised female pilgrim turning out to be a male royal. In fact, his/her existence was not strange, merely wondrous. It was what propelled the imposture forward. The miraculous was what made the conspiracy possible.

Another alleged brother appeared in the course of this affair, equally sketchy, equally unresolved.[134] This development, one of the last in the Madrigal investigation, takes us outside the convent and back onto the busy roads of the Iberian peninsula, where spies, disguised travelers, hoodwinkers, and dispossessed royals all seemed to wander at will. It turned out that a minor judicial official named Bernardino de Galarza, a colleague of Rodrigo de Santillán's, encountered a foot messenger in Extremadura who told him he was on his way to Madrigal with a sheaf of letters for Ana, Philip II, Prince Philip, and Infanta Isabel Clara Eugenia, all sent by a prisoner disguised as a friar currently sitting in a Portuguese jail cell under the jurisdiction of the archbishop of Evora. Galarza knew about the Madrigal events, and he proposed that he accompany this courier, thinking that once they arrived, he could hand over the letters directly to Santillán. The courier, whose name was Manoel Gonzalves, told him the letter-writer, a "dark-haired, lean-faced man with good eyes and delicate hands," claimed to be the son of don Juan of Austria and the duchess of Niza (which could be Nisa, Portugal, near the Spanish border, or Nice in Savoy, present-day France). In the courier's opinion, the man was Castilian, though he wrote in Portuguese. (In the opinion of Galarza, the courier was Portuguese, "judging by his speech and dress.") For some reason, Galarza and Gonzalves got only as far as a tavern on the estates of the duke of Alba, where there was an altercation, and the courier was detained and examined by the duke's officials.[135] Galarza nonetheless managed to send the relevant information on to Santillán, who forwarded it to the king. Santillán wanted the archbishop of Evora to send the prisoner to Madrigal immediately so he and his men could "extract his sinful soul and uncover his life." "From what I can tell," Santillán said, "it must be yet another branch from Fray Miguel's seed, some deceitfulness, and the messenger says this prisoner had another prisoner write the letters while yet more prisoners observed, which I surmise was so the archbishop would let him go."[136] The archbishop was unlikely to do that, however, because when he first encountered the phony friar in the streets of Evora and asked the man's name, the stranger told him he was a grander prince than the archbishop himself, triggering his immediate arrest. (But it was also unlikely the archbishop would go out of his way anyway to cooperate with Castilian authorities. On another occasion, Juan de Silva had complained to the king that the prelate was in cahoots with members of the clergy who supported don António: "The archbishop of Evora's natural condition makes him liable to cause bothers and difficulties," he wrote.)[137] After his letter-writing performance, the prisoner in Evora somehow summoned Gonzalvez to his jail cell, and the courier accepted the job because he needed to eat. The prisoner paid the courier eighty *reales* and promised that Ana would compensate him with more once he arrived in Madrigal. In his letters, signed "don Juan of Austria," he variously explained to the king, prince, infanta, and Ana that he was their unjustly imprisoned relative, which he said he could prove "with counts and dukes." He referred to some mysterious error he had committed, for which he asked the king's and prince's forgiveness, and said the duke of Alburquerque had been unjust to him in Saragossa.

Ana never knew this man existed. If she had read his letter to her, it surely would have touched her, though by that time, in late July, she may have been impervious. "My sister," he began, "traveling through this Kingdom of Portugal very different than I am, the archbishop of Evora jailed me because I did not want to say who I am." He told her and the infanta he had three siblings: one was Ana, another was in Naples, and the third lived with their most illustrious mother, the duchess. He had jewels and a portrait of their father he could send to her as proof of his claims. He was "very alone," he wrote. Here was yet another figure tragically unable to reveal his true identity, using jewels and portraits to aid his case.[138] Santillán, thinking outside the box, wondered if the prisoner in Evora might be one of Espinosa's sons. Luckily for him, Espinosa was still alive, and Santillán paid him a visit the day before his execution, partly to question him about the little girl, as we have seen, but also to inquire about any older children he might have. "He told me he had other children but he did not want to tell me where they were in case I wanted to find them and hang them, but I gathered it is possible that the archbishop of Evora's prisoner is his son and that Fray Miguel is using him in this tragedy to play doña Ana's brother,"[139] he told the king, though it is hard to believe Fray Miguel could still have been directing the drama from his prison cell. But Philip II was inclined to think the prisoner was just not right in the head. "*Poco seso,*" he opined.

The Rebellion of the Nuns

Since October, the interrogations had completely disrupted the life of the convent, home to some sixty women, most of whom had lived there since they were teenagers and knew just about everything there was to know about each other. The more they were questioned, the more detailed their stories grew, and each new tantalizing nugget gave Juan de Llano a new reason to requestion them. Over and over again they told him about the jewels and the linens, the mysterious visitors who spoke with Ana, Ana's inappropriate hospitality, and the lax supervision of the entrance to the convent. Ana's rooms were of particular interest, and the two nuns who attended Ana, Isabel Ramírez and Francisca de Roda, had an excellent view of the goings-on.[140] Isabel said Ana cooked for Fray Miguel in her rooms (in theory the quid pro quo for jewels), and the two fed each other little bites. María Tascón said Ana called the vicar "little grandfather" (*abuelito*) during their evening repasts. (Llano later wrote that the vicar called Ana *angel* and she called him *angelito.*)[141] When Ana was well, she and Fray Miguel visited every morning and afternoon, and when she was ill (she was quite sick in April 1594), Fray Miguel spent the night in her room along with three doctors and her maids, according to various witnesses. Even though there was a mattress on the floor, he rarely used it, "causing scandal and murmurs throughout the monastery." Llano was quite direct with the vicar on this point: was there inappropriate activity such that they knew each other carnally in the convent or outside? Everyone in the convent as well as in town knew that Ana and Espinosa had pledged themselves to each other. Isabel Ramírez reported that once after nightfall, when Ana, María Nieto, and she were in the *grada,* Ana told Isabel to go fetch Juan Roderos, which she did, and Ana then told her to go back upstairs, which she also did. She went to Ana's rooms, where she drifted off to sleep, and was awakened between nine and ten when Ana, Luisa, and María all came in. They said they had been talking to another nun, but later Isabel found out that was the night of the marriage vows. Ana was very fond of Portuguese people, Francisca de Roda said, so much so that she had heard Ana wanted to be queen of Portugal, and she once heard her say "she had her hopes pinned on that kingdom and her fate was there" (*y también su estrella en él*). And there was worse: Ana once told Catalina de Espinosa (probably the same as Ana de Espinosa) that she wanted to get pregnant.

Clearly, the nuns could not attend to their spiritual duties in this atmosphere. The vicar and several of his friars were under arrest. Llano and his army of notaries were in and out on a daily basis, keeping a close watch on Ana, her confidantes, and her guards. Llano had wanted to remove Luisa and María when he first arrived, but a couple of weeks later he reported one of them was sick ("They're probably sick so they don't have to leave," the king jotted in the margin). He finally managed to move them late one night after Christmas, draped in blankets to avoid detection, installing them and two servants in a house in town where a "very honest, old hidalgo from out of town" would watch over them.[142] The little girl was gone. So, obviously, was Espinosa. Goldaraz had been dismissed. The convent appeared to have fallen under the supervision of Llano, who, rather than interview the nuns in the receiving area, where their stories might be overheard, took their statements in closed rooms. By February, complaints were beginning to circulate, and the king's aide, Cristóbal de Moura, was obliged to call the judge to order. "I must tell you, I have heard that you and your notary enter the convent more than is necessary and spend long periods of time there," he wrote.[143] Llano responded, "I have spent as many as four or five days each questioning some of the nuns, and as there are more than sixty, you can see how long this is taking." Moura also was fielding complaints from Augustinian authorities, though according to Llano himself, he was liberating the nuns from the captivity and tyranny of the provincial: "God has been merciful in allowing me to return the nuns to peace and quiet," he told Moura, and there is no denying that Goldaraz's management had been lacking.[144]

The nuns, however, neither regarded their previous state as one of captivity nor their present one as evidence of God's mercy, and by spring they had had enough. They, too, could take advantage of the busy roads leading out of Madrigal. In April, after Ana and her guard, the subprioress María Belón, were prohibited from attending Mass or going to the infirmary, they tried to smuggle letters to Rodrigo de Santillán in Medina del Campo describing the indignities to which the apostolic judge was subjecting them. Unfortunately for them, the letters fell into the hands of Llano, who took the opportunity to stage a show trial. He began with Leonor Enríquez, the concierge, who testified that Isabel de Azebes had given her the two letters, sealed with colored wax and tied with a linen ribbon, asking her to pass them to Pedro de Huerta, Leonor's brother-in-law, who lived in town and knew where to take them. But Pedro was not feeling well, so he didn't deliver them, and Leonor returned to the convent and told Isabel de Azebes of the mishap. Llano somehow obtained the letters and entered them into the record as evidence. Pedro de Huerta testified that he had carried two or three letters previously from the convent to Medina, and, even more interesting, had carried replies the other way. This was followed by testimony from Isabel de Azebes, who denied she gave ink and paper to Ana; from Ana herself, who confessed she wrote the letter; and from María Belón, who said she had no idea how Ana had obtained ink and paper. Asked to explain how she could have offended God and his ministers by helping to write this letter suggesting that Llano was behaving improperly, María Belón resorted to an old strategy: "She was moved by anger, for no good reason, and didn't know what she was saying, like a crazy woman with no judgment." Never ever had she seen Llano or his notaries behave improperly, she said. Never ever had they spoken to nuns outside the designated interview areas; never had they done so without the prioress present; and Llano had always "set the grandest example of honesty and propriety and decency and restraint, behaving as a saint in Heaven would if he were present." María Belón, who had been a nun for forty years, was then ordered to make a public confession of guilt and repentance, declare that she esteemed Llano as if he were Saint Peter, and prostrate herself at his feet.[145]

But the nuns continued writing letters and talking. In late June, Ana wrote to the king and his personal chaplain, García de Loaysa (it is not clear how she got the letters out) complaining about Llano's rough treatment and once again pleading for forgiveness.[146] "I am the daughter of Your Majesty's brother," she reminded Philip, "and it does not speak well of Your Majesty's Christianity that, because of my failures and ignorance, past services be forgotten." Without someone to represent her interests truly, she could not defend herself against lies and slander, she said. "I beg of Your Majesty, for God's sake, to provide me with a person of good conscience who does not wish me harm." It was in the king's interest that she be proven innocent, she correctly pointed out, one of the early indications that she was, after all, clever. To Loaysa, she wrote, "The more Dr. Juan de Llano is made aware of my innocence, the more he mistreats me, and these offenses have become intolerable, for they endanger my honor. Every day, his bad intentions are made manifest, and I am treated with the strangest judicial rigor." She wrote on her own behalf, but also to reiterate that Llano was behaving very badly with her fellow nuns.

As if to confirm her complaints, in early July, Llano seems to have come unhinged. He had ordered the nuns to refrain from contact with Ana, to speak with no one about the investigation, to write no letters, and to abide by their house arrest, he said. But the women, "obstinate and having forgotten the Lord and their conscience and the natural obedience we owe to apostolic authorities," persisted in their talking and writing, spreading stories throughout the town "as if they were town criers." Therefore, he decided, he had no choice but to excommunicate the whole damn convent.[147] On July 3, he sent a tertiary nun off to get the prioress, Catalina de Espinosa, so he could formally serve her with the order. A few minutes later, the tertiary returned with the sad news that the prioress was indisposed. Llano then summoned a subprioress, María de San Vicente, who dutifully received word from the notary of the order and was told to gather the nuns together and relay his excommunication order, which she did. The congregation of nuns, using a common legal tactic of the time, then demanded that everything be put in writing, which Llano appears to have refused. Showing that he was worthy of María Belón's praise and indeed an honest and saintly man, Llano told the nuns he would wait up that night in the chapter in case anyone wanted to come by and request absolution. Not a single nun appeared.

The king received word of all this immediately, of course, and four days later Llano wrote to defend himself.[148] His was a very difficult job, he insisted, and one thing after another had impeded his search for the truth. The job got even more difficult a few days later when he discovered that the friars also were writing letters, confirming the women's complaints. The nuns' confessor, Alonso Rodríguez, testified that the new vicar (Fray Miguel's replacement), Andrés Ortiz, had dispatched him to Madrid with letters for Moura, Rodrigo Vázquez de Arce (president of the Council of Castile), Loaysa, and Enrique Enríquez, prior of the monastery of San Augustín in Madrid.[149] As if that were not bad enough, Rodríguez said he and Ortiz stopped off to visit Santillán in Medina the very day the nuns were excommunicated. Llano, naturally, ordered Rodriguez imprisoned in the men's portion of the convent.

Why were the nuns and friars so upset? Details of their complaints appear in the sixteen-point memorandum from Ortiz to Moura, and the judge does not come out looking quite as restrained as he had claimed.[150] Despite "the case being closed," Ortiz said (an interesting observation; Ortiz did not know the case was still open because of Philip's interest in *la niña* and Fray Miguel's accomplices), Llano continued visiting the convent every day, saying he needed to ratify statements. He and his notary spent their afternoons chatting with their devotees (*devotas*), to whom they gave presents, including taffeta petticoats. (The prioress and the new vicar demanded that the women relinquish the petticoats, which they did, but Llano returned them.) He stayed with his *devotas* long after it was dark. He hugged the nuns and sheltered them under his cloak as they walked. Llano had even offered Rodrigo de Santillán the services of a *devota*, which Santillán sensibly declined. The other nuns were scared to death (*temorosísimas*) of Llano, according to Ortiz, and no wonder; Llano called the women "worse than Lutherans" and said they were living "as if they were in Geneva, apostates, and shameless rogues." "These ladies are pleading [to] God for mercy and freedom," Ortiz wrote, "because [Llano] has enslaved them and threatened that he will take them elsewhere and that those who have been excommunicated will be transported in an Inquisition cart." (His rough treatment appears to have had royal approval; in December, one of the king's secretaries wrote up instructions for the apostolic judge, telling him that doña Ana must be treated with kid gloves, "but the rest of the nuns . . . can be threatened with torment and with everything permitted by law if you think it will help in obtaining information.")[151]

Earlier, the well-informed author of the anonymous letters hinted at Llano's previous bad behavior: "I seem to have heard something about your needing to stay here awhile," he wrote, the implication being that Llano was in some sort of professional exile in Madrigal after similar indiscretions elsewhere.[152] At any rate, things had gone too far, and Vázquez de Arce ordered an investigation, putting Santillán in charge. Given Santillán's antipathy toward the clergy in general, the choice was an odd one, and the secular judge demurred. "It would be less noisy and less awkward if an ecclesiastic were to do it," he wrote the king in July, but the king did not agree.[153] So after Llano left Madrigal in late July to accompany Fray Miguel to Madrid, Santillán commenced retracing his former colleague's steps in the convent. Among other things, he discovered that letters of support from nuns that Llano had sent to Moura and the king in his own defense had been signed by nuns who had no idea what they were signing.[154] In August, Llano told Martín de Idiáquez that Santillán was taking too long (Santillán himself complained that if he had to interview sixty nuns all over again, he would never finish) and asked that the matter be turned over to the Augustinians, who had offered to intervene and who Llano for some reason thought would be more lenient.[155] The result of the inquest is unknown to me. The following year, however, Llano and his brother, also an inquisitor (they were related to the famed archbishop of Seville and inquisitor general Fernando de Valdés), sued the Oviedo cathedral over money, and one of the plaintiffs' tactics was a familiar one: in 1598 the Llano Valdés brothers excommunicated the entire cathedral chapter.[156]

Ana's Punishment

Andrés Ortiz, in a way, was right to say the case was over. Insofar as the convent was concerned, it had ended long ago. Though they didn't know it, the inhabitants were simply waiting for Philip to learn to live with the loose ends. Ana's role was manifestly clear, even to Llano: she had been vilely used by Fray Miguel and Gabriel Espinosa. She had not shown good judgment, but her virtue was never in question. In March, five months after the interrogations began, Llano told the king there was absolutely no reason to question Ana's honesty and modesty. On the contrary, he found "only virtue and religion," he said, "except for saying she was not really a nun because she professed against her will. . . . As for doña Ana's maids [Francisca and Isabel], whom I have held prisoner outside the monastery, they are blameless and should be thanked for telling us what they knew."[157]

On March 7, 1595, Ana was officially accused.[158] "Persuaded by Fray Miguel," the indictment stated, "she believed that a lowly man who lived in this town of Madrigal working as a baker, whose name was Gabriel de Espinosa, was the King of Portugal" and she "consented that Fray Miguel speak of marriage" between the two. She asked Espinosa for a written commitment, which he signed as king of Portugal, and she gave an oral commitment, and this was all witnessed by Fray Miguel, Luisa del Grado, and María Nieto. She also gave Espinosa presents. She had been "deceived and persuaded by Fray Miguel that Espinosa was King Sebastian and that she would be queen of Portugal, which they had spoken about and concealed without informing His Majesty, as she was obliged to do, nor

Figure 8. Ana of Austria's autograph in a 1594 letter to Rodrigo de Santillán (AGS E, leg. 172, doc. 89). Courtesy of Archivo General de Simancas, Ministerio Español de la Cultura.

anyone else who could set her straight." She believed Fray Miguel because she respected him and because she wanted to be free of her vows, the indictment noted. The fantasy was a solution to her entrapment. Llano ended by listing the mitigating circumstances, among which was that she had been cloistered since she was six, and by asking for Philip's clemency for this young woman whose life had been turned upside down. The following month, Vázquez de Arce wrote the king in similar terms, also suggesting lenience because of Ana's youth, "the fragility of her sex," and the relentless pressures from Fray Miguel attesting to "the power that vicars have over nuns in their monasteries." As her punishment, Vázquez suggested four years' confinement, forced silence inside her own monastery, and a lifetime ban against holding positions of responsibility.[159]

On July 17, at last, Llano met with Ana to read her the indictment, and the following day she wrote a remarkable letter to Philip. "The justice observed with me was nothing but ceremony," she stated flatly before responding to the accusations one by one, noting that in her previous confessions she had gone easy on Fray Miguel out of respect. "When King Sebastian died seventeen years ago, I was ten years old, and I knew so little that Fray Miguel's account was the first I ever heard. I thought he was alive because the friar told me he was." For four long years, he introduced her to alleged eyewitnesses from the battle, showed her letters from people who had seen Sebastian, told her the story of Dr. Mendes, who had cured the hidden king, recounted holy visions, and recited prophecies from the saints and the *trovas* of the Portuguese messianic poet Bandarra. "The friar believed Bandarra's words were true, and his reasons and all that he said would have persuaded anyone older and far more experienced than I," Ana wrote. "This happened not once nor four times but nearly all year, with so many lies that anyone would have been taken in." She never could have imagined he was lying. He led a devoted and modest life, underwent self-flagellation three times a week, and, incidentally, was "better looking than any friar who had ever been in this house, and he had the same reputation in town."[160]

Credulity in the face of an apparently honest holy person was not that unusual, Ana pointed out, venturing bravely onto thin ice and showing she had ways of obtaining useful news from outside. "With less cause, Your Majesty and the Emperor were deceived by the nuns of the Anunciada of Lisbon and Magdalena de la Cruz, to whom your majesties both did considerable favors. If monarchs can give credit to younger, unlettered women, then how is it surprising that I should believe a man whose words and exemplary life had been so admired by the kings of Portugal and everyone who knew him?"[161]

Ana's point is worth pausing over. The two nuns she named were among the most famous of the sixteenth-century false mystics. Magdalena was a Franciscan abbess in Córdoba who died in 1560 in solitary confinement in an Inquisitorial prison after years of claiming prophetic powers later deemed to be the workings of the devil. In 1527, during the reign of Charles V, the empress sent the future Philip II's baby blankets to Córdoba to be blessed by Magdalena to ensure that the future monarch would be protected from the devil.[162] More interesting for our purposes is Sor María de la Visitación, also called the "nun of Lisbon." She was the daughter of Francisco Lobo, an ambassador at the court of Charles V, and became prioress of the aristocratic Anunciada convent in Lisbon, where she lived since she was orphaned at the age of eleven.[163] Her time in the spotlight coincided with that of Lucrecia de León and just preceded the years in which Fray Miguel was seeding Ana's path. Sor María first sported stigmata, in the form of five wounds, in 1584, and soon became all the rage among the elites of Spain, Portugal, and beyond. The duke of Medina Sidonia asked her blessing before setting off for England with the Armada fleet. Philip II's sister, the empress María, saw the nun several times when she visited her son Albert in Lisbon.[164] The famed Castilian preacher Luis de Granada, the nun's confessor (whom we last saw during don António's assault on Lisbon in 1580), wrote a glowing biography of her in 1586, complete with a description of iron nails appearing in the middle of her hands as a shaft of light carried Jesus' wounds to her. She bled religiously every Friday, and she performed miracles. Had she remained merely holy, she might have survived, but in addition to arousing suspicion and jealousy in the religious community, she began attracting the support of the don António camp and undergoing visions and raptures of a political nature concerning none other than King Sebastian. She saw Sebastian pointing to his wounds and saying, "I bleed for you," and had a revelation that an angel had tugged at Sebastian's hair during the battle of Alcazarquivir to draw him to the safe side of the river. At her 1588 trial, she said her lies had all been inspired by don António's partisans "so she could persuade everyone to rise up against the Catholic King [Philip] because not he, but António was their true king, and this was God's revelation, and she was just waiting for her sainthood to be widely known before writing to the Catholic King to tell him he could not rule a kingdom that was not his, and he should give it to its rightful owner, which she knew was true because she had had a heavenly revelation."[165] Philip's enthusiasm for Sor María by then had diminished, of course, but Ana's point, to return to Madrigal, was that, for a time, even he believed in her. If Fray Luis de Granada could believe María de la Visitación, if Fray Luis de León could believe Miguel de Piedrola, if monarchs could believe frauds, then certainly Ana could not be judged imprudent for doing the same.

"This man arrived here," Ana resumed, referring to Espinosa, "whether by design, I know not." Espinosa echoed what Fray Miguel had told her, his presence offering physical proof of what until then had been just stories. "The schemes and inventions were so many and so artful that, if it were not so painful for me, I could write a long history that would not fail to astound you," she said. Again and again, Fray Miguel told her that Espinosa was Sebastian. When she asked why Espinosa's face looked so changed, he said it was the sea, which makes people look very different. (According to the *Historia de Gabriel de Espinosa*, Fray Miguel ran that same theory by Llano: he said that when he asked Espinosa why he looked so old, the baker replied, "tribulations can age one more than years.")[166] She never signed anything, she insisted; she only gave her word that she would marry him. When she suffered doubts, the incessant encouragement of her religious guide "gave me more faith than my imagination." In explaining how it was that she could entertain thoughts of marriage, Ana said, "I did not regard myself as a nun because I was a novice for six years before professing entirely against my will, and was still within the five years allowed by the Council of Trent to protest one's profession, and I had done only three or four." Finally, she returned to the question of her honor, responding to the vile rumors of her alleged maternity. "I have committed no mortal sin, either in thought or in word," she said, adding that she released her confessors from their vows of confidentiality to confirm this. And again she insisted that the only reason for not telling Philip all this before, an omission she begged him to forgive, was that she was waiting to meet her brother. Had Espinosa not brought him to her (and we have no idea whom he was planning to bring, if anyone), she would have "returned to my old suspicion that it was all a lie." Fray Miguel and Espinosa never spoke badly about Philip, she reassured the king—"that was the key to their edifice," she pointed out—and rarely even mentioned Portugal.[167] Theirs was a story of Africa.

"I beg Your Majesty to look upon me with the great Christianity that God granted you and to see that harshness would only prove right those who have dishonored me, which would greatly dishonor your brother, the most faithful servant Your Majesty ever had and who now stands before God asking Him to inspire Your Majesty. Do not punish me except as a pious father," Ana begged, "allow me to practice my religion and serve the Lord, for there is little time and I have little life. . . . May God guard your Catholic Majesty as the world wishes and as this unworthy servant begs from this prison."[168]

On July 22 she heard her sentence. She was to leave Madrigal for another convent, where she was to be confined to a cell for four years. She could leave her cell only to hear Mass on holy days, when she was to walk directly to the chorus, accompanied by two elderly nuns appointed for this purpose, and return to her cell in the same fashion, speaking to no one. Every Friday for four years she was to have only bread and water. She was never to have a supervisorial position in her new convent nor in any other, and was to employ no nuns as her servants; rather, she was to use common servants like everyone else. She was to be addressed as if she were an ordinary nun.[169]

Immediately she wrote to her uncle, beside herself with sorrow and contrition. The chaotic letter is nearly impossible to read, but even the smudges and rips betray her desperation.[170] "With this I dare to declare, if words can, how deeply pained I am to have offended Your Majesty," she began. Once again she threw herself at the king's feet, pleading for mercy and for him to restore her honor. "I am an ant, I am nothing but a dried splinter" (*astilla seca*), she wrote. "What does Your Majesty gain from my perdition and dishonor?" Nearly blind from weeping, she begged forgiveness for her sins. "I am the granddaughter of your father," she reminded him, "and the daughter of the most loyal slave anyone ever had, and when a man has a loyal slave, he frees the slave's children and gives them freedom and sustenance." Instead, she had been a prisoner since she was six years old, she was serving a life sentence. Why could the king not kill her honorably instead of making her the target of public infamy? She was an orphan, with no one to help her except her uncle. Lost and defeated, she closed by signing, "this wretched woman, doña Anna de Austrya."

Sometime in the spring, Philip or one of his aides had requested a list of Augustinian convents and the number of nuns in each. Twenty-two institutions appeared on the list. One of them, Nuestra Señora de Gracia, just outside the famous walls of Avila, would be Ana's new home.[171] She remained in Madrigal all of August, surely aware of Espinosa's execution and the noisy and macabre death procession through the small town. On September 5 the king told the new provincial, Pedro Manríquez, to arrange for Ana's transport to Avila. "Make sure they travel with the decency and modesty required by their profession," the king admonished.[172] The provincial reported back three days later that Ana had left in a carriage at midnight, accompanied by María Gaytan, a lay sister, and a common servant, along with three male religious. Her closest friends, Luisa del Grado and María Nieto, who enabled most of Ana's follies, had been ordered, respectively, to convents in Toledo and Ciudad Rodrigo, where they were to be held in isolation, with bread and water on Fridays, for eight years. Manríquez said María was gravely ill, and the doctors were not sure she would survive; Luisa, however, was to be taken to Toledo that week. They probably had never been apart.[173]

EPILOGUE

Mutilated bodies mark the beginning and end of this tale. On August 4, 1578, King Sebastian was stabbed and shot to death at the end of the battle of Alcazarquivir, and soon the work of vandals and the summer heat left his body unrecognizable. On August 1, 1595, Gabriel de Espinosa met his awful end in Madrigal de las Altas Torres, the town where he had arrived fifteen months earlier with his companion and their little girl in the hope of setting up a more profitable pastry shop than the one he had in Nava. The tragedy and then the farce marked the end of some sort of dream, a fantasy lodged in politics, and the beginning of a never-ending cycle of tales.

Espinosa spent his last few days in the company of a Jesuit confessor, Juan de Fuensalida, who was passing through town accompanied by the man believed to have written the first *Historia de Gabriel de Espinosa*, which closely parallels Fuensalida's own version.[1] For some reason, Santillán enlisted Fuensalida for the crucial task of ensuring that the prisoner died a Christian death; thus the false Sebastian ended his days under the tutelage of a member of the Company of Jesus, just as the true Sebastian spent his childhood in their thrall. To oversee a prisoner's death was an esteemed post, described by a fellow Jesuit in Seville as "more honorable than honorable preachers and scholars of theology [and] than their own superiors."[2] There could be no greater satisfaction than ensuring that a sinner, even the most vile sinner imaginable, would meet God. Fuensalida's account of Espinosa's last days is remarkable for its detail and dreadful poignancy. It is written in the third person, addressed to the royal secretary Martín de Idiáquez.

On July 28, Espinosa learned from Fuensalida what his sentence was. He was to be taken from his jail cell, placed in a basketlike container called a *serón,* and then dragged "in the usual manner through the usual public streets." Then, in the plaza, he would be hanged until dead, and then quartered. Each of the four quarters would be exhibited in a public spot to be decided upon by the judge, and his head would be placed in an iron cage atop a pike and displayed.[3] But such a death was not proper for a man of his standing, Espinosa protested. "Imagine I had entered the monastery waving my standard—how much worse could the punishment possibly be?" he asked. "Ah, Philip! Your day will come! You should pray that this ends with my death!"[4] As always, hints of a more vast conspiracy. When a court official entered his cell to deliver the sentence formally, Espinosa insisted that he wanted to appeal. The official pointed out that the king himself had signed the sentence, so there was nobody to appeal to, and he reminded Espinosa that he had confessed without (as well as with) torture. Back he went to protesting against being dragged, to which Fuensalida responded that Jesus Christ had died an even more undignified death. Think of this as an opportunity to enter eternity, he counseled.

The next day, a Saturday, the Jesuit went back to the cell for more talks, hoping to administer the last sacraments. Now Espinosa said he would request a delay. He was not ready, he said; he was too weak to go down on his knees and recite a Hail Mary. But then he exclaimed, very excited, "If you could see me amid an army!" Grasping Fuensalida's hand, he cried, "Oh what I could do! This is not the time for such stories, I know, but I can say that when I was surrounded by soldiers in the port of Ferrol [in Galicia, perhaps during Drake's assault], I snatched a lance, and with one thrust one corporal fell to one side and another to the other." Another time he spoke to the Jesuit about the little girl. "She is the daughter, . . ." he said, his voice drifting off, still suggesting, of course, that her parentage was mysterious. (Two days later Santillán paid Espinosa his last visit to discuss, precisely, *la niña.*) Tell us who you are, Fuensalida insisted. If

I do not know who you are, I cannot hear your confession, to which the prisoner replied that he had given his name and was not going to be executed on Tuesday. "I am amazed," Espinosa said, "that such knowledgeable people, seeing who I am, are still convinced I am an ignoramus. Do you really think a low and common man would behave like this? Do you think I am so crazy as to undertake such a plan with no basis? After I am dead, you will see who I am and what this is all about, and what makes me even sorrier than my own death is what will happen next."[5] Fuensalida was desperate at Espinosa's refusal to confess; by law (albeit always flexible) a prisoner should be executed no more than three days after hearing the sentence. Rodrigo de Santillán, meanwhile, was suspicious of the Jesuit's attempts to delay; this was a typical dispute in which the state wanted the body and the church the soul. After Fuensalida once again voiced fears that a sinner was going to his death without the proper rites, Santillán's solution was to bring the *serón* and the rope to Espinosa's cell and tie his hands. That, finally, made the baker realize that his delay tactics were futile, because the end indeed was near. Monday he confessed his sins and received the last rites at the hands of two Franciscans whom Santillán trusted more than the Jesuit, who was proving far too susceptible to Espinosa's stories.

The execution took place on Tuesday between five and six in the afternoon. It must have been broiling, yet the streets and squares were packed with an "infinite number" of people who had poured into Madrigal from the entire district. Santillán said it was as if there were an Inquisition auto-da-fé. Espinosa spent the morning pacing in his cell. He took a nap and snored. He could hear the crowds outside. "What is that noise?" he complained. "The clopping of the horses hammers at my heart." What is today identified as the old jail sits on the Plaza de San Nicolás, the main square, where the execution also took place. As Espinosa left his cell on his way to be placed into the *serón,* one final opportunity, the very last one, presented itself for him to bargain with inevitability. A stranger entered the room, prompting the prisoner to call out to the guards and the friars, "'The king has sent this gentleman to recognize me, for surely Fray Miguel has told him who I am,' and he rose from his chair . . . and said, 'Sir, tell my uncle [Philip II] how don Rodrigo [de Santillán] treats his own

Figure 9. Present-day Plaza de San Nicolás, Madrigal de las Altas Torres; site of Espinosa's execution. Photograph by Javier Alvarez Dorronsoro.

blood.'"[6] Fuensalida's account says he calmed Espinosa down, telling him the gentleman actually was just a member of the Medina del Campo city council who was there to console him and pray for his salvation. The exchange now prompted the Franciscans to plead with Santillán to postpone the execution, as Espinosa clearly was not ready to meet his maker, but the judge had had enough.

Espinosa was placed into the *serón* with the assistance of a crowd of religious who had come from all over, and the procession began. The basket was dragged as the prisoner looked out through the bars, though it might also have been placed on a wheeled carriage and pulled. (The verb is *arrastrar*). The macabre cortege wound its way through the town as the *pregonero,* the town crier who doubled as torturer, walked alongside shouting out the sentence. Those who accompanied the basket later told Fuensalida that when the crier said the words "a traitor to His Majesty," Espinosa murmured, "not so." And when the *pregonero* said the prisoner had impersonated a royal person "when he is a low and lying man," Espinosa said, "God knows."[7] To the very end, the double refused to relinquish control over his identity.

Finally they were back at the square. He was removed from the basket. He looked around at the crowd and slowly walked to the stairway leading up to the scaffold. He went down on his knees and was absolved, after which a Franciscan and the Jesuit helped him up the steps. The rope was put over his head; the author of the Escorial version of the *Historia de Gabriel de Espinosa* said he adjusted it as if he were adjusting an elegant ruff, as if he were laughing at death. Then he looked over to the balcony where Santillán sat watching; the judge had positioned himself there to preclude any last-minute speechifying from the prisoner or, worse, a retracted confession. As it was, Santillán later wrote, Espinosa emerged from the *serón* displaying enormous self-possession, "as if they were about to give him an award." According to the *Historia de Gabriel de Espinosa*, he arrived as if at a joust. His eyes fixed on the judge, Espinosa cried out twice, "Ah! Señor don Rodrigo!" And a third time, with rage in his eyes, "Ah, don Rodrigo." Quickly the Jesuit or the friar placed a crucifix on his mouth, Espinosa asked forgiveness, and the hangman did his job. "He took a long time to die," Fuensalida said.[8] In Santillán's words to Cristóbal de Moura, "Espinosa died well."[9]

Public executions after nearly a year of manic obsession with secrecy might appear incongruent. But secrecy was of importance only as long as there was any real threat. Once the king was sure there was no dangerous popular support for don António or Sebastian, he apparently wanted to make the end of this convoluted case a demonstration of royal remorselessness. It was Philip's turn to make some noise, simply a different way of controlling information. Espinosa's execution received attention, to be sure, but though the streets of Madrigal were packed, it was still, after all, Madrigal. Fray Miguel de los Santos, in contrast, would be hanged in Madrid's Plaza Mayor, the capital city's greatest and most theatrical square.

As soon as the apostolic judge Juan Llano de Valdés notified Ana of her sentence in July, he prepared to accompany the vicar to Madrid, where the prize prisoner was to be cross-examined with two of his alleged Portuguese accomplices, Antonio Fonseca and Francisco Gomes. Heavily guarded, the entourage traveled southeast and scaled the mountains outside Madrid, where they were forced to stay put for several very uncomfortable days in the town of Galapagar. Llano wrote a barrage of letters from there to Madrid asking how long they would have to stay and demanding that a carpenter be hired immediately to secure the doors and windows of Fray Miguel's house to stop him from escaping now that he knew his stories would get him nowhere. Finally, whatever problems were preventing their entry into the capital were resolved, and Llano and the former vicar traveled to Madrid.[10] Once the cross-examination of the two men from Lisbon confirmed (as Juan Silva had said it would) that they knew nothing of the plot, the authorities turned their attention to the punishment.

Fray Miguel had received his formal accusation already in March. This was a list of all his wicked deeds: how he enlisted Espinosa to persuade Ana that he was her cousin and then marry him, and how he called Espinosa "Your Majesty" and wrote to accomplices in Portugal, all because "for many years the said Fray Miguel had wanted there to be a new king in Portugal." His principal crime was lèse majesté.[11] Once the prisoner was safely in Madrid and the various authorities got down to discussing legalities, Llano explained that royal imposture called for the harshest punishment imaginable, never mind that it had failed, and that Fray Miguel should be publicly degraded, that is, stripped of his religious habit and privileges and passed over to the secular realm. To grease the wheels of justice a bit, the president of the Council of Castile suggested that the words "atrocious crimes suspected of heresy" be added to his *pregón* (until then the crimes were just *graves y gravísimos, enormes y enormísimos*) so as to guarantee that church authorities or the pope would not get in the way and try to stop the execution.[12]

But in the end the church made itself felt by omission, rather than commission. The Portuguese witnesses had been sent home, and Fray Miguel's sentence was all ready, but Llano could not persuade any church authority to oversee the degradation. Without a bishop, the ceremony could not go forward.[13] The papal nuncio, the bishops of Málaga, Córdoba, and Ciudad Rodrigo, and a Portuguese bishop all happened to be in Madrid right then, but Llano had no takers. The king might have to simply order their participation, he said. A week later matters remained stuck, and three days after that, he still had no good news. "As this is an unpleasant matter, they're all hiding," he told Martín de Idiáquez.[14] Bishops throughout Spain appear deliberately to have been staying away from the capital for the two weeks or so during which Llano was searching, but finally one came wandering into his trap. The unlucky man was from Oristano, in Sardinia, and he agreed to preside over the ceremony, which took place on Monday, October 16, 1595, at the church of San Martín, next to the Descalzas Reales, the splendid convent established by Sebastian's mother, Juana.

Fray Miguel was placed inside a carriage and taken to San Martín at around two in the afternoon. Llano told the king the next day he had done everything he could to make as little fuss (*ruido*) as possible, but even so, "there was such a crowd it was amazing." Fray Miguel alighted from the carriage dressed in his ordinary habit, and he entered the church and approached the high altar, where Llano formally stated his and the bishop's authority. The vicar then got down on his knees to hear his degradation sentence, which was read aloud by a notary. The immediate victims of his deceit were identified as "a nun" (no name) and Espinosa, "a native of Toledo, left at the door of the church." The lies, the phony marriage, the false visions, the network of accomplices, the "deceit and horror" he caused the unnamed nun, and the *graves y gravísimos, enormes y enormísimos* crimes all meant that he must be perpetually deprived of his habit and office and then passed over to secular authorities. The prisoner said he had heard the sentence, which he formulaically appealed and protested. Then the bishop, "in the presence of many people and guards and a large crowd actually and truly degraded the said Fray Miguel, first dressing him as if he were going to say Mass and then removing each item one by one until he removed the surplice and the Augustinian habit and put on him a secular habit, and a barber removed his crown [of hair]." He was now dressed in an old black cape, carrying a hat in his hand, "his venerable baldness displayed." It was the last disguise of this tale. Then Llano took him by the arm and handed him over to the secular authority in the person of alcalde Diego de la Canal, who acknowledged custody. The prisoner then was handed to two guards, who took him back to the royal jail in a carriage. The ceremony took around two hours. Fray Miguel was no longer Fray Miguel.[15]

Like Espinosa, the former vicar was attended by friars in his last days. But it was thought that the prisoner, unlike Espinosa, might still have something to say, and Llano told the two Franciscans as well as the guards to be on alert in case he revealed "anything of importance." He said nothing new, though a fragmentary document, apparently copied in the early seventeenth century, indicates that Fray Miguel told one of the Franciscans that all his previous confessions had been false. In an exchange similar to that which occurred nearly three months earlier in Madrigal, the Franciscan, worried he could not absolve someone who would not confess, relayed this new information to the president of the Royal Council. But the president insisted that the hanging must go forward.[16]

Three days later, on Thursday, October 19, Fray Miguel was executed in the Plaza Mayor, a few steps from the jail.[17] Again, the streets were packed, as was the plaza itself. "So many people were there, people of all social groups, it was astonishing, and everyone was so stunned to see such an unbelievable spectacle," Llano wrote to Moura. As the prisoner approached the steps to the scaffold, he turned to the notary who was recording the ceremony and spoke to him for several moments. He was dying with no guilt, and his confessions obtained under torture had all been false, he said, reiterating what he had told the Franciscan. In Llano's opinion, the conversation was his last attempt to delay death or avoid it altogether. "My understanding is that he never thought he would die," the apostolic judge told one of the Idiáquezes. An anonymous witness of the former vicar's death recorded all the true and important things known about the prisoner: he had been Ana's and Catherine's confessor, Sebastian's preacher, and provincial of his order. He arranged the marriage between Ana and the baker with the ultimate aim of putting António on the throne and killing Espinosa. And—that essential part of the story, which one year after the fact was known even to someone standing in the crowd—the conspiracy was discovered after Espinosa's heedless exhibition of the jewels. "The friar was hanged on the 19th in this court [Madrid], and it was a thing of wonder to see such a proud and venerable man die," wrote the correspondent.[18] After Fray Miguel's body was cut down, the head was cut off. The following day it was sent to Madrigal de las Altas Torres where, in the town square, it was displayed on a pike for ten hours. "And with that," Llano told the king, in his very last letter regarding the case, "the said Fray Miguel's life was over, and so too was this matter, which has brought so much worry and trouble to Your Majesty."

"This morning news has arrived that don António of Portugal is dead," the Venetian ambassador in France wrote home in late August 1595. "I saw him the day before I left, quite well, in a carriage in Paris. The poor gentleman died in great poverty, and frequent collections have been made on his behalf at court. Although the king gave him certain revenues, yet as those were not paid regularly, don António was obliged to throw himself on the charity of others." Indeed, the list of António's belongings was thin; he owned a few weapons, clothing, boots and shoes, hats, linens, nineteen books (including one on the Portuguese people's right to elect their kings), personal papers, silver objects, a coach with horses, and a broken mirror.[19]

The man whose followers called him the eighteenth king of Portugal lived in a humble home in the Marais district of Paris. His last will and testament, dated June 5, sheds crucial and puzzling light on the Madrigal case.[20] Before six witnesses, he begged God to show mercy and forgive his sins (among which he mentioned his sexual excess, *liberdade da carne*), and then he named two religious men of "great virtue and prudence" who were to provide guidance to the six witnesses if doubts arose regarding execution of the will. One was Luís de Sotomayor, a Dominican professor at Coimbra who had been singled out and condemned by Fray Luis de Granada for having, "with his letters and his authority, persuaded don António he was the true king." Sotomayor was captured by the Castilians during the war and excluded from the general pardon, but in September 1582, when Philip left Portugal and published his last pardon, Sotomayor was allowed to return to the university. Seven years later, however, there is evidence that he was corresponding with priests in Rome who were plotting on don António's behalf.[21]

The other virtuous and prudent religious was none other than Fray Miguel de los Santos. At that point, the Augustinian vicar had spent nine months in prison, had repeatedly been tortured, and stood accused of lèse majesté. He obviously was going nowhere except to the scaffold. Did don António not know this? How could he not have received news of an event that was being discussed throughout Spain and beyond? Certainly the Augustinian order knew that its former provincial was involved in high political scandal and was facing execution, and don António had plenty of friends in the Augustinian order. The papacy knew. The Jesuits knew. Anyone who knew anyone in Madrigal or Medina del Campo or Valladolid knew, and they all told people elsewhere. And if don António did know what had happened to his old confessor, did he think Fray Miguel could somehow escape? Were there plans to that end?

In the weeks leading up to his death, the pretender, who was sixty-four years old, was busy remembering the past. On July 13 he made a list of all the people who had supported him through his public struggles and passions.[22] He had not traveled this long road unaccompanied. He distinguished his closest aides, those who went with him to France, all the regular (among them Fray Miguel) and secular clergy; all told he named 253 men and women. And unlike just about every other parent in this tale, don António remembered his children, whose guardian would be Diogo Botelho. In his will he mentioned the four children he knew best: Manoel and Cristóvão, and Filipa and Luisa. It had always been his intention that Luisa should marry "in accordance with her bloodline," he said, so perhaps her mother was very well born and perhaps, unlike Filipa, she had been placed in a convent only at the time of the annexation; that would explain her vehement protests upon arriving in Tordesillas. But, her father said, if she now preferred being a nun, that was fine too.

As the days passed and death approached, don António remembered he had six children more, and on August 8 he dictated a codicil providing for them. He had a son named Luís who lived with a Portuguese man in Jeréz de la Frontera; he may have been a monk. He had two more sons in Castile, perhaps named João and Bernardo, who don António believed were being held captive by Philip II. There was another son whose name he could not remember. Another daughter, whose name also escaped him, could be a nun if she wished; he left her money. And there was yet another daughter whose name and place of residence he did not know, but one of his servants knew, he said. All this was set down as an addendum to his will.

Finally, on August 22, four days before his death, he wrote to Queen Elizabeth, overcome with sorrow that he had been unable to free his country from Spanish tyranny. He could trust only in the incomprehensible judgment of God, he said, and in the goodness and protection of the queen, whom he begged to look after his children.[23] The queen, for years moved more by self-interest than by altruism when it came to don António, wrote to Henry IV, king of France, essentially passing the buck once the pretender had died: "If the spirit of one departed could disturb a living friend, I should fear that the late King Anthony (whose soul may God pardon) would pursue me in all places if I did not perform his last request, which charged me, by all our friendship, that I should remind you after his death of the good and honourable offers which you made to him while living, that you might be pleased to fulfil them in the persons of his orphans and son [*sic*]." Neither monarch appears to have done much, for a year later an English correspondent in Guise wrote to Philip that the two sons were desperately poor and begged the king for his pardon.[24]

Don António died on August 26, 1595. He was buried in the Cordeliers convent, a Franciscan establishment. Two hundred years later, over António's dead body, Danton and his revolutionary comrades noisily debated in that same convent what to do with yet another king denied his throne. Though don António's body lay in the Cordeliers, the Portuguese pretender's heart was deposited in the walls of the convent of Ave Maria. Twelve years later, his loyal aide Diogo Botelho died and was buried at António's feet, and in 1638 Cristóvão joined them.[25] Both the Cordeliers and Ave Maria were later razed, and the remains of don António never returned home as he had wished.

Two Moroccan kings died at Alcazarquivir. One was the cultured and cosmopolitan Abd al-Malik, who was succeeded by his brother, Ahmad al-Mansur. The other, Abu Abdallah Muhammed, who unwisely sought

Portuguese protection against his own uncles, had a son, and the son also (though he had no choice, given the desecration of his father) turned to the Christians. He was known as Muley Xeque and later as Philip of Africa. His story has no direct relationship to that of the *pastelero* of Madrigal, but there are reasons to include it here. His life was irreparably changed by the battle of Alcazarquivir. Like others in this story, he became itinerant, going from Morocco to Portugal, Spain, and finally to Italy, always dependent on the Spanish crown. He converted from Islam to Christianity, providing a worthy conclusion to the conflict. He was another orphaned son, another man who changed his costume, another exiled royal heir unable to assume his throne.[26]

During the battle of Alcazarquivir, Muley Xeque, then around twelve, was held captive in Asilah as a guarantee of his father's loyalty to the Portuguese. After the disaster, he and an uncle were taken to Portugal, where they were useful pieces in Philip's continual and delicate three-way negotiations with Morocco and England. The two princes and their large entourage lived well in Portugal throughout the 1580s, occasionally receiving invitations from don António's emissaries, which they spurned. But a year after the defeat of the Spanish Armada, they were moved to Andalucia, in southern Spain, where the Spanish king kept a closer watch to ensure they did not get too friendly with Moriscos or their countrymen across the water. Then, in 1593, the young Muley Xeque underwent a sudden, well-timed revelation while watching a religious procession in Carmona. As one chronicler put it, "After he was in Spain for several years, God touched him, and as he already knew the Castilian language, he said he wanted to be a Christian."[27] Muley Xeque was baptized in an elaborate ceremony in El Escorial at which his godparents were Philip II and the infanta, Isabel Clara Eugenia, and he was renamed Philip of Africa. His conversion brought him stability and status. He was made a member of the Order of Santiago and a grandee.[28] He had a palace on Calle de las Huertas and was a fixture on the royal social scene for around a decade. During the early years of the reign of Philip III, however, he was reduced to begging for the royal subsidies that the late king had set aside for him. He sent a stream of appeals to the duke of Lerma, who forwarded them to the Council of Portugal. "He's dying of hunger," Lerma told the council.[29]

As the new regime prepared for the 1609 expulsion of the Moriscos, the former Moroccan prince thought it best to leave, and Lerma arranged for him to go to Milan, where he died in 1621. His only heir was his illegitimate daughter, Josefa de Africa, who became a nun in Zamora.

It is striking that Lope de Vega chose to tell the story of Alcazarquivir through the story of Philip of Africa. He knew the Moroccan, and probably attended his baptism. The play, *The Tragedy of King Sebastian and the Baptism of the Prince of Morocco*, was written sometime between 1593 and 1603.[30] It has been criticized for its structural incoherence, but it does not lack interest for us. A few of the characters are familiar—the count of Vimioso and Cristóvão de Tavora are there, for example. Much of the first act, a mash-up of Lisbon, Guadalupe, and Morocco, reads like the well-circulated chronicles of the debacle, and in fact Lope appropriated entire passages from the chronicler Gerolamo Franchi di Conestaggio in his dialogues, including the duke of Alba's letter to Sebastian on the eve of the battle. The play includes the familiar account of the young king's death, as he rode round and round on his horses until he finally went down with the fourth one, shot dead, in this version, by arrows. ("If these arrows flew straight because of my name . . ." Sebastian murmurs as he expires. Finally he could die like the saint.) But there is redemption. Act 2 features Muley Xeque's epiphany as he witnesses the procession of Santa María de la Cabeza. Disguised as a Christian, he tells another character how a certain Father Mendoza once told him all about the manifestations of the Virgin (a conversation in which don Juan of Austria is mentioned apropos nothing), and the play concludes, in act 3, with the prince embracing the true church and being baptized by Philip II. If King Sebastian could not survive, then Christ could be reborn in the soul of an infidel. By embracing the orphaned son, Philip II restores some of what was lost by his foolhardy nephew in the desert. Conversion and transformation were constant elements of the late sixteenth-century imagination, and there was no better transformation than that of a Muslim becoming a Christian.

Philip II died in El Escorial on September 13, 1598. His long and gruesome death "became a lesson in death and the art of dying."[31] For nearly two months he suffered excruciating pain, with fevers, chills, abscesses, diarrhea, swelling, and insomnia. He literally lay in his own excrement during much of the ordeal. Yet he remained stoic and pious, a heroic example of Christian faith despite the many indications that God had not been his ally. On his deathbed, he ordered Masses to be said for a long list of relatives, but his half-brother don Juan of Austria, whom he never called Your Highness, was not among them. He forgave certain people, even the wife of Antonio Pérez, but not his niece Ana.

Philip's pitilessness is hard to explain, but Ana's father's behavior was just as reprehensible. In January 1573, don Juan wrote to his half-sister Margaret in Naples in amusement and joy that he was about to be a father and would give the child to her to raise.[32] He wrote as if it were his first child. It was his second. Possibly, don Juan's amnesia and Philip's cruelty can be attributed to the fact that Ana's mother was a Mendoza; that is why I have pointed to all the Mendozas as they have appeared in this account. They had conspired against Philip II, and he loathed them. In contrast, the mother of don Juan's second child was a beautiful Italian noblewoman, Diana Falangola. She brought no shame or turmoil to the royal house, just sexual entanglement, generally forgiven. Many contemporaries knew about "la donna Giovanna," as Ana's sister Juana was called, but Ana's existence was largely unknown. Historians and archivists from the seventeenth century onward often referred to Ana as Juana. Philip II's viceroy in Naples, Juan de Zúñiga, believed the second daughter was the only daughter.[33] Ana was quite simply eliminated. Though her father visited Castile several times during Ana's childhood, there is no trace of his ever having seen her.

The second daughter, however, was raised by her aunt Margaret, who made sure don Juan never forgot about her. Margaret wrote him frequent letters describing Juana's progress, and she urged don Juan to urge their brother the king to legitimize her. Margaret's reminders worked; though don Juan did not mention either of his children as he lay dying in 1578, in the previous year, confessing what he called his *amor de padre*, he repeatedly begged his sister to send him a recent portrait of the girl. After don Juan's death, Juana received recognition; like Ana and her father, she was given the title of Excellency. The king later ordered his niece to enter the

Santa Clara convent in Naples, and she spent her adolescence trying to get out of it. (She did not profess as a nun.) Margaret died in 1586, but even without Margaret to protect her, for some reason Juana, unlike Ana, was allowed to seek a husband, though she was never allowed to go to court. An attempt in 1590 to marry her to the nephew of Pope Sixtus V foundered once the pope died, and it was not until after Philip II's death, by which time she had an ally in her cousin Philip III, who clearly wanted to do right by his cousins, that she finally succeeded in leaving the convent. After long negotiations, in 1603 she married Francesco Branciforti, duke of Petrabona. They lived in the Sicilian town of Militello, where they established a court, and to this day guidebooks celebrate "Giovanna" as the person responsible for the town's golden age. She and her husband had a daughter, Margaret, who married the duke of Colonna. Juana died in 1630.

As for her sister . . .

When Ana was young, she wanted to leave religious life and marry. That was not to be. But she nonetheless survived, and eventually she triumphed. And she did not have to wait long.

Just two months after her unforgiving uncle died, she was appointed to direct her new convent in Avila, so she must quickly have overcome her punishment and isolation. It is possible that the strict terms of her exile were not even enforced. Like her distant cousin the unhappy Filipa, whom she never met, Ana wrote letters from her cell. "It was my destiny and God's plan to make me His," she wrote to a religious personage who appears to have been a protector. Perhaps relationships such as this one helped her finally accept that her life would be spent behind convent walls.[34] By 1599 she was back at Madrigal—now as prioress. According to one account, all the noblemen of Avila accompanied her for the first ten kilometers of her journey.[35] It is tempting to wonder about her state of mind four years after her shameful ordeal and harsh exile as she traveled in her carriage back along the same roads. She governed Nuestra Señora de Gracia la Real for around a decade, overseeing nuns who had been witnesses to her disgrace. (I do not know if Luisa del Grado and her sister María Nieto ever returned or if Ana did anything to help them.) Among the women who took orders under her rule was Barbara del Píramo, daughter of Conrad and, like Ana, granddaughter of Barbara Blomberg. In 1611 she helped establish a municipal granary in Madrigal, an act she performed in thanksgiving for having survived a serious illness and which she announced while standing at the very grille where years earlier she had pledged herself in marriage.[36]

One of Ana's ancestors, one of the two Marías de Aragón who were prioresses of Madrigal in the early sixteenth century, had left the convent to govern the great royal monastery of Santa María la Real de las Huelgas in Burgos. When she was forty-two years old, Ana followed in María's footsteps. Las Huelgas, founded in 1187, was one of the most important seats of power in Spanish Christendom. The abbess oversaw not just the convent but all Cistercian nuns in Castile and León, and furthermore governed the towns and villages within the convent's jurisdiction. She appointed religious authorities, heard legal cases, and disciplined priests. When Ana still resided in Madrigal, Las Huelgas became the center of a power struggle among church officials and nobles. Philip III got involved in 1609, and he suggested that his cousin Ana take over as abbess. She was not well, he told his ambassador in Rome, Madrigal being a poor and sterile place with inadequate medical services, so Ana would be better off in Burgos, and Las Huelgas would be better off with her.[37] Philip III fought hard for her, insisting to his ambassador on several occasions that Ana's promotion would bring him singular happiness and pushing him to get the pope to approve the necessary briefs. After much correspondence and foot-dragging, the pope finally allowed Ana to switch from the Augustinian to the Cistercian order. In August 1611, Ana de Austria was named perpetual abbess, the highest female post in the Spanish church.

The following summer, on the day devoted to Spain's patron saint, Santiago, Ana left Madrigal, accompanied by the bishop of Osma and members of the local aristocracy. She arrived in Burgos some ten days later, where she was greeted ceremoniously by the archbishop and the chapter of the great cathedral, who awaited her along with the entire city council, the royal governor, and the aristocracy, all of them dressed in their finest clothes. On August 7 Ana went to Las Huelgas and formally

Figure 10. Anon., *Doña Ana de Austria*. Convent of Nuestra Señora de Gracia la Real.

took possession of it amid gun salutes, triumphal arches, dancing, music, "and all sorts of festivities showing the general delight and rejoicing."[38] The new abbess humbly declined the offer to enter through a doorway reserved for royalty, saying she was just a nun.

By all accounts, this woman who brought so much turmoil to her first convent brought peace and stability to Las Huelgas. She was an excellent leader, fighting for her sisters' interests against those of the powerful bishops. When necessary, Ana enlisted the aid of her cousin the king, who visited on several occasions and continued supporting her until his death in 1618. In 1615, Philip III wrote to the governor of Salamanca, who for some reason had Juan de Llano's old papers, including the case file from Madrigal. Some of these papers concerned Ana, the king said, and were unsuitable to be seen by outsiders. He instructed the official to gather them together and send them to his secretary of state.[39] The duke of Lerma probably also helped her, by omission if not by commission; one of his sons in 1603 married Luisa de Mendoza, heir to the house of Infantado. Another of Ana's supporters was Antonio Zapata de Cisneros, an archbishop and later a cardinal, viceroy of Naples, inquisitor general—and son of the counts of Barajas. His mother the countess, María de Mendoza y Mendoza, was part of the Coruña branch of the family that Ana's mother, also named María de Mendoza, came from and to which she had looked for assistance when she was alone and dying with a baby girl.

Don Juan of Austria's biographer, Baltasar Porreño, mentioned neither Ana nor her younger sister in his life of their father, but he dedicated the volume (and others) to her, the *excelentísima señora doña Ana de Austria*, the "perpetual, worthy, and blessed" abbess. Ana wrote her own autobiography, but not a single copy survives. A seventeenth-century biographer of don Juan, Antonio Ossorio, said he read the copy owned by the duchess of Petrabona, so we know the two sisters finally were in touch. Ossorio, as it happens, lived at the Jesuit institute founded by Luis de Quijada and Magdalena de Ulloa, the caretakers of Juan of Austria and his illegitimate daughter Ana, who died in her last home on November 28, 1629, and was buried in a chapel built in her honor at the foot of the convent's central nave.

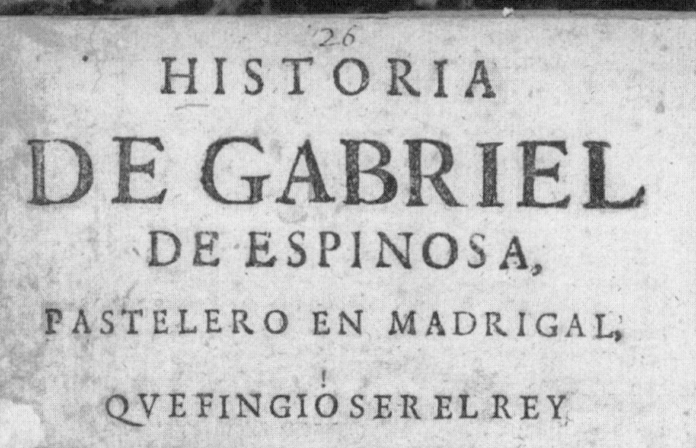

HISTORIA
DE GABRIEL
DE ESPINOSA,
PASTELERO EN MADRIGAL,
QVE FINGIO SER EL REY
D. SEBASTIAN
DE PORTVGAL:
Y ASSIMISMO LA DE FRAY MIGVEL
de los Santos, de la Orden de San Agustin,
en el año de 1595.

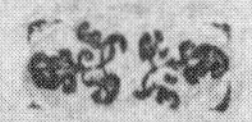

IMPRESSO,
En Xerez: Por Iuan Antonio de Tarazona,
Año de 1683.

Figure 11. Cover of the 1683 pamphlet "Historia de Gabriel de Espinosa, Pastelero en Madrigal, Que Fingio Ser El Rey D. Sebastian de Portugal." Courtesy of the Bancroft Library, University of California, Berkeley.

APPENDIX

The 1683 Pamphlet and Other Chronicles

In describing the events that took place in Madrigal de las Altas Torres, I frequently have cited the *Historia de Gabriel de Espinosa*. Its complete title is *Historia de Gabriel de Espinosa, pastelero en Madrigal, que fingió ser el Rey D. Sebastian de Portugal, y asismismo la de Fray Miguel de los Santos, de la Orden de San Agustín, en el año de 1595*. It was published in Jeréz in 1683 in both cuarto and octavo editions with various similar titles. I have seen printed copies of this pamphlet in the Biblioteca Nacional in Madrid, the Real Academia de la Historia in Madrid, the Biblioteca Nacional in Lisbon, the British Library, the Newberry Library, the Hispanic Society of America, and the Bancroft Library at the University of California, Berkeley. I do not know the reasons for the variations among printed editions or if all the pamphlets were indeed published by Juan Antonio de Tarazona, as the title page states.

Though it was published in 1683, it obviously was written much earlier. At the end of chapter 3, I quoted a Jesuit correspondent whose language is exactly repeated in the pamphlet. His fragmentary *relación*, held in the Real Academia de la Historia, was written between November 1594 and February 1595. This probable author of the pamphlet has been identified as Fernando de la Cerda. He was rector of the Jesuit college in Medina del Campo and was in Madrigal accompanying Juan de Fuensalida, with whom Espinosa spent his last days. De la Cerda (or whoever the Jesuit was) probably wrote his full account in 1595, whether printed or manuscript. He died in 1605. Between then and 1683, a variety of manuscripts about the Madrigal case with similar, sometimes identical, organization and content circulated; I have seen handwritten versions at the Biblioteca Nacional in Madrid (which has as many as ten), the El Escorial library, the Real Biblioteca del Palacio, the Biblioteca Regional de Madrid, the Instituto de Valencia de don Juan in Madrid, the Real Academia de la Historia, the Torre do Tombo archives in Lisbon, and the British Library.

There are reasons to doubt the existence of a 1595 printed pamphlet, though they are speculative.[1] First, no copies survive, though there are always good reasons why they might have disappeared. Second, it is unlikely that a pamphlet on such a delicate subject would have received permission to be printed in 1595. Third, given that the title of the 1683 pamphlet ends with the words "in the year 1595," I suggest that someone misinterpreted this as a publication date. And fourth, there is indeed a 1596 pamphlet called *Histoire du patissier de Madrigal en Espagne*, published in France, but it concerns not Sebastian but don Carlos, the prematurely dead son of Philip II, a confusion alluded to in chapter 3 where Pedro (aka Luís) Silva recounted a conversation he heard in a Salamanca bar. According to the French pamphlets, the baker was don Carlos, who had been stashed away in rural Spain twenty-six years earlier by noblemen who did not want to carry out Philip II's orders to kill his son. Don Carlos had revealed his identity to his first cousin, Ana of Austria, who was protecting him, according to this version, which also includes the baker's arrest for carrying a suspicious amount of jewels. (The pamphlet has no resolution, leaving the prince/imposter sitting in a well-guarded cell in La Mota on the king's orders.) Bibliographies, however, mistakenly list this French pamphlet as an early version of the 1683 pamphlet.[2]

Just as one traces backwards to land on the first publication, one does the same to find the first mention of a publication that may not exist. George Ticknor's 1863 *History of Spanish Literature*, which appears to be the origin of the tale, says the *pastelero* story "was first printed in 1595 at Cadiz."[3] The catalog of the book collection that Ticknor gave to the Boston Public Library refers to Patricio Escosura's 1835 novel about the case, *Ni Rey ni Roque*, as being "almost entirely founded upon the *Historia* . . . , the first edition of which was printed at Xerez in 1595."[4] Benito Sánchez Alonso's three-volume bibliography of Spanish and Latin American history lists the 1683 edition of the *Historia de Gabriel de Espinosa* with a note that "the first edition of this work, a transcript of the original trial, was published in Madrid in 1595 or 1596."[5] Palau y Dulcet repeated the assertion in his 1951 bibliography (though he also says a version of the 1683 pamphlet was published in Tarragona, a likely confusion with the publisher, named Tarazona.)[6] Julián Zarco Cuevas also repeats it in his Escorial catalog.[7] So, too, do editors of subsequent literary works about Madrigal, who generally tuck the assertion into a footnote with no explanation; for example, the editor of one of the most famous dramatic adaptations of the Madrigal story, José Zorrilla's *Traidor, inconfeso y martir* (1849), gives as one of Zorrilla's sources the 1683 pamphlet, "a revision of one of the versions of the events that appeared in 1595 and 1596," and the editor makes clear he is not talking about manuscripts.[8]

Mary Elizabeth Brooks, author of the only other English-language account of the Madrigal events, tacitly accepted the existence of the lost 1595 pamphlet, though she acknowledged the contradictory bibliographic information. She argued that the undated manuscript version in El Escorial, *Tratado del Suceso del fingido Rey Don Sebastian, del qual hasta oy se supo qué hombre era, escrito por un Padre de la Compañía* (Z-IV-2) is, chronologically, the version closest to the original. She reached this conclusion by comparing the case file, the El Escorial manuscript, and the 1683 publication, studying variations and omissions.[9]

Pamphlet or no pamphlet, news of the Madrigal case certainly traveled quickly. Luis Cabrera de Córdoba, for example, writing in the very early seventeenth century, included events and conversations in his account that do not appear in the case file as it has survived but do appear in the 1683 pamphlet. So either he had privileged access to papers, or he had seen a manuscript version. The same is true for Conestaggio. According to the editor of the works of the English dramatist George Peele, who in 1594 printed a play about Alcazarquivir, "At least as early as 1598 the interest in the false Sebastian had reached England, for in that year there was entered in the Stationers' Registers a book or pamphlet called *Strange Newes of the Retourne of Don Sebastian*."[10]

All the printed and manuscript versions follow a similar format. They generally have a prologue, around eighteen chapters, and copies of many of the letters contained in this book. Many start with the same sentences, which instruct the reader that this, and not previous versions, is the true account.

The Escorial prologue, repeated in most of the other versions, is as follows:

> Prologue: Being that the events that occurred in Madrigal in the year 1595 are so well known, and seeing that they are being recounted in very different ways, with different versions and even contradicting themselves without telling the truth about the same things, I have decided to write a true account of everything, starting at the beginning, because I can speak as an eyewitness to most of the events and as someone who was there at his death. Regarding things that took place in his life and the rest, I can also address these, being no less certain, because I consulted with reliable people who saw him and touched him with their hands.[11]

The printed 1683 prologue is as follows:

> Prologue for the curious and inquisitive Reader: Being that the events that occurred in the Town of Madrigal, in Old Castile, in the year 1595 are so well known, and the accounts of the events are so varied, disagreeing on the same point and all of them so distant from the truth, I have decided to write a complete and true exposition, starting at the beginning, and I can vouch for it as an eyewitness, both at the time of death and of many things that happened in life, and of those things I did not see I am no less certain because I consulted with reliable people who saw him and touched him.[12]

A few of the manuscripts have completely different introductions; this is true of BNM, MS 9324; RAH 9-3762/5, and ANTT, Miscelánea Manuscrita 964, for example. Most accounts then explain the structure of the narrative, saying that rather than order the events chronologically, the author prefers to present them as they were discovered. And nearly all say that Gabriel de Espinosa arrived in Valladolid (some say in 1595, though it was 1594) dressed as a common man, *con hábito y traje de hombre común*.

The publication history (as opposed to the manuscript history, which appears to have been continual) raises questions for which I have no answers. Why was it published in 1683? Why in Jeréz? Who would benefit from such a publication? And who would read it? The historian María José del Río has suggested to me that we think about don Juan José of Austria, bastard son of Philip IV and half-brother of King Charles II. Just six years before the pamphlet was published, in 1677, don Juan José (who, like the famous earlier don Juan of Austria, was raised not knowing he was a royal) staged a well-organized coup against Charles, who had no heirs—another reminder of how dangerous half-siblings could be in times of dynastic crisis. Don Juan José died suddenly at the age of fifty in 1679. Charles ruled badly for twenty more years, and after that the Spanish Hapsburgs were finally extinguished. So possibly there was renewed interest in the 1680s in half-brothers and shaky successions.

The 1683 pamphlet was reprinted in 1785, this time by Alonso del Riego in Valladolid. Again, it is worth asking what prompted a publisher then and there to consider this a worthy venture. The uncontroversial Bourbon reformer Charles III was on the throne, a healthy heir was in place, the Spanish Enlightenment was under way. No works of literature on the subject that I know of were printed any time close to this date (the only eighteenth-century version to survive was that of José Cañizares [1706], and the next one was Fredrick Reynolds's 1812 adaptation of John Dryden's 1690 play), so it was not an effort to piggyback on someone else's literary success. Perhaps it was just that readers and publishers continued to love a good story.

ACKNOWLEDGMENTS

As always, it is a pleasure to recognize the support of friends and colleagues. They gave me ideas, criticism, clues, sustenance, translations, rides, time, money, photocopies, and lodging. They are Rayne Allinson, Javier Alvarez Dorronsoro, Jim Amelang, Laura Bass, Emilie Bergmann, Fernando Bouza, Heath Dillard, Ignacio Fernández Terricabra, Paula Findlen, Cornell Fleischer, José Luis García de Paz, Mike Hannigan, Tamar Herzog, Richard Kagan, Santiago Martínez Hernández, Satoko Nakajima, Ignacio Navarrete, Geoffrey Parker, Mother Pilar of the Madres Agustinas de Nuestra Señora de Gracia, Carla and Wim Phillips, Teo Ruiz, Magdalena Sanchez, Lisa Surwillo, Tony Thompson, and Jack Weiner.

Jeff Sklansky made this book happen, so he gets his own paragraph.

Librarians and archivists who went out of their way for me include Mary Munill and Ben Stone at Stanford's Green Library; Luis Barrio Cuenca Romero at the Biblioteca Histórico Municipal de Madrid; Isabel Aguirre at the Archivo General de Simancas; José Manuel Calderón at the Archivo de los Duques de Alba; Tony Bliss at the Bancroft Library at the University of California, Berkeley; John O'Neill at the Hispanic Society of America; María Jesús Herrero Sanz at Patrimonio Nacional; and the staff of the Newberry Library.

ABBREVIATIONS

ACC	*Actas de las Cortes de Castilla*
ADA	Archivo de los Duques de Alba (Madrid)
AGS	Archivo General de Simancas
E	Sección Estado
PR	Sección Patronato Real
AHN	Archivo Histórico Nacional (Madrid)
AHPA	Archivo Histórico Provincial de Avila
AMAEC	Archivo del Ministerio de Asuntos Exteriores y de Cooperación (Madrid)
ANTT	Arquivo Nacional Torre do Tombo (Lisbon)
BL	British Library (London)
Eg.	Egerton
Add.	Additional manuscripts
BNL	Biblioteca Nacional (Lisbon)
BNM	Biblioteca Nacional (Madrid)
CODOIN	*Colección de Documentos Inéditos para la Historia de España*, ed. Martín Fernández et al. 112 vols. Madrid: Calera and others, 1841–95.
Escorial	Real Biblioteca de San Lorenzo de El Escorial
FN	Fernán Nuñez Collection, Banc MS UCB 143, The Bancroft Library, University of California, Berkeley

FZ	Fundación Francisco de Zabálburo y Basabe (Madrid)
IVDJ	Instituto Valencia de Don Juan (Madrid)
RAH	Real Academia de la Historia (Madrid)
RBP	Real Biblioteca del Palacio (Madrid)

NOTES

Chapter 1

1. Luís Vaz de Camões, *The Lusiads*, trans. Landeg White (Oxford: Oxford University Press, 1997), canto 1, st. 6. All subsequent references are to this edition.

2. Harold B. Johnson, "A Horoscope Cast Upon the Birth of King Sebastian of Portugal (1554–1578)." Online at http://people.virginia.edu/~hbj8n/horoscope.pdf.

3. The expression is Richard Kagan's, from *Lucrecia's Dreams: Politics and Prophecy in Sixteenth-Century Spain* (Berkeley and Los Angeles: University of California Press, 1990), 3.

4. Luis Cabrera de Córdoba, *Historia de Felipe II, Rey de España*, ed. José Martínez Millán and Carlos Javier de Carlos Morales (Salamanca: Junta de Castilla y León, 1998), 2:756. Most chronicles of Sebastian's life recount similar versions of his mother's visions. A similar tale of in utero predestination was told about Prince Henry, "the Navigator," who reportedly "emerged from his mother's womb embracing a simulacrum of the Holy Cross, a piece of information that the chronicler [Gomes Eanes de Zurara] seems to attribute to Henry himself [and which] was seen as proof positive that the young prince's dedication to religion and to crusading against the infidel was prenatally arranged" (Peter Russell, *Prince Henry 'the Navigator': A Life* [New Haven, CT: Yale Note Bene, 2001], 13). "Moors" is a translation of *moros*, a highly unscientific contemporary term referring to the peoples of North Africa and, sometimes, to Muslims in general.

5. Gerónimo Gascón de Torquemada, *Compendio de los Reyes que ha tenido España desde Adam hasta el Rey don Phelipe el quarto, nuestro señor* (1625) FN, vol. 123, fols. 123v–129r. On Juana, see Anne J. Cruz, "Juana of Austria: Patron of the Arts and Regent of Spain, 1554–59," in Anne J. Cruz and Mihoko Suzuki, eds., *The Rule of Women in Early Modern Europe* (Urbana: University of Illinois Press, 2009), 103–22; José Martínez Millán, "Elites de poder en las Cortes de las Monarquías española y portuguesa en el

siglo XVI: Los servidores de Juana de Austria," *Miscelánea Comillas* 61, no. 118 (2003): 169–202; José Martínez Millán, "Familia real y grupos políticos: La princesa doña Juana de Austria (1535–1573)," in *La corte de Felipe II*, ed. José Martínez Millán (Madrid: Alianza Universidad, 1994), 73–105.

6. *Epitome del compendio historeal de España de Garibay, recopilado por don Antonio Pelhcer [sic]* . . . , FN, vol. 88, libro 34, ch. 8, fol. 829. This is a handwritten copy of a late sixteenth-century history of Iberia since the Romans.

7. Fernand Braudel, *The Mediterranean and the Mediterranean World in the Age of Philip II* (New York: Harper and Row, 1973), 1:352. At the end of the seventeenth century, the British ambassador, Alexander Stanhope, was told that indeed Philip II had wanted to move his capital to Lisbon after the annexation but that "the Grandees of Castile would not hear of residing so far from their estates and vassals." See Alexander Stanhope, *Spain under Charles the Second; or, Extracts from the Correspondence of the Hon. Alexander Stanhope, British Minister at Madrid, 1690–1699*, ed. Lord Mahon (London: Murray, 1844), 75–76.

8. For Sebastian's early life, I have relied on J. M. de Queiroz Velloso, *Don Sebastián, 1554–1578*, trans. Ramón de Garciasol (Madrid: Espasa Calpe, 1943).

9. Ibid., 82.

10. Juan de Silva to Philip II, 6 March 1576, AGS E, leg. 393, widely cited (e.g., in Alfonso Dánvila, *Felipe II y el Rey Don Sebastián de Portugal* [Madrid: Espasa Calpe, 1954], 298). Harold Johnson has suggested Sebastian was sexually abused by his tutors see "A Pedophile in the Palace or the Sexual Abuse of King Sebastian of Portugal (1554–1578) and Its Consequences," in *Pelo Vaso Traseiro: Sodomy and Sodomites in Luso-Brazilian History*, ed. Harold Johnson and Francis A. Dutra (Phoenix, AZ: Fenestra Books, 2006), 195–230; and *Camponeses e Colonizadores: Estudos de História Luso-Brasileira* (Lisbon: Editorial Estampa, 2002), 158–162. There is no doubt that the young Sebastian was strictly controlled by his tutor and confessor, Luís Gonzalvez de la Cámara, and Luís's brother Martín.

11. Fray Luis Nieto, *Relación de las guerras de Berbería y del suceso y muerte del Rey Don Sebastián*, in *CODOIN* (1891), 100:433. Nieto's account was first published in French in 1579 and in Portuguese only three hundred years later. (For *CODOIN* and other abbreviations used in the notes, see the list of abbreviations preceding the endnotes.)

12. Luis Vélez de Guevara, *Comedia famosa del Rey Don Sebastián*, ed. Werner Herzog (Madrid: Anejos del Boletín de la Real Academia Española, 1972), 88–89, ll. 925–34): "My heart / does not desire such things. / I am warlike and do not wish / to spend two hours or three / beating my body and my feet / to the rhythms of a fool. / My destiny points to weapons / and I loathe repose, / and if I love hunting / it is because it imitates warfare."

13. *Crónicas del Rey Dom Sebastião*, FN, vol. 147, fol. 146.

14. Silva, who joined Philip's court as a page in 1538, descended from prominent families in the Castilian-Portuguese circle of advisers to the Spanish crown. See Silva to Gabriel de Zayas, 1 May 1576, AGS E, leg. 393, cited in Antonio Villacorta Baños-García, *Don Sebastián, Rey de Portugal* (Barcelona: Editorial Ariel, 2001), 56; Silva to Philip II, 25 May 1576, cited in Dánvila, *Felipe II y el Rey Don Sebastián*, 297; Borja to

Silva, December 1575, AGS E, leg. 392, fol. 217, cited in Alfonso Dánvila y Burguero, *Don Cristóbal de Moura, Primer Marqués de Castel Rodrigo (1538–1613)* (Madrid: Fortanet, 1900), 855.

15. For a more favorable account, see Rafael Valladares, *La conquista de Lisboa. Violencia militar y comunidad política en Portugal, 1578–1583* (Madrid: Marcial Pons, 2008), ch. 7. Valladares argues that Sebastian was less interested in Morocco than in re-establishing absolute rule in Portugal and that political imperative, not anachronism, governed his actions.

16. Valladares, *Conquista de Lisboa*, 212.

17. Diogo Barbosa Machado, *Memorias para a historia de Portugal, que comprehendem o governo del Rey D. Sebastião, unico em o nome, e decimo sexto entre os Monarchas Portuguezes* (Lisbon: Officina de Joseph António da Sylva, 1736–51), 3:149. Barbosa does not cite sources. The conversation may never have taken place, of course, but it was described in one form or another in most contemporary accounts of Sebastian's life. It also appears in Queiroz Velloso, *Don Sebastián*, 97. Machado could have been channeling Camões, who at that very time was writing *The Lusiads*: "that ravenous hunger / That reckless, insatiable greed / Which, to possess what is another's / Exposes wretches to the pangs of Hell." (canto 4, st. 44). On the 1569 epidemic, see Mario Da Costa Roque, "A 'peste grande' de 1569 em Lisboa," *Anais*, 2nd. ser., 28, (1982): 74–90.

18. The literature on Lepanto is huge; for Braudel, the spectacular battle with few immediate consequences (though many rippling effects) was a perfect example of the limitations of *l'histoire événémentielle* (*Mediterranean*, 2:1088–142). For the Actium comparison and the problem of narrating heroic actions undertaken to build empires, a question that has later relevance for the battle of Alcazarquivir, see Elizabeth R. Wright, "Narrating the Ineffable Lepanto: The *Austrias Carmen* of Joannes Latinus (Juan Latino), *Hispanic Review* 77, no. 1 (Winter 2009): 71–91.

19. Antonio de Herrera y Tordesillas, *Historia general del mundo . . . del tiempo del Señor rey Don Felipe II el Prudente. . . .* (Valladolid, 1606), 1:155.

20. Joaquim Veríssimo Serrão, *Itinerários de El-Rei D. Sebastião* (Lisbon: Academia Portuguesa da Historia, 1962), 2:65–67; Dánvila, *Felipe II y el Rey Don Sebastián*, 275.

21. Cabrera de Córdoba, *Historia de Felipe II*, 2:756.

22. Barbosa Machado, *Memorias*, 3:603–4. No source given.

23. The entire account is bound at the end of Barbosa Machado, *Memorias*, vol. 4. I do not think there is an original. Portions, taken from Barbosa Machado, appear in Queiroz Velloso, *Don Sebastián*, 153. See also Herrera y Tordesillas, *Historia general*, 1:155.

24. Miguel de Cervantes, *Los baños de Argel* (Madrid: Taurus, 1983), 140. Malik was a character in this short play, published in 1615. Cervantes enlisted in the Holy League's army in 1571 and spent four years fighting in the Mediterranean with don Juan of Austria. He was captured by pirates in 1575 and held captive in Algiers for five years.

25. Lope de Vega, "La tragedia del Rey don Sebastián y Bautismo del Príncipe de Marruecos," in *Biblioteca de Autores Españoles*, vol. 225 (Madrid: Atlas, 1969), 124.

26. Manuel Fernández Alvarez emphasizes the remarkable fact that Philip went to Guadalupe at all. Unlike his father, Philip much preferred to send envoys to speak with other rulers. See "Objetivo: Lisboa. La unión de Portugal y Castilla bajo Felipe II," in

Las relaciones entre Portugal y Castilla en la época de los descubrimientos y la expansión colonial (Salamanca: Ediciones Universidad, 1994). A late seventeenth-century fictional account of the life and death of Sebastian says Philip brought along his daughter Catalina Micaela to tempt Sebastian—decidedly untrue: see Ferrand Spence, *Don Sebastian, King of Portugal. An Historical Novel in Four Parts* (London: Printed for R. Bentley and S. Magnes, 1683), 119.

27. "Relación de las vistas [*sic*] de los Reyes Don Phelipe 2 y Don Sebastian en Nuestra Señora de Guadalupe, año de 1576," Hispanic Society of America (New York), HC 411–209, 15r–17v. For a description of Sebastian's journey, see Barbosa Machado, *Memorias*, 4:55–63.

28. "Coplas del gran peña sobre los dichos de los portugueses en Guadalupe," in Antonio Rodríguez Moñino, *Viaje a España del Rey Don Sebastián de Portugal (1576–1577)* (Valencia: Editorial Castalia, 1956), 127. This book includes a transcription of the "Relación escrita por un músico de la Real Capilla y enviada por éste a un señor de Toledo," 87–114, and other contemporary accounts. The "Relación" can also be found in *Relaciones históricas de los siglos XVI y XVII* (Madrid: Sociedad de Bibliófilos Españoles, 1896), 114–152; and in RAH, Salazar N-44, fols. 407–21v. My quotations and descriptions come from Rodríguez Moñino and from the "Relación." See also Queiroz Velloso, *Don Sebastián*, 175, for other accounts.

29. Joachim Romero de Cepeda, *Famossisimos romances. El primero trata de la venida a Castilla del muy alto y muy poderoso señor don Sebastian primero. . . .* (2009 facsimile of 1577 original pamphlet; Badajoz: Ayuntamiento de Badajoz, 2009).

30. Vélez de Guevara, *Comedia famosa*, 105, ll. 1410–14.

31. Much of the correspondence regarding marriage plans is in *CODOIN*, vol. 28, with scattered references in vols. 26 and 27. The originals are mostly in AGS E, legs. 385–88. See Queiroz Velloso, *Don Sebastián*, ch. 5, on the negotiations.

32. Fernando Carrillo to Gabriel de Zayas, 22 September 1569, *CODOIN*, 28:543.

33. Sebastian to Juana, 27 September 1569, ibid., 552.

34. Fernando Carrillo to Gabriel de Zayas, 22 September 1569, ibid., 521.

35. Borja to Philip, 24 January 1570, cited in Dánvila, *Felipe II y el Rey Don Sebastián*, 189. Sebastian's biographer reports on some of the more extravagant tales regarding Sebastian's supposed love interests at this time. For example, he was actually in love with a Moorish princess whom he met during the 1574 episode in Tangiers, and he received messages from her via a courier whom Sebastian would meet on a beach near Lisbon. Or, he was in love with the noblewoman Juliana de Lencastre (Lancaster), whose father, the duke of Aveiro, was later killed at Alcazarquivir. Or he was in love with Juana de Castro, another noblewoman. See Queiroz Velloso, *Don Sebastian*, 141–42.

36. Silva to Philip, 20 March 1576, cited in Dánvila, *Felipe II y el Rey Don Sebastián*, 297.

37. RAH, Salazar, N-44, fols. 421r and 418v.

38. For Sebastian's state, see Rodríguez Moñino, *Viaje a España del Rey Don Sebastián*, 62. For the cat and the cistern, see RAH, Salazar, N-44, fols. 408r and 419r. For Philip's conditions, see Rodríguez Moñino, *Viaje a España del Rey Don Sebastián*, 62. For Sebastian's plan to leave early, see Baltasar Porreño, *Dichos y hechos del Señor Rey Don Felipe Segundo. . . .* (Madrid: Melchor Sánchez, 1663), fols. 61v–62r.

39. Silva, cited in Joaquim Veríssimo Serrão, *Itinerarios de El-Rei D. Sebastião* (Lisbon: Academia Portuguesa da Historia, 1962), 2:169. Aldana, whom Cervantes called "el Divino," was recently termed "the best mid-century poet" in Spain; see Julian Weiss, "Renaissance Poetry," in *The Cambridge History of Spanish Literature*, ed. David T. Gies (Cambridge: Cambridge University Press, 2004), 165. Aldana's attempts to dissuade Sebastian are generally included in the chronicles and literary works about Alcazarquivir.

40. Silva to Philip II, 16 January 1578, *CODOIN*, 39:479. A publicly circulated appeal to Sebastian to desist was written by the bishop of Silves: see Jerónimo Osorio, *Cartas portuguezas de D. Hieronymo Osorio* (Paris: P. N. Rougeron, 1819), 3–17.

41. Medinaceli to Philip II, RAH, Salazar y Castro, M-20, fol. 95; see also BNM, MSS 12866, *Papeles referentes al gobierno del Rey Sebastián I de Portugal y a las expediciones a la India y Africa*, fol. 440v.

42. Anonymous, *Crónica do Xarife Mulei Mahamet e d'el-rey D. Sebastião, 1573–1578*, ed. Francisco de Sales de Mascarenhas Loureiro (Odivelas: Heuris, 1987), 83. The author of this chronicle, a member of don António's entourage, wrote the account in Fez after he was taken captive.

43. Gerolamo Franchi di Conestaggio, *The historie of the uniting of the kingdom of Portugall to the crowne of Castill. . . .* (London: Imprinted by A. Hatfield for E. Blount, 1600), 15. I have modernized Conestaggio's spelling here and throughout. This chronicle was first published in Genoa in 1585 and was widely and quickly translated and disputed. It was never translated into Portuguese. Conestaggio's principal source is generally assumed to have been Juan de Silva; some authors have said Silva in fact wrote it. The chronicle's bald recounting of Philip's Machiavellian approach to the annexation led the king to prohibit its circulation. The critical tone of the chronicle prompted a Portuguese chronicler to reply with a fiercely patriotic version of his own: see Jeronymo de Mendonça, *A jornada d'Africa. Resposta a Jeronymo Franqui e a outros. . . .* (1607; Oporto: Imprensa Recreativa do Instituto Escholar de S. Domingos, 1878). A similarly combative tone appears in Sebastián de Mesa, *Iornada de Africa por el Rey Don Sebastián y Unión del Reyno de Portugal a la Corona de Castilla* (Barcelona: Pedro Lacavallería, 1630); the author, an Inquisition official, was a Spaniard but admired the Portuguese monarch's sacrifice for the faith.

44. Mesa, *Iornada de Africa*, 48.

45. Fr. Antonio San Román de Ribadeneyra, *Jornada y muerte del rey Don Sebastián de Portugal, sacada de las obras del Franchi, ciudadano de Genova, y de otros muchos papeles auténticos* (Valladolid: Por los herederos de Juan Yñiguez de Lequerica, 1603), 40–42. On the reaction to the comet, see Barbosa Machado, *Memorias*, 4:177–87.

46. Hieronymo Muñoz Valenciano, *Libro del nuevo cometa y del lugar donde se hazen. . . .* (Valencia, 1573). Muñoz was a professor of Hebrew and mathematics at the University of Valencia.

47. San Román, *Jornada y muerte*, 40–42.

48. Baltasar Gracián, *Agudeza y Arte de Ingenio*, ed. Evaristo Correa Calderón (Madrid: Clásicos Castalia, 1969), 1:190–91.

49. Fernando de Goes Loureiro, *Breve Summa y Relación de las Vidas y Hechos de los Reyes de Portugal, y cosas succedidas en aquel Reyno desde su principio hasta el año de*

MDXCV (Mantua: Osana, 1596), fols. 83–84. This book also was written to counter Conestaggio's.

50. Pero Roiz Soares, *Memorial*, ed. M. Lopes de Almeida (Coimbra: Universidade de Coimbra, 1953), 90. This anti-Spanish chronicle, about whose author nothing appears to be known, was written in the early seventeenth century. The original is in BNL, Fundo Geral MS 938.

51. Fr. Bernardo da Cruz, *Crónica del-Rei D. Sebastião*, Bibliotheca de Clásicos Portuguezes, vol. 36 (Lisbon: Escriptorio, 1903), 111–13. Other accounts say the soldiers in the sky appeared the day of the battle: see Lucette Valensi, *Fables de la Mémoire: La glorieuse bataille des trois rois* (Paris: Editions du Seuil, 1992), 140, citing Thome Roiz Quaresma, "Memorias históricas de Portugal dos Reynados de El Rey D. Sebastião do Cardeal Rey D. Henrique e dos Phelipes," BNL, cod. 591, fol. 85. Penamacor, perhaps not coincidentally, was where the first false Sebastian arose, two years before Cruz wrote his chronicle.

52. Silva to Zayas, 12 November 1577, from AGS E, leg. 394, fol. 278, cited in Veríssimo Serrão, *Itinerários*, 2:177.

53. Escorial, L.I.12, 173–76.

54. ANTT, Gaveta XVI, 3–21, 14 March 1578; Barbosa Machado, *Memorias*, 4:279.

55. Anonymous, *Crónica do Xarife*, 87.

56. *CODOIN*, 40:9.

57. Ibid., 40. The Silva correspondence from these months is in vols. 39, 40, and 59; the originals are in AGS E, leg. 396. Some copies are also in *Papeles referentes al gobierno*; RAH, Salazar y Castro Z-9; and in *Les sources inédites de l'histoire du Maroc de 1530 a 1845*, Espagne, vol. 3 (Paris: E. Leroux, 1961).

58. Nieto, *Relación de las guerras*, 454–55.

59. *Papeles referentes al gobierno*, fol. 85.

60. *Crónicas del Rey Dom Sebastião*, FN, vol. 147, fol. 147. Malik's beautiful wife was fictionalized by Cervantes as Zoraida in *Don Quixote*, vol. 1, ch. 40.

61. See Queiroz Velloso, *Don Sebastian*, 242–45, for a discussion of the letters and their translations.

62. Barbosa Machado, *Memorias*, 4:198–99. Barbosa Machado says Sebastian did not reply. Malik also wrote to Philip II around this time, asking him to stop the expedition.

63. *Papeles referentes al gobierno*, fols. 12–14.

64. There are multiple and varied copies in BNM; BL; Escorial; RAH; the Hispanic Society of America (New York); ANTT; *Les sources inédites. . . .* (*Espagne*, 3:424–27); most chronicles; and in modern secondary sources. I do not know in which language Malik wrote his letters. I am citing from BL Eg., 357, no. 7; and BNM, MS 773 fols. 135v–137r, both in Spanish.

65. Anonymous, *Crónica do Xarife*, 87.

66. The men were the archbishop of Lisbon, João Mascarenhas, and Francisco de Sá de Meneses. Sebastian's will, drawn up on June 13, 1578, is in Antonio Caetano de Sousa, *Provas da história genealógica da casa real portuguesa* (Coimbra: Atlântida, 1948), 3:249–58; and in Barbosa Machado, *Memorias*, 4:55–63 (pages bound at the end of

the volume). Sousa, whose book was first published in 1744 and therefore may be the source for Barbosa Machado, says the will is false.

67. Nieto, *Relación de las guerras*, 439–40. A preliminary list of the Portuguese noblemen and hidalgos called up is in Joaquim Veríssimo Serrão, "Documentos inéditos para a historia do reinado de D. Sebastião," *Boletim da biblioteca da Universidade de Coimbra* 24 (1960): 236–43.

68. Juan de Silva to Philip II, 1 June 1578, *CODOIN*, 40:26; Anonymous, *Crónica do Xarife*, 62.

69. Anonymous, *Historia de Portugal desde el tiempo del Rey Don Sebastian. . . .* , BL Eg., 522, fol. 26. In the BL catalog, Pascual de Gayangos attributes this chronicle to Juan de Villegas.

70. Camões, *Lusiads*, canto 4, st. 84.

71. *Ayer fuiste rey de Hespaña, Oy no tienes un castillo*; the anecdote is reported frequently, here from Manoel dos Santos, *Historia sebastica, contem a vida do augusto principe o senhor D. Sebastião, Rey de Portugal* (Lisbon: A. Pedrozo Galram, 1735), 436.

72. The bumpy departure appears in all the accounts: BL Eg., 522, *Historia de Portugal*, fol. 26; Anonymous, *Crónica do Xarife*, 89; *Crónicas del Rey Dom Sebastião*, FN, vol. 147, fol.149; Conestaggio, *Historie*, 29; and Cruz, *Crónica del-Rei D. Sebastião*, 112–13. A sermon preached to the departing ships can be found in BL Add. 28.483, fols. 232–35v. Vélez de Guevara's *Comedia famosa del Rey Don Sebastián* relies on Conestaggio, putting entire passages in his characters' mouths, including an account of the departure spoken by don António, the prior of Crato.

73. Camões, *Lusiads*, canto 4, st. 89; canto 5, st. 1; canto 4, st. 97. The Spanish Baroque poet Luís de Góngora's first "Soledad" (381–85) also depicts an old man weeping and railing away as the imperial fleet departs: "These monsters of the deep with planks for scales, / more treacherous than Greece's wooden gift / that brought fire and confusion to Troy's walls, / have transported so much pain / to worlds so many seas apart!" Later (409–11) he laments, "Today Greed is at the helm / not of single ships alone / but of whole restless fleets." From Luis de Góngora, *Selected Poems*, ed. and trans. John Dent-Young (Chicago: University of Chicago Press, 2007). The poem dates from around 1610.

74. Silva to Philip II, 6 July 1578, *CODOIN*, 40:58–63, from AGS E, leg. 396. Asilah is also written Arcila, Arzila, and Asila.

75. Conestaggio says Vimioso was in favor of marching inland, but he is the only chronicler to say so. Given that Conestaggio's principal source was Juan de Silva, who for good reason disliked Vimioso and his family, Queiroz believes Conestaggio is wrong. See Queiroz Velloso, *Don Sebastian*, 237. There is an alleged verbatim transcript of Vimioso's argument in Barbosa Machado, *Memorias*, 4:346–51.

76. Barbosa Machado says Sebastian ordered the arrest of a renegade who appeared in his camp with news of the size of Malik's forces (*Memorias*, 4:352).

77. RAH, Salazar y Castro K-19, fols. 7–12. This wonderfully descriptive anonymous chronicle, most commonly known as "Los ytenes de Portugal" (and so cited hereafter) or "Respuesta que se hizo a una carta de un abbad de la Vera," is widely reproduced; see also *Les sources inédites* (*Espagne*, 3:476–488); António Sérgio, ed., *O Desejado:*

Depoimentos de contemporaneos de D. Sebastião sobre este mesmo rei e sua jornada de Africa (Paris and Lisbon: Livrarias Aillaud e Bertrand, 1924), 13–36; and Miguel Angel de Bunes Ibarra and Enrique García Hernán, "La muerte de D. Sebastian de Portugal y el mundo mediterráneo de finales del siglo XVI," *Hispania* 54, no. 187 (May/August 1994), 463–65, taken from the Biblioteca Casanatense de Roma.

78. Conestaggio, *Historie*, 31; Mesa, *Iornada de Africa*, fol. 46. The chronicler likewise wrote of Malik, "Seeing he could not reach an agreement with the Catholic King, he determined to defend himself [though he] knew how much better it is to have a bad agreement than a good war" (BL Eg. 522, *Historia de Portugal*, fol. 27v.).

79. Silva to Philip II, 17 July 1578, AGS E, leg. 396, fol. 79, cited in Veríssimo Serrão, *Itinerários*, 2:223.

80. E. W. Bovill says Malik had between sixty thousand and seventy thousand men; see *The Battle of Alcazar. An Account of the Defeat of Don Sebastian of Portugal at El-Ksar el-Kebir* (London: The Batchworth Press, 1952), 110. Queiroz estimates he had fifty thousand (*Don Sebastian*, 278); "Los ytenes de Portugal" says there were one hundred twenty thousand.

81. Camões, *Lusiads*, canto 1, st. 17.

82. Alba to Sebastian, 22 July 1578, RAH, Jesuitas, vol. 188, *Floreto de anécdotas y noticias diversas que recopiló un fraile dominico residente en Sevilla a mediados del siglo XVI*, fol. 177. The letter also appears in *Papeles referentes al gobierno*, fol. 33v; Hispanic Society of America (New York), HC411/209, *Papeles varios sobre acaecimientos politicos y eclesiasticos de los reinados de Felipe II, Felipe III y Felipe IV*, fol. 18; Vélez de Guevara, *Comedia famosa*, 130–31; and BNM, MS 1753, *Descripción de las cosas sucedidas en los Reynos de Portugal desde la Jornada que el Rey Don Sebastián hizo en Africa. . . .*, fol. 11.

83. *Sucesos notables. . . .*, FN, vol. 72, fol. 191.

84. *Papeles referentes al gobierno*, fol. 38.

85. Juan Bautista de Morales, *Jornada de Africa del Rey Don Sebastian de Portugal* (Seville, 1622), fols. 38–38v, in *Tres relaciones históricas: Gibraltar, Los Xerves, Alcazarquivir* (Madrid: Imprenta de M. Ginesta Hermanos, 1889). The book is in large part a celebration of the Jesuits.

86. Nieto, *Relación de las guerras*, 448.

87. *Papeles referentes al gobierno*, fol. 51v.

88. "Los ytenes de Portugal," RAH, Salazar y Castro K-19, fols. 7–12. For English-language descriptions of the battle, see Bovill, *Battle of Alcazar*; and Weston F. Cook Jr., *The Hundred Years War for Morocco: Gunpowder and the Military Revolution in the Early Modern Muslim World* (Boulder, CO: Westview Press, 1994), ch. 9. In French, see Valensi, *Fables de la Mémoire*, 26–35. The eyewitness accounts in Portuguese are by Jeronymo de Mendonça, Fr. Bernardo da Cruz, and Miguel Leitão de Andrade, whose works are collected in Sérgio, *O Desejado*. José María de Queirós Veloso disputes Cruz's identity; see his "Fr. Bernardo da Cruz e a 'Chronica d'el-rei D. Sebastião,'" in *Estudos históricos do século XVI* (Lisbon: Academia Portuguesa da Historia, 1950), 137–96, a study of all the chronicles.

89. Queiroz Velloso, *Don Sebastian*, 246–47, on theories regarding the poisoning.

90. George T. Matthews, ed., *News and Rumor in Renaissance Europe (The Fugger*

Newsletters) (New York: G. P. Putnam's Sons, 1959), 48–50. The son of the duke of Braganza was António, prior of Crato, whose survival is discussed in the following chapter.

91. On the death of Sebastian, see Nieto, *Relación de las guerras*, 451; Conestaggio, *Historie*, 50–51; *Sucesos notables. . . .* , FN, vol. 72, fols. 199–205v; San Román, *Jornada y muerte*, 157–66; Morales, *Jornada de Africa*, 49–55.

92. "Los ytenes de Portugal."

93. Luís Coello de Barbuda, *Empresas militares de Lusitanos* (Lisbon: Pedro Craesbeeck, 1624), 297v.

94. "Those killed in late medieval and early modern battles were always naked because specialized units stripped them immediately of their clothes and arms for resale" (Valentin Groebner, *Who Are You? Identification, Deception, and Surveillance in Early Modern Europe*, trans. Mark Kyburz and John Peck [New York: Zone Books, 2007], 96). For a summary of all the evidence regarding Sebastian's body, see Pedro José de Figueiredo, *Carta em resposta de certo amigo da cidade de Lisboa a outro da villa de Santarém, em que se lançam os fundamentos sobre a verdade ou incerteza da morte d'ElRei D. Sebastião* (Lisbon: Off. de João Evangelista Garcez, 1808).

95. Nieto, *Relación de las guerras*, 453. On the relationship between the bodies of King Sebastian and St. Sebastian, see Marsha Swislocki, "De cuerpo presente: El Rey don Sebastián en el teatro áureo," in *En torno al teatro del Siglo de Oro (Actas)* (Almería: Instituto de Estudios Almerienses, 1999), 45–54; and Marsha Swislocki, "Cuerpo de santo, cuerpo de Rey: El 'martirio' del rey Don Sebastián en la literatura áurea," in *Homenaje a Henri Guerreiro. La hagiografía entre historia y literatura en la España de la Edad Media y del Siglo de Oro*, ed. Marc Vitse, 1059–68 (Madrid: Iberoamericana, 2005).

96. The handover of the body is recounted in San Román, *Jornada y muerte*, 166. Sometime in 1579, Philip II sent a new ambassador to Morocco and instructed Silva to tell him to tell the sharif how much Philip appreciated his generosity and courtesy in delivering Sebastian's body, made known to Philip through Andrea Gasparo Corso; see "Instruccion que mandó formar Su Magestad al Conde," undated, RAH, Z-9, fol. 108; see also Silva to Zayas, 4 October 1578, AGS E, leg. 396, fol. 87, cited in Veríssimo Serrão, *Itinerários*, 2:223.

97. BL Eg. 522, *Historia de Portugal*, 47. The very last lines of Camões's *Lusiads* also compare Alexander and Sebastian. And, in Vélez de Guevara's *Comedia famosa*, 76, l. 515, the sharif asks, "Is your king powerful?" "He is another Alexander," replies a Portuguese. The comparison was tempting, given the young leaders' headstrong nature, bravery, and untimely death, but Alexander's nasty despotism made him "a dangerous weapon that always threatened to cut both ways." See Vincent Barletta, *Death in Babylon: Alexander the Great and Iberian Empire in the Muslim Orient* (Chicago: University of Chicago Press, 2010), 23.

98. Paul Fussell, *The Great War and Modern Memory* (Oxford: Oxford University Press, 1975), 29–35; Valensi, *Fables de la Mémoire*, 142, makes a similar comparison.

99. Sebastián de Covarrubias Orozco, *Tesoro de la Lengua Castellana o Española* (Madrid: Editorial Castalia, 1995).

100. Aviso de Antonio Manso, in *Les sources inédites* (*Espagne*, 3:451).

101. BL Add 28.262, fols. 632–35v, cited by Geoffrey Parker, *Felipe II: La biografía definitiva* (Madrid: Planeta, 2010), 708; *Memorias de Fray Juan de San Gerónimo, CODOIN*, 7:229–34.

102. *Sucesos notables. . . .* , FN, vol. 72, fols. 211–11v.

103. For Teresa's vision, see Barbosa Machado, *Memorias*, 4:425–27. The bishop indeed was killed in the battle. The distraught Teresa found consolation by vowing to establish Carmelite houses in the martyred Portugal (Santos, *Historia sebástica*, 431–32).

104. João Francisco Marques, *A parenética portuguesa e a dominação filipina* (Oporto: Instituto Nacional de Investigação Científica, 1986), 29, citing José de Castro, *D. Sebastião e D. Henrique* (Lisbon: Tip. União Gráfica, 1942), 188, who quotes a letter to the Vatican from Roberto Fontana in Lisbon, August 18, 1578. In fact, the duke of Aveiro (Jorge de Lencastre) was killed; so were the poet Francisco de Aldana, Cristóvão de Tavora and his brother, and the famed English soldier of fortune Thomas Stukeley. See Bunes Ibarra and García Hernán. "La muerte," 458, citing from Archivo Secreto Vaticano, Nunciatura de Portugal. This article has a detailed account of the immediate reception of the news.

105. "Los ytenes de Portugal." Lucrecia de León (see chapter 4) had visions of an apocalypse that would "turn Spain into Troy" (María V. Jordán Arroyo, *Soñar la Historia: Riesgo, creatividad y religión en las profecías de Lucrecia de León* [Madrid: Siglo XXI, 2007], 3). It was Lisbon's founder, Ulysses, "through whose cunning Troy was burned" (Camões, *Lusiads*, canto 3, st. 57).

106. *Sucesos notables. . . .* , FN, vol. 72, fol. 211v.

107. Conestaggio, *Historie*, 56–57.

108. St. Teresa to Fray Jerónimo Gracian, 19 August 1578, in *Cartas*, 3rd ed., 2:342, Maestros Espirituales Carmelitas (Burgos: Editorial Monte Carmelo, 1983).

109. Matthews, *News and Rumor*, 50.

110. Thucydides, *History of the Peloponnesian War*, 8.1.

111. Plutarch, *Nicias*, trans. John Dryden. Available online at http://classics.mit.edu/Plutarch/nicias.html.

112. Margaret Meserve, "News from Negroponte: Politics, Popular Opinion, and Information Exchange in the First Decade of the Italian Press," *Renaissance Quarterly* 59, no. 2 (2006), 449–51, citing contemporary chronicles.

113. "Relación del llanto y ceremonias que se hicieron por la muerte del rey de Portugal. . . . ," RAH, Salazar N-4, fols. 60–61; Juan de Baena Parada, *Epítome de la vida, y hechos de Don Sebastian Dezimo Sexto Rey de Portugal y Unico deste Nombre. . . .* (Madrid: Antonio Gonzalez de Reyes, 1692), fols. 155–57.

114. *Crónicas del Rey Dom Sebastião*, FN, vol. 147, fol. 40; also in Roiz Soares, *Memorial*, 104–05. Here and throughout, I use the Spanish version of the friar's name rather than the Portuguese, dos Santos. According to the Torre do Tombo (p. 238) and Escorial (p. 27) versions of the chronicle (the *Historia de Gabriel de Espinosa*), Fray Miguel said Sebastian watched his own funeral: "Father, I have seen myself buried."

115. The BNL has two sermons by Alvares for Sebastian, MSS 3030 and 6590, fols.

49–56. They are in Marques, *A parenética portuguesa*, 29–38, 349–50. Excerpts are also transcribed in Queirós Veloso, *A perda da independencia*, vol. 1, *O reinado do Cardeal D. Henrique* (Lisbon: Empresa Nacional de Publicidade, 1946), 26–30; Jacqueline Hermann, *No Reino do Desejado. A construção do sebastianismo em Portugal, séculos XVI e XVII* (Sao Paulo: Companhia das Letras, 1998), 159; and Francisco Caeiro, *O Arquiduque Alberto de Austria, vice-rei de Portugal* (Lisbon, 1961). The entire September 19 (*sic*) sermon attributed to Fray Miguel is in Camilo Castelo Branco, *As virtudes antigas; ou a freira que fazia chagas e o frade que fazia reis* (1868; 2nd ed., Lisbon: Livraría de Campos Junior, 1904), 89–116, citing a copy in his possession. An account of the October 8, 1578, funeral for Sebastian in Madrid in the presence of the Spanish royal family is in AHN, Nobleza, Frias 24/105, fols. 65–69. The transcript of that sermon (October 9) is in ADA, caja 115, no. 88.

116. Peter McNiven, "Rebellion, Sedition and the Legend of Richard II's Survival in the Reigns of Henry IV and Henry V," *Bulletin of the John Rylands University Library of Manchester* 76, no. 1 (Spring 1994): 93–117.

117. BNM MS 12866, fol. 321; Porreño, *Dichos y hechos*, fol. 103. Philip II similarly collected his dynasty's corpses from throughout Spain to rebury them in El Escorial; see Carlos Eire, *From Madrid to Purgatory: The Art and Craft of Dying in Sixteenth-Century Spain* (Cambridge: Cambridge University Press, 1995), 260.

118. Luis de Herrera to Philip II, *Les sources inédites* (*Espagne*, 3:457).

119. Moura to Philip II, 26 August 1578, *CODOIN*, 40:136–140. The reference to Moura's brother appears in a letter to the king cited in Fernando Bouza, ed., *Cartas de Felipe II a sus hijas* (Madrid: Akal, 2008), 59. On Moura, see Dánvila, *Don Cristóbal de Moura*. The Spanish historian Santiago Martínez Hernández is preparing a new biography of this diplomat and courtier, who became viceroy of Portugal under Philip III.

120. *Papeles referentes al gobierno*, fol. 68.

121. The Asilah story appears everywhere; here I am using Herrera y Tordesillas, *Historia general*, 1:345–46; and Morales, *Jornada de Africa*, fols. 57–58.

122. *Crónicas del Rey Dom Sebastião*, FN, vol. 147, fol. 40.

123. Martha Walker Freer, *The Married Life of Anne of Austria, Queen of France, Mother of Louis XIV. And Don Sebastian, King of Portugal*. Historical Studies, vol. 2 (London: Tinsley Brothers, 1864), 405. This story then segues into the account of the false Sebastian of Venice, on which see H. Eric R. Olsen, *The Calabrian Charlatan, 1598–1603: Messianic Nationalism in Early Modern Europe* (New York: Palgrave Macmillan, 2003).

124. Spence, *Don Sebastian, King of Portugal*, bk. 4.

125. José Pereira Bayão, *Portugal cuidadoso, e lastimado com a vida, e perda do senhor rey Dom Sebastiaõ, o desjado de saudosa memoria* (Lisbon: Officina de Antonio de Sousa da Sylva, 1737), 723.

126. *Historia de Gabriel de Espinosa, Pastelero en Madrigal, que fingió ser el rey Don Sebastian de Portugal, y asimismo la de Fray Miguel de los Santos, en el año de 1595* (Jeréz: Juan Antonio de Tarazona, 1683), 15 (hereafter *Historia de Gabriel de Espinosa*).

127. AGS E, leg. 173, doc. 226; Mary Elizabeth Brooks, *A King for Portugal: The Madrigal Conspiracy, 1594–95* (Madison: University of Wisconsin Press, 1964), 92–93, 109;

Miguel d'Antas, *Les faux Don Sébastien. Etude sur l'histoire de Portugal* (Paris: Chez Auguste Durand, libraire, 1866), 147–57. For a vastly more detailed account of the Mendes story than that in the case file itself, see *Historia de Gabriel de Espinosa*, 23–26.

128. *Historia de Gabriel de Espinosa*, 11–13. In his testimony in 1594–95, Fray Miguel sometimes said Sebastian was alive and sometimes that he was dead. This nine-point list, which also appears in manuscript versions of the chronicle, was not part of the case file. It might have existed in an alleged earlier edition of the pamphlet, or in case papers that did not survive but which the author of the 1683 edition saw, or it might have been added in 1683, based on stories which by then had all appeared in literary or historical accounts.

129. Bovill says the fleet commander heard the noise of the battle from the port of Larache as he was awaiting the king. Once it was clear the king was not coming, the fleet sailed north past Asilah, stopping at Tangiers to pick up survivors before returning to Lisbon. He was criticized later for having not saved enough people (Bovill, *Battle of Alcazar*, 143, 146). Cabrera de Córdoba names the admiral as Diego de Soussa and says some people believed the ship returned the day of the battle with the king on board.

Chapter 2

1. 17 March 1578, RAH, Salazar M-20, fol. 89.

2. The story of the servant is widely repeated; see J. M. de Queiroz Velloso, *Don Sebastian, 1554–1578*, trans. Ramón de Garciasol (Madrid: Espasa Calpe, 1943), 225.

3. *Descripción de las cosas sucedidas en los Reynos de Portugal desde la Jornada que el Rey Don Sebastian hizo en Africa. . . .*, BNM, MS 1753, fol. 12v.

4. Moura to Philip II, 2 September 1578, *CODOIN*, 40:144.

5. The following year, Abraham Gibre's son, Jacobo, fell victim to a prisoner-swap scam in which, he explained to don António in a letter written from his prison cell, a Spanish gentleman in alleged need of money had passed himself off as a nephew of the duke of Medina Sidonia. None other than Juan de Silva had told him the man was Medina Sidonia's nephew, Jacobo said. So he loaned the swindler six thousand ducats and waited three weeks for the man's servant to appear with the money. Finally someone showed up, telling him Jacobo would have to go with him to Ceuta to collect the money. They boarded a ship, and the unlucky mediator was dropped off in the Spanish town of Tarifa and promptly imprisoned. The duke of Medina Sidonia washed his hands of the matter, claiming he had no idea who the culprit was. Jacobo wrote to don António, reminding him of all that his father had done for the pretender and asking for his help. ADA, caja 115, doc. 64. I do not know if António rescued Jacobo, but I doubt it, given how busy he was. A letter in the Torre do Tombo written in August 1592 describes the plight of a Jew in Ceuta who also helped ransom Portuguese soldiers after Alcazarquivir and was never paid (ANTT, Gaveta 20,15–22).

6. Carlos José Margaça Veiga, "Entre o rigor do castigo e a magnanimidade da clemencia: Os perdões concedidos por Filipe II a Portugal," *Mare Liberum* 10 (December 1995): 153; Queiroz Velloso, *Don Sebastian*, 311; Anonymous, "Los ytenes de Portugal"; Yves-Marie Bercé, *Le roi caché: Sauveurs et imposteurs. Mythes politiques populaires dans*

l'Europe moderne (Paris: Fayard, 1990), 28–29; Louise-Geneviève Gillot de Sainctonge, *Histoire secrete de dom Antoine, Roy de Portugal, tirée des memoires de Dom Gomes Vasconcellos de Figueredo* (Paris: Chez Jean Guignard, 1696), 13. This is a French version of António's memoirs.

7. Bernardo Maschi to duke of Urbino, 10 January 1580, cited by Geoffrey Parker in *Felipe II: La biografía definitiva* (Madrid: Planeta, 2010), 712.

8. Letters and accounts in RAH, 9/3723 describe the legitimacy struggle and others of António's travails and victories in 1579–80. See also Agostino Borromeo, "La Santa Sede y la candidatura de Felipe II al trono de Portugal," in *Las sociedades ibéricas y el mar a finales del siglo XVI*, vol. 5, *El área Atlantica: Portugal y Flandes* (Madrid: Sociedad Estatal Lisboa '98, 1998), 41–57; and "Relaçaõ de algunas accoens do e Senhor D. António," FN, vol. 48, fols. 216–37.

9. 19 April 1579, RBP, II/2226 fol. 83; Osuna to Pérez, 10 April 1579, *CODOIN*, 6:326,. Osuna was named extraordinary ambassador in February 1579. His sister Magdalena was the widow of the second duke of Aveiro, killed at Alcazarquivir. The Portuguese Cortes comprised representatives of dozens of cities and towns but was dominated by Lisbon, Oporto, Evora, Coimbra, and Santarém. See Antonio Manuel Hespanha, "Cities and the State in Portugal," in *Cities and the Rise of States in Europe, AD 1000 to 1800*, ed. Charles Tilly and Wim P. Blockmans (Boulder, CO: Westview Press, 1994), 184–95.

10. Such was the case of the López Marmolejo brothers, from Marbella, both captured at Alcazarquivir. Their family managed to come up with money for one of them in 1583, but the Moroccans demanded that a particular Moor from Constantinople serving on the Spanish galleys be produced in exchange for the second brother; see José Antonio Martínez Torres, *Prisioneros de los infieles: Vida y rescate de los cautivos cristianos en el Mediterráneo musulmán (siglos XVI–XVII)* (Barcelona: Ediciones Bellaterra, 2004), 118, citing documents from AGS. The Bennassars tracked thirty-seven commoners taken prisoner at Alcazarquivir, of whom twelve managed to return to Portugal in less than five years; see Bartolomé and Lucile Bennassar, *Les Chrétiens d'Allah. L'histoire extraordinaire des renegats. XVI et XVII siècles* (Paris: Perrin, 1989), 226–51.

11. "Sentencia que el Rey Don Henrique dió contra Don Antonio . . . ," BNM, MS 11261/33; also in Antonio Caetano de Sousa, ed., *Provas da história geneaológica da casa real portuguesa* (Coimbra: Atlântida, 1948), vol. 2, pt. 2, 127–29.

12. Rodrigo de la Cerda to Philip (7 January 1580), IVDJ, envío 93, doc. 142.

13. "A haver mas tarde nacido / o mas temprano reynado." From Manuel de Faria e Sousa, *Fuente de Aganipe. Rimas Varias* (Hispanic Society of America [New York], B2509, n.d.), fol. 93v. 17C.

14. Victor von Klarwill, ed., *The Fugger News-Letters, 2nd series. Being a further Selection from the Fugger papers specially referring to Queen Elizabeth. . . .* (New York: G. P. Putnam's Sons, 1926), 35–38.

15. ADA, caja 115, scattered letters, January–April 1580.

16. Ibid., no. 173.

17. "Relaçaõ de algunas accoens do e Senhor D. Antonio," FN, vol. 48, fols. 222–23.

18. ADA, caja 115, doc. 58. Moura also pressured Cárcamo, Antonio's chief steward, who ended up serving in Philip's court. See Alfonso Dánvila y Burguero, *Don Cristobal de Moura, Primer Marqués de Castel Rodrigo (1538–1613)* (Madrid: Fortanet, 1900), 653–54; and Gerolamo Franchi di Conestaggio, *The historie of the uniting of the kingdom of Portugall to the crowne of Castill. . . .* (London: Imprinted by A. Hatfield for E. Blount, 1600), 204–5. Don António remembered Cárcamo in his will.

19. ADA, caja 115, doc. 75, 6 April 1580.

20. Cited in Rafael Valladares, *La conquista de Lisboa. Violencia militar y comunidad política en Portugal, 1578–1583* (Madrid: Marcial Pons, 2008), 46.

21. "Revelaciones de la visionaria de Alburquerque," 3 May 1580, IVDJ, Envío 5 (2) 3–6. Transcribed in Gregorio de Andrés, "Las revelaciones de una visionaria de Alburquerque sobre Felipe II," in *Homenaje a Luis Morales Oliver* (Madrid: Fundación Universitaria Española, 1986), cited in Richard Kagan, "Politics, Prophecy, and the Inquisition in Late Sixteenth-Century Spain," in *Cultural Encounters: The Impact of the Inquisition in Spain and the New World*, ed. Mary Elizabeth Perry and Anne J. Cruz (Berkeley and Los Angeles: University of California Press, 1991), 105–26.

22. The sermon is referenced in many sources; I am using the transcript in Francisco Caeiro, *O Arquiduque Alberto de Austria, vice-rei de Portugal* (Lisbon, 1961), 522–31; the original is BNL, cod. 3030.

23. Isidro Velázquez Salamantino, *La entrada que en el Reino de Portugal hizo la S.C.R.M. de Don Philippe* (Lisbon, 1582), fol. 37v.

24. P. Juan de Mariana, *Historia General de España* (Madrid: Imprenta y Librería de Gaspar y Roig, Editores, 1852), 2:491. The first edition, in Latin, was published in 1592.

25. Conestaggio, *Historie*, 160–61. The story is also told in Pedro Batalha Reis, *Numária d'el Rey dom António, décimo oitavo Rei de Portugal, O ídolo do povo* (Lisbon: Academia Portuguesa da História, 1947), 62, citing the Vatican Secret Archive. Barachio and his brother Gabriel both landed on the list of those excluded from the general amnesty.

26. There is a description in *CODOIN*, 40:324–25, though the source is unclear. Convent reference is from Velázquez Salamantino, *La entrada*, RAH, 9/3723, fol. 12, which describes António's liberation of Henry's belongings.

27. Conestaggio, *Historie*, 165–66.

28. The edict is in AGS E, leg. 412, reproduced in *CODOIN*, 7:300–304; in the *Memorias de Fray Juan de San Gerónimo*; and in RAH, 9/3723, fol. 56.

29. On the fall of Lisbon, see Valladares, *La conquista de Lisboa*, ch. 3. On the Moroccans, see Mário Domingues, *O Prior do Crato contra Filipe II* (Lisbon: Romano Torres, 1965), 181. On the noblemen, see "Memoria de las personas principales que se hallaron con Don Antonio en la batalla sobre Lisboa," AGS E, leg. 422. On the women, see Conestaggio, *Historie*, 176.

30. Pero Roiz Soares, *Memorial*, ed. M. Lopes de Almeida (Coimbra: Universidade de Coimbra, 1953), 182.

31. Fernando Bouza, ed. *Cartas de Felipe II a sus hijas* (Madrid: Akal, 2008), 99.

32. AGS E, leg. 173, doc. 149.

33. Ibid., doc. 28.

34. Ibid., doc. 146.

35. Alba to Philip II, 26 August 1580, *CODOIN*, 32:465.

36. Velázquez Salamantino, *La entrada*, fols. 59–60; António, prior of Crato, *The Explanation of the True and Lawful Right and Tytle of the Moste Excellent Prince Anthonie. . . .* (Leyden [*sic*; probably London]: In the Printing House of Christopher Plantyn, 1585). Conestaggio's version had don António walking back through Lisbon and opening all the prisons before leaving (*Historie*, 216–18); see also Gillot de Sainctonge, *Histoire secrete*.

37. RAH, 9/3723. According to one biographer, Cervantes, who was in Lisbon during Philip II's residency, wanted to join the army against don António but for some reason did not enlist, though his brother Rodrigo did; see Jean Canavaggio, *Cervantes* (Madrid: Espasa-Calpe, 1986), 90–92.

38. Antonio Herrera y Tordesillas, *Historia general del mundo . . . del tiempo del Señor rey Don Felipe II el Prudente. . . .* (Valladolid: 1606), 1:440.

39. AGS E, leg. 413, fol. 109, cited in J. A. Pinto Ferreira, ed., *A campanha de Sancho de Avila em perseguição do Prior do Crato. Alguns documentos de Simancas* (Oporto: Camara Municipal, 1954), 74–76.

40. Ibid., fol. 104, cited in Pinto Ferreira, *A campanha de Sancho de Avila*, 82.

41. Ibid., fol. 82, cited in Pinto Ferreira, *A campanha de Sancho de Avila*, 102.

42. *CODOIN*, 31:338–44.

43. Ibid., 236. The threats included house-burnings, sometimes carried out.

44. For example, "Edicto de Felipe II contra el rebelde de Portugal," 26 April 1581, AGS PR, leg. 51, no. 4.

45. Von Klarwill, *Fugger News-Letters*, 47–50.

46. Fernando de Goes Loureiro, *Breve Summa y Relación de las Vidas y Hechos de los Reyes de Portugal, y cosas succedidas en aquel Reyno desde su principio hasta el año de MDXCV* (Mantua: Osana, 1596), fols. 104–7; Von Klarwill, *Fugger News-Letters*, 50. When Philip II heard that don António had managed to stroll among the Spanish soldiers near the Viana marina, he instructed Sancho Dávila to get the names of the soldiers and punish them; see Pinto Ferreira, *A campanha de Sancho de Avila*, 122. The Viana escapade is also in Conestaggio, *Historie*, 235–37.

47. Domingues, *O Prior do Crato*, 281–82; António, prior of Crato, *Explanation*, 35. The date of his final departure from Portugal was probably May 10, but could have been a few days earlier. Don António remembered Gonçalves in his will; see Sousa, *Provas da história genealógica*, 173.

48. One of Philip II's aides expressed concern over the site of the Tomar meeting, a convent, which he said once belonged to don António's father, don Luís. Caesar's killers, he reminded the king, dared to act only when their prey was enclosed with no hope of outside help. Philip disagreed. See Bouza, *Cartas de Felipe II a sus hijas*, 36. For the street incident, see Fernando Bouza, *Imagen y propaganda: Capítulos de historia cultural del reinado de Felipe II* (Madrid: Akal, 1998), 58, citing IVDJ, envío 5, fols. 184–86.

49. Luis Cabrera de Córdoba, *Historia de Felipe II, Rey de España*, ed. José Martínez Millán and Carlos Javier de Carlos Morales (Salamanca: Junta de Castilla y León, 1998), 3:1013.

50. ADA, caja 115, doc. 27.

51. Cabrera de Córdoba, *Historia*, 3:1139. Albert was the son of Maximilian II of Austria and Philip's sister María, though he was raised by Philip from the age of eleven.

52. José Pedro Paiva, "Bishops and Politics: The Portuguese Episcopacy during the Dynastic Crisis of 1580," *e-Journal of Portuguese History* 4, no. 2 (2006); online at www.brown.edu/Departments/Portuguese_Brazilian_Studies/ejph/html/Winter 06.html. João of Portugal's antipathy toward Philip stemmed from a squabble in the 1570s in which the monarch took Henry's side against him and his family. That account is also in Valladares, who cites Conestaggio; see Valladares, *La conquista de Lisboa*, 202.

53. ADA, caja 118, doc. 7. Another orthographic error came earlier, on July 14, 1580, in the general pardon Philip issued in Badajoz. The usual wording of "Philip, by the grace of God" appeared as "Philip, by the race of God," suggesting that the invading king was divine. The edict was not distributed. See Bouza, *Imagen y propaganda*, 135–36, citing FZ, 126.8.

54. João Francisco Marques, "Fr. Miguel dos Santos e a luta contra a união dinástica o contexto do falso D. Sebastião de Madrigal," *Revista da Faculdade de Letras: Historia*, series 2, 14 (1997), 348.

55. Bishop of Tuyd to Zayas, 23 May 1581, AGS E, leg. 412.

56. Luis de Granada to Zayas, 23 November 1580, AGS E, leg. 419, fol. 22, cited in João Francisco Marques, *A parenética portuguesa e a dominação filipina* (Oporto: Instituto Nacional de Investigação Científica, 1986), 403–7. Fray Luis had been the confessor of both Catherine and the duke of Alba, and author of two of the century's bestsellers, *The Book of Prayer and Meditation* (1554) and *The Sinner's Guide* (1555).

57. Marques, "Fr. Miguel dos Santos e a luta," 348.

58. AGS E, leg. 172, doc. 110.

59. Luís Vaz de Camões, *The Lusiads*, trans. Landeg White (Oxford: Oxford University Press, 1997), 85 (canto 4, st. 41).

60. Luis Vélez de Guevara, *Comedia famosa del Rey Don Sebastián*, ed. Werner Herzog (Madrid: Anejos del Boletín de la Real Academia Española, 1972), 76, 97.

61. António, prior of Crato, *Explanation*, 54–55.

62. Marques, "Fr. Miguel dos Santos e a luta," 333.

63. AGS E, leg. 172, doc. 63.

64. AGS E, leg. 173, doc. 1.

65. Juan de Borja to Philip II, 12 December 1575, BNM, MS 12866, fol. 266v. For more on stereotypes and categorizations of the Portuguese, see Miguel Herrero García, *Ideas de los españoles del siglo XVII* (Madrid: Editorial Gredos, 1966), 134–78.

66. Geoffrey Parker, "David or Goliath? Philip II and His World in the 1580s," in *Spain, Europe and the Atlantic World: Essays in honour of John H. Elliott*, ed. Richard L. Kagan and Geoffrey Parker (Cambridge: Cambridge University Press, 1995), 249.

67. Jean Frédéric Schaub, "Conflictos y alteraciones en Portugal en le época de la unión de coronas: Marcos de interpretación," in *Ciudades en conflicto (siglos XVI–XVIII)*, ed. José I. Fortea and Juan E. Gelabert (Valladolid: Junta de Castilla y León, 2008), 397–410.

68. Pedro Cardim, "Los portugueses frente a la monarquía hispánica," in *La monar-*

guía de las naciones. Patria, nación y naturaleza en la monarquía de España, ed. Antonio Alvarez-Ossorio Alvariño and Bernardo J. García García (Madrid: Fundación Carlos de Amberes, 2004), 355–83.

69. Letter from Doctor Rui López, 1595, ANTT, Arquivo de D. António, doc. 341. Unless the date is incorrect, this cannot be the same Portuguese Dr. Rodrigo López who was in the pay of Philip II, physician to Queen Elizabeth, and convicted of trying to poison her. But he also worked for don António, so perhaps it is the same man. He was hanged, drawn, and quartered on June 7, 1594.

70. Llano to Philip II, 29 January 1595, AGS E, leg. 173, doc. 2. Biographical information from Marques, *A parenética portuguesa*, 321; Thomas de Herrera, *Breve compendio de los prelados eclesiásticos y ministros de sumos pontífices, reyes, y príncipes de quienes haze mención en su Alfabeto Agustiniano el M. F. Tomas de Herrera. . . .* (Madrid: I. Maroto, 1643), fol. 31; Carlos Alonso, OSA, "Documentación inédita sobre Fr. Agustín de Jesús, OSA, Arzobispo de Braga (1588–1609), *Analecta Augustiniana* 34 (1971): 126–28.

71. Santillán to Idiáquez, 7 March 1595, AGS E, leg. 173, doc. 137.

72. Carlos Alonso, OSA, "Las profesiones religiosas en la provincia de Portugal durante el período 1513–1631," *Analecta Augustiniana* 48 (1985): 338.

73. Marques, "Fr. Miguel dos Santos e a luta," 331–88; Marques cites J. S. da Silva Dias, *O Erasmismo e a Inquisição em Portugal: O processo de Fr. Valentim da Luz* (Coimbra: Universidade de Coimbra, 1975), which describes the testimony in that case of our friar, referring to him as Miguel Todos-os-Santos.

74. Marques. *A parenética portuguesa*, 321; J. M. Queirós Veloso, in *A perda da independencia*, vol. 1 of *O Reinado deo Cardeal D. Henrique* (Lisbon: Empresa Nacional de Publicidade, 1946), 29, also says Fray Miguel publicly condemned the African expedition from his pulpit. Neither writer gives sources for the assertion.

75. A list of the *exceptuados* appears in Mario Brandão, "Alguns documentos relativos a 1580," *Boletim da Biblioteca da Universidade de Coimbra* 16 (1944): 38–43, but Fray Miguel's name is again erroneously noted as "dos Anjos" rather than "dos Santos." For a study of Philip's Portuguese pardons, see Margaça Veiga, "Entre o rigor do castigo e a magnanimidade da clemecia." Of the fifty-two exclusions from the amnesty, five were secular clergy (including the bishops of La Guarda, Evora, and Coimbra), and thirteen were regular clergy.

76. Philip to provincial, 9 August 1581, AGS E, leg. 426.

77. AGS E, leg. 173, doc. 206.

78. Printed in Marques, "Fr. Miguel dos Santos e a luta," 331–88. I do not know why (or if) he was in Valladolid and not Salamanca.

79. AGS E, leg. 172, unnumbered document, Philip to prior, by Zayas. The paper is ripped, and the date is 158—, but a nineteenth-century hand added the "6," which makes sense.

80. AGS E, leg. 173, doc. 52.

81. Peter Burke, "Early Modern Venice as a Center of Information and Communication," in *Venice Reconsidered: The History and Civilization of an Italian City-State, 1297–1979*, ed. John Martin and Dennis Romano (Baltimore, MD: Johns Hopkins University Press, 2000), 396.

82. The English also referred to "noise" and "murmur," and Ovid describes *murmura* in *Metamorphosis*; see Adam Fox, *Oral and Literate Culture in England 1500–1700* (Oxford: Clarendon Press, 2000), 336. The *avisos* published in late sixteenth-century Spain were often just translations from the Italian. There is a broad literature on seventeenth-century Spanish newsletters, or *relaciones de sucesos*: see Jean-Pierre Etienvre, "Entre relación y carta: Los Avisos," in *Les 'relaciones de sucesos' (canards) en Espagne (1500–1750). Actes du premier colloque international (Alcalá de Henares, 8–10 juin 1995)* (Alcalá de Henares, 1996); for an excellent study of an earlier case, see Pedro M. Cátedra, *Invención, difusión y recepción de la literatura popular impresa (Siglo XVI)* (Badajoz: Editorial Regional de Extremadura, 2002).

83. 20 December 1581, AGS E, leg. 428.

84. "Las personas que se deben sacar de Portugal," August 1581, AGS E, leg. 428. The duke of Francavilla was an important member of the Mendoza family; see ADA, caja 117, doc. 7; Luiz Augusto Rebello da Silva, *Historia de Portugal nos seculos XVII e XVIII* (Lisbon: Imprensa National, 1867), 3:485–87; and Batalha Reis, *Numária d'el Rey dom António*, 383. Silva and Reis both reproduce an alleged confession obtained by the Spaniards from Francisco before his death, which they say is false. Francisco and brother Manoel (to whom the duke of Alba wrote before the invasion) were both on the list of *exceptuados*.

85. Rebello da Silva, in *Historia de Portugal*, 3:20, says the count of Vimioso had seven sisters, all of whom Philip confined in convents.

86. AGS E, legs. 426 and 428 contain several of these announcements.

87. P. José de Castro, *O Prior do Crato* (Lisbon: Tip. União Gráfica, 1942), 359–62. Another version has the bishop being taken to Castile and confined in the "convent of Calatrava," where he died. See Cabrera de Córdoba, *Historia*, 3:1140.

88. E. García España and Annie Molinié-Bertrand, eds., *Censo de Castilla de 1591: Vecindarios* (Madrid: Instituto Nacional de Estadística, 1986), 75–76; Catastro de Ensenada, 20 January 1751, available online at http://pares.mcu.es/catastro/. Today, the town has around two thousand inhabitants.

89. Firmo Zurdo Manso and Esther del Cerro Calvo, *Madrigal de las Altas Torres: Recuerdos para una historia* (Avila, 1996), 40.

90. AGS E, leg. 173, doc. 5. The *extramuros* monastery today is in ruins.

91. Alberto Marcos Martín, "Medina del Campo 1500–1800: An Historical Account of Its Decline," in I. A. A. Thompson and Bartolomé Yun Casalilla, eds. *The Castilian Crisis of the Seventeenth Century: New Perspectives on the Economic and Social History of Seventeenth-Century Spain* (Cambridge: Cambridge University Press, 1994), 244.

92. AGS E, leg. 172, doc. 242; BL Eg., 2059 fol. 252. The position of vicar does not seem to exist anymore in the Augustinian order; the Recollect Augustinians have vicars, but their jurisdiction does not seem to be a single monastery, as was the case with Fray Miguel.

93. *Collecção de memorias e casos raros*, ANTT, Miscelánea manuscrita 964, fol. 230. The same description is in the version in Escorial, *Historia del fingido Rey de Portugal*, Z-4-2, fol. 6v.

94. Cabrera de Córdoba, *Historia*, 3:1520.

95. AGS E, leg. 173, unnumbered document between docs. 251 and 252. The document contains the questions, but not the answers.

96. AGS E, leg. 172, doc. 112. Throughout the case, testimony veers between first-person and third-person narrative, with the mediating presence of the judge always felt.

97. Juan de Aranda, *Lugares comunes de conceptos, dichos, y sentencias, en diversas materias* (Seville, 1595), fol. 81v.

98. AGS E, leg. 172, doc. 100. These copies are illegible to me; I used transcriptions in María Remedios Casamar, *Las dos muertes del Rey Don Sebastián* (Granada, 1995), 79–84; and in the pamphlet *Historia de Gabriel de Espinosa, Pastelero en Madrigal, que fingió ser el rey Don Sebastian de Portugal, y asimismo la de Fray Miguel de los Santos, en el año de 1595* (Jeréz: Juan Antonio de Tarazona, 1683), 53–54 (hereafter *Historia de Gabriel de Espinosa*). Casamar used the same bad copy I have, but whoever compiled the 1683 pamphlet must have had access to a clearer version.

99. AGS E, leg. 172, doc. 29.

100. Martin Hume, *True Stories of the Past* (London: E. Nash, 1910), 85.

101. AGS E, leg. 173, doc. 227, but taken here from BL Eg., 2059, fols. 252–55v.

102. *Historia de Gabriel de Espinosa*, 23.

103. BL Eg, 2059, fol. 254r.

104. AGS E, leg. 173, doc. 226.

105. Ibid., docs 11, 12, 18, and unnumbered documents between docs. 251 and 252; BL Eg., 2059, fols. 255v–259v; *Historia de Gabriel de Espinosa*, 43–44. Santillán was sometimes present at Fray Miguel's torture sessions, though he did not have jurisdiction. See AGS E, leg. 173, doc. 37.

106. *Historia de Gabriel de Espinosa*, 43–44.

107. BL Eg., 2059, fols. 256v–57r.

108. AGS E, leg. 173, doc. 233 lists eight *confesiones*, or testimonies, by Fray Miguel between March and August; there may have been more.

109. Santillán to Philip, 26 June 1595, AGS E, leg. 173, doc. 174.

110. AGS E, leg. 172, docs. 4 and 5.

111. Ibid., doc. 11.

112. AGS E, leg. 173, doc. 227. I am using the version in BL Eg., 2059 fol. 254.

113. Harry Kelsey, *Sir Francis Drake: The Queen's Pirate* (New Haven, CT: Yale University Press, 1998), 342–56; Gordon K. McBride, "Elizabethan Foreign Policy in Microcosm: The Portuguese Pretender, 1580–89," *Albion: A Quarterly Journal Concerned with British Studies*5, no. 3 (Autumn 1973), 193–210; Cabrera de Córdoba. *Historia*, 3:1256. A more positive spin on the Drake adventure can be found in an account held by the Hispanic Society of America (New York), possibly written by Sir Walter Raleigh: *A true coppie of a discourse written by a Gentleman employed in the late Voyage of Spaine and Portingale* (London, 1589).

114. BFZ, 219.D.141/1 (n.d.).

115. António, prior of Crato, *Explanation*, 49.

116. *Calendar of Letters and State Papers Relating to English Affairs, preserved in, or originally belonging to, the Archives of Simancas*, vol. 4, *Elizabeth, 1587–1603*, ed. Martin A. S. Hume (London: Public Record Office, 1899), 5–50.

117. Ibid., 50.

118. AGS E, leg. 172, docs. 94 and 95.

119. AGS E, leg. 173, docs. 27 and 229.

120. *Historia de Gabriel de Espinosa*, 45.

121. AGS E, leg. 173, unnumbered document between docs. 251 and 252.

122. Ibid., doc. 52.

123. Ibid., doc. 46.

124. Ibid., doc. 145.

125. Von Klarwill, ed., *Fugger News-Letters*, 143.

126. Silva to Idiáquez, 13 May 1595, AGS E, leg. 173, doc. 201; Silva to Philip II, 2 June 1595, AGS E, leg. 433. His appointment as governor would appear to violate Philip II's pledge to appoint only Portuguese, as Silva was mostly Castilian. On this point and in general on Silva's career, see Fernando Bouza, "Corte es decepción: Don Juan de Silva, conde de Portalegre," in *La corte de Felipe II*, ed. José Martínez Millán (Madrid: Alianza Universidad, 1994), 451–502.

127. AGS E, leg. 173, doc. 25; AGS E, leg. 173, docs. 62 and 85 for subsequent retractions.

128. Llano to Philip II, 23 May 1595, AGS E, leg. 173, doc. 48.

129. On his accomplices, see ibid., docs. 12, 18, 27, 46, 52, 163, and 165.

130. Ibid., doc. 46.

131. Ibid., doc. 52.

132. Jaime Oliver Asín, *Vida de Don Felipe de Africa, príncipe de Fez y Marruecos (1566–1621)*, ed. Miguel Angel de Bunes Ibarra and Beatriz Alonso Acero (Granada: University of Granada, 2008), 60.

133. AGS E, leg. 173, docs. 209 and 267.

134. Ibid., doc. 175.

135. Ibid., docs. 83 and 85.

136. AGS E, leg. 173, doc. 85.

137. Henry Kamen, *Inquisition and Society in Spain in the Sixteenth and Seventeenth Centuries* (Bloomington: Indiana University Press, 1985), 175–77; Henry Charles Lea, *Torture* (Philadelphia: University of Pennsylvania Press, 1973), 37–41; Francisco Tomás y Valiente, *La tortura en España: Estudios históricos* (Barcelona: Editorial Ariel, 1973), 134, citing *ACC*, vol. 16, 646. The leading manual was Antonio Quevedo y Hoyos, *Libro de indicios y tormentos; que contiene toda la práctica criminal y modo de sustanciar el proceso indicativamente. . . .* (Madrid: Francisco Martínez, 1632).

138. AGS E, leg. 173, doc. 283.

139. Ibid., docs. 26 and 298.

140. Rodrigo Vázquez de Arce, AGS E, leg. 173, doc. 382.

141. ANTT, Arquivo de don António, doc. 341.

142. Gregorio Marañon, *Antonio Pérez (el hombre, el drama, la época)*, 2 vols., 5th ed. (Madrid: Espasa Calpe, 1954), 2:822, testimony in Pérez's Inquisition trial.

143. Gregorio Marañón, *Antonio Pérez, 'Spanish Traitor,'* trans. Charles David Ley (London: Hollis and Carter, 1954), 308. Again, this may be the same López executed by Elizabeth in 1594; see note 69 above.

144. Julieta Teixeira Marques de Oliveira, *Fontes documentais de Veneza referentes a Portugal* (Lisbon: Comissão Nacional para as Comemorações dos Descobrimentos Portugueses, 1997), 609. The author mistakenly gives the year as 1590; it was 1591.

145. The Bernardo del Río story is in AGS E, leg. 173, docs. 127, 128, 154, 155, 188, 237, and 238.

146. AGS E, leg. 173, docs. 202 and 327.

147. The letters are transcribed or discussed in AGS E, leg. 173, docs. 6, 119, 125, 130, 140, 244–48, 289, and 294.

148. AGS E, leg. 173, doc. 289.

149. AGS E, leg. 173, doc. 244.

150. Ibid., doc. 140.

151. RAH, 9–3675/86 (Jesuitas, vol. 102).

152. AGE E, leg. 173, docs. 128 and 129.

153. Ibid., doc. 140.

154. On the Zúñiga affair, see Thomas de Herrera, *Historia del convento de S. Augustin de Salamanca* (Madrid: G. Rodríguez, 1652), 399; Conrado Muiños Sáenz, *Fray Luis de Leon y Fray Diego de Zúñiga* (El Escorial: Imprenta Helénica, 1914), discusses the various Zúñigas and concludes it is nearly impossible to know which was which. James Fitzmaurice-Kelly reaches the same conclusion in *Fray Luis de León, a Biographical Fragment* (Oxford: Oxford University Press, 1921), available online at http://www.gutenberg.org/files/16148/16148-8.txt; on Fray Luis's trial, see *CODOIN*, vols. 10 and 11, and also Marcelino Gutiérrez, "Fray Diego de Zúñiga," *Ciudad de Dios* 14 (1887): 298.

155. AGS E, leg. 173, docs. 393, 348, and 396. The investigation commenced in early August, and the results are unknown to me.

156. *Calendar of State Papers and Manuscripts Relating to English Affairs, Existing in the Archives and Collections of Venice*, vol. 9, 1592–1603 (London: Public Record Office, 1897), 158 (April 22, 1595).

Chapter 3

1. Francesco Vendramino, quoted in Luigi Firpo, ed., *Relazioni di ambasciatori veneti al Senato*, vol. 8, *Spain (1497–1598)* (Turin: Bottega D'Erasmo, 1981), 451.

2. Mário Domingues. *O Prior do Crato contra Filipe II* (Lisbon: Romano Torres, 1965), 215.

3. *The Coppie of the Anti-Spaniard made at Paris by a French man, a Catholique. Wherein is directly proved how the Spanish king is the onely cause of all the troubles in France. Translated out of French into English* (London, 1590), 19, 4.

4. J. Ignacio Tellechea Idígoras, *El ocaso de un rey. Felipe II visto desde la Nunciatura de Madrid, 1594–1598* (Madrid: Fundación Universitaria Española, 2001), 139.

5. IVDJ, 45/452 (5 February 1591).

6. On the *millones*, see José Ignacio Fortea Pérez, *Monarquía y Cortes en la corona de Castilla* (Valladolid: Cortes de Castilla y León, 1990), 271–98; Charles Jago, "Habsburg

Absolutism and the Cortes of Castile," *American Historical Review* 86, no. 2 (April 1981): 307–26; Felipe Ruiz Martín, "Credit procedures for the Collection of Taxes in the Cities of Castile During the Sixteenth and Seventeenth Centuries: The Case of Valladolid," in I. A. A. Thompson and Bartolomé Yun Casalilla, eds., *The Castilian Crisis of the Seventeenth Century: New Perspectives on the Economic and Social History of Seventeenth-Century Spain* (Cambridge: Cambridge University Press, 1994), 169–81; José Ignacio Ruiz Rodríguez, "Estructura y recaudación del servicio de millones 1590–1691," *Hispania* 52, no. 3 (1992): 1073–88; I. A. A. Thompson, "Crown and Cortes in Castile 1590–1665," *Parliaments, States and Representation* 2, no. 1 (June 1982): 29–45.

7. *ACC*, vol. 12, 63 (26 May 1595).

8. *Calendar of State Papers and Manuscripts Relating to English Affairs, Existing in the Archives and Collections of Venice*, vol. 9, 1592–1603 (London: Public Record Office, 1897), 68.

9. I. A. A. Thompson, "Oposición política y juicio del gobierno en las Cortes de 1592–98," *Studia Historica*, no. 17 (1997): 37–62.

10. *ACC*, vol. 12, 473; AGS E, leg. 173, doc. 129. I. A. A. Thompson, in "La respuesta castellana ante la política internacional de Felipe II," in *La monarquía de Felipe II a debate* (Madrid: Sociedad Estatal para la Conmemoración de los Centenarios de Felipe II y Carlos V, 2000), 121–34, argues that the Cortes in these years disengaged from the monarchy's imperial mission. Another scholar has argued that contemporary playwrights also were opposed to Philip's policies regarding Portugal and North Africa; see Aaron M. Kahn, "Moral Opposition to Philip in Pre-Lopean Drama," *Hispanic Review* 74, no. 3 (Summer 2006): 227–50.

11. See, for example, Geoffrey Parker, "The Messianic Vision of Philip II," in *The World Is Not Enough: The Imperial Vision of Philip II of Spain*, the Twenty-second Charles Edmundson Historical Lectures (Waco, TX: Baylor University, 2000), 29.

12. *Documentos para la Historia: Avila 1085–1985* (Avila: Museo Provincial de Avila, 1985), 119. The Argentine novelist Enrique Larreta included the Avila protests in *La Gloria de Don Ramiro: Una vida en tiempos de Felipe II* (Madrid: Victoriano Suárez, 1908).

13. Luis Cabrera de Córdoba, *Historia de Felipe II, Rey de España*, ed. José Martínez Millán and Carlos Javier de Carlos Morales (Salamanca: Junta de Castilla y León, 1998), 3:1367. The king had a long memory; in what became known as the "farce of Avila," a group of noblemen in 1465 deposed Henry IV in effigy and replaced him with his half-brother Alfonso. Avila did indeed side with the *comuneros*, and Padilla, who was married to a noblewoman of the Mendoza family, was beheaded in 1521 for his role in the revolt.

14. Fernando Bouza, "Corte y Protesta. El Condestable de Castilla y el 'insulto' de los maestros y oficiales de Madrid en 1591," in *Madrid, Felipe II y las ciudades de la monarquía*, vol. 2, *Capitalismo y economía*, ed. Enrique Martínez Ruiz, 17–32 (Madrid: Actas Editorial, 2000); Tellechea Idígoras, *El ocaso de un rey*, 126; P. Fr. Jerónimo de Sepúlveda, *Historia de varios sucesos y de las cosas notables que han acaecido en España. . . .*, vol. 4 of *Documentos para la Historia del Monasterio de San Lorenzo el Real de El Escorial*, ed. Julián Zarco Cuevas (Madrid: Imprenta Helénica, 1924), 119–20.

15. The stories of the "king of Penamacor" and the "king of Ericeira" are recounted in many primary and secondary sources. See Mary Elizabeth Brooks, *A King for Portugal: The Madrigal Conspiracy, 1594–95* (Madison: University of Wisconsin Press, 1964), 41–43; Julián María Rubio, *Felipe II de España, Rey de Portugal* (Madrid: Cultura Española, 1939), 157–64; Antonio de Herrera y Tordesillas, *Historia general del mundo . . . del tiempo del Señor rey Don Felipe II el Prudente. . . .* (Valladolid, 1606–12), 1:599–604; and especially Miguel d'Antas, *Les Faux Don Sébastien. Etude sur l'histoire de Portugal* (Paris: Chez Auguste Durand, libraire, 1866), 95–123.

16. *Calendar of State Papers [. . .] Venice*, vol. 8, 1581–1591, 173, 178.

17. RAH, Salazar y Castro, Z-9, 6v–7.

18. Fernando Bouza, "De las alteraciones de Beja (1593) a la revuelta lisboeta *dos ingleses* (1596): Lucha política en el último Portugal del primer Felipe," *Studia Historica: Historia Moderna*, no. 17 (1997), 91–120; correspondence from Juan de Silva to Philip, Moura, and Alberto, in RAH, Salazar y Castro, Z-9.

19. Fernando Bouza, "Corte es decepción: Don Juan de Silva, conde de Portalegre," in *La corte de Felipe II*, ed. José Martínez Millán (Madrid: Alianza Universidad, 1994), 484, citing BNM, MS 1439, fol. 4r.

20. *CODOIN*, 43:529–42.

21. Pero Roiz Soares, *Memorial*, ed. M. Lopes de Almeida (Coimbra: Universidade de Coimbra, 1953), 295, 301.

22. The following discussion is taken from Richard Kagan and Abigail Dyer, eds. and trans., *Inquisitorial Inquiries: Brief Lives of Secret Jews and Other Heretics* (Baltimore, MD: Johns Hopkins University Press, 2004), 60–87; and Richard Kagan, *Lucrecia's Dreams: Politics and Prophecy in Sixteenth-Century Spain* (Berkeley and Los Angeles: University of California Press, 1990), 95–101.

23. Kagan and Dyer, *Inquisitorial Inquiries*, 85.

24. Ibid., 79.

25. *CODOIN*, 39:468–69.

26. Bouza, "De las alteraciones de Beja," 107; María de la Visitación appears in the next chapter.

27. Kagan, *Lucrecia's Dreams*. See also María V. Jordán Arroyo, *Soñar la historia: Riesgo, creatividad y religión en las profecías de Lucrecia de León* (Madrid: Siglo XXI, 2007).

28. Richard L. Kagan, *Clio and the Crown: The Politics of History in Medieval and Early Modern Spain* (Baltimore, MD: Johns Hopkins University Press, 2009), 127–33. Philip took their advice and also commissioned works about the history of Portugal.

29. Juan de Aranda, *Lugares comunes de conceptos, dichos, y sentencias, en diversas materias* (Seville, 1595), fol. 25.

30. Satoko Nakajima, "Breaking Ties: Marriage and Migration in Sixteenth-Century Spain" (PhD diss., University of Tokyo, 2011). Nakajima looked at all 354 existing trials (the full case files, not just the summaries) in the Inquisition of Toledo (stored at the AHN) between 1560 and 1600 for secondary offences (i.e., not heresy). Most frequently, the crime was simple fornication, blasphemy, or scandalous words. I am grateful to Nakajima for sharing her data with me.

31. Fernand Braudel, *The Mediterranean and the Mediterranean World in the Age of Philip II*, 2 vols. (New York: Harper and Row, 1973), 1:91.

32. Miguel de Cervantes, *Los trabajos de Persiles y Sigismunda*, ed. Carlos Romero Muñoz (Madrid: Cátedra, 2002), 4.1, 630.

33. Adam Fox, *Oral and Literate Culture in England, 1500–1700* (Oxford: Clarendon Press, 2000), 353, 370. See also chap. 4 of Beat Kümin's *Drinking Matters: Public Houses and Social Exchange in Early Modern Central Europe* (New York: Palgrave Macmillan, 2007). Innkeepers also ran coach services and hosted military recruitment.

34. AGS E, leg. 173, docs. 190 and 266.

35. It is unclear if Silva also was riding or traveled on foot. Just a few months before his arrival in Medina, the Cortes debated whether to ask the king to allow clerics in Castile to travel on horseback. The Italian clergy did it, even the pope did it, argued don Alonso de Godoy, adding that it would be an excellent stimulus for horse-raising, which was in dangerous decline. See *ACC*, vol. 13, 459 (Madrid, 1887), 25 February 1595.

36. See the appendix for a brief discussion of the don Carlos connection.

37. AGS E, leg. 172, doc. 4, and leg. 173, doc. 239; *Historia de Gabriel de Espinosa, Pastelero en Madrigal, que fingió ser el rey Don Sebastian de Portugal, y asimismo la de Fray Miguel de los Santos, en el año de 1595* (Jerez: Juan Antonio de Tarazona, 1683), 17 and 42 (hereafter *Historia de Gabriel de Espinosa*); Philip II noted (AGS E, leg. 173, doc. 139) that Sebastian would have been forty-one, not forty-three.

38. AGS E, leg. 172, doc. 94.

39. AGS E, leg. 172, docs. 195 and 245. The tenth count of Niebla was don Alonso Pérez de Guzmán El Bueno, also the seventh duke of Medina Sidonia, an infamously poor naval commander. He was married to Ana de Silva y Mendoza, daughter of the princess of Eboli, who was four years old when they were engaged. Some transcriptions refer to the count of Nieva, which is less likely.

40. Ibid., doc. 245.

41. Cabrera de Córdoba. *Historia*, 3:1520.

42. AGS E, leg. 173, doc. 239.

43. Probably Nava del Rey, near Medina del Campo. The stay in Nava was known to the Jesuit correspondent quoted at the end of chapter 2.

44. AGS E, leg. 173, doc. 119.

45. *Historia de Gabriel de Espinosa*, 5.

46. Ibid., 9–10.

47. AGS E, leg. 173, docs. 239 and 240, a summary of the confession. All subsequent quotations from Llano's February interview with Espinosa are from these documents.

48. AGS E, leg. 172, doc. 1; *Historia de Gabriel de Espinosa*, 4.

49. AGS E, leg. 173, doc. 239.

50. AGS E, leg. 172, doc. 105.

51. Ibid., docs. 120 and 122.

52. Ibid., doc. 254.

53. Ibid., doc. 133.

54. Ibid., doc. 19.

55. Ibid., doc. 28 (2).

56. Ibid., doc. 45.

57. Ibid., doc. 261.

58. Ibid., doc. 254.

59. Ibid., doc. 81.

60. Valentin Groebner, *Who Are You? Identification, Deception, and Surveillance in Early Modern Europe*, trans. Mark Kyburz and John Peck (New York: Zone Books, 2007), 281.

61. RAH, 9-3675/86 (Jesuits, vol. 102), fols. 280–81v.

62. AGS E, leg. 172, doc. 105.

63. Jan Bondeson, *The Great Pretenders: The True Stories behind Famous Historical Mysteries* (New York: W. W. Norton, 2004), 34–35; Natalie Zemon Davis, *The Return of Martin Guerre* (Cambridge, MA: Harvard University Press, 1983), 54, 79.

64. *Historia de Gabriel de Espinosa*, 27.

65. AGS E, leg. 173, doc. 227, though I am using BL Eg., 2059, fols. 252–62v. Geoffrey Parker has pointed out to me that this exchange proves definitely that Espinosa was not Sebastian because, whereas Spanish kings signed "Yo el Rey," Portuguese kings signed "ElRey." Ana later burned this paper; see AGS E, leg. 173, doc. 234.

66. AGS E, leg. 173, doc. 139.

67. Ibid., doc. 189.

68. AGS E, leg. 172, doc. 1.

69. *Historia de Gabriel de Espinosa*, 8. Cabrera de Córdoba repeats the exchange in his *Historia*, 3:1523.

70. AGS E, leg. 172, docs. 94 and 95.

71. Marta Madero, "Savoirs féminins et construction de la vérité: Les femmes dans la preuve testimoniale en Castille au XIII siècle," *Crime, Histoire et Sociétés* 3, no. 2 (1999): 5–21; Antonio Quevedo y Hoyos, *Libro de indicios y tormentos; que contiene toda la práctica criminal y modo de sustanciar el proceso indicativamente. . . .* (Madrid: Francisco Martínez, 1632), fol. 53.

72. "To give the subjective measure of distance from the speaker's present was more natural for them than to mark an objective point in a sequence of the years," one historian has written; see Robert Bartlett, *The Hanged Man: A Story of Miracle, Memory and Colonialism in the Middle Ages* (Princeton, NJ: Princeton University Press, 2004), 55. This excellent book is about fourteenth-century Wales, but the principle holds true for sixteenth-century Spain.

73. AGS E, leg. 172, doc 95.

74. Ibid.

75. Ibid., doc. 78.

76. *Historia de Gabriel de Espinosa*, 22.

77. Roiz Soares, *Memorial*, 310. It is highly unlikely that Ana's father ever gave her jewels—or anything else, for that matter.

78. AGS E, leg. 172, doc. 1

79. Ibid., doc. 94.

80. Tellechea Idígoras, *El ocaso de un rey*, 144 (5 November 1594), citing Archivio Se-

greto Vaticano, Segreteria di Stato, Nunziatura di Spagna 45, fols. 667r–69v. In August 1595, Santillán told the king he still had Ana's jewel case and her other valuables he had taken from Espinosa. Ana requested their return, but he said he did not think that was appropriate to her station (see AGS E, leg. 173, doc. 187).

81. Examples from Cervantes alone include Aurestela in *Persiles* (1.9); Zoraida (1.39–41) and Ana Felix (2.63) in *Don Quixote*; and Preciosa in "La Gitanilla," one of the *Novelas Ejemplares*.

82. AGS E, leg. 173, doc. 234.

83. Ibid., doc. 249, unnumbered document between docs. 251 and 252.

84. Fernando Bouza, "Letters and Portraits: Economy of Time and Chivalrous Service in Courtly Culture," in *Cultural Exchange in Early Modern Europe*, vol. 3, *Correspondence and Cultural Exchange in Europe, 1400–1700*, ed. Francisco Bethencourt and Florike Egmond, 145–62 (Cambridge: Cambridge University Press, 2007).

85. See for example, the portrait of his sister Juana by Alonso Sánchez Coello in the Monasterio de las Descalzas Reales (plate 2); the Prado portrait of his wife Isabel of Valois attributed to Juan Pantoja de la Cruz, Sofonisba Anguissola, or Sánchez Coello; and the portraits of Isabel Clara Eugenia in the Prado and in the Museo de Santa Cruz in Toledo. See Jorge Sebastián Lozano, "Lo privado es político. Sobre género y usos de la imagen en la corte de los Austrias," in *Luchas de género en la historia através de la imagen. Ponencias y comunicaciones*, ed. María Teresa Sauret Guerrero and Amparo Quiles Faz (Málaga: Diputación Provincial, 2001), 1:683–99.

86. Patricia Fumerton, *Cultural Aesthetics: Renaissance Literature and Practice of Social Ornament* (Chicago: University of Chicago Press, 1991), chap. 3.

87. AGS E, leg. 172, doc. 49.

88. Ibid., doc. 74.

89. Ibid., doc. 124. Antolínez went on to a brilliant career, ending up in 1624 as archbishop of Santiago de Compostela.

90. Ibid., doc. 144.

91. BL Eg., 2059, fol. 252, "Relación de la confesión . . ."

92. AGS E, leg. 172, doc. 93.

93. AGS E, leg. 173, docs. 13 and 249.

94. AGS E, leg. 172, docs. 28 and 29.

95. Ibid., docs. 188 and 212. I do not know if Ruiz was ever actually in the house at the same time as the prisoners and judicial staff; he also had a home in Valladolid. By this time he was around seventy years old and quite ill. His biographer says he was often away; see Henri Lapeyre, *Une famille de marchands. Les Ruiz* (Paris: Colin, 1955), 76–77.

96. AGS E, leg. 172, doc. 43.

97. Ibid., doc. 28.

98. Ibid., doc. 226.

99. Ibid., doc. 259.

100. Ibid., doc. 54; *Historia de Gabriel de Espinosa*, 43, 47.

101. AGS E, leg. 173, doc. 120.

102. Ibid., docs. 131, 140, and 294.

103. Ibid., docs. 11, 21–24, 136, and 149.

104. AGS E, leg. 172, docs. 206, 217, and 261.

105. *Historia de Gabriel de Espinosa*, 47.

106. See, for example, ibid., 27.

107. Ibid., 41.

108. AGS E, leg. 173, doc. 194.

109. Roiz Soares, *Memorial*, 311.

110. AGS E, leg. 172, doc. 144.

111. *Historia de Gabriel de Espinosa*, 22.

112. Camilo Castelo Branco. *As virtudes antigas; ou a freira que fazia chagas e o frade que fazia reis* (1868; 2nd ed., Lisbon: Livraría de Campos Junior, 1904), 126–27.

113. Cabrera de Córdoba, *Historia*, 3:1521.

114. Davis, *Return of Martin Guerre*, 84.

115. AGS E, leg. 173, doc. 270.

116. Ibid., doc. 271.

117. *Calendar of State Papers [. . .] Venice*, vol. 9, 1592–1603, 164. I did not see the original, but compared this version to the Italian version in Julieta Teixeira Marques de Oliveira, *Fontes documentais de Veneza referentes a Portugal* (Lisbon: Comissão Nacional para as Comemorações dos Descobrimentos Portugueses, 1997), 648–49, who cites Achivio Segreto Vaticano, Senato Secreta, Dispacci Ambasciatori, Spagna, fila 27, fol. 37.

118. Cabrera de Córdoba, *Historia*, 3:1528–29. Another ambassador in Madrid at the time, the imperial envoy Hans Khevenhüller, did not mention the case of the *pastelero* at all, though he did write about one of the earlier false Sebastians in Portugal and also the subsequent false Sebastian in Venice; see his *Diario de Hans Khevenhüller, embajador imperial en la corte de Felipe II*, ed. Sara Veronelli and Félix Labrador Arroyo (Madrid: Sociedad Estatal para la Conmemoración de los Centenarios de Felipe II y Carlos V, 2001).

119. *List and Analysis of State Papers, Foreign Series. Elizabeth I. Preserved in the Public Record Office*, vol. 7, January to December 1596, ed. Richard Bruce Wernham (London: Public Record Office, 2000), 223 (Item 266, cited from NL73, Advertisements, from Rome, Cologne, and Antwerp, fol. 170).

120. RBP, II/2149, doc. 108. Gondomar went on to become one of Spain's most prominent diplomats. Gasca de la Vega vanishes, but his sister married Francisco de Contreras, president of the Royal Council. See her biography: Manuel Francisco de Hinojosa y Montalvo, *Libro de la Vida, Loables Costumbres, y Santa Muerte de la Ilustrisima Señora doña María Gasca de la Vega* (Madrid, 1626).

121. *Historia de Gabriel de Espinosa*, 28; see also the account by the Jesuit discussed at the end of chapter 2. The pamphlet seems to suggest the confession indeed was heard by multiple witnesses, though the case file says nothing about this.

122. Sara T. Nalle, "The Millennial Moment: Revolution and Radical Religion in Sixteenth-Century Spain," in *Toward the Millennium: Messianic Expectations from the Bible to Waco*, ed. Peter Schafer and Mark R. Cohen (Leiden: Brill, 1998), 151–71.

123. In the years just before the *pastelero* case, Bandarra was rediscovered by João de

Castro, a disillusioned noble comrade of don António, who made the *trovas* the documentary basis for what became the *sebastianista* movement. Castro was the chief organizer of the subsequent and far more serious apparition in Italy of a false Sebastian: see H. Eric R. Olsen, *The Calabrian Charlatan, 1598–1603: Messianic Nationalism in Early Modern Europe* (New York: Palgrave MacMillan, 2003). In Portuguese, see Antonio Machado Pires, *D. Sebastião e o Encoberto. Estudo e antologia* (Lisbon: Fundação Calouste Gulbenkian, 1971); and J. Lucio de Azevedo, *A evoluçao do Sebastianismo*, 2nd ed. (Lisbon: Livraría Clássica, 1947). In French, see Lucette Valensi, *Fables de la Mémoire: La glorieuse bataille des trois rois* (Paris: Editions du Seuil, 1992), and Yves-Marie Bercé, *Le roi caché. Saveurs et imposteurs. Mythes politiques populaires dans l'Europe moderne* (Paris: Fayard, 1990).

124. Antonio Ubieto Arteta, "La aparición del falso Alfonso I el Batallador." *Argensola: Revista de Ciencias Sociales del Instituto de Estudios Altoaragoneses*, no. 33 (1958): 29–38.

125. For a fascinating analysis of how Lope de Vega and other Spanish writers adapted the Russian tales of usurpation with the deaths of Sebastian and don Carlos in mind, see Jack Weiner, "Un episodio de la historia rusa visto por autores españoles del Siglo de Oro. El pretendiente Demetrio," *Journal of Hispanic Philology* 2, no. 3 (Spring 1978): 175–201.

126. Switched babies led to a royal imposture in fourteenth-century France: see the excellent account by Tommaso di Carpegna Falconieri, *The Man Who Believed He Was King of France: A True Medieval Tale*, trans. William McCuaig (Chicago: University of Chicago Press, 2008). Two Augustinian friars were key players in that imposture. For a case of the escaped mother and baby, there is Jachia ben Mehmet, who in the early seventeenth century claimed to be the son of the Ottoman Sultan Mehmet III; see Dorothy M. Vaughan, *Europe and the Turk: A Pattern of Alliances, 1350–1700* (Liverpool: Liverpool University Press, 1954), 219–36.

127. See, for example, Antonio Caetano de Sousa, *Provas da história genealógica da casa real portuguesa* (Coimbra: Atlântida, 1946–48), vol. 2, pt. 2, 139.

128. Roberto González Echevarría, *Myth and Archive: A Theory of Latin American Narrative* (Durham, NC: Duke University Press, 1998), 38. Many literary conventions, such as identity tests, accidental reunions, subsequent recognition, disguises, and abductions, are frequent in folk tales; see Stith Thompson, *Motif-Index of Folk Literature*, 6 vols. (Bloomington: Indiana University Press, 1934).

129. "Relación de las vistas [*sic*] de los Reyes Don Phelipe 2 y Don Sebastian en Nuestra Señora de Guadalupe, año de 1576," Hispanic Society of America (New York), HC 411–209, 15v.

130. AGS E, leg. 173, unnumbered document between docs. 251 and 252, probably March 1595.

131. Robert Southwell, *The History of the Revolutions of Portugal, from the Foundation of That Kingdom to the Year [1667], with Letters of Sir Robert Southwell. . . .* (London: Printed for John Osborn at the Golden Ball in Pater-Noster Row, 1740), 34. The ambassador was familiar with three of the four false Sebastians; he said nothing about Madrigal.

132. See the introduction to Terence Cave, *Recognitions: A Study in Poetics* (Oxford: Clarendon Press, 1988).

Chapter 4

1. Juan Vallafañe, *La limosnera de Dios. Relación histórica de la vida, y virtudes de la excelentíssima señora Doña Magdalena de Ulloa Toledo Ossorio y Quiñones* (Salamanca: Imprenta de Francisco García Onorato, 1723); Baltasar Porreño, *Historia del sereníssimo Señor don Juan de Austria*, ed. Antonio Rodríguez Villa (Madrid: Sociedad de Bibliófilos Españoles, 1899). On Ana's entrance into the convent on June 28, 1575, see Mercedes Formica, *María de Mendoza (Solución a un enigma amoroso)* (Madrid: Editorial Caro Raggio, 1979), 21, citing AHN, Clero, leg. 580.

2. Formica, *María de Mendoza*. Formica discovered Ana's mother by working in notarial archives; the following discussion is based on her book.

3. Mercedes Formica, *La hija de Don Juan de Austria. Ana de Jesús en el proceso al pastelero de Madrigal* (Madrid: Revista de Occidente, 1973), 66–67.

4. Saint Teresa, *The Complete Works of Saint Teresa of Jesus*, trans. and ed. E. Allison Peers (London: Sheed and Ward, 1946), "Constitutions Which the Mother Teresa of Jesus gave to the Discalced Carmelite Nuns," 3:223; Elizabeth A. Lehfeldt, *Religious Women in Golden Age Spain: The Permeable Cloister* (Aldershot: Ashgate, 2005), 177.

5. IVDJ, envío 63, fols. 125, 130, 131; the vow of profession is transcribed in Firmo Zurdo Manso and Esther del Cerro Calvo, *Madrigal de las Altas Torres: Recuerdos para una historia* (Avila, 1996), 122. The Augustinian provincial was Pedro de Rojas; the following year, Fray Luis de León was elected provincial, but he died a week later, at which point Gabriel de Goldaraz got the job.

6. Teófilo Viñas Román, "El convento agustiniano, extramuros de Madrigal de las Altas Torres," *Ciudad de Dios* 214, no. 3 (2001): 705–32; Quirino Fernández, OSA, "Las dos Agustinas de Madrigal, hijas de Fernando el Católico llamadas ambas Doña María de Aragón," *Analecta Augustiniana* 53 (1990): 361–407; Jesús Miguel Benítez, OSA, "Agustinas de Madrigal de las Altas Torres del siglo XVI al XVII," in *La clausura femenina en España: Actas del simposium, 1/4-IX-2004*, ed. Francisco Javier Campos and Fernández de Sevilla, Escorial, 1:363–98. This Juana, not to be confused with Charles V's legitimate daughter Juana (Sebastian's mother), lived at the convent with her mother, whose identity is unknown to me. According to one local history, the child drowned in the convent well; see Zurdo Manso and Cerro Calvo, *Madrigal de las Altas Torres*, 40.

7. Richard L. Kagan, *Lucrecia's Dreams: Politics and Prophecy in Sixteenth-Century Spain* (Berkeley and Los Angeles: University of California Press, 1990), 121–22.

8. AGS E, leg. 172, docs. 58, 73, and 207. The gossipy friars wrote a letter to the king relaying stories they heard about Gabriel de Goldaraz. Quiroga was buried in the *extramuros* monastery; his remains were moved to the nuns' convent in 1835 after government disentailment of church properties.

9. James Casey, *Family and Community in Early Modern Spain: The Citizens of Granada, 1570–1739* (Cambridge: Cambridge University Press, 2007), 213; David Gutiérrez, *The Augustinians from the Protestant Reformation to the Peace of Westphalia, 1518–1648*, trans. John J. Kelly, OSA (Villanova, PA: Augustinian Historical Institute, 1979), 91.

10. Bartolomé Bennassar, *Valladolid en el Siglo de Oro: Una ciudad de Castilla y su entorno agrario en el siglo XVI* (Valladolid: Ambito, 1983), 359.

11. AGS E, leg. 172, doc. 7.

12. *ACC*, 1592–1595, vol. 13 (Madrid, 1887), 436–37.

13. AGS E. leg. 172, doc. 95.

14. AGS E, leg. 173, doc. 220; Elizabeth A. Lehfeldt, "Spatial Discipline and Its Limits: Nuns and the Built Environment in Early Modern Spain," in *Architecture and the Politics of Gender in Early Modern Europe*, ed. Helen Hills (Aldershot: Ashgate, 2003), 143.

15. AGS E, leg. 424. Bad behavior in convents, often apocryphal, is a long-standing trope. See Craig Monson's books *Disembodied Voices: Music and Culture in an Early Modern Italian Convent* (Berkeley and Los Angeles: University of California Press, 1995), and *Nuns Behaving Badly: Tales of Music, Magic, Art, and Arson in the Convents of Italy* (Chicago: University of Chicago Press, 2010).

16. AMAEC, Santa Sede, leg. 49, docs. 293–300.

17. *Historia de Gabriel de Espinosa, Pastelero en Madrigal, que fingió ser el rey Don Sebastian de Portugal, y asimismo la de Fray Miguel de los Santos, en el año de 1595* (Jerez: Juan Antonio de Tarazona, 1683), 19 (hereafter *Historia de Gabriel de Espinosa*).

18. Silva to the Marques de Poza, March 15, 1593, BL Add., 28.377.

19. AGS E, leg. 172, doc. 96.

20. AGS E, leg. 173, doc. 234. This group of Portuguese visitors would not be the same as those who supposedly came in July 1594; the latter had no contact with Ana. But they might be the ones mentioned by the Jesuit correspondent discussed in chapter 3.

21. AGS E, leg. 172, docs. 242 and 257.

22. Ibid., doc. 211.

23. Ibid., doc. 191.

24. AGS E, leg. 173, docs. 26, 28, and 146.

25. Ibid., doc. 239.

26. Ibid., doc. 249. "Doctors" here does not imply medical doctors.

27. AGS E, leg. 172, doc. 251.

28. Ibid., doc. 1.

29. Ibid., docs. 2 (also BL Eg., 2059, fol. 241) and 3.

30. AGS E, leg. 173, doc. 133.

31. AGS E, leg. 172, docs. 110 and 145.

32. Ibid., docs. 94 and 95.

33. Ibid., doc. 215. This was probably Martín de Idiáquez.

34. Ibid., doc. 8.

35. Ibid., docs. 13 and 121.

36. Ibid., doc. 159.

37. Ibid., docs. 30 and 237.

38. José Ignacio Tellechea Idígoras, *El ocaso de un rey: Felipe II visto desde la Nunciatura de Madrid, 1594–1598* (Madrid: Fundación Universitaria Española, 2001), 144.

39. AGS E, leg. 172, docs. 74 and 75.

40. Ibid., docs. 56–58, 60–61, 73, 75, and 99.

41. Ibid., docs. 94 and 95.

42. Ibid.

43. Ibid., doc. 94.

44. Ibid., doc. 25.

45. Ibid., doc. 42.

46. Ibid., doc. 20.

47. Ibid., doc. 203.

48. Ibid. In seventeenth-century Venice, involuntary nuns insisted (and canonists agreed) that they were not nuns at all; one said "she wasn't a nun but [wearing] a mask." See Anne Jacobson Schutte, "Between Venice and Rome: The Dilemma of Involuntary Nuns," *Sixteenth Century Journal* 41, no. 2 (2010): 425 and 429.

49. Ibid., doc. 180.

50. Ibid., doc. 91.

51. Ibid., doc. 196.

52. Ibid., doc. 208.

53. Ibid., doc. 211; and BL Eg., 2059, fols. 240v–41.

54. AGS E, leg. 172, doc. 191.

55. Ibid., doc. 211.

56. Ibid., docs. 49 and 54. He told Barbara Blomberg he was raised in the convent. Sebastianillo, mentioned below, could be another such case; possibly both were illegitimate.

57. AGS E, leg. 173, unnumbered document between docs. 251 and 252.

58. AGS E, leg. 172, doc. 49.

59. Ibid.

60. Luís Cabrera de Córdoba. *Historia de Felipe II, Rey de España*, ed. José Martínez Millán and Carlos Javier de Carlos Morales (Salamanca: Junta de Castilla y León, 1998), 3:1523; *Historia del fingido Rey de Portugal*, Escorial, Z-IV-2, fol. 47r.

61. AGS E, leg. 128, doc. 184; also reported by Louis Prosper Gachard, *Don Juan d'Autriche: Etudes historiques* (Brussels: M. Hayez, 1868), 11, with no citation.

62. Perhaps Philip II renamed his brother Juan because he remembered a brother of that name when he was a small child; the first Juan died in 1537; see Manuel Fernández Alvarez, *La Princesa de Eboli* (Madrid: Espasa Calpe, 2009), 83–84.

63. Correspondence on Blomberg in Brussels and her move to Spain, AGS E, leg. 545; María del Rosario Falcó y Osorio, ed., *Documentos escogidos del Archivo de la Casa de Alba. Los publica la Duquesa de Berwick y de Alba* (Madrid, 1891); Porreño, *Historia del serenissimo Señor*; Antonio Rodríguez Villa, "Documentos sobre la estancia de Madame Barbara de Blombergh," *Boletín de la Real Academia de la Historia* 36 (1900): 69–81; Gachard, *Don Juan d'Autriche*.

64. I do not know how or why Escobedo's house was chosen. See correspondence on Blomberg in Colindres, IVDJ, envíos 36, 41, and 46; Porreño, *Historia del serenissimo Señor*, 311–18, 575; BNM, MS 20058/52, fols. 133–34; Gachard, *Don Juan d'Autriche*.

65. IVDJ, envío 46.

66. Formica, *María de Mendoza*, 371, citing Catalina's will, in Archivo Histórico Provincial de Madrid, Protocolo 390, escr. Diego Méndez (November 23, 1571). Also

according to Formica, who cites no sources, accounts show Blomberg occasionally sent her granddaughter dried cod. See Formica, *La hija de Don Juan*, 215.

67. AGS E, leg. 172, doc. 165.

68. AGS E, leg. 172, doc. 100; I used *Historia de Gabriel de Espinosa*, 6.

69. *Historia de Gabriel de Espinosa*, 6; also ANTT, Miscelánea Manuscrita 964, *Collecção de Memorias e Casos Raros*, 228; the original is AGS E, leg. 172, doc. 100. On Mazateve, Angel Rodríguez Villa, "Documentos sobre la estancia de Madama Barbara Blombergh en España," *Boletín de la Real Academia de la Historia* 36 (1900): 69–81. Ana's letter is taken from the transcription in Formica, *La hija de Don Juan de Austria*, 401.

70. Andrés María Mateo was convinced there was more to Roderos's visit to Blomberg than meets the eye. Ana and Blomberg were not on good terms, so it is unlikely Ana would turn to her grandmother for help, he said. Rather, he suggested, Blomberg was somehow involved in the plot, and she turned Roderos in as a way of extricating herself. I believe Blomberg would not have wanted to anger Philip, given her financial dependence on the crown; Mateo suggests she was already so angry with him she was willing to conspire: Andrés María Mateo, "Barbara Blomberg y el Pastelero de Madrigal, 7 octubre 1594–19 octubre 1595" (PhD diss., Universidad Complutense de Madrid, 1945), 226–41.

71. AGS E, leg. 173, doc. 120.

72. AGS E, leg. 173, docs. 187 and 270. By the late sixteenth century, virtually all galley oarsmen were serving a sentence: see José Luis de las Heras Santos, *La justicia penal de los Austrias en la Corona de Castilla* (Salamanca: Ediciones Universidad, 1991), 304–16; and Ruth Pike, *Penal Servitude in Early Modern Spain* (Madison: University of Wisconsin Press, 1983), 3–26.

73. AGS E, leg. 172, doc. 78.

74. Ibid., doc. 242.

75. AGS E, leg. 173, doc. 234.

76. AGS E, leg. 172, doc. 46.

77. ANTT, Miscelánea Manuscrita 964, *Collecção de Memorias e Casos Raros*, 230. The author of this unusual variant implies that Ana was Philip II's daughter. I have not found the original of this letter in the case file; it may never have existed.

78. For a description of the chair and the helplessness it brought the king, see Geoffrey Parker, *Philip II*, 3rd ed. (Chicago: Open Court, 1995), 192–93.

79. Mark Eccles, *Christopher Marlowe in London* (Cambridge, MA: Harvard University Press, 1934), 145–57; I found this reference in Keith Thomas, *Religion and the Decline of Magic* (New York: Charles Scribner's Sons, 1971), 426.

80. P. Fr. Jerónimo de Sepúlveda, *Historia de varios sucesos y de las cosas notables que han acaecido en España. . . .*, vol. 4 of *Documentos para la historia del Monasterio de San Lorenzo el Real de El Escorial*, ed. Julián Zarco Cuevas (Madrid: Imprenta Helénica, 1924), 121–22. Philip's best-known illegitimate siblings are don Juan and Margaret of Parma, but there was at least one more. A woman named Tadea della Penna, who lived in Rome, contacted the king in December 1560 soon after Philip learned of don Juan's existence to tell him she was his half-sister. See José Ignacio Tellechea Idígoras, "La Mesa de Felipe II," *Ciudad de Dios* 218, no. 1 (2005): 187–88.

81. Rafael Valladares, *La conquista de Lisboa: Violencia militar y comunidad política en Portugal, 1578–1583* (Madrid: Marcial Pons, 2008), 121.

82. António's instructions to Cristóvão on how to behave at the Moroccan court are in Pedro Batalha Reis, *Numária d'el Rey dom António, décimo oitavo Rei de Portugal, O ídolo do povo* (Lisbon: Academia Portuguesa da História, 1947), 406–11; and Antonio Caetano de Sousa, *Provas da história genealógica da casa real portuguesa*, vol. 2, pt. 2 (Coimbra: Atlântida, 1948), 175–81. See also Jaime Oliver Asín, *Vida de Don Felipe de Africa, príncipe de Fez y Marruecos (1566–1621)*, ed. Miguel Angel de Bunes Ibarra and Beatriz Alonso Acero (Granada: University of Granada, 2008), 83. Unlike his brother Manoel, Cristóvão never made his peace with Philip II.

83. These two daughters possibly were named Violante (António's mother's name) and Antonia or María: António de Portugal, Viscount of Faria, *Descendance de D. António, Prieur de Crato* (Livorno: Imprimerie Raphaël Giusti, 1908).

84. On Luisa and Filipa, see AGS E, leg. 426; Antonio de Portugal, *Descendance*; Francisco Marquez de Sousa Viterbo, *O Prior do Crato ea invasão hespanhola de 1580* (Lisbon, 1897), 19–25, with transcriptions of don António's letters granting the allowances.

85. Philip to doña Catalina Barahona, 20 July 1581, AGS E, leg. 426.

86. AGS E, leg. 172, doc. 4.

87. Philip II to Francisco Hernández de Liévana, 8 June 1581, AGS E, leg. 426.

88. May 8, 1590, IVDJ, envío 38.

89. BFZ, Altamira 219.D.150/1; BFZ, Altamira 219.D.149/1; Diogo Barbosa Machado, *Biblioteca Lusitana histórica, crítica e cronólogica* (Ridgewood, NJ: Gregg Press, 1962), 1:190–94; facsimile (orig. pub. Lisbon, 1741).

90. February 8, 1605, ANTT, Arquivo de don António, doc. 347. The letter is very difficult to read.

91. Gregorio Marañon, *Antonio Pérez (el hombre, el drama, la época)*, 5th ed. (Madrid: Espasa Calpe, 1954), 2:872; letter from Pérez to Chateau Martín, transcribed from AGS E, leg. 363, fol. 270.

92. ANTT, doc 347.

93. Silva to Gabriel de Zayas, February 1580, RAH, Z-9, fol. 198.

94. AGS E, leg. 424, doc. 339.

95. AGS E, leg. 428; AGS E, leg. 424, doc. 338. The incident took place in November 1582.

96. RAH, Salazar y Castro, Z-9, fol. 188 (October 1598).

97. AGS E, leg. 172, docs. 94 and 95.

98. Ibid.

99. *Historia de Gabriel de Espinosa*, 10, 22. The *Historia*'s version of Fray Miguel's (false) confession also says it was through the child that the vicar supposedly detected *la casta* of the father.

100. AGS E, leg. 172, doc. 242.

101. Ibid., doc. 78.

102. AGS E, leg. 173, docs. 236 and 275; Lehfeldt, "Spatial Discipline," 143.

103. AGS E, leg. 173, doc. 338.

104. Ibid., doc. 263.

105. Ibid., doc. 189.

106. His four books were a life of St. Catherine of Siena, a life of St. Amadeus, an astrology text, and a manual on converts to Christianity. Santillán sold them all. See AGS E, leg. 173, doc. 68.

107. AGS E, leg. 172, doc. 29.

108. Ibid., doc. 31. *In caput alienum* meant that torture was used to obtain information about third parties. This was also applied to Roderos. It was a controversial step, and it was not included in Spain's medieval law code, called the *Partidas*; see Francisco Tomás y Valiente, *La tortura en España: Estudios históricos* (Barcelona: Editorial Ariel, 1973), 117–20.

109. AGS E, leg. 173, doc. 275.

110. AGS E, leg. 172, doc. 54.

111. AGS E, leg. 173, docs. 120 and 123.

112. Ibid., doc. 181.

113. For a couple to obtain a marriage license, witnesses had to testify that they were free to marry. There are plenty of documented cases of perjury, but perhaps because Epinosa and Cid were itinerant, they did not have friends they could draw on. On these licenses, see Satoko Nakajima, "Breaking Ties: Marriage and Migration in Sixteenth-Century Spain" (PhD diss., University of Tokyo, 2011).

114. AGS E, leg. 173, docs. 263 and 264, both interrogations.

115. Ibid., doc. 189.

116. There was a local lord in Toro named don Juan de Ulloa, probably the descendant of a man of the same name who built two imposing fifteenth-century castles in the province of Zamora. The timing and geography make it likely this was the man Espinosa knew.

117. AGS E, leg. 173, doc. 350.

118. It is unclear why Santillán hired *pregoneros* from Valladolid; Madrigal had at least two of its own in 1594, judging from records of oral announcements of land sales at this time. See AHPA, Protocolos, leg. 3787.

119. AGS E, leg. 173, doc. 264.

120. *Historia de Gabriel de Espinosa*, 47.

121. AGS E, leg. 173, doc. 264. For an even more terrible transcript of torture, this one of a woman accused of theft in 1648 in Madrid, see Francisco Tomás y Valiente, *El derecho penal de la monarquía absoluta* (Madrid: Editorial Tecnos, 1969), 414–19.

122. AGS E, leg. 173, doc. 270.

123. Kagan, *Lucrecia's Dreams*, 145, 150, 155. Lucrecia also was tortured.

124. BNM, MS 3784, *Papeles varios en prosa*, "Historia de Gabriel de Espinosa," fols. 1–60. This is a composite account drawn from the 1683 pamphlet and other writings. The description of the child is on fol. 47v.

125. AGS E, leg. 172, docs. 94 and 95.

126. Ibid., doc. 144.

127. Ibid.

128. Ibid., doc. 94.

129. Ibid., doc. 144.

130. *Historia de Gabriel de Espinosa*, 16. Don Juan of Austria had a son by Zenobia Sarotosio in Naples who died as a baby; see Gachard. *Don Juan d'Autriche*, 166. With no real evidence, Mercedes Formica speculates that Francisco existed and was born after María de Mendoza allegedly traveled to the mountains of Granada to be with don Juan before the Alpujarras war (*María de Mendoza*, 315–22).

131. "Open the doors and the windows, / the balconies and the galleries, / because instead of bringing a wife, / I bring you my sister!" The traditional poem is variously called "Don Bueso," "Don Bueso y su hermana," or "Una tarde de verano." For a discussion of the versions, see George K. Zucker, "Some Considerations on the Sephardic Treatment of the 'Romancero,'" *Anuario de estudios filológicos* 14 (1991): 519–24.

132. In 1618, one Jerónimo de Dueñas, captured at Alcazarquivir forty years earlier, fled when his galley ship docked in Malta. He then wrote to the Council of Portugal requesting his pension: Diogo Ramada Curto, "O Bastião! O Bastião! (Actos políticos e modalidades de crença, 1578–1603)," in *Portugal: Mitos revisitados*, ed. Yvette Kace Centeno (Lisbon: Edições Salamandra, 1993), 144, citing ANTT, Conselho Geral do Santo Oficio, liv. 216, docs. 149 and 153.

133. Teresa loved reading chivalric romances when she was a girl: "I was so completely taken up with this reading that I didn't think I could be happy if I didn't have a new book." See Saint Teresa, *The Autobiography of St. Teresa of Avila*, trans. Kieran Kavanaugh, OCD, and Otilio Rodríguez, OCD (New York: One Spirit, 1995), 57, 55.

134. AGS E, leg. 173, docs. 182, 187, 261, 262, 350, and 401–06.

135. Ibid., doc. 262; nearly illegible.

136. AGS E, leg. 173, doc. 182.

137. RAH, Salazar y Castro, Z-9, fol.162 (March 1594). A former bishop of Evora had been on the list of people excluded from the 1580 general amnesty.

138. AGS E, leg. 173, doc. 403.

139. AGS E, leg. 173, doc. 187.

140. The following discussion is based on AGS E, leg. 173, docs. 236, 249, and an unnumbered packet between leg. 173, docs. 251 and 252.

141. BL Eg., 2059, fol. 246v.

142. AGS E, leg. 172, docs. 88, 238, and 242. The sisters were both "more or less" forty years old, considerably older than Ana, who was twenty-seven. Their brother, Blas Nieto, was one of the few characters in this story to be acquitted.

143. AGS E, leg. 173, doc. 289.

144. AGS E, leg. 172, docs. 196 and 238; leg. 173, docs. 1 and 8.

145. AGS E, leg. 173, doc. 258. Some twenty years earlier, Belón had been the founding prioress of an Augustinian monastery in Talavera de la Reina; see Tomás Cámara, *Vida y escritos del Beato Alonso de Orozco del Orden de San Agustín, Predicador de Felipe II* (Valladolid: Imp. y Lib. de la V. de Cuesta e Hijos, 1882), 172.

146. AGS E, leg. 173, docs. 218 and 219. Loaysa was Prince Philip's tutor and later cardinal and archbishop of Toledo. He came from a family of high church officials; his uncles included Seville archbishop García de Loaysa y Mendoza, a friar named Domingo de Mendoza, who went to America, and Lima Archbishop Jerónimo de Loaysa; all were

Dominicans. See Javier Malagón-Barceló, "Toledo and the New World in the Sixteenth Century," *The Americas* 20, no. 2 (October 1963): 107; Angel Fernández Collado, *La Catedral de Toledo en el siglo XVI: Vida, arte y personas* (Toledo: Diputación Provincial, 1999), 254–56. My thanks to Ignacio Fernández Terricabra for help on this point.

147. AGS E, leg. 173, doc. 59.

148. Ibid., doc. 60.

149. Ibid., doc. 259.

150. Ibid., doc. 391. Andrés María Mateo describes the accusations as *calumnia*, but I see no reason to doubt the charges ("Barbara Blomberg," 193).

151. AGS E, leg. 172, doc. 230.

152. AGS E, leg. 173, doc. 248.

153. Ibid., docs. 115 and 178.

154. Ibid., docs. 187 and 192.

155. Ibid., doc. 81.

156. AHN, Inq., leg. 5142, caja 3. The archbishop left Juan de Llano two thousand ducats: José Luis González Novalin, *El inquisidor general Fernando de Valdés (1483–1568)* (Oviedo: Universidad de Oviedo, 1971), 2:377. There is a family tree in vol. 1 of this biography.

157. AGS E, leg. 173, doc. 11.

158. Ibid., doc. 13.

159. Ibid., doc. 313.

160. Ibid., doc. 220.

161. Ibid.

162. Geoffrey Parker, *Felipe II: La biografía definitiva.* Madrid: Planeta, 2010, 46.

163. Stephen Haliczer, *Between Exaltation and Infamy: Female Mystics in the Golden Age of Spain* (Oxford: Oxford University Press, 2002), 22; Richard L. Kagan, "Politics, Prophecy, and the Inquisition in Late Sixteenth-Century Spain," in *Cultural Encounters: The Impact of the Inquisition in Spain and the New World*, ed. Mary Elizabeth Perry and Anne J. Cruz (Berkeley and Los Angeles: University of California Press, 1991), 118–19; Fray Luis de Granada, *Historia de Sor María de la Visitación y Sermón de las caídas públicas*, ed. Bernardo Velado Graña (Barcelona: Juan Flors, 1962).

164. Fernando Bouza, ed. *Cartas de Felipe II a sus hijas* (Madrid: Akal, 2008), 96.

165. Jesús Imirizaldu, ed., *Monjas y beatas embaucadoras* (Madrid: Editora Nacional, 1977), 130–33; João Francisco Marques, *A parenética portuguesa e a dominação filipina* (Oporto: Instituto Nacional de Investigação Científica, 1986), 93–94; Sepúlveda, *Historia de varios sucesos*, 66–69 [fols. 104v–106v]. The criminal sentence, handed down by Cardinal Archduke Albert, was widely circulated in pamphlet form; see BNM, VE 49–161, published in 1590; also BL Eg., 357 no. 10, fols. 124–42.

166. *Historia de Gabriel de Espinosa*, 17.

167. AGS E, leg. 173, doc. 220.

168. Ibid.

169. AGS E, leg. 173, doc. 72.

170. Ibid., doc. 221. That same day she sent a similar plea to someone addressed as "señora," probably her cousin Isabel Clara Eugenia; see ibid., doc. 222.

171. Ibid., doc. 70. The future St. Teresa lived there briefly in around 1531, when she was a somewhat wild teenager in need of discipline. See Saint Teresa, *Autobiography*, 59, n. 5.

172. AGS E, leg. 173, doc. 377.

173. Ibid., doc. 95. Their sentence is in doc. 74 and, with the charges, in BL Eg., 2059 fols. 245–48v.

Epilogue

1. On Espinosa's death, see AGS E, leg. 173, docs. 178, 187, 189–97, and 271; *Historia de Gabriel de Espinosa, Pastelero en Madrigal, que fingió ser el rey Don Sebastian de Portugal, y asimismo la de Fray Miguel de los Santos, en el año de 1595* (Jeréz: Juan Antonio de Tarazona, 1683), chapters 15 and 16 (hereafter *Historia de Gabriel de Espinosa*).

2. Pedro de León, *Grandeza y miseria en Andalucia. Testimonio de una encrucijada histórica (1578–1616)*, ed. Pedro Herrera Puga (Granada: Facultad de Teología, 1981), 251. For the recollections of another late sixteenth-century Jesuit who guided prisoners to their death in Madrid, see AGS, Clero Jesuits, leg. 5, no. 35, "Traslado de la vida del Padre Tomás de Soto."

3. This was also the usual punishment for treason in England, where the head was cut off "which had imagined the mischief . . . and the quarters set up in some high and eminent place, to the view and detestation of men, and to become a prey for the fowls of the air"; see *Public Execution in England, 1573–1868*, vol. 1, *Public Execution in England, 1573–1674* (London: Pickering and Chatto, 2009), xi–xix.

4. AGS E, leg. 173, doc. 194.

5. *Historia de Gabriel de Espinosa*, 52.

6. AGS E, leg. 173, doc. 192.

7. *Historia de Gabriel de Espinosa*, 53.

8. AGS E, leg. 173, doc. 194.

9. AGS leg. 173, doc. 190. Subsequent chronicles spent far more time discussing Espinosa's confession and his preparation for a Christian death than the execution itself, which also was typical of English literature; see *Public Execution in England*, 1:xxviii.

10. AGS E, leg. 173, docs. 76–81.

11. BL Eg., 2059, fols. 252–59v.

12. AGS E, leg. 173, docs. 382–83.

13. Ibid., docs. 99–104.

14. Ibid., doc. 102.

15. For the ceremony, see BL Add., 8708, fol. 87v; AGS E, leg. 173, docs. 105, 108, and 109. For the sentence, see BL Eg., 2059, fols. 259v–62v.

16. BNL, cod. 863, fols. 587r–87v.

17. The story of the execution is in AGS E, leg. 173, docs. 110–12. The royal jail was in the Plaza de Santa Cruz, today the site of the Ministry of Foreign Affairs.

18. "Colección de papeles históricos sobre los años 1542 a 1596," BNM, MS 3827, fol. 227.

19. *Calendar of State Papers and Manuscripts Relating to English Affairs, Existing in the Archives and Collections of Venice and in Other Libraries of Northern Italy*, vol. 9,

1592–1603 (London: Public Records Office, 1897), doc. 365, p. 166 (August 31, 1595); Pedro Batalha Reis, *Numária d'el Rey dom António, décimo oitavo Rei de Portugal, O ídolo do povo* (Lisbon: Academia Portuguesa da História, 1947), 450–53; the inventory is also in Antonio Caetano de Sousa, *Provas da história genealógica da casa real portuguesa*, vol. 2, pt. 2 (Coimbra: Atlântida, 1948), 141–44. The Venetian ambassador's colleague in Madrid once again mangled the story: six weeks after don António's death, he wrote that the news "was communicated to the [Spanish] ministers by a Portuguese who hoped for a reward, which was promised him if the news proved true," an unlikely story (see *Calendar of State Papers*, 9:169).

20. ANTT, Arquivo de don António, docs. 267 and 270; see also Batalha Reis, *Numária d'el Rey dom António*, 152–56 and 420–40; Júlio Dantas, "Testamento e morte do Rei D. António," *Anais das Bibliotecas e Arquivos* 11 (1936): 92–109; and Sousa, *Provas da história*, 144–59.

21. João Francisco Marques, *A parenética portuguesa e a dominação filipina* (Oporto: Instituto Nacional de Investigação Científica, 1986), 64, 326, and 406; AMAEC, Santa Sede, leg. 9, exp. 12, fols. 243–76; an excellent example of a seditious epistolary network centered in Rome. As it happens, the next (and last) false Sebastian appeared in Italy.

22. Sousa, *Provas da história*, 160–67.

23. Batalha Reis, *Numária d'el Rey dom António*, 445–50. That same day don António wrote to Henry IV of France (also about his children), the Estates General of Holland, the count of Nassau, the princess of Orange, and the count of Essex.

24. G. B. Harrison, ed., *The Letters of Queen Elizabeth* (London: Cassell, 1935), 236–37. The Guise letter appears in Gregorio Marañón, *Antonio Pérez (el hombre, el drama, la época)*, 2 vols., 5th ed. (Madrid: Espasa Calpe, 1954), 2:851–52; it contradicts other sources who say that Cristóvão never sought reconciliation with Philip II.

25. Antonio de Portugal, *D. Antonio, Prieur de Crato, XVIII Roi de Portugal* (Milan: Impr. Nationale de V. Ramperti, 1909), 1–3; Cesar da Silva, *O Prior do Crato e a sua epoca* (Lisbon: João Romano Torres, 192[?]), 269. Cristóvão wrote a biography of his father, published in 1629 in Paris.

26. Jaime Oliver Asín, *Vida de Don Felipe de Africa, príncipe de Fez y Marruecos (1566–1621)*, ed. Miguel Angel de Bunes Ibarra and Beatriz Alonso Acero (Granada: University of Granada, 2008). (Oliver Asín's work was first published in 1948; the new version has a very informative introductory essay by the editors.) See also Luis Cabrera de Córdoba, *Historia de Felipe II, Rey de España*, ed. José Martínez Millán and Carlos Javier de Carlos Morales (Salamanca: Junta de Castilla y León, 1998), 3:1269.

27. P. Fr. Jerónimo de Sepúlveda. *Historia de varios sucesos y de las cosas notables que han acaecido en España. . . .*, vol. 4 of *Documentos para la historia del Monasterio de San Lorenzo el Real de El Escorial*, ed. Julián Zarco Cuevas (Madrid: Imprenta Helénica, 1924), 148. Sepúlveda called him "the true king of Africa."

28. Jehan Lhermite, *El pasatiempos de Jehan Lhermite. Memorias de un Gentilhombre Flamenco en la corte de Felipe II y Felipe III*, ed. Jesús Sáenz de Miera, trans. José Luis Checa Cremades (Madrid: Doce Calles, 2005), 440–41.

29. BL Add., 28.422, fols. 292, 386–87, 391; BL Add., 28.423, fols. 211–12, 264.

30. Lope de Vega, *La tragedia del Rey don Sebastián y Bautismo del Príncipe de Marrue-*

cos, in *Biblioteca de Autores Españoles*, vol. 225 (*Obras de Lope de Vega*, vol. 27) (Madrid: Atlas, 1969), 121–82; Melchora Romanos, "Felipe II en la *Tragedia del Rey don Sebastián y el Bautismo del príncipe de Marruecos* de Lope de Vega," *Edad de Oro* 18 (1999) 177–91. George Mariscal says the play opened in 1593 at the Corral del Príncipe ("Symbolic Capital in the Spanish *Comedia*," in *Disorder and the Drama*, ed. Mary Beth Rose [Evanston, IL: Northwestern University Press], 143–69).

31. Carlos Eire, *From Madrid to Purgatory: The Art and Craft of Dying in Sixteenth-Century Spain* (Cambridge: Cambridge University Press, 1995), 258.

32. Baltasar Porreño, *Historia del sereníssimo Senor don Juan de Austria. . . .* , ed. A. Rodríguez Villa (Madrid: Sociedad de Bibliófilos Españoles, 1899), 356–71; Louis Prosper Gachard, *Don Juan d'Autriche: Etudes historiques* (Brussels: M. Hayez, 1868), 149–204. More correspondence to, from, and about Juana is in IVDJ, envío 46, docs. 20–22; and AMAEC, Santa Sede, leg. 44, exp. 1.

33. Gachard, *Don Juan d'Autriche*, 196.

34. IVDJ, envío 46, doc. 19. Possible identities of the recipient of the letter, addressed as "Vuestra Paternidad Reverendisima," are Philip II's chaplain García de Loaysa, or the duke of Lerma's uncle Bernardo de Sandoval y Rojas (future archbishop of Toledo), or the future Cardinal Zapata. All were related to the Mendozas.

35. BNM, MS 3784, *Papeles varios en prosa*, "Historia de Gabriel de Espinosa . . . ," fol. 48.

36. For the foundational document of the granary, containing Ana's motivations and her relationship with the town council, see Román Moreno y Rodrigo, *Madrigal de las Altas Torres, Cuna de Isabel la Católica* (Avila: Editorial Medrano, 1949).

37. Amancio Rodríguez López, *El Real Monasterio de las Huelgas de Burgos y el Hospital del Rey* (Burgos, 1907), vol. 2, chap. 6; royal correspondence in AMAEC, Santa Sede, leg. 31, exp. 7, and leg. 55, fols. 80–84; AGS E, legs. 991 and 993. Geoffrey Parker has pointed out in correspondence with me that the letters from Philip to ambassador Francisco de Castro were countersigned by Andrés de Prada, Juan of Austria's last secretary.

38. The account of the journey is in "Fundación y demás cosas tocantes al Real Monasterio de las Huelgas de Burgos," RAH, Salazar M-76, fols. 20–25v. Santiago's feast day is July 25.

39. AGS E, leg. 172, doc. 269.

Appendix

1. The controversy is discussed briefly in *Catálogo Razonado de Obras Anónimas y Seudónimas de autores de la Compañía de Jesus*, ed. P. J. Eugenio de Uriarte, 5 vols. (Madrid: Rivadeneyra, 1904), 1:324–25; and in Rafael Lozano Miralles's introduction to José de Cañizares, *El pastelero de Madrigal, rey Don Sebastian fingido* (Parma: Edizioni Zara, 1995), 8–9, which is also where I found the bibliographic information on De la Cerda.

2. The pamphlets I have seen are *Histoire du patissier de Madrigal en Espagne, estimé estre Dom Carles fils du roy Philippe* (Lyon: Thibaud Ancelin, 1596), 8vo; *Le patissier de Madrigal en Espaigne, estimé. . . .* (Paris: Jean le Blanc, 1596), 8vo; and *Le patissier de*

Madrigal en Espaigne. Estimé. . . . (Paris: Jean le Blanc, 1596), 12vo. All are in the Bibliotheque Nationale de France. Philip II's alleged order to murder his son was one of the linchpins of the Black Legend, so the tale of the young man's survival can be read as an implicit attack on the king.

3. George Ticknor, *History of Spanish Literature*, vol. 3, pt. 1 (Boston: Houghton, Mifflin, 1863), 10, n. 19.

4. George Ticknor, *Catalogue of the Spanish Library and of the Portuguese Books Bequeathed by George Ticknor to the Boston Public Library*, ed. James Lyman Whitney (Boston: Boston Public Library, 1879; repr., Boston: G. K. Hall, 1970), 128.

5. Benito Sánchez Alonso, *Fuentes de la historia española e hispanoamericana*, 3 vols. (Madrid: CSIC, 1952), 2:200. The pamphlet, of course, is not a transcript.

6. Antonio Palau y Dulcet, *Manual del librero hispanoamericano*, vol. 5 (E–F) (Oxford and Madrid, 1951), 142.

7. Julian Zarco Cuevas, ed., *Catálogo de los Manuscritos Castellanos de la Real Biblioteca de el Escorial* (Madrid: Imprenta del Real Monasterio, 1924–29), 3:150.

8. José Zorrilla, *Traidor, inconfeso y martir*, ed. Ricardo Senabre (Madrid: Cátedra, 1976), 23.

9. Mary Elizabeth Brooks, *A King for Portugal: The Madrigal Conspiracy, 1594–95* (Madison: University of Wisconsin Press, 1964), ch. 5.

10. John Yoklavich, "The Battle of Alcázarquivir," in George Peele, *The Dramatic Works of George Peele*, ed. John Yoklavich (New Haven, CT: Yale University Press, 1961), 2:257.

11. Prólogo: Por haber sido tan notable el caso que el año de 1595 sucedió en Madrigal y ver que se cuenta de maneras muy diferentes, refiriéndose en diversas partes y aun contradiciéndose sin decir verdad en unas mismas cosas, me ha parecido hacer una fiel relación de todo, tomándolo desde su principio, por que del mayor parte de sus sucesos puedo hablar como testigo de vista que me hallé a su muerte, y en cosas que pasaron en su vida y de lo demas podré asimismo tratar de que no estoy menos cierto por haberme informado de personas fididignas que lo vieron y tocaron con las manos.

12. Prólogo al curioso y noticioso Lector: Por haber sido tan notable el caso que sucedió en la Villa de Madrigal, en Castilla la Vieja, el año de 1595 y ver las diligencias tan varias que en el hecho se cuentan, diferentemente aún en una misma cosa y todo tan lejos de la verdad, me ha parecido hacer una muy entera y fiel relación, tomándolo desde su principio, y lo puedo asegurar como testigo de vista, ansi a la muerte como a muchas cosas que pasaron en vida, y de algunas que no vi no estoy menos cierto por haberme informado de personas fididignas que lo vieron y tocaron.

BIBLIOGRAPHY

Abad, Camilo María, S. I. *Doña Magdalena de Ulloa. La educadora de Don Juan de Austria y la fundadora del Colegio de la Compañía de Jesús de Villagarcía de Campos (1525–1598)*. Comillas: Universidad Pontificia, 1959.

Abun-Nasr, Jamil M. *A History of the Maghrib*. 2nd ed. Cambridge: Cambridge University Press, 1975.

Actas de las Cortes de Castilla. Vols. 12–13. Madrid, 1887.

Alonso, Carlos, OSA. "Documentación inédita sobre Fr. Agustín de Jesús, OSA, Arzobispo de Braga (1588–1609). *Analecta Augustiniana* 34 (1971): 85–170.

———. "Las profesiones religiosas en la provincia de Portugal durante el período 1513–1631." *Analecta Augustiniana* 48 (1985): 331–89.

Alonso Romero, María Paz. *El proceso penal en Castilla, siglo XIII–XVIII*. Salamanca: Ediciones Universidad de Salamanca, 1982.

Anonymous. *Crónica do Xarife Mulei Mahamet e d'el-rey D. Sebastião, 1573–1578*. Ed. Francisco de Sales de Mascarenhas Loureiro. Odivelas: Heuris, 1987.

———. *Historia de Portugal desde el tiempo del Rey Don Sebastián. . . .* BL Eg., 522.

———. "Los ytenes de Portugal" [or] "Respuesta que se hizo a una carta de un abbad de la Vera."

Antas, Miguel d'. *Les faux Don Sébastien. Etude sur l'histoire de Portugal*. Paris: Chez Auguste Durand, libraire, 1866.

Antonio de Portugal, Viscount of Faria. *Antonio I, Prieur do Crato, XIII Roi de Portugal. Bibliographia*. Livorno: Imprimerie Raphaël Giusti, 1910.

———. *Descendance de D. António, Prieur de Crato*. Livorno: Imprimerie Raphaël Giusti, 1908.

———. *D. Antonio, Prieur do Crato, XVIII Roi de Portugal (Extraits, Notes et Documents)*. Vol. 1. Milan: Impr. Nationale de V. Ramperti, 1909.

———. *D. António I, Prior do Crato, XVIII Rei de Portugal (1534–1595) e seus descendentes*. Livorno: Imprimerie Raphaël Giusti, 1910.

António, prior of Crato. *The Explanation of the True and Lawful Right and Tytle of the Moste Excellent Prince Anthonie. . . .* Leyden [*sic*; probably London]: In the Printing House of Christopher Plantyn, 1585.

Aranda, Juan de. *Lugares comunes de conceptos, dichos, y sentencias en diversas materias*. Seville, 1595.

Azevedo, J. Lucio de. *A evoluçao do Sebastianismo*. 2nd ed. Lisbon: Liv. Clássica, 1947.

Baena Parada, Juan de. *Epitome de la vida, y hechos de Don Sebastian Dezimo Sexto Rey de Portugal y Unico deste Nombre. . . .* Madrid: Antonio Gonzalez de Reyes, 1692.

Barbarics, Zsuzsa, and Renate Pieper. "Handwritten Newsletters as a Means of Communication in Early Modern Europe." In Bethencourt and Egmond, *Cultural Exchange in Early Modern Europe*, 3:53–79.

Barbosa Machado, Diogo. *Biblioteca Lusitana histórica, crítica e cronológica*. 4 vols. Ridgewood, NJ: Gregg Press, 1962; facsimile. (Orig. pub in Lisbon, 1741–59.)

———. *Memorias para a historia de Portugal, que comprehendem o governo del Rey D. Sebastião, unico em o nome, e decimo sexto entre os Monarchas Portuguezes*. 4 vols. Lisbon: Officina de Joseph António da Sylva, 1736–51.

Barletta, Vincent. *Death in Babylon: Alexander the Great and Iberian Empire in the Muslim Orient*. Chicago: University of Chicago Press, 2010.

Bartels, Emily C. *Speaking of the Moor: From Alcazar to Othello*. Philadelphia: University of Pennsylvania Press, 2008.

Bartlett, Robert. *The Hanged Man: A Story of Miracle, Memory and Colonialism in the Middle Ages*. Princeton, NJ: Princeton University Press, 2004.

Batalha Reis, Pedro. *Numária d'el Rey dom António, décimo oitavo Rei de Portugal, O ídolo do povo*. Lisbon: Academia Portuguesa da História, 1947.

Bellany, Alastair. *The Politics of Court Scandal in Early Modern England: News Culture and the Overbury Affair, 1603–1660*. Cambridge: Cambridge University Press, 2000.

Benítez, Jesús Miguel, OSA. "Agustinas de Madrigal de las Altas Torres del siglo XVI al XVII." In *La clausura femenina en España: Actas del simposium, 1/4-IX-2004*, ed. Francisco Javier Campos and Fernández de Sevilla, 1:363–98. Vol. 1. San Lorenzo del Escorial, 2004.

Bennassar, Bartolomé. *Don Juan de Austria*. Madrid: Temas de Hoy, 2000.

———. *Valladolid en el Siglo de Oro: Una ciudad de Castilla y su entorno agrario en el siglo XVI*. Valladolid: Ambito, 1983.

Bennassar, Bartolomé, and Lucile Bennassar. *Les Chrétiens d'Allah. L'histoire extraordinaire des renegats. XVI et XVII siècles*. Paris: Perrin, 1989.

Bercé, Yves-Marie. *Le roi caché. Saveurs et imposteurs. Mythes politiques populaires dans l'Europe moderne*. Paris: Fayard, 1990.

Bethencourt, Francisco. "Political Configurations and Local Powers." In *Portuguese Oceanic Expansion, 1400–1800*, ed. Francisco Bethencourt and Diogo Ramada Curto, 197–254. Cambridge: Cambridge University Press, 2007.

Bethencourt, Francisco, and Florike Egmond, eds. *Cultural Exchange in Early Modern*

Europe. Vol. 3. *Correspondence and Cultural Exchange in Europe, 1400–1700*. Cambridge: Cambridge University Press, 2007.
Bilinkoff, Jodi. *The Avila of Saint Teresa: Religious Reform in a Sixteenth-Century City*. Ithaca, NY: Cornell University Press, 1989.
Birmingham, David. *A Concise History of Portugal*. 2nd ed. Cambridge University Press, 2003.
Bondeson, Jan. *The Great Pretenders: The True Stories behind Famous Historical Mysteries*. New York: W. W. Norton, 2004.
Borromeo, Agostino. "La Santa Sede y la candidatura de Felipe II al trono de Portugal." In *Las sociedades ibéricas y el mar a finales del siglo XVI*. Vol. 5. *El área Atlántica: Portugal y Flandes*. Madrid: Sociedad Estatal Lisboa '98, 41–57.
Bouza, Fernando, ed. *Cartas de Felipe II a sus hijas*. Madrid: Akal, 2008.
———. "Los contextos materiales de la producción cultural." In *España en tiempos del Quijote*, ed. Antonio Feros and Juan Gelabert, 309–44. Madrid: Taurus, 2004.
———. *Corre manuscrito: Una historia cultural del Siglo de Oro*. Madrid: Marcial Pons, 2001.
———. "Corte es decepción: Don Juan de Silva, conde de Portalegre." In *La corte de Felipe II*, ed. José Martínez Millán, 451–502. Madrid: Alianza Universidad, 1994.
———. "Corte y Protesta. El Condestable de Castilla y el 'insulto' de los maestros y oficiales de Madrid en 1591." In *Madrid, Felipe II y las ciudades de la monarquía*, ed. Enrique Martínez Ruiz. Vol. 2. *Capitalismo y economía*, 17–32. Madrid: Actas Editorial, 2000.
———. "De las alteraciones de Beja (1593) a la revuelta lisboeta *dos ingleses* (1596): Lucha política en el último Portugal del primer Felipe." *Studia Histórica: Historia Moderna*, no. 17 (1997): 91–120.
———. *Imagen y propaganda: Capítulos de historia cultural del reinado de Felipe II*. Madrid: Akal, 1998.
———. "Letters and Portraits: Economy of Time and Chivalrous Service in Courtly Culture." In Bethencourt and Egmond, *Cultural Exchange in Early Modern Europe*, 3:145–62.
Bovill, E. W. *The Battle of Alcazar. An Account of the Defeat of Don Sebastian of Portugal at El-Ksar el-Kebir*. London: Batchworth Press, 1952.
Boxer, C. R. *Four Centuries of Portuguese Expansion: A Succint Survey*. Berkeley and Los Angeles: University of California Press, 1969.
———. *The Portuguese Seaborne Empire, 1415–1825*. 2nd ed. Manchester: Carcanet and the Calouste Gulbenkian Foundation, 1991.
Brandão, Mario. "Alguns documentos relativos a 1580." In *Boletim da Biblioteca da Universidade de Coimbra*. Vol. 16. Coimbra: Universidade de Coimbra, 1944.
———. *Coimbra e D. António, Rei de Portugal*. Coimbra: Universidade de Coimbra, 1939.
Braudel, Fernand. *The Mediterranean and the Mediterranean World in the Age of Philip II*. 2 vols. New York: Harper and Row, 1973.
Brooks, Mary Elizabeth. *A King for Portugal: The Madrigal Conspiracy, 1594–95*. Madison: University of Wisconsin Press, 1964.

———. "From Military Defeat to Immortality: The Birth of Sebastianism." *Luso-Brazilian Review* 1, no. 2 (Winter 1964): 41–49.

Bunes Ibarra, Miguel Angel de, and Enrique García Hernán. "La muerte de D. Sebastián de Portugal y el mundo mediterráneo de finales del siglo XVI." *Hispania* 54, no. 187 (May/August 1994): 447–65.

Burke, Peter. "Early Modern Venice as a Center of Information and Communication." In *Venice Reconsidered: The History and Civilization of an Italian City-State, 1297–1979*, ed. John Martin and Dennis Romano, 389–419. Baltimore, MD: Johns Hopkins University Press, 2000.

Cabrera de Córdoba, Luis. *Historia de Felipe II, Rey de España*, ed. José Martínez Millán and Carlos Javier de Carlos Morales. 4 vols. Salamanca: Junta de Castilla y León, 1998.

Caeiro, Francisco. *O Arquiduque Alberto de Austria, vice-rei de Portugal*. Lisbon, 1961.

Calendar of Letters and State Papers Relating to English Affairs, preserved in, or originally belonging to, the Archives of Simancas. Vol. 4. *Elizabeth, 1587–1603*, ed. Martin A. S. Hume. London: Public Record Office, 1899.

Calendar of State Papers and Manuscripts Relating to English Affairs, Existing in the Archives and Collections of Venice and in Other Libraries of Northern Italy. Vols. 8–9 [1581–1603]. London: Public Record Office, 1894 and 1897.

Cámara, P. Fr. Tomás. *Vida y escritos del Beato Alonso de Orozco del Orden de San Agustín, Predicador de Felipe II*. Valladolid: Real Colegio de PP. Agustinos Filipinos (Imp. y Lib. de la V. de Cuesta e Hijos), 1882.

Camões, Luís Vaz de. *The Lusiads*. Trans. Landeg White. Oxford: Oxford University Press, 1997.

Canavaggio, Jean. *Cervantes*. Madrid: Espasa-Calpe, 1986.

Cañizares, José de. *El pastelero de Madrigal, rey Don Sebastian fingido*. Ed. Rafael Lozano Miralles. Parma: Edizioni Zara, 1995.

Cardim, Pedro. "Los portugueses frente a la monarquía hispánica." In *La monarquía de las naciones. Patria, nación y naturaleza en la monarquía de España*, ed. Antonio Alvarez-Ossorio Alvariño and Bernardo J. García García, 355–83. Madrid: Fundación Carlos de Amberes, 2004.

Casamar, María Remedios. *Las dos muertes del Rey Don Sebastián*. Granada, 1995.

Casey, James. *Family and Community in Early Modern Spain: The Citizens of Granada, 1570–1739*. Cambridge: Cambridge University Press, 2007.

Castelo Branco, Camilo. *As virtudes antigas; ou a freira que fazia chagas e o frade que fazia reis*. 2nd ed. Lisbon: Livraría de Campos Junior, 1904. (Orig. pub. 1868.)

Castro, P. José de. *O Prior do Crato*. Lisbon: Tip. União Gráfica, 1942.

Cátedra, Pedro M. *Invención, difusión y recepción de la literatura popular impresa (siglo XVI)*. Badajoz: Editorial Regional de Extremadura, 2002.

Cave, Terence. *Recognitions: A Study in Poetics*. Oxford: Clarendon Press, 1988.

Cervantes, Miguel de. *Los baños de Argel*. Madrid: Taurus, 1983.

———. *El ingenioso hidalgo Don Quijote de La Mancha*. 2 vols. Madrid: Clásicos Castalia, 1978.

———. *Novelas ejemplares*. 2 vols. Madrid: Colección Austral, 1996.

———. *Los trabajos de Persiles y Sigismunda*. Ed. Carlos Romero Muñoz. Madrid: Cátedra, 2002.

Coello de Barbuda, Luís. *Empresas militares de Lusitanos*. Lisbon: Pedro Craesbeeck, 1624.

Colección de documentos inéditos para la historia de España. 112 vols. Madrid: Calera and others, 1841–95.

Conestaggio, Gerolamo Franchi di. *The historie of the uniting of the kingdom of Portugall to the crowne of Castill. . . .* London: Imprinted by A. Hatfield for E. Blount, 1600.

Cook, Alexandra Parma, and Noble David Cook. *The Plague Files: Crisis Management in Sixteenth-Century Seville*. Baton Rouge: Louisiana State University Press, 2009.

Cook, Weston F., Jr. *The Hundred Years War for Morocco: Gunpowder and the Military Revolution in the Early Modern Muslim World*. Boulder, CO: Westview Press, 1994.

The Coppie of the Anti-Spaniard made at Paris by a French man, a Catholique. Wherein is directly proved how the Spanish king is the onely cause of all the troubles in France. Translated out of French into English. London, 1590.

Covarrubias Orozco, Sebastián de. *Tesoro de la Lengua Castellana o Española*. Madrid: Editorial Castalia, 1995.

Coward, Barry, and Julian Swann, eds. *Conspiracies and Conspiracy Theory in Early Modern Europe. From the Waldensians to the French Revolution*. Aldershot: Ashgate, 2004.

Crane, Mark, Richard Raiswell, and Margaret Reeves, eds. *Shell Games: Studies in Scams, Frauds, and Deceits (1300–1650)*. Toronto: Centre for Reformation and Renaissance Studies, University of Toronto, 2004.

Crónicas del Rey Dom Sebastião (multiple authors). Fernán Nuñez Collection, Banc MS UCB 143, vol. 147. The Bancroft Library, University of California, Berkeley.

Cruz, Anne J. "Juana of Austria: Patron of the Arts and Regent of Spain, 1554–59." In *The Rule of Women in Early Modern Europe*, ed. Anne J. Cruz and Mihoko Suzuki, 103–22. Urbana: University of Illinois Press, 2009.

Cruz, Fr. Bernardo da. *Crónica del-Rei D. Sebastião*. Bibliotheca de Clásicos Portuguezes, vol. 36. Lisbon: Escriptorio, 1903.

Curto, Diogo Ramada. "O Bastião! O Bastião! (Actos políticos e modalidades de crença, 1578–1603)." In *Portugal: Mitos revisitados*, ed. Yvette Kace Centeno, 141–76. Lisbon: Edições Salamandra, 1993.

Da Costa Roque, Mario. "A 'peste grande' de 1569 em Lisboa." *Anais*, 2nd ser., 28 (1982): 74–90.

Dantas, Júlio. "Testamento e morte do Rei D. António." *Anais das Bibliotecas e Arquivos* 11 (1936): 92–109.

Dánvila, Alfonso. *Felipe II y el Rey Don Sebastián de Portugal*. Madrid: Espasa Calpe, 1954.

Dánvila y Burguero, Alfonso. *Don Cristóbal de Moura, Primer Marqués de Castel Rodrigo (1538–1613)*. Madrid: Fortanet, 1900.

Davis, Natalie Zemon. *Fiction in the Archives: Pardon Tales and Their Tellers in Sixteenth-Century France*. Stanford, CA: Stanford University Press, 1987.

———. "From Prodigious to Heinous: Simon Goulart and the Reframing of Imposture." In *L'histoire grande ouverte. Hommages à Emmanuel Le Roy Ladurie*, 274–83. Paris: Fayard, 1997.

———. *The Return of Martin Guerre*. Cambridge, MA: Harvard University Press, 1983.

Descripción de las cosas sucedidas en los Reynos de Portugal desde la Jornada que el Rey Don Sebastián hizo en Africa. . . . BNM MS 1753.

Di Carpegna Falconieri, Tommaso. *The Man Who Believed He Was King of France: A True Medieval Tale*. Trans. William McCuaig. Chicago: University of Chicago Press, 2008.

Documentos para la Historia: Avila, 1085–1985. Avila: Museo Provincial de Avila, 1985.

Domingues, Mário. *O Prior do Crato contra Filipe II*. Lisbon: Romano Torres, 1965.

Dooley, Brendan. *The Social History of Skepticism. Experience and Doubt in Early Modern Culture*. Baltimore, MD: Johns Hopkins University Press, 1999.

Dooley, Brendan, and Sabrina Baron, eds. *The Politics of Information in Early Modern Europe*. Routledge Studies in Cultural History. London: Routledge, 2001.

Dover, Paul. "Good Information, Bad Information and Misinformation in Fifteenth-Century Italian Diplomacy." In Crane, Raiswell, and Reeves, *Shell Games*, 81–102.

Dubert García, Isidro. "Don Antonio, realidad y mito: El Prior do Crato, de la pretensión al trono de los Avis a Les Psaeumes Confessionales franceses." In *Universitas: Homenaje a Antonio Eiras Roel*, ed. Camilo Fernández Cortizo, 133–53. Santiago de Compostela: Universidad de Santiago de Compostela, 2002.

Durand-Lapie, Paul. *Dom Antoine I, Roi de Portugal, 1580–1595*. Paris: Typ. Plon-Nourrit, 1905.

Eccles, Mark. *Christopher Marlowe in London*. Cambridge, MA: Harvard University Press, 1934.

Edouard, Sylvène. *L'Empire Imaginaire de Philippe II: Pouvoir des images et discours du pouvoir sous les Habsbourg d'Espagne au XVIe siècle*. Paris: Honoré Champion Editeur, 2005.

Eire, Carlos. *From Madrid to Purgatory: The Art and Craft of Dying in Sixteenth-Century Spain*. Cambridge: Cambridge University Press, 1995.

Escriva de Balaguer, José María. *La abadesa de Las Huelgas: Estudio teológico jurídico*. 2nd ed. Madrid: Ediciones Rialp, 1974.

Etienvre, Jean-Pierre. "Entre relación y carta: Los Avisos." In *Les 'relaciones de sucesos' (canards) en Espagne (1500–1750). Actes du premier colloque international (Alcalá de Henares, 8–10 juin 1995)*. Alcalá de Henares: Universidad de Alcalá de Henares, 1996.

Ettinghausen, Henry. "The News in Spain: *Relaciones de sucesos* in the Reigns of Philip III and Philip IV." *European History Quarterly* 14, no. 1 (January 1984): 1–20.

———. "Phenomenal Figures: The Best-Selling First Newsletter Attributed to Andrés de Almansa y Mendoza." *Bulletin of Spanish Studies* 81, nos. 7–8 (2004): 1051–67.

———. "Politics and the Press in Spain." In Dooley and Baron, *Politics of Information*, 199–215.

Falcó y Osorio, María del Rosario, ed. *Documentos escogidos del Archivo de la Casa de Alba. Los publica la Duquesa de Berwick y de Alba*. Madrid, 1891.

Faria e Sousa, Manuel de. *Fuente de Aganipe. Rimas Varias*. Hispanic Society of America, B2509, n.d.

Fernández, Quirino, OSA. "Las dos Agustinas de Madrigal, hijas de Fernando el Católico llamadas ambas Doña María de Aragón. *Analecta Augustiniana* 53 (1990): 361–407.

Fernández Alvarez, Manuel. "Objetivo: Lisboa. La unión de Portugal y Castilla bajo

Felipe II." In *Las relaciones entre Portugal y Castilla en la época de los descubrimientos y la expansión colonial*, ed. Ana María Carabias Torres, 327–36. Salamanca: Ediciones Universidad, 1994.

———. *La Princesa de Eboli*. Madrid: Espasa Calpe, 2009.

Fernández Collado, Angel. *La Catedral de Toledo en el siglo XVI. Vida, arte y personas*. Toledo: Diputación Provincial, 1999.

Fernández Conti, Santiago, and Félix Labrador Arroyo. '"Entre Madrid y Lisboa.' El servicio de la nación portuguesa a través de la Casa Real, 1581–1598." In *La monarquía de las naciones. Patria, nación y naturaleza en la monarquía de España*, eds. Antonio Alvarez-Ossorio Alvariño and Bernardo J. García García. Madrid: Fundación Carlos de Amberes, 2004, 163–91.

Fernández Fernández, Maximiliano. *Prensa y comunicación en Avila (siglos XVI–XIX)*. Avila: Institución Gran Duque de Alba, 1998.

Fernández y González, Manuel. *El pastelero de Madrigal: Novela histórica*. Madrid: Editorial Tesoro, 1952. (Orig. pub. 1863.)

Figueiredo, Pedro José de. *Carta em resposta de certo amigo da cidade de Lisboa a outro da villa de Santarém, em que se lançam os fundamentos sobre a verdade ou incerteza da morte d'ElRei D. Sebastião*. Lisbon: Officina de João Evangelista Garcez, 1808.

Firpo, Luigi, ed. *Relazioni di ambasciatori veneti al Senato*. Vol. 8. *Spain (1497–1598)*. Turin: Bottega D'Erasmo, 1981.

Fitzmaurice-Kelly, James. *Fray Luis de León, a Biographical Fragment*. Oxford: Oxford University Press, 1921. Available online at http://www.gutenberg.org/files/16148/16148-8.txt.

Floreto de anécdotas y noticias diversas que recopiló un fraile domínico residente en Sevilla a mediados del siglo XVI. RAH, Jesuitas, vol. 188.

Fonseca, Antonio Belard da. *Dom Sebastião, antes e depois de Alcácer-Quibir*. 2 vols. Lisbon: Tip. Ramos, Alfonso, e Moita, 1978.

Formica, Mercedes. *La hija de Don Juan de Austria. Ana de Jesús en el proceso al pastelero de Madrigal*. Madrid: Revista de Occidente, 1973.

———. *María de Mendoza (Solución a un enigma amoroso)*. Madrid: Editorial Caro Raggio, 1979.

Fortea Pérez, José Ignacio. *Monarquía y cortes en la corona de Castilla*. Valladolid: Cortes de Castilla y León, 1990.

Fox, Adam. *Oral and Literate Culture in England, 1500–1700*. Oxford: Clarendon Press, 2000.

Freer, Martha Walker. *The Married Life of Anne of Austria, Queen of France, Mother of Louis XIV, and Don Sebastian, King of Portugal*. Vol. 2. London: Tinsley Brothers, 1864.

Freire de Oliveira, Eduardo, ed. *Elementos para a historia do Municipio de Lisboa*. Lisbon: 1932.

Friedman, Ellen. *Spanish Captives in North Africa in the Early Modern Age*. Madison: University of Wisconsin Press, 1983.

Fuchs, Barbara. *Passing for Spain: Cervantes and the Fictions of Identity*. Urbana: University of Illinois Press, 2003.

Fumerton, Patricia. *Cultural Aesthetics: Renaissance Literature and the Practice of Social Ornament*. Chicago: University of Chicago Press, 1991.

Fussell, Paul. *The Great War and Modern Memory*. Oxford: Oxford University Press, 1975.

Gachard, Louis Prosper. *Don Juan d'Autriche: Etudes historiques*. Brussels: M. Hayez, 1868.

———. *Relations des ambassadeurs vénitiens sur Charles-Quint et Philippe II*. Brussels: M. Hayez, 1855.

Garcés, María Antonia. *Cervantes in Algiers: A Captive's Tale*. Nashville, TN: Vanderbilt University Press, 2002.

García Carraffa, Alberto, and Arturo García Carraffa. *Enciclopedia heráldica y genealógica Hispano-Americana*. Vol. 56. Madrid, 1935.

García España, E., and Annie Molinié-Bertrand, eds. *Censo de Castilla de 1591: Vecindarios*. Madrid: Instituto Nacional de Estadística, 1986.

Garrido Camacho, Patricia. *El tema del reconocimiento en el teatro español del siglo XVI: La teoría de la anagnórisis*. London: Editorial Támesis, 1999.

Garzón Garzón, Juan María. *El real hospital de Madrigal*. Avila: Institución Gran Duque de Alba, 1985.

Gillot de Sainctonge, Louise-Geneviève. *Histoire secrete de dom Antoine, Roy de Portugal, tirée des memoires de Dom Gomes Vasconcellos de Figueredo*. Paris: Chez Jean Guignard, 1696.

Goes Loureiro, Fernando de. *Breve Summa y Relación de las Vidas y Hechos de los Reyes de Portugal, y cosas succedidas en aquel Reyno desde su principio hasta el año de MDXCV.* Mantua: Osana, 1596.

Góngora, Luis de. *Selected Poems*. Ed. and trans. John Dent-Young. Chicago: University of Chicago Press, 2007.

González Echevarría, Roberto. *Love and the Law in Cervantes*. New Haven, CT: Yale University Press, 2005.

———. *Myth and Archive: A Theory of Latin American Narrative*. Durham, NC: Duke University Press, 1998.

González Marcos, Isaac. "Datos para una biografía de Agustín Antolinez, OSA." *Revista Agustiniana* 30, nos. 91–92 (1989): 101–42.

González Novalin, José Luis. *El inquisidor general Fernando de Valdés (1483–1568)*. 2 vols. Oviedo: Universidad de Oviedo, 1971.

Gracián, Baltasar. *Agudeza y arte de ingenio.* Ed. Evaristo Correa Calderón. 2 vols. Madrid: Clásicos Castalia, 1969.

Granada, Fray Luis de. *Historia de Sor María de la Visitación y Sermón de las caídas públicas*. Ed. Bernardo Velado Graña. Barcelona: Juan Flors, 1962.

Groebner, Valentin. "Describing the Person, Reading the Signs in Late Medieval and Renaissance Europe: Identity Papers, Vested Figures, and the Limits of Identification, 1400–1600." In *Documenting Individual Identity: The Development of State Practice in the Modern World*, ed. Jane Caplan and John Torpey, 15–27. Princeton, NJ: Princeton University Press, 2001.

———. *Who Are You? Identification, Deception, and Surveillance in Early Modern Europe.* Trans. Mark Kyburz and John Peck. New York: Zone Books, 2007.

Güell, Monique. "La défaite d'Alcazarquivir et la mort du roi Don Sébastien de Portugal (1578): Sa mise en écriture par les poètes Fernando de Herrera et Luis Barahona de Soto." In *L'actualité et sa mise en écriture aux XV–XVI et XVII siècles. Espagne, Italie, France et Portugal*, ed. Pierre Civil and Danielle Boillet, 251–67. Paris: Presses Sorbonne Nouvelle, 2005.

Gutiérrez, David. *The Augustinians from the Protestant Reformation to the Peace of Westphalia, 1518–1648*. Trans. John J. Kelly, OSA. Villanova, PA: Augustinian Historical Institute, 1979.

Gutiérrez, Marcelino. "Fray Diego de Zúñiga." *Ciudad de Dios* 14 (1887): 293–304.

Gutiérrez Coronel, Diego. *Historia genealógica de la Casa de Mendoza*. 2 vols. Ed. Angel González Palencia, vol. 2. Cuenca: CSIC, 1946.

Haliczer, Stephen. *Between Exaltation and Infamy: Female Mystics in the Golden Age of Spain*. Oxford: Oxford University Press, 2002.

———. *Sexuality in the Confessional: A Sacrament Profaned*. Oxford: Oxford University Press, 1996.

Hampton, Timothy. *Fictions of Embassy: Literature and Diplomacy in Early Modern Europe*. Ithaca, NY: Cornell University Press, 2009.

Harrison, G. B., ed. *The Letters of Queen Elizabeth*. London: Cassell, 1935.

Heras Santos, José Luis de las. *La justicia penal de los Austrias en la Corona de Castilla*. Salamanca: Ediciones Universidad, 1991.

Hermann, Jacqueline. *No Reino do Desejado: A construção do sebastianismo em Portugal, séculos XVI e XVII*. São Paulo: Companhia das Letras, 1998.

Herrera, Fernando de. *Poesías*. Ed. Victoriano Roncero López. Madrid: Clásicos Castalia, 1992.

Herrera, Thomas de. *Breve compendio de los prelados eclesiásticos y ministros de sumos pontífices, reyes, y príncipes de quienes haze mención en su Alfabeto Agustiniano el M. F. Tomas de Herrera. . . .* Madrid: I. Maroto, 1643.

———. *Historia del convento de S. Augustín de Salamanca*. Madrid: G. Rodríguez, 1652.

Herrera y Tordesillas, Antonio de. *Historia general del mundo . . . del tiempo del Señor rey Don Felipe II el Prudente. . . .* 3 vols. Valladolid, 1606–12.

Herrero García, Miguel. *Ideas de los españoles del siglo XVII*. Madrid: Editorial Gredos, 1966.

Hespanha, Antonio Manuel. "Cities and the State in Portugal." In *Cities and the Rise of States in Europe, AD 1000 to 1800*, ed. Charles Tilly and Wim P. Blockmans, 184–95. Boulder, CO: Westview Press, 1994.

Hess, Andrew C. "The Battle of Lepanto and Its Place in Mediterranean History." *Past and Present*, no. 57 (November 1972): 53–73.

Hinojosa y Montalvo, Francisco. *Libro de la vida, loables costumbres, y santa muerte de la Ilustríssima Señora doña María Gasca de la Vega*. Madrid, 1626.

Historia del fingido Rey de Portugal. Real Biblioteca del Monasterio de San Lorenzo de El Escorial, Z-IV-2.

Historia de Gabriel de Espinosa, pastelero en Madrigal, que fingió ser el rey Don Sebastian de Portugal, y asimismo la de Fray Miguel de los Santos, en el año de 1595. Jeréz: Juan Antonio de Tarazona, 1683; repr. Valladolid: Alonso del Riego, 1785.

Homem, Fr. Manoel de. *Memoria da disposiçam das armas castelhanas, que injustamente invadirão o Reyno de Portugal no Anno de 1580*. Lisbon: 1655.

Hume, Martin. *True Stories of the Past*. London: E. Nash, 1910.

Imirizaldu, Jesús, ed. *Monjas y beatas embaucadoras*. Madrid: Editora Nacional, 1977.

Les imposteurs fameux ou histoires extraordinaires et singulieres. Paris: Eymery, 1818.

Infelise, Mario. *Prima dei giornali: Alle origini della pubblica informazione (secoli XVI e XVII)*. Rome: Editori Laterza, 2002.

———. "Professione reportista: Copisti e gazzettieri nella Venezia del Seicento." In *Venezia: Itinerari per la storia della città*, ed. Stefano Gasparri, Giovanni Levi, and Pierandrea Moro, 193–219. Bologna: Società editrice il Mulino, 1997.

Johnson, Harold B. *Camponeses e Colonizadores: Estudos de História Luso-Brasileira*. Lisbon: Editorial Estampa, 2002.

———. "A Horoscope Cast Upon the Birth of King Sebastian of Portugal (1554–1578)." Online at http://people.virginia.edu/~hbj8n/horoscope.pdf.

———. "A Pedophile in the Palace; or, the Sexual Abuse of King Sebastian of Portugal (1554–1578) and Its Consequences." In *Pelo Vaso Traseiro: Sodomy and Sodomites in Luso-Brazilian History*, ed. Harold Johnson and Francis A. Dutra, 195–230. Phoenix, AZ: Fenestra Books, 2006.

Johnson, James H. "Deceit and Sincerity in Early Modern Venice." *Eighteenth-Century Studies* 38, no. 3 (2005): 399–415.

Jordán Arroyo, María V. *Soñar la historia: Riesgo, creatividad y religión en las profecías de Lucrecia de León*. Madrid: Siglo XXI, 2007.

Juárez Almendros, Encarnación. *El cuerpo vestido y la construcción de la identidad en las narrativas autobiográficas del Siglo de Oro*. London: Editorial Támesis, 2006.

Kagan, Richard L. *Clio and the Crown: The Politics of History in Medieval and Early Modern Spain*. Baltimore, MD: Johns Hopkins University Press, 2009.

———. *Lucrecia's Dreams: Politics and Prophecy in Sixteenth-Century Spain*. Berkeley and Los Angeles: University of California Press, 1990.

———. "Politics, Prophecy, and the Inquisition in Late Sixteenth-Century Spain." In *Cultural Encounters: The Impact of the Inquisition in Spain and the New World*, ed. Mary Elizabeth Perry and Anne J. Cruz, 105–26. Berkeley and Los Angeles: University of California Press, 1991.

Kagan, Richard L., and Abigail Dyer, eds. and trans. *Inquisitorial Inquiries: Brief Lives of Secret Jews and Other Heretics*. Baltimore, MD: Johns Hopkins University Press, 2004.

Kahn, Aaron M. "Moral Opposition to Philip in Pre-Lopean Drama." *Hispanic Review* 74, no. 3 (Summer 2006): 227–50.

Kamen, Henry. *Inquisition and Society in Spain in the Sixteenth and Seventeenth Centuries*. Bloomington: Indiana University Press, 1985.

———. *Philip of Spain*. New Haven, CT: Yale University Press, 1997.

Kelsey, Harry. *Sir Francis Drake: The Queen's Pirate*. New Haven, CT: Yale University Press, 1998.

Khevenhüller, Hans. *Diario de Hans Khevenhüller, embajador imperial en la corte de Felipe II*. Ed. Sara Veronelli and Félix Labrador Arroyo. Madrid: Sociedad Estatal para la Conmemoración de los Centenarios de Felipe II y Carlos V, 2001.

Klarwill, Victor von, ed. *The Fugger News-Letters, 2nd series. Being a further Selection from the Fugger papers especially referring to Queen Elizabeth. . . .* Trans. L. S. R. Byrne. New York: G. P. Putnam's Sons, 1926.

Kümin, Beat. *Drinking Matters: Public Houses and Social Exchange in Early Modern Central Europe*. New York: Palgrave Macmillan, 2007.

Lapeyre, Henri. *Une famille de marchands: Les Ruiz*. Paris: Colin, 1955.

Lea, Henry Charles. *Torture*. Philadelphia: University of Pennsylvania Press, 1973.

Lecuppre, Gilles. *L'imposture politique au Moyen Age: La seconde vie des rois*. Paris: Presses Universitaires de France, 2005.

Lehfeldt, Elizabeth A. *Religious Women in Golden Age Spain: The Permeable Cloister*. Aldershot: Ashgate, 2005.

———. "Spatial Discipline and Its Limits: Nuns and the Built Environment in Early Modern Spain." In *Architecture and the Politics of Gender in Early Modern Europe*, ed. Helen Mills, 131–49. Aldershot: Ashgate, 2003.

León, Pedro de. *Grandeza y miseria en Andalucia. Testimonio de una encrucijada histórica (1578–1616)*. Ed. Pedro Herrera Puga. Granada: Facultad de Teología, 1981.

Lhermite, Jehan. *El pasatiempos de Jehan Lhermite: Memorias de un Gentilhombre Flamenco en la corte de Felipe II y Felipe III*. Ed. Jesús Sáenz de Miera, trans. José Luis Checa Cremades. Madrid: Doce Calles, 2005.

Lima Cruz, Maria Augusta. *D. Sebastião*. Lisbon: Círculo de Leitores, 2006.

List and Analysis of State Papers, Foreign Series. Elizabeth I. Preserved in the Public Record Office. Vol. 7. *January to December 1596*. Ed. Richard Bruce Wernham. London: Public Record Office, 2000.

Lozano, Jorge Sebastián. "Lo privado es político: Sobre género y usos de la imagen en la corte de los Austrias." In *Luchas de género en la historia através de la imagen: Ponencias y comunicaciones*, ed. María Teresa Sauret Guerrero and Amparo Quiles Faz, 1:683–99. Málaga: Diputación Provincial, 2001.

Macedo, Jose Agostinho de. *Os sebastianistas*. Lisbon: Officinas Antonio Rodrigues Galhardo, 1810.

Machado Pires, Antonio. *D. Sebastião e o Encoberto: Estudo e antologia*. Lisbon: Fundação Calouste Gulbenkien, 1971.

Machado de Sousa, Maria Leonor, ed. *D. Sebastião na literatura inglesa*. Lisbon: Minsterio da Educação, 1985.

Madero, Marta. "Savoirs féminins et construction de la vérité: Les femmes dans la preuve testimoniale en Castille au XIII siècle." *Crime, Histoire et Sociétés* 3, no. 2 (1999): 5–21.

Malagón-Barceló, Javier. "Toledo and the New World in the Sixteenth Century." *The Americas* 20, no. 2 (October 1963): 97–126.

Marañon, Gregorio. *Antonio Pérez (el hombre, el drama, la época)*. 2 vols. 5th ed. Madrid: Espasa Calpe, 1954.

———. *Antonio Pérez, 'Spanish Traitor.'* Trans. Charles David Ley. London: Hollis and Carter, 1954.

Marcos Martín, Alberto. "Medina del Campo 1500–1800: An Historical Account of Its Decline," in Thompson and Yun Casalilla, *Castilian Crisis of the Seventeenth Century*, 220–48.

Margaça Veiga, Carlos José. "Entre o rigor do castigo e a magnanimidade da clemecia: Os perdões concedidos por Filipe II a Portugal." *Mare Liberum* 10 (December 1995): 141–55.

Mariana, P. Juan de. *Historia General de España*. 3 vols. Madrid: Imprenta y Librería de Gaspar y Roig, Editores, 1852.

Mariscal, George. "Symbolic Capital in the Spanish *Comedia*." In *Disorder and the Drama*, ed. Mary Beth Rose, 143–69. Renaissance Drama, n.s., 21. Evanston, IL: Northwestern University Press, 1990.

Marques, João Francisco. *A parenética portuguesa e a dominação filipina*. Oporto: Instituto Nacional de Investigação Científica, 1986.

———. "Fr. Miguel dos Santos e a luta contra a união dinástica o contexto do falso D. Sebastião de Madrigal." *Revista da Faculdade de Letras: Historia* (Oporto), 2nd series, 14, (1997): 331–88.

Martínez Hernández, Santiago. *El marqués de Velada y la corte en los reinados de Felipe II y Felipe III: Nobleza y cultura política en la España del Siglo de Oro*. Valladolid: Junta de Castilla y León, 2004.

Martínez Millán, José. "Elites de poder en las Cortes de las Monarquías española y portuguesa en el siglo XVI: Los servidores de Juana de Austria." *Miscelánea Comillas* 61 (2003): 169–202.

———. "Familia real y grupos políticos: La princesa doña Juana de Austria (1535–1573)." In *La corte de Felipe II*, ed. José Martínez Millán, 73–105. Madrid: Alianza Universidad, 1994.

Martínez Torres, José Antonio. *Prisioneros de los infieles: Vida y rescate de los cautivos cristianos en el Mediterráneo musulmán (siglos XVI–XVII)*. Barcelona: Ediciones Bellaterra, 2004.

Matar, Nabil. *Turks, Moors, and Englishmen in the Age of Discovery*. New York: Columbia University Press, 2000.

Mateo, Andrés María. "Antonio Pérez en la conspiración del pastelero de Madrigal." Madrid: Escuela Diplomática, 1949.

———. "Barbara Blomberg y el Pastelero de Madrigal, 7 octubre 1594–19 octubre 1595." PhD diss., Universidad Complutense de Madrid, 1945.

Matthews, George T., ed. *News and Rumor in Renaissance Europe (The Fugger Newsletters)*. New York: G. P. Putnam's Sons, 1959.

McBride, Gordon K. "Elizabethan Foreign Policy in Microcosm: The Portuguese Pretender, 1580–89." *Albion: A Quarterly Journal Concerned with British Studies* 5, no. 3 (Autumn 1973): 193–210.

McNiven, Peter. "Rebellion, Sedition and the Legend of Richard II's Survival in the Reigns of Henry IV and Henry V." *Bulletin of the John Rylands University Library of Manchester* 76, no. 1 (Spring 1994): 93–117.

Mendonça, Jeronymo de. *A jornada d'Africa. Resposta a Jeronymo Franqui e a outros*.

Ed. F. María Rodrigues. Oporto: Imprensa Recreativa do Instituto Escholar de S. Domingo, 1878. (Orig. pub. 1607.)
Menéndez Pidal, Gonzalo. *Los caminos en la historia de España*. Madrid: Ediciones Cultura Hispánica, 1951.
Menezes, Manoel de. *Chronica do muito alto e muito esclarecido principe D. Sebastião, decimosexto Rey de Portugal*. Lisbon, 1730.
Merriman, Roger. *The Rise of the Spanish Empire in the Old World and in the New*. Vol. 4. *Philip the Prudent*. 4 vols. New York: Macmillan, 1934.
Mesa, Sebastian de. *Iornada de Africa por el Rey Don Sebastián y Unión del Reyno de Portugal a la Corona de Castilla*. Barcelona: Pedro Lacavallería, 1630.
Meserve, Margaret. "News from Negroponte: Politics, Popular Opinion, and Information Exchange in the First Decade of the Italian Press." *Renaissance Quarterly* 59, no. 2 (2006): 440–80.
Michener, James A. *Iberia: Spanish Travels and Reflections*. New York: Random House, 1968.
Montáñez Matilla, María. *El correo en la España de los Austrias*. Madrid: CSIC, 1953.
Morales, Juan Bautista de. *Jornada de Africa del Rey Don Sebastián de Portugal*. In *Tres relaciones históricas: Gibraltar, Los Xerves, Alcazarquivir.* Madrid: Imprenta de M. Ginesta Hermanos, 1889. (Orig. pub. in Seville, 1622.)
Moreno Sánchez, Consuelo. "Los mentideros de Madrid." *Torre de los Lujanes*, no. 18 (1991): 155–72.
Moreno y Rodrigo, Román. *Madrigal de las Altas Torres, Cuna de Isabel la Católica*. Avila: Editorial Medrano, 1949.
Muiños Sáenz, Conrado. *Fray Luis de León y Fray Diego de Zúñiga*. El Escorial: Imp. Helénica, 1914.
Muñoz Valenciano, Hieronymo. *Libro del nuevo cometa y del lugar donde se hazen. . . .* Valencia, 1573.
Myscofski, Carole A. "Messianic Themes in Portuguese and Brazilian Literatures in the Sixteenth and Seventeenth Centuries." *Luso-Brazilian Review* 28 (1991): 77–93.
Nakajima, Satoko. "Breaking Ties: Marriage and Migration in Sixteenth-Century Spain." PhD diss., University of Tokyo, 2011.
Nalle, Sara T. "The Millennial Moment: Revolution and Radical Religion in Sixteenth-Century Spain." In *Toward the Millennium: Messianic Expectations from the Bible to Waco*, ed. Peter Schafer and Mark R. Cohen, 151–71. Leiden: Brill, 1998.
Neubauer, Hans-Joachim. *The Rumour: A Cultural History*. Trans. Christian Braun. London: Free Association Books, 1999.
Nieto, Fr. Luis de. *Relación de las guerras de Berbería y del suceso y muerte del Rey Don Sebastián*. In *CODOIN*, 100:411–58. Madrid, 1891.
Norton, Mary Beth. *In the Devil's Snare: The Salem Witchcraft Crisis of 1692*. New York: Alfred A. Knopf, 2002.
Olivari, Michele. "Note sul sebastianismo portoghese al tempo di Filippo II. *Studi Storici* 41, no. 2 (April–June 2000): 451–70.
Oliveira, Antonio de. "Sociedade e conflitos sociais em Portugal nos finais do século

XVI." In *Las sociedades ibéricas y el mar a finales del siglo XVI*. Vol. 5. *El área Atlántica: Portugal y Flandes*, 7–40. Madrid, 1998.

Oliveira Marques, A. H. de. *History of Portugal*. 2 vols. New York: Columbia University Press, 1972.

Oliveira Martins, J. P. *Historia de Portugal*. 7th ed. 2 vols. Lisbon: Parcería Antonio María Pereira, 1908.

Oliver Asín, Jaime. *Vida de Don Felipe de Africa, príncipe de Fez y Marruecos (1566–1621)*. Ed. Miguel Angel de Bunes Ibarra and Beatriz Alonso Acero. Granada: University of Granada, 2008.

Olsen, H. Eric R. *The Calabrian Charlatan, 1598–1603: Messianic Nationalism in Early Modern Europe*. New York: Palgrave Macmillan, 2003.

Osorio, Jerónimo. *Cartas portuguezas de D. Hieronymo Osorio*. Paris: P. N. Rougeron, 1819.

Ossorio, P. Antonio, S. I. *Modelo del inclito héroe, del príncipe, del general y del excelente soldado, o sea, vida de Don Juan de Austria*. Madrid: Blass S. A. Tipográfica, 1946.

Paiva, José Pedro. "Bishops and Politics: The Portuguese Episcopacy during the Dynastic Crisis of 1580." *e-Journal of Portuguese History* 4, no. 2 (2006). Online at http://www.brown.edu/Departments/Portuguese_Brazilian_Studies/ejph/html/issue8/html/jpaiva_main.html

Papeles referentes al gobierno del Rey Sebastián I de Portugal, y a las expediciones a la India y Africa. BNM, MS 12866.

Parker, Geoffrey. "David or Goliath? Philip II and His World in the 1580s." In *Spain, Europe and the Atlantic World: Essays in Honour of John H. Elliott*, ed. Richard L. Kagan and Geoffrey Parker, 245–66. Cambridge: Cambridge University Press, 1995.

———. *Felipe II: La biografía definitiva*. Madrid: Planeta, 2010.

———. *Philip II*. 3rd ed. Chicago: Open Court, 1995.

Peele, George. *The Dramatic Works of George Peele*. Ed. John Yoklavich. New Haven, CT: Yale University Press, 1961.

Pereira Bayaõ, José. *Portugal cuidadoso e lastimado com a vida, e perda do senhor rey Dom Sebastiaõ, o desjado de saudosa memoria*. Lisbon: Officina de Antonio de Sousa da Sylva, 1737. [Note: this is a revision of the author's *Chronica do muito alto e muito esclarecido principe D. Sebastiaõ*. . . . Lisbon, 1730, published under the name of Manoel de Menezes.]

Peres, Damião. *1580: O Governo do Prior do Crato*. 2nd ed. Barcelos: Companhia Editora do Minho, 1929.

Peters, Edward. *Torture*. New York: Basil Blackwell, 1985.

Pike, Ruth. *Penal Servitude in Early Modern Spain*. Madison: University of Wisconsin Press, 1983.

Pinto Ferreira, J. A., ed. *A campanha de Sancho de Avila em perseguição do Prior do Crato: Alguns documentos de Simancas*. Oporto: Camara Municipal, 1954.

Platelle, Henri. "Erreur sur la personne: Contribution à l'histoire de l'imposture au Moyen Age." In *Universitas: Philosophie, théologie, lettres, histoire, questions d'aujourd'hui*, 117–45. Lille, 1977.

Porreño, Baltasar. *Dichos y hechos del Señor Rey Don Felipe Segundo, el prudente, poten-*

tisimo y glorioso monarca de las Españas y de las Indias. Madrid: Melchor Sánchez, 1663.

———. *Historia del sereníssimo Señor don Juan de Austria. . . .* Ed. Antonio Rodríguez Villa. Madrid: Sociedad de Bibliófilos Españoles, 1899.

Porter, Anna Maria. *Don Sebastian; or, the House of Braganza: An Historical Romance*. 4 vols. London: Longman, 1809.

Public Execution in England, 1573–1868. Ed. Leigh Yetter. Vol. 1. *Public Execution in England, 1573–1674*. London: Pickering and Chatto, 2009.

Queiroz Velloso, J. M. de. *Don Sebastián, 1554–1578*. Trans. Ramón de Garciasol. Madrid: Espasa Calpe, 1943.

Queirós Veloso, José María de [*sic*; author's name has variations]. "Fr. Bernardo da Cruz e a 'Chronica d'el-rei D. Sebastião.'" In *Estudos históricos do século XVI*, 137–96. Lisbon: Academia Portuguesa da Historia, 1950.

———. *A perda da independencia*. Vol. 1 of *O reinado do Cardeal D. Henrique*. Lisbon: Empresa Nacional de Publicidade, 1946.

Quevedo y Hoyos, Antonio. *Libro de indicios y tormentos; que contiene toda la práctica criminal y modo de sustanciar el proceso indicativamente. . . .* Madrid: Francisco Martínez, 1632.

Ramírez, Manuel D. "The Pastelero de Madrigal Theme Revisited." In *Papers on Romance Literary Relations*. West Point: U.S. Military Academy, 1982.

Randall, David. *Credibility in Elizabethan and Early Stuart Military News*. London: Pickering and Chatto, 2008.

Rebelo, P. Amador. *Crónica de El-Rei Dom Sebastião*. Ed. António Ferreira de Serpa. Lisbon, 1925.

Rebello da Silva, Luiz Augusto. *Historia de Portugal nos seculos XVII e XVIII*. Vol. 3. Lisbon: Imprensa National, 1867.

"Relación de las vistas [*sic*] de los Reyes Don Phelipe 2 y Don Sebastián en Nuestra Señora de Guadalupe, año de 1576." Hispanic Society of America (New York), HC 411–209.

Relaciones históricas de los siglos XVI y XVII. Madrid: Sociedad de Bibliófilos Españoles, 1896.

Ricard, Robert. "La cloche de Velilla et le mouvement sébastianiste au Portugal." *Bulletin Hispanique* 56 (1954), 175–77.

Roche, Daniel. *The Culture of Clothing: Dress and Fashion in the 'Ancien Regime.'* Trans. Jean Birrell. Cambridge: Cambridge University Press, 1994.

Rocoles, Jean-Baptiste de. *Of Infamous Impostors; or, the Lives and Actions of Several Notorious Counterfeits Who From the Most Abject and Meanest of the People Have Usurped the Titles of Emperours, Kings, and Princes*. London, 1683.

Rodríguez López, Amancio. *El Real Monasterio de las Huelgas de Burgos y el Hospital del Rey*. Vol. 2. Burgos, 1907.

Rodríguez Marín, Francisco. "Cervantes y el mentidero de San Felipe." In *Viaje del Parnaso*, by Miguel de Cervantes, 443–50. Madrid: C. Bermejo, 1935.

Rodríguez Moñino, Antonio. *Viaje a España del Rey Don Sebastián de Portugal (1576–1577)*. Valencia: Editorial Castalia, 1956.

Rodríguez Villa, Antonio. "Documentos sobre la estancia de Madame Barbara de Blombergh." *Boletín de la Real Academia de la Historia* 36 (1900): 69–81.
Roiz Soares, Pero. *Memorial.* Ed. M. Lopes de Almeida. Coimbra: Universidade de Coimbra, 1953.
Romanos, Melchora. "Felipe II en la *Tragedia del Rey don Sebastián y el bautismo del príncipe de Marruecos* de Lope de Vega." *Edad de Oro* 18 (1999): 177–91.
Romero de Cepeda, Joaquín. *Famossísimos romances* [2009 facsimile of 1577 original pamphlet]. Badajoz: Ayuntamiento de Badajoz, 2009.
Rosenbach Museum and Library. *The Spanish Golden Age in Miniature.* Catalog, March 25–April 23, 1988. New York: Spanish Institute, 1988.
Rothwell, Phillip. *A Canon of Empty Fathers: Paternity in Portuguese Narrative.* Lewisburg, PA: Bucknell University Press, 2007.
Rubio, Julián María. *Felipe II de España, Rey de Portugal.* Madrid: Cultura Española, 1939.
Ruiz Ibáñez, José Javier, and Bernard Vincent. *Los Siglos XVI–XVII: Política y sociedad.* Madrid: Editorial Síntesis, 2007.
Russell, Peter. *Prince Henry 'the Navigator': A Life.* New Haven, CT: Yale Note Bene, 2001.
Sánchez Alonso, Benito. *Fuentes de la historia española e hispanoamericana.* 3 vols. Madrid: CSIC, 1952.
San Román de Ribadeneyra, Fr. Antonio. *Jornada y muerte del rey Don Sebastián de Portugal, sacada de las obras del Franchi, ciudadano de Genova, y de otros muchos papeles auténticos.* Valladolid: Por los herederos de Juan Yñiguez de Lequerica, 1603.
Santos, Manoel dos. *Historia sebástica, contem a vida do augusto principe o senhor D. Sebastião, Rey de Portugal.* Lisbon: A. Pedrozo Galram, 1735.
São Mamede, José Pereira Ferreira Felicio, comte de. *Don Sébastien et Philippe II: Exposé des négociations entamées en vue du mariage du roi de Portugal avec Marguerite de Valois.* Paris, 1884.
Schaub, Jean Frédéric. "Conflictos y alteraciones en Portugal en la época de la unión de coronas: Marcos de interpretación." In *Ciudades en conflicto (siglos XVI–XVIII)*, ed. José I. Fortea and Juan E. Gelabert, 397–410. Valladolid: Junta de Castilla y León, 2008.
Schutte, Anne Jacobson. "Between Venice and Rome: The Dilemma of Involuntary Nuns." *Sixteenth Century Journal* 41, no. 2 (2010): 415–39.
Sepúlveda, P. Fr. Jerónimo de. *Historia de varios sucesos y de las cosas notables que han acaecido en España. . . .* Vol. 4 of *Documentos para la historia del Monasterio de San Lorenzo el Real de El Escorial.* Ed. Julián Zarco Cuevas. Madrid: Imprenta Helénica, 1924.
Sérgio, António, ed. *O Desejado: Depoimentos de contemporaneos de D. Sebastião sobre este mesmo rei e sua jornada de Africa.* Paris: Livrarias Aillaud e Bertrand, 1924.
Serrão, Joaquim Veríssimo. "Documentos inéditos para a historia do reinado de D. Sebastião." *Boletim da biblioteca da Universidade de Coimbra* 24 (1960): 139–272.
———. *Fontes de direito para a história da sucessão de Portugal (1580).* Coimbra, 1960.

———. *Itinerários de El-Rei D. Sebastião*. 2 vols. Lisbon: Academia Portuguesa da Historia, 1962.

———. *O reinado de D. António Prior do Crato*. 2 vols. PhD diss., Universidade de Coimbra, 1956.

Shapiro, Barbara J. *A Culture of Fact: England, 1550–1720*. Ithaca, NY: Cornell University Press, 2000.

Silva, Cesar da. *O Prior do Crato e a sua epoca*. Lisbon: João Romano Torres, 192[?].

Silva Dias, J. S. da. *O Erasmismo e a Inquisição em Portugal: O processo de Fr. Valentim da Luz*. Coimbra: Universidade de Coimbra, 1975.

Les sources inédites de l'histoire du Maroc de 1530 a 1845. Ed. Henry de Castries, Chantal de la Véronne, et al. 27 vols. Paris: E. Leroux, 1905–61.

Sousa, Antonio Caetano de. *História genealógica da casa real portuguesa* (12 vols.) and *Provas da história genealógica da casa real portuguesa* (7 vols.). Revised eds. by M. Lopes de Almeida and César Pegado. Coimbra: Atlântida, 1946–48.

Sousa Viterbo, Francisco Márquez de. *O Prior do Crato e a invasão hespanhola de 1580*. Lisbon, 1897.

Southwell, Robert. *The History of the Revolutions of Portugal, from the Foundation of That Kingdom to the Year [1667], with Letters of Sir Robert Southwell*. . . . London: Printed for John Osborn at the Golden Ball in Pater-Noster Row, 1740.

Spence, Ferrand. *Don Sebastian, King of Portugal. An Historical Novel in Four Parts*. London: Printed for R. Bentley and S. Magnes, 1683.

Stanhope, Alexander. *Spain under Charles the Second; or, Extracts from the Correspondence of the Hon. Alexander Stanhope, British Minister at Madrid, 1690–1699*. Ed. Lord Mahon. 2nd ed. London: Murray, 1844.

Stirling-Maxwell, Sir William. *Don John of Austria, or Passages from the History of the Sixteenth Century, 1547–1578*. 2 vols. London: Longmans, Green, 1883.

Suárez Inclán, Julián. *Guerra de anexión en Portugal durante el reinado de Don Felipe II*. 2 vols. Madrid: Imp. y Litog. del Depósito de la Guerra, 1898.

Sucesos notables. . . . [1567–1600]. Fernán Nuñez Collection, Banc MS UCB 143, vols. 69–76. The Bancroft Library, University of California, Berkeley.

Swislocki, Marsha. "Cuerpo de santo, cuerpo de Rey: El 'martirio' del rey Don Sebastián en la literatura áurea." In *Homenaje a Henri Guerreiro: La hagiografía entre historia y literatura en la España de la Edad Media y del Siglo de Oro*, ed. Marc Vitse, 1059–68. Madrid: Iberoamericana, 2005.

———. "De cuerpo presente: El Rey don Sebastián en el teatro áureo." In *En torno al teatro del Siglo de Oro (Actas)*, 45–54. Almería: Instituto de Estudios Almerienses, 1999.

Tapia, Serafín de. "Las fuentes demográficas y el potencial humano de Avila en el siglo XVI." *Cuadernos Abulenses*, no. 2 (July–December 1984): 31–88.

Tausiet, María. *Abracadabra Omnipotens: Magia urbana en Zaragoza en la Edad Moderna*. Madrid: Siglo XXI, 2007.

Tazón, Juan E. *The Life and Times of Thomas Stukeley (c.1525 78)*. Aldershot: Ashgate, 2003.

Teixeira Marques de Oliveira, Julieta. *Fontes documentais de Veneza referentes a Portugal*. Lisbon: Comissão Nacional para as Comemorações dos Descobrimentos Portugueses, 1997.

Tellechea Idígoras, José Ignacio. "La Mesa de Felipe II." *Ciudad de Dios* 218, no. 1 (2005): 181–215.

———. *El ocaso de un rey: Felipe II visto desde la Nunciatura de Madrid, 1594–1598*. Madrid: Fundación Universitaria Española, 2001.

Tenace, Edward. "A Strategy of Reaction: The Armadas of 1596 and 1597 and the Spanish Struggle for European Hegemony." *English Historical Review* 118, no. 478 (September 2003): 855–82.

Teresa, Saint. *The Autobiography of St. Teresa of Avila*. Trans. Kieran Kavanaugh, OCD, and Otilio Rodríguez, OCD. New York: One Spirit, 1995.

———. *Cartas*. 3rd ed. Vol. 2. *Maestros Espirituales Carmelitas*. Burgos: Editorial Monte Carmelo, 1983.

———. *The Complete Works of Saint Teresa of Jesus*. Vol. 3. Trans. and ed. E. Allison Peers. London: Sheed and Ward, 1946.

Terpstra, Nicolas, ed. *The Art of Executing Well: Rituals of Execution in Renaissance Italy*. Kirksville, MO: Truman State University Press, 2008.

Thomas, Keith. *Religion and the Decline of Magic*. New York: Charles Scribner's Sons, 1971.

Thompson, I. A. A. "Oposición política y juicio del gobierno en las Cortes de 1592–98." *Studia Histórica*, no. 17 (1997): 37–62.

———. "La respuesta castellana ante la política internacional de Felipe II." In *La monarquía de Felipe II a debate*, 121–34. Madrid: Sociedad Estatal para la Conmemoración de los Centenarios de Felipe II y Carlos V, 2000.

Thompson, I. A. A., and Bartolomé Yun Casalilla, eds. *The Castilian Crisis of the Seventeenth Century: New Perspectives on the Economic and Social History of Seventeenth-Century Spain*. Cambridge: Cambridge University Press, 1994.

Thompson, Stith. *Motif-Index of Folk Literature*. 6 vols. Bloomington: Indiana University Press, 1934.

Ticknor, George. *Catalogue of the Spanish Library and of the Portuguese Books Bequeathed by George Ticknor to the Boston Public Library*, ed. James Lyman Whitney. Boston: Boston Public Library, 1879; repr., Boston: G. K. Hall, 1970.

———. *History of Spanish Literature*. Boston: Houghton, Mifflin, 1863.

Tomás y Valiente, Francisco. *El derecho penal de la monarquía absoluta*. Madrid: Editorial Tecnos, 1969.

———. *La tortura en España: Estudios históricos*. Barcelona: Editorial Ariel, 1973.

Tornatore, Matthew G. C. "The Spanish Byzantine Novel." In *Sixteenth-Century Spanish Writers*. Vol. 318 of *Dictionary of Literary Biography*, 273–83. Farmington Hills, MI: Thompson Gale, 2006.

Ubieto Arteta, Antonio. "La aparición del falso Alfonso I el Batallador." *Argensola: Revista de Ciencias Sociales del Instituto de Estudios Altoaragoneses*, no. 33 (1958): 29–38.

Uriarte, P. J. Eugenio de, ed. *Catálogo Razonado de Obras Anónimas y Seudónimas de Autores de la Compañia de Jesus*. 5 vols. Madrid: Rivadeneyro, 1904–16.

Valensi, Lucette. *Fables de la Mémoire: La glorieuse bataille des trois rois*. Paris: Editions du Seuil, 1992.

———. "The Making of a Political Paradigm: The Ottoman State and Oriental Despotism." In *The Transmission of Culture in Early Modern Europe*, ed. Anthony Grafton and Ann Blair, 173–203. Philadelphia: University of Pennsylvania Press, 1990.

———. "Silence, dénégation, affabulation: Le souvenir d'une grande défaite dans la culture portugaise." *Annales* 46, no. 1 (1991): 3–24.

Valladares, Rafael. *La conquista de Lisboa: Violencia militar y comunidad política en Portugal, 1578–1583*. Madrid: Marcial Pons, 2008.

Vallafañe, Juan. *La limosnera de Dios. Relación histórica de la vida, y virtudes de la excelentíssima señora Doña Magdalena de Ulloa Toledo Ossorio y Quiñones*. Salamanca: Imprenta de Francisco García Onorato, 1723.

Vañes, Carlos Alonso. *Doña Ana de Austria: Abadesa del Real Monasterio de las Huelgas*. Madrid: Editorial Patrimonio Nacional, 1990.

Vassberg, David E. *The Village and the Outside World in Golden Age Castile: Mobility and Migration in Everyday Rural Life*. Cambridge: Cambridge University Press, 1996.

Vaughan, Dorothy M. *Europe and the Turk: A Pattern of Alliances, 1350–1700*. Liverpool: University Press, 1954.

Vega, Lope de. *La tragedia del Rey don Sebastián y bautismo del príncipe de Marruecos*. In *Biblioteca de Autores Españoles*. Vol. 225 (*Obras de Lope de Vega*, vol. 27), 121–82. Madrid: Atlas, 1969.

Vega Carnicero, Jacinto de la, and Nuria González Hernández. *Madrigal de las Altas Torres: El secreto de Madrigal*. Valladolid: Ambito, 1996.

Velázquez Salamantino, Isidro. *La entrada que en el Reino de Portugal hizo la S.C.R.M. de Don Philippe*. Lisbon, 1582.

Vélez de Guevara, Luis. *Comedia famosa del Rey Don Sebastián*. Ed. Werner Herzog. Madrid: Anejos del Boletín de la Real Academia Española, 1972.

Vidal, Fr. Manuel. *Augustinos de Salamanca: Historia del observantíssimo convento de S. Augustín*. 2 vols. Salamanca: Eugenio García de Honorato i S. Miguel, 1751.

Villacorta Baños-García, Antonio. *Don Sebastián, Rey de Portugal*. Barcelona: Editorial Ariel, 2001.

Viñas Román, Teófilo. "El convento agustiniano, extramuros de Madrigal de las Altas Torres." *Ciudad de Dios* 214, no. 3 (2001): 705–32.

Vivo, Filippo de. *Information and Communication in Venice: Rethinking Early Modern Politics*. Oxford: Oxford University Press, 2007.

———. "Pharmacies as Centres of Communication in Early Modern Venice." *Renaissance Studies* 21, no. 4 (2007): 505–21.

Weber, Alison. "'Little Angels': Young Girls in Discalced Carmelite Convents (1562–1582)." In Wyhe, *Female Monasticism*, 211–26.

Weiner, Jack. "Un episodio de la historia rusa visto por autores españoles del Siglo de Oro: El pretendiente Demetrio." *Journal of Hispanic Philology* 2, no. 3 (Spring 1978): 175–201.

Weiss, Julian. "Renaissance Poetry." In *The Cambridge History of Spanish Literature*, ed. David T. Gies, 159–77. Cambridge: Cambridge University Press, 2004.

White, Richard. *Remembering Ahanagran: Storytelling in a Family's Past*. New York: Hill and Wang, 1998.

Wright, Elizabeth R. "Narrating the Ineffable Lepanto: The *Austrias Carmen* of Joannes Latinus (Juan Latino). *Hispanic Review* 77, no. 1 (Winter 2009): 71–91.

Wyhe, Cordula, ed. *Female Monasticism in Early Modern Europe*. Aldershot: Ashgate, 2008.

Yahya, Dahiru. *Morocco in the Sixteenth Century: Problems and Patterns in African Foreign Policy*. Essex: Longman, 1981.

Yañez Neira, Fr. María Damián. "Doña Ana de Austria, abadesa de las Huelgas de Burgos." *Anuario jurídico y económico escurialense*, no. 29 (1996): 1036–78.

Yoklavich, "The Battle of Alcázarquivir," in Peele, *Dramatic Works*, 2:257.

Zagorin, Perez. *Ways of Lying: Dissimulation, Persecution, and Conformity in Early Modern Europe*. Cambridge, MA: Harvard University Press, 1990.

Zorrilla, José. *Traidor, inconfeso y martir*. Ed. Ricardo Senabre. Madrid: Cátedra, 1976.

Zucker, George K. "Some Considerations on the Sephardic Treatment of the 'Romancero.'" *Anuario de estudios filológicos* 14 (1991): 519–24.

Zurdo Manso, Firmo, and Esther del Cerro Calvo. *Madrigal de las Altas Torres: Recuerdos para una historia*. Avila, 1996.

INDEX